Reasons and Arguments

Reasons and Arguments

Gerald M. Nosich

University of New Orleans

Wadsworth Publishing Company
Belmont, California
A Division of Wadsworth, Inc.

Philosophy Editor: Kenneth King
Production Service: Mary Forkner, Publication Alternatives
Cover Designer: Bruce Kortebein, Design Office
Text Designer: Hal Lockwood, Bookman Productions
Copy Editor: Steve Sorensen

ISBN 0-534-01076-8

Printed in the United States of America

2 3 4 5 6 7 8 9 10 – 86 85 84 83

Library of Congress Cataloging in Publication Data

Nosich, Gerald M.
  Reasons and arguments.

  Includes index.
  1. Reasoning. I. Title.
BC177.N67   168   81-19709
ISBN 0-534-01076-8   AACR2

Contents

Preface

Reasons and Arguments is designed primarily for use as the main textbook in undergraduate introductory courses in reasoning or informal logic. It is also suitable as a supplementary text in those courses as well as in low-level philosophy courses generally and in basic English composition courses.

Briefly, reasoning is the ability to construct arguments for positions one believes, to meet objections with reasons, to analyze arguments and criticize them effectively. In more general terms, it's the ability to think cogently and critically about issues.

I've tried in *Reasons and Arguments* to help teach not just the specific skills being discussed but also this more general ability. For no matter what other skills are taught in a reasoning text — skills of picking out fallacies, or being clever, or manipulating truth-tables — the worth of these skills has to be evaluated in terms of the student's increased ability to think logically and hard about the things he or she believes and encounters.

A number of features distinguish *Reasons and Arguments* from other texts in the area. An important one, and a feature that makes *Reasons and Arguments* unique, is that it explains how to construct arguments. A good portion of what it means to be rational or reasonable is being able to defend one's own point of view with a good argument — and that means being able to construct an argument on one's own. Three chapters in *Reasons and Arguments* are devoted primarily to constructing arguments. In Chapter 2 a three-step method is presented: clarify the meaning of what one is trying to prove, break it down into its component parts, think up a reason to cover each part. In Chapters 3 and 4 the techniques for carrying out this method are explained in detail. By introducing basic concepts and techniques, these chapters also lay the groundwork for Chapters 5 and 6, in which analysis and criticism are covered. In Chapter 5 a five-step method for analyzing arguments is presented, and in Chapter 6 a number of the more difficult tasks — filling in missing premises is the most difficult of all — are explained in greater depth. The examples used throughout are the kind one encounters in everyday life, in newspaper editorials, textbooks, advertising, and political campaigns.

In addition to the emphasis on constructing arguments, there are other salient features of *Reasons and Arguments*. First, the book is intended to help teach people to think critically, reasonably, and not just about arguments, but about a broader range of topics. There is a logic to things — institutions, automobile engines, games, interpersonal relations — and it would be well to be critical about them also. This seems genuinely a part of reasoning. And it is a part that is usually entirely neglected by reasoning textbooks in favor of the more easily encompassable problems having to do specifically with arguments.

In Chapter 7, "Reasoning Things Out," construction, analysis, and criticism are combined under the topic "Issues and Strategies." Skills already learned are applied not just to arguments but to broader aspects of the student's personal, social, and cultural life. A method is given for analyzing personal actions and habits reasonably: figure out the goals of the action and the likelihood of its achieving those goals; reason out alternative ways of achieving them; weigh comparative advantages and costs; and finally question the goals themselves. The method is then expanded to one for reasoning out a broader range of social, legal, and cultural issues. A conscientious application of the methods yields a strategy for dealing with a complex network of interrelated problems, only a few of which are straightforwardly arguments.

Second, the language of *Reasons and Arguments* is informal, often colloquial, and pitched at a level for introductory students. I have tried to make it as free from technical jargon as possible. The few "technical" words the book does contain — words like "valid" and "sound" — are there because they sometimes make concepts easier for students to remember. There they are always explained in ordinary terms.

Third, the examples used in *Reasons and Arguments* are realistic. This includes the examples in the exercises as well as those used in the body of the text. They progress from easy cliches like "people are the same the world over" to more incisive issues like the relation (if any) between justice and trial by jury. The examples used are not philosophical (though some philosophical issues arise when the structure of a particular argument requires it), and they are not geared to the schema for formal logic. Numerous examples are used in the text to teach as well as to illustrate techniques of reasoning. Often they are done intricately and at length. The examples in the exercises are also often done at length, comments are written out in detail, and alternative possible analyses are discussed. (See "A Note on the Exercises," immediately following the preface.)

Fourth, *Reasons and Arguments* covers real and practical difficulties of argument construction and analysis. At the end of Chapter 4, for instance, there is a section called "A Realistic Example." In it, I go through the actual construction of an argument, bit by bit, as a student would have to do it. This requires giving comments and suggestions on very many small practical difficulties which the student must overcome — difficulties of phrasing premises, connecting assumptions, imagining alternative possibilities, breaking conclusions down in the most helpful way, and so forth.

I want to thank those who contributed to this book: Ken King, the philosophy editor at Wadsworth, and John Tice for help and for suggesting that I do this book in the first place.

In addition, I would like to thank the publisher's readers: Jerome A. Stone, Kendall College; E. Jay Hilty, Jr., Maple Woods Community College; Donovan J. Ochs, University of Iowa; Elizabeth Ranken, Auburn University; J.T. Howald, Franklin College; S.K. Wertz, Texas Christian University; Roger Ariew, Virginia Polytechnic Institute and State University; and especially Tryg A. Ager of Stanford University for his incisive and detailed comments on the entire manuscript. Special thanks go to Edward Johnson, John Christmas, Deborah Rosen, Randall Curren, and Norton Nelkin for suggestions and encouragement. I would also like to thank Eileen Long, Linda Giessinger, and Hubert Fernandez. Finally, I am grateful to the College of Liberal Arts at the University of New Orleans for providing organized research funds at several critical stages in the writing of this book.

Gerald M. Nosich

A Note on the Exercises

The exercises in *Reasons and Arguments* are designed to contribute centrally to the actual teaching of reasoning, not just to testing what has been learned. One major way students learn how to reason well is by trying examples, having them carefully corrected, and understanding specifically where they went wrong and specifically where they succeeded. For this learning procedure to be useful, exercises should contain more than just questions, or questions plus answers. They should contain explanations and reasons as well. The exercises at the end of each chapter (except the first and last chapter) have a four-part structure that incorporates this procedure.

Part A consists of short selections — statements, arguments, paragraphs — for the student to analyze (construct, criticize, etc.) using the reasoning techniques in the chapter just finished. The selections are presented here without comments or hints at the right answer.

In Part B the same set of selections is given, only this time with various possible answers attached. Sometimes these answers are in multiple-choice or true-or-false form, but usually they are simply answers that a student might give. The students not only develop critical skills from this, but they also can compare the answers they got on their own in Part A with a range of possibilities. Thus, they can come to see aspects of the problem they may have been mistaken about or overlooked. So skills of argument construction are also developed.

Part C contains comments on the selections in Parts A and B. It usually includes correct (or at least reasonable) answers as well as reasons and explanations. Part C also contains further questions about the selections. The comments and answers in this part of the exercises are sometimes long. But this is likely to be what will help students the most. The various answers considered in Part C are similar to answers students themselves give, and thus the comments are like the comments teachers write in the margin of students' tests.

Part D consists of another set of selections — this time without any corresponding answers or comments. If the material in the chapter requires any questions other than selections for analysis, these will also be asked in Part D.

In addition there is a short list of questions, labeled "Problems," following most sections within chapters. These are given without answers and are generally closely related to the material just covered. They can serve as mileage markers of progress. Instructors can, of course, augment these with assignments from the exercises at the end. Indeed, given the number of questions, instructors can freely choose those they feel most beneficial or appropriate as pre-tests, class work, homework, tests, or extra-credit work.

Chapter One

Reasoning and Arguments

1. What Reasoning Is

Reasoning is something you're probably already familiar with. It is, after all, a process you engage in every day in practical life. In its most general sense reasoning is simply thinking clearly about things.

More specifically, reasoning has to do with reasons: giving reasons to back up your position, understanding the reasons behind someone else's position, criticizing that position by bringing up reasons against it, and trying to figure out if the reasons given on either side succeed in establishing or refuting the position. It's thinking hard about something, thinking your way through a problem, trying to solve it by giving and evaluating reasons.

Reasons

It's something you already do a good deal of the time. If your car won't start and you try to figure out why, you are reasoning. You may try the lights. If they don't work, the chances are that what's wrong is the battery. If the lights work as well as before, you are going to consider some other possibility to explain why your car doesn't start. That's reasoning your way through alternatives, and it is something you do naturally, without thinking that it's reasoning.

Trying to understand the plot of a novel is another instance of reasoning. You reason about many more things than you pay attention to. Interpersonal relations, for example. When you try to figure out why somebody means a lot to you, or why you hate somebody, you are probably reasoning. The loving or the hating in themselves are not instances of reasoning. They are mostly emotional. But when you try to figure out *why* you love or hate, that's reasoning.

Reasoning and emotions

Unfortunately, there are other areas where people *should* reason but don't — or at least they don't reason well, or enough. You can tell that easily enough by looking at the results of political campaigns. Often candidates who are clearly better do not win. People sometimes vote for a candidate even though they believe the other candidate ought to win. And they do it for irrelevant reasons: because the candidates look a certain way, or because they have a catchy campaign slogan. A reason people frequently gave for voting for Nixon in 1972 is that they thought Nixon would win. That is *not* a thought-out reason.

When you try to decide which candidate to vote for in an election, presumably you should try to figure out which candidate is going to do the things you want done, and then vote for that one. Simple. But it is doubtful that people in general do vote that way.

An even clearer case of reasoning badly, or not at all, is with regard to advertising. There are many products on the market that are popular and, by any reasonable standard, are no good. Not only do they fail to do what the advertisers say they will do, they may even do harm. It is perplexing that people can buy a product that does not do them any good, that they know does not do them any good, and that they do not even especially like. There are many products that fit this description. We will discuss several of them, but you can easily think of your own examples. People often do not reason well, and they do not reason enough.

Learning to Reason

It is wise, then, to learn how to reason in both these senses: to reason *more* and to reason *better*. A good way to learn how to reason better is

Reasoning better

by learning a technique for reasoning. This consists of learning a series of steps for constructing arguments of your own, or for analyzing and evaluating arguments by others. Following the steps carefully will help you get to the root of an argument and enable you to see exactly what is right or wrong about it. This will not guarantee arriving at the truth, however; nothing guarantees truth. But it will give you an insight into truth and the best chance you have at arriving at it.

Merely learning the method, though, is not enough to become

Reasoning is a skill

good at reasoning. That is because reasoning is a skill, not a body of knowledge. In that way it is different from most other courses you take in school. It is the difference between mastering something like tennis versus mastering something like history. When you learn history, you acquire a number of facts, causes, explanations, and theories: That *is* mastering history. Mastering tennis, on the other hand, is not just knowing that you should grip the racket a certain way; rather it is *being able* to hold it that way.

Similarly, you will not become good at reasoning merely by memorizing the steps involved in constructing or analyzing arguments. You have to be able to apply the steps; you have to be able to perform the constructing and analyzing yourself. So learning how to

Practice is necessary

reason, like learning tennis, requires a good deal of *practice*. Therefore, much of the material in this text will consist of examples: arguments to construct and analyze, statements to evaluate for truth, misleading claims to clarify and criticize. And it is practicing these tasks, as well as the exercises at the ends of chapters, that will *be* reasoning.

So much for reasoning better. As for reasoning *more*, about more

Reasoning more

topics, there is no independent method for learning it. Once you practice the steps and see how helpful they are, you will come to think more and apply the steps to areas of your daily life that you haven't analyzed. The hope is that after a while you will acquire the habit of reasoning things out, that you will do it as easily and naturally as a tennis player holds a racket.

2. The Uses of Reasoning

Reasoning is useful for many purposes, but it has three major, general uses. First, it helps keep you from being fooled; second, it helps you understand things better; and third, it helps you defend positions you hold.

Not Being Fooled

By enabling you to analyze and evaluate the arguments people give you, reasoning helps you avoid being fooled. Are the reasons good reasons? Do they hold water? And even if they do, do they establish what the people are trying to convince you of? What assumptions underlie their argument?

Learning how to reason well probably will not prevent you from being fooled in all cases. Reasoning is not a universal cure. Subtle cases may still get by you; you may continue to accept deeply in-grained ways of thinking, even if they are not accurate. But it will help you to be fooled *less*. Quite a bit less.

As it is, you are probably fooled by a lot more things than you think you are. The most straightforward case of this, but not the most difficult, is when people try to trick you or at least seriously mislead you intentionally. There are some people who have a stake in fooling you; they stand to gain by it. Many advertisers are in this position. "Fooling" is undoubtedly too strong a word to use for advertising in general. But advertisers have a stake in getting you to believe something. The point of advertising is to get you to do something, buy a product, that you would not do without the advertising. Advertisements do this by trying to sway you. Sometimes they appeal to your emotions, but sometimes they attempt to give you *reasons* why you should buy the product. Some of the reasons given may be good ones, but often they are bad reasons indeed.

People intentionally mislead you

Advertising

Consider Bayer aspirin. Bayer is the largest-selling aspirin in the United States. If you ask people what reasons they have for taking Bayer, you are likely to hear a medley from Bayer's advertisements. They say,

Bayer is pure aspirin

Bayer is 100% aspirin

Bayer works

or even

Bayer works wonders.

The last two, of course, simply mean that

Bayer cures headaches.

Now are these good reasons for buying Bayer? They sound like it. You want to have your headache cured; aspirin does it; so you want a pill that is all aspirin ("100% aspirin, pure aspirin" — they say the same thing). Notice also that the reasons they give are *true*: Bayer *is* 100% aspirin, and it *does* cure headaches.

In advertising what is actually said is usually not false: The falsehoods are in the statements that are left unsaid. An unstated assumption in this argument is that Bayer is the only brand of aspirin that is 100% pure. They do not actually say this, of course. It does not even follow from what they *have* said. But without this assumption they have given you no reason to prefer Bayer over other brands of aspirin.

And the assumption is false. *All* aspirin is "pure aspirin, 100% aspirin." That is because all aspirin is made in the same way, out of the same materials. Except for the name stamped on each pill, Bayer is no different from any other brand. They all work — work wonders, even — equally well.

Reasoning and knowledge

Reasoning about the advertisement would have helped you not be taken in by it. Reasoning by itself will not tell you that all brands are 100% pure aspirin; that requires also some *knowledge* of the composition of aspirin tablets. But one of the prime tasks in reasoning is to pick out the missing premises, the reasons that are needed but not stated. In this advertisement the missing premise is the assumption, "Bayer is the only brand that is 100% pure aspirin." Just having your attention drawn to this claim makes you suspect it; probably it would lead you to check its truth (by looking at the labels, for example). The advertisement succeeds only by your *not noticing* that this claim is involved in the argument. Reasoning makes you notice it.

Sometimes people are fooled even when they already have all the requisite knowledge. Anacin advertises itself as containing "more of the pain reliever doctors recommend most." Now what *is* the pain reliever doctors recommend most? Everyone already knows it is just aspirin. (There is even a standing joke that for any ailment doctors always tell you to take two aspirins and go to bed.) Anacin never says that its main ingredient is aspirin because that would make it sound too ordinary and it would not sell as well as it does. It's as if people had one piece of knowledge in one part of their heads (that Anacin contains the pain reliever doctors recommend most) and another piece of knowledge in another part of their heads (that doctors' favorite remedy is aspirin), and they simply do not put the two pieces of knowledge together. It is hard to see how people fail to connect these two things. They *would* connect them if they asked themselves the question: "Let's see, which pain reliever *is* recommended most by doctors?" All they have to do is ask the question and they'll realize the answer. That's one of the things reasoning gets you to do: It gets you to ask the question.

Product advertising is one area in which reasoning keeps you from being fooled; political advertising is another. Successful campaigns are sometimes run on the basis of slogans that say almost nothing. This is especially true of local elections (where your vote and opinion are more likely to count than in national elections). If a billboard says, "Vote for X — He's good people," the slogan will have a pleasant ring to it. It may even incline people to vote for X. But if you stop and think about it for a second, you realize instantly that it is not a *reason* at all. It says nothing. It does not tell you what X will do, what he is for, whether he is honest; it does not give you any concrete information about X. It's merely a catchy phrase. The problem with such slogans is not in analyzing them. That is ridiculously easy and may change your view of X entirely. The problem is to notice how empty the slogan is in the first place.

In many other cases, though, people are fooled by things even though no one in particular is intentionally trying to fool them. In such cases it is almost as if people are fooling themselves. More accurately, people are taken in by misleading habits of thinking and by ideas that are unexamined and accepted uncritically. A primary part of reasoning is to learn to substitute rational ways of thinking for misleading ways, and to examine ideas instead of simply accepting the ones we are taught.

Bayer's advertising furnishes an example of this also. There is one quite significant difference between Bayer and other brands of aspirin: price. Bayer costs more. Instead of this counting *against* using Bayer, however, in many cases it is taken as a reason *in favor of* using Bayer. If Bayer lowered its prices to the level of its competitors, there is a good chance it would lose sales. That is because people have an ingrained belief that the more you pay, the better a thing is. Recognizing that people hold this principle, Freud advised psychoanalysts to charge higher prices so patients would think there was a higher likelihood of being cured. Yet a little reasoning will show that the principle is not trustworthy in general and that it is certainly not true in these cases, when the products are identical.

No one in particular, however, has tried to convince you that more expensive things are better. Both Bayer and Freud rely on your already believing it. It is just part of a general way people have of thinking about things, but it is a way of thinking that needs to be examined rationally.

Sometimes it is not just an advertisement or an isolated belief that needs to be reasoned out but a significant aspect of one's life. There are large-scale ideas and institutions that determine patterns of behavior and the rules we follow. These ideas and institutions can be fundamentally unreasonable.

Consider the idea of *fashion*. The essence of fashion is that at one point in time you like X (say, a style of clothes) and dislike Y; at a later point in time you no longer like X, and you do like Y. Think about your own experience. Typically, when a new fashion is just beginning to become popular, it looks ugly to you. But if you wait a while, it starts to look good. What *now* looks ugly (besides your old clothes, of course) is the new fashion on the next horizon. But pretty soon *it* begins to look good (and the *two* previous fashions now look ugly). There seems to be something basically irrational in all these pointless changes. They are not based on what function the things serve because that, for the most part, stays the same. It would be hard to say what these changes are based on other than changing tastes. But why should your tastes change? More suspiciously, why do they change in the same direction in which other people's tastes change?

There might be something in us that causes us to like different things periodically (the possibility merits some reasoning out), but not so often, so uniformly, or so expensively. The custom of following fashions has several earmarks of a custom shaped by people who stand to gain from it.

The rational procedure is not to be subject to fashion but to buy things with an eye to how useful they are. Reasoning certainly does not dictate that questions of taste be excluded entirely, but at least the look of a shoe should not interfere with your ability to walk in it. Tastes can be followed as long as they don't lead you to harmful or expensive extremes. A good test is to match the life of the item with the duration of your liking for it. If a well-made item wears out at the same time you begin to tire of it, the changing fashions are not hurting you too much. If your clothes last longer than your liking for them, you may be being fooled by fashions and should probably try to educate your tastes.

There are many other ways of living that warrant reasoning out. Some of them, like the custom of changing fashions each year, support large industries. They succeed in misleading us primarily because we haven't examined them closely enough.

Understanding

The function of reasoning is not merely to keep you from being fooled, though. It also helps you simply to understand things. There are issues that you just want to get clear about (problems you want to solve, explanations you want to evaluate) in which the question of being fooled or not doesn't enter.

You want to know, for example, about gun control. Should guns be prohibited? That seems like an important question. It seems like something you ought to be able to reason out objectively and come to the right answer about. (You also need some information, but you do not necessarily need any sophisticated statistics.) Primarily, it seems a matter to be understood by clear and careful thinking.

There are things you might just wonder about. Take a different kind of example. An explanation you often hear for the fall of the Roman Empire is that Rome fell because of internal decay. On first hearing that sounds like a perfectly adequate explanation, and in the end it may be. But it should make you pause and wonder. Just how does internal decay make a nation fall? Doesn't a nation "fall" because it's invaded successfully? And if so, how is that affected by "internal decay"? That is, how does internal decay *work* in the actual fall? The explanation can make it sound like the Romans were too fat or too drunk to fight in the army, but that does not sound plausible. Were they so inclined to sensual pleasure that they neglected to spend money to hire an army? (That does not sound plausible either; the Romans' problem then would be stupidity, not decadence.)

"Falling from internal decay" is not a literal explanation. It is a metaphor that compares Rome to an apple on a tree. When an apple gets overripe, the cells in the stem begin to break down, lose their fluid, and dry up. Eventually, the stem breaks and gravity pulls the apple down to the ground. The apple falls because of internal decay. What you have to understand is how that could apply to a nation, which has no stem, no cells, does not ripen, cannot "fall," and has no gravity pulling on it. In the end the explanation about Rome *may* make sense, but it takes a considerable amount of thinking to understand it. It may be that the metaphor actually makes it harder to understand.

There are many other issues and problems that are of practical importance to figure out. And reasoning is the primary tool for figuring things out. Should you marry so and so? That is a question that is crucial to reason out so that you can decide rationally. Being rational doesn't mean excluding emotional considerations; it means weighing them in as a factor in your decision. You have to let your emotions come into play, but you do not want them to rule you completely. Spontaneity may be important, but getting married, because it is supposed to last a long time, is not the sort of thing you should just do spontaneously. It's not something you want to do without having good reasons. And that takes some hard and careful thinking out.

There is a logic to things (man-made things, that is). The better made a thing is, the more its parts "fit together." By understanding the point of a thing, having the necessary knowledge, and reasoning it out, you can come to understand how each part contributes to the point.

Understanding how a fine car works, or appreciating a well-played game of chess or a well-constructed novel, is seeing how no part or move or word is without a function in the whole, and that none interferes with another. Understanding in this deeper sense requires a number of talents — an ability to observe mechanical workings intelligently, a knowledge of electrical principles or the rules of the game, a large vocabulary maybe — but one indispensable skill in understanding anything is reasoning.

Defending Your Own Position

Constructing arguments

In addition to helping you understand things and not be fooled so often, reasoning is eminently useful for defending your own point of view. That is, reasoning is concerned not only with reacting to what others say, but also with thinking out your own positions and constructing arguments to support them. You can think of your own examples of things you want to argue for. To give a good argument in favor of your position, you have to understand your position well, know the reasons for it and how to make them convincing, and be able to state the further reasons you need to draw your conclusion.

Learning how to construct arguments for things you believe is also a good foundation for understanding and evaluating the positions and arguments of others. It will serve, then, as an introduction to the basic skills involved in all the tasks of reasoning.

Exercises to Chapter One

The exercises to Chapter One do not have the same format as the exercises to later chapters. The questions are mostly diagnostic, and they are supposed to make you think out a few things you may not have considered before. They do not all have definite answers, and you should not automatically think that there is something wrong with a selection just because it is contained in a question. Where you can, give reasons — good, solid, true reasons — to back up what you say.

1. A famous saying, attributed to Ralph Waldo Emerson, is that if a person builds a better mousetrap, the world will beat a path to the person's door. What does that mean? Is it true?

2. The United States gives money and goods to many underdeveloped countries. It is often claimed that such foreign aid is a gift. Is it?

3. In a nutshell, you have inflation when the price of the same products keeps increasing. So a basic remedy for inflation is to decrease the price of goods. One way to do this is by "increasing productivity": Getting a worker to produce more goods for the same wage. That will decrease the cost of making the product and so will decrease the price of the product to the consumer. So far so good. The problem is *how* best to increase productivity?

   Now one major Conservative program is to give an income-tax cut, thus increasing the workers' *incentive*, thus increasing their productivity. The reasoning behind the program is that with a tax cut workers will gain an incentive to work harder and produce more goods because they will be receiving more take-home pay.

   Evaluate this reasoning. Is the program a plausible one? That is, if people are given a tax cut, is it likely that they will turn out more goods per hour? If *you* were given a tax cut by the government, would you work harder at your job?

4. Newscasters often analyze rises and falls in the stock market as being caused by nonfinancial news events, like an American diplomat being kidnapped or a rash of terrorist bombings. Does that seem like a believable analysis? If you know people who own stocks, is that why *they* buy or sell?
   How would you tell if this kind of analysis were true?

5. There are many ads on television about deodorants. How often does a normal person need to use a deodorant?

6. What is the trick in this ad?

   Comtrex is better. The ingredients in Comtrex make it better than Dristan, Contac, or Bayer in relieving this complete combination of cold symptoms: (1) nasal and sinus congestion, (2) sneezing, (3) runny nose, (4) coughing, (5) fever, (6) postnasal drip, (7) watery eyes, (8) minor sore-throat pain, (9) headache, and (10) body aches and pains.

   All by itself, Comtrex gives more kinds of relief than Dristan or Contac or Bayer. Because only Comtrex has a cough suppressant.

   So, the ingredients in Comtrex make it better in relieving this complete combination of symptoms.

   Try new Comtrex from Bristol-Myers. Available in tablet or liquid.

7. "Nothing has been found better for pain than Tylenol. Nothing,"
   Tylenol has almost certainly run some tests to back up its claim in this ad. What, precisely, *is* the claim, and what do you suppose were the findings on those tests? How might this ad be misleading?

8. Colonel Sanders' fried chicken is advertised as "finger-lickin' good." What *exactly* is it about fried chicken that makes you lick your fingers after each bite?

Here are six arguments about raising the minimum drinking age. They are taken from an article in *Nutshell*[1] (1979–80), a magazine distributed free to college students.
Evaluate each of the arguments. Which are good? Bad? Miss the point?
This is really a diagnostic test of the skills you have in evaluating arguments before receiving any appreciable instruction in reasoning. Later on, you should return to these arguments. You will be impressed by the improvement in your ability to give precise, well-thought-out criticisms.

9. A Connecticut legislator who is an undertaker by profession: I favor the higher drinking age because I'm tired of seeing the mutilated bodies of teenagers killed in drunken-driving car accidents.

10. A senior at Tufts University: "If kids want to get liquor, they'll get it. Raising the drinking age won't make a difference."

---

[1]Reprinted with publisher's permission from *Nutshell 1979/80* © 1979, 13–30 Corporation, Knoxville, TN 37902.

11. "In legislative chambers and elsewhere, two arguments are repeated time and time again: The lower the minimum drinking age, the higher the rate of alcohol-related traffic deaths; and the lower this age, the higher the drinking rate among still younger teens."

12. A health official: "The thing that concerns me is the civil-liberties aspect of the situation. You have a person at 18, old enough to die for his country, responsible enough to vote for the president. You have to assume he's responsible enough to do other things — like drink — that adults are permitted to do."

13. The same health official: "I say sure, if you want to have an impact on traffic fatalities, raise the age. But why stop at 21? Put it up to 25 or 30 or higher. There's no question that the rate of fatalities will fall."

14. A senior at the University of Missouri: "Eighteen-year-olds are treated as second-class citizens. Age 21 has no reasonable basis other than tradition for being the determinate level of adult rights and responsibilities. Twenty-one as the age of majority rights came from English common law. It was the age at which a man became fully grown and could physically carry a full suit of armor. But in other societies, the age of adult rights has ranged from 14 to 30."

Reasoning deals not only with criticizing arguments of others but also with making up good arguments to back up what you believe. Later you should be able to return to these topics and do a better job on them also.

15. Find three beliefs that a lot of people hold but that you think are false. Then give the best argument you can in favor of your position regarding each of the three beliefs. (To make the exercise worthwhile, the beliefs you choose should not be false because of a mere technicality, nor should your argument rely on very specialized knowledge you may have.)

Developed reasoning skills are of crucial importance in doing well on most standardized tests, including intelligence tests, comprehension tests, civil-service exams, and many admissions tests. The Law School Admission Test is a good example. Taking the tests in an LSAT guide is a good way to practice one's reasoning skills while in a reasoning course. According to one study guide, the LSAT consists of some, but not all, of the following question categories.[1]

1. *Reading comprehension.* A thirty-minute test that includes four passages of 500 to 1000 words each and approximately twenty-five questions about the readings.

2. *Reading recall.* A thirty-minute test in which you are given fifteen minutes to read three or four passages, absorbing as much information as possible, and then fifteen minutes to answer twenty-five

---

[1]This list and the subsequent questions are taken from Candrilli and Slawsky, *LSAT* (Arco, 1979). Used by permission of Arco.

to thirty questions about the readings without looking back at them.

3. *Data interpretation.* A thirty-minute test of approximately twenty-five questions based upon the information presented in four or five graphs, charts, or tables.

4. *Quantitative comparison.* A fifteen-minute test consisting of twenty-five mathematical comparisons in which you must determine the relationship that exists between two given quantities. Are they equal? Is one greater than the other? Or is the information given insufficient to establish any relationship?

5. *Principles and cases.* A forty-minute test of about thirty questions that involve applying given principles to specific cases or determining the reasoning that underlies the decisions of the court as indicated for a variety of cases.

6. *Logical reasoning.* A twenty-minute test of approximately fifteen to twenty questions that require you to read brief passages and then analyze, interpret, criticize, or draw conclusions from them.

7. *Practical judgment.* A forty-five-minute test that presents two long and highly detailed case studies of practical business situations and then poses questions that require you to evaluate, classify, and apply the data given.

8. *Error recognition.* A twenty-minute test of approximately thirty-five questions in which you must demonstrate your ability to distinguish between well- and poorly written sentences and to recognize errors in diction, verbosity, or grammar.

9. *Sentence correction.* A twenty-minute test of twenty-five questions that indicate your ability to recognize the most correct and effective way to express a particular thought.

Comments:

As you can see, categories 1, 5, 6, and 7 are direct tests of reasoning skills, while in categories 2, 3, 4, and, perhaps, 9, improved reasoning skills will greatly aid your performance.

The following questions from category 5 are patterned after questions on the LSAT. Answer in accordance with the instructions. Answers follow.

Directions: Each principle of law given below is followed by several law cases. These principles may be either real or imaginary, but for purposes of this test you are to assume them to be valid. Following each law case are four statements regarding the possible applicability of the principle to the law case. You are to select the one statement that most appropriately describes the applicability of the principle to the law-case decision. These questions do not presuppose any specific legal knowledge on your part; you are to arrive at your answers entirely by the ordinary processes of logical reasoning.

PRINCIPLE OF LAW

When a police officer observes unusual conduct that leads him reasonably to conclude, in light of his experience, that criminal activity may be afoot and that persons with whom he is dealing may be armed and presently dangerous, when in the course of investigating this behavior he identifies himself as a policeman and makes reasonable inquiries, and when nothing in the initial stages of the encounter serves to dispel his reasonable fear for his own or others' safety, he is entitled, for the protection of himself and others in the area, to conduct a carefully limited search of the outer clothing of such person in an attempt to discover weapons that might be used to assault him. An officer may put a hand beneath a suspect's clothes if he feels what appears to be a weapon.

16. Clancy O'Toole, a New York policeman, while walking his beat in a bad neighborhood observed Polonius Punk, a known narcotics addict, consorting with three other men. All four men were standing in front of the First National Town Bank. During this period Clancy observed that one of the men handed Punk an object of some sort, which Punk put into his jacket pocket. When Clancy approached Punk and asked him what he was doing, Punk simply mumbled something unintelligible. At that point Clancy stuck his hand into Punk's pocket and pulled out a nonregistered gun.

   When Punk moves to have a charge of possessing a nonregistered firearm dismissed, he will

   (a) win because Clancy had no right to stick his hand into Punk's pocket at that point;
   (b) win because Clancy did not know what the object was that Punk put into his pocket;
   (c) lose because Punk did have a gun and he was acting suspiciously in front of a bank;
   (d) lose because Punk was guilty of both conspiracy to rob a bank and attempt to rob a bank.

17. While on his way home from the station house, Burny Guardino, an off-duty police officer, spotted three men cruising in a car up and down in front of a jewelry store. When the men finally stopped in front of the store, Burny approached the driver, Kelly Klinker, and asked to see his license and registration; Kelly refused. Burny ordered the men out of the car and patted them down. Under Kelly's jacket he felt what appeared to be a crumpled ball of paper. When Burny stuck his hand into Kelly's pocket, he found a small package containing heroin. Kelly is arrested for possession of narcotics.

   When Kelly moves to have the charges against him dismissed, he will

   (a) win because he was not really trying to rob the jewelry store;
   (b) win because Burny did not feel what appeared to be a weapon beneath Kelly's clothes;

(c) lose because Burny could really believe that criminal
   activity was afoot;

(d) lose because Burny first made a limited search of Kelly's
   outer clothing.

18. Casey, an ex-convict, was employed as a handyman in a pawnshop.
Officer Fogarty spotted Casey staring into the window of the pawnshop.
Suspecting that Casey was about to rob the shop, Fogarty approached
Casey and began to question him. Casey told Fogarty that he was the
handyman and was about to wash the windows. The owner of the store
corroborated Casey's story. Nevertheless, Fogarty patted Casey down
and, upon feeling what appeared to be a gun, went inside Casey's clothing
and did in fact find an unregistered firearm. Casey is charged with illegal
possession of a weapon.

   When Casey moves to have the charge against him dismissed, he will

(a) win because the owner corroborated Casey's story;

(b) win because Fogarty should have first asked the shop-
   keeper if he knew Casey;

(c) lose because Casey did in fact have an unregistered gun;

(d) lose because it is reasonable to search an ex-convict
   under almost any circumstances.

19. Smith was locked out of his apartment one day and the superintendent,
who had the only passkey, was nowhere to be found. Realizing that his
window was unlocked, Smith went to the roof of the building, climbed
down the fire escape, and entered his apartment through the open
window. Officer Jones saw Smith climb in the window and decided to
investigate. Jones knocked on Smith's door, and when Smith answered,
Jones identified himself as a policeman and asked Smith why he was on
the fire escape. Smith refused to answer, so Jones searched his outer
clothes and, upon feeling what appeared to be an ice pick, Jones went into
Smith's pocket and removed an ice pick and a small quantity of
marijuana. Smith is charged with the possession of marijuana.

   When Smith moves to have the charges dismissed, he will

(a) win because it was his own apartment that he entered;

(b) win because he had a right to remain silent;

(c) lose because Jones' suspicions were reasonable in the
   light of the facts available to him;

(d) lose because it is unlawful to be on a fire escape except
   in an emergency.

20. Roger, a plainclothes policeman, saw Lefty keeping a close watch on the
activity of the store clerk in Julius's Diamond Exchange. Roger approached Lefty and asked him to state the nature of his business, but
Lefty merely sneered at him. Roger searched Lefty's outer clothing and
felt what appeared to be a sharp object. Upon reaching into Lefty's
trouser pockets, Roger found a glass cutter. Lefty is charged with
attempted robbery.

When Lefty moves to have the charge against him dismissed, he will

  (a) win because Roger did not identify himself as a police-
       man;
  (b) win because he had a right to be where he was;
  (c) lose because all the elements of this particular case do
       not appear to add up to an attempt to rob the store;
  (d) lose because all elements of the search were carried out
       properly.

Answers

16. (A) is correct because Clancy did not first make a search of Punk's
    outer clothing. (B) is incorrect because it·is not knowledge of a
    weapon that is important, but rather the procedure that is fol-
    lowed. (C) is incorrect because it is not the possession of a weapon
    that is important, but rather the procedure by which the search is
    carried out. (D) is incorrect because guilt is not relevant to the
    manner of searching the suspect.

17. (B) is correct because there was no real evidence of a weapon. (A)
    is incorrect because the principle stresses not the motive, but the
    manner in which the search is carried out. (C) is incorrect. It is
    true, but Burny did not feel what might be a weapon. (D) is
    incorrect because it ignores the requirement that the officer feel
    something that appears to be a weapon.

18. (A) is correct because the owner's statement made Fogarty's fear
    unreasonable. (B) is incorrect because it contradicts the facts. The
    owner did corroborate Casey's story. (C) is incorrect because it is
    the manner of the search, not the possession of a weapon, that is
    important. (D) is incorrect because the principle does not make a
    special exception for ex-convicts.

19. (C) is correct. There was suspicion that Smith did nothing to
    dispel and a reasonable belief of a weapon on the part of Jones.
    (A) is incorrect because innocence alone will not dismiss suspicion
    of a crime. (B) is incorrect because the right to remain silent is not
    covered by the principle. (D) is incorrect and irrelevant to the
    principle.

20. (A) is correct. The principle calls for self-identification by the
    policeman. (B) is incorrect because a right alone will not quell
    suspicion. (C) is incorrect because although there appears to be
    an attempt, it was an improper search. (D) is incorrect because
    Roger did not identify himself as a policeman.

Chapter Two

Constructing Arguments

Reasoning involves a number of closely related skills. It involves being able to understand clearly what you are reading or what someone is saying; this is true of reading anything or listening to anyone about anything. The first step in any intelligent appraisal is understanding. When you are confronted with an argument for a conclusion, more aspects of reasoning come into play. In these cases it involves being able not only to understand, but also to evaluate. After you understand what is being said, you have to figure out if it is true, if the reasons the people have given are good ones, and if the argument proves its point. In other words, *you have to evaluate the argument.*

But reasoning does not apply only to arguments or positions of other people; it applies also to finding reasons to back up what *you* say and then being able to put those reasons together into a sound argument for something *you* believe. It involves understanding the implications of your beliefs, knowing what the strong points and weak points of your position are, and being able to evaluate your reasons and the conclusions they support.

Learning how to construct a sound, logical argument on your own can serve as a good foundation for learning how to understand and evaluate arguments given by others. Both skills are closely related. Both are built on the same concepts of logic, the same kind of ability to think your way through an issue by closely examining reasons and arguments.

1. *Arguments and Criticism*

Imagine that a number of people are trying to construct arguments that marijuana should be legalized and that they give reasons like the following:

1. It just doesn't make sense that you should have to go to *prison* for having a little bit of marijuana.

2. Marijuana has been used successfully by doctors to treat glaucoma and other diseases of the eye.

3. If marijuana is legalized, organized crime will stop making so much money out of it.

4. If it were legal, the government could tax marijuana sales, and the revenue from this could be used for many good purposes, including treatment of people who are addicted to hard drugs.

5. Jimmy Carter said it should be legalized.

6. Almost everybody agrees nowadays that there's nothing wrong with it.

7. It should be legalized. Marijuana isn't any worse for you than tobacco or alcohol. Smoking tobacco causes lung cancer and emphysema. Alcohol causes damage to your liver. Those are the really hazardous drugs, tobacco and alcohol. Marijuana doesn't do anything nearly as bad as either of them.

8. It is simply a myth that marijuana is addictive.

9. Marijuana is harmless. It should be legal.

10. Nobody has *proved* that marijuana is harmful. It should be legal.

11. You shouldn't have legislation against a thing that the majority of the population does. And today the majority smokes marijuana. So marijuana should be legalized.

Definition of "premise"

Each of these statements is intended as an argument for the conclusion that marijuana should be legalized. Each of them contains one or more stated *premises*. A premise is a reason used in trying to argue for a conclusion. Some of the arguments are better than others. Some are simply bad arguments. Some are incomplete. Some of the reasons given are true. Some are false. Some are irrelevant.

Now, legalization of marijuana is an issue about which you may have very decided opinions. You may think marijuana should be legal for reasons like the ones given here, or for other reasons. You may disagree entirely and think that marijuana should remain illegal, and you may have strong reasons for that position.

No matter what your position is, though, you should be able to analyze the issue logically, to understand and evaluate the reasons given, and to construct as good an argument as possible for the conclusion. Figuring out what is right and wrong about the reasons given here will help to open up some of the general techniques of logical analysis. These techniques will be applicable to building (and criticizing) arguments for any position.

Constructing a sound argument for the conclusion begins with being able to make plausible and relevant statements, premises, that support the conclusion. Ideally, these premises should prove the conclusion. But even if positive proof remains only an ideal, it is an ideal that can be approached. The premises we give should be true, or at least as likely to be true as we can make them. They should cover the whole conclusion and not omit anything.

Let's consider the arguments one by one.

1. It just doesn't make sense that you should have to go to *prison* for having a little bit of marijuana.

The statement in argument 1 may be true; in fact it probably is true. The trouble with the premise is that it is irrelevant to the conclusion. What is to be argued for is that marijuana should be *legalized*. The fact that it is senseless to put someone in prison for possession may be a good reason for making possession less than a criminal offense; it is not a good reason for making it not an offense at all. It may be senseless to put someone in prison for going through a red light, but that doesn't mean going through a red light should be legalized. *Irrelevance*

2. Marijuana has been used successfully by doctors to treat glaucoma and other diseases of the eye.

The single premise in argument 2 is irrelevant in the same way as argument 1. Treatment of glaucoma may be a reason for making marijuana a prescription drug for certain illnesses (the way morphine is), but that doesn't constitute a reason for believing that it should be legalized.

3. If marijuana is legalized, organized crime will stop making so much money out of it.

4. If it were legal, the government could tax marijuana sales, and the revenue from this could be used for many good purposes, including treatment of people who are addicted to hard drugs.

Argument 3 is more relevant. So is argument 4. Both of them contain premises that support the conclusion, at least a little, and the premises may be true too. Yet neither of them is a very good argument for the conclusion. To see this, notice that both of them could be used in the same way to justify almost any crime, no matter how serious. Legalizing prostitution and hit men would take money away from organized crime, and taxing them would bring revenue to the government. Legalizing marijuana may also do both these things. But these are, at best, unimportant, extra reasons for legalization; they could never be the main reasons.

5. Jimmy Carter said it should be legalized.

Argument 5 is an argument from authority. Its premise is also probably false because it is based on a much more guarded statement that Jimmy Carter did make. But even if Jimmy Carter did say exactly this, that still doesn't give you any reason at all for believing that *Arguments from authority* marijuana should be legalized. Jimmy Carter's opinion on legalization is no better than the reasons on which that opinion is based. The important thing, then, is to know not what Jimmy Carter said, but what reasons there are for believing that marijuana should be legalized.

6. Almost everybody agrees nowadays that there's nothing wrong with it.

Argument 6 is very similar to argument 5. It too is an argument from authority. The mere fact that everyone agrees about a statement doesn't mean that the statement is true. At one time everyone agreed that the earth was flat, but it isn't. It never was. Everyone was mistaken. Again, what is needed are the reasons on which this universal agreement is based, and these reasons must then be evaluated.

7. It should be legalized. Marijuana isn't any worse for you than tobacco or alcohol. Smoking tobacco causes lung cancer and emphysema. Alcohol causes damage to your liver. Those are the really hazardous drugs, tobacco and alcohol. Marijuana doesn't do anything nearly as bad as either of them.

Argument 7 contains five connected premises that compare marijuana to tobacco and alcohol. There is not as much evidence yet about the long-term harmfulness of marijuana as there is about the long-term effects of tobacco and alcohol. But no matter how much better marijuana appears than the other two, these reasons will not go far toward proving the conclusion. They are actually not very good reasons at all. The most that can be proved on the basis of argument 7 is that marijuana should be legal *if* tobacco and alcohol should be legal. But why should we think that "if" is true? After all, what argument 7 says is that both tobacco and alcohol cause serious diseases. That seems more like a reason for outlawing *them* than for legalizing marijuana. The fact (if it is a fact) that we allow two dangerous drugs to be sold legally is not a good reason for allowing what may be a third. It may be that alcohol and tobacco use are ingrained too deeply in our society to be abolished: The thing to do then may be to root out marijuana use before it becomes ingrained deeply also.

8. It is simply a myth that marijuana is addictive.

Argument 8 comes a little closer to the heart of the matter. Some evidence is required to back it up, of course, and it is by no means clear what amounts to "addictiveness". But if argument 8 is true, it does support the legalization of marijuana. The trouble with argument 8 as it stands, though, is that the stated premise is only a *partial* argument for the conclusion. An essential step in the reasoning process has been left out. The argument needs a second premise, one that is now missing from the argument. Until we fill in that missing premise, it will be impossible to evaluate how strong or weak argument 8 is. What's missing is this: Nothing in argument 8 says how important the addictiveness of marijuana is in the issue of whether marijuana should be legalized. That it is important is assumed — not stated. Obviously, if addictiveness is the major reason for keeping marijuana illegal, then argument 8 contains a major reason for legalizing it. On the other hand, if addictiveness is only a side issue, then argument 8 is not a very good reason. In any case, to take argument 8 as an argument for the conclusion is to make this assumption:

> PREMISE 2 (missing).   Addictiveness is a key issue in whether marijuana should be legalized.

Without such an assumption, argument 8 is only an incomplete argument. To evaluate argument 8 as an argument, we have to fill in the gap between it and the conclusion with a missing premise; then we have to see how plausible that missing premise is. Here it is not very plausible. Addictiveness is not really a key issue in the fight over legalization. Many of the people on both sides of the issue agree that marijuana is not seriously addictive. So even if argument 8 is true, it fails as an argument for legalization. It is only *part* of an argument. It needs a missing premise like premise 2 to complete it. And premise 2 is false.

9. Marijuana is harmless. It should be legal.

10. Nobody has *proved* that marijuana is harmful. It should be legal.

Arguments 9 and 10 are similar to argument 7 about tobacco and alcohol use in that all three concentrate on the supposed harmfulness of marijuana. But arguments 9 and 10 avoid making their claims hinge on a contrast between marijuana and anything else. They give more direct reasons. They say that marijuana has a certain property, and they assume that in virtue of that property marijuana should be legalized. Argument 9 makes a much more ambitious claim than argument 10. It says that marijuana is actually harmless, whereas all argument 10 says is that it has not been *proved* to be harmful. Which of these reasons makes the better argument? It is a tricky question. Notice that the premise in argument 9 — precisely because it is more ambitious — is more likely to be false than the premise in argument 10. Surely there are *some* bad effects; marijuana is *sometimes* harmful. And we haven't done enough study yet to know that there have not been appreciable bad effects. So we would be doubtful, at least, that the premise in argument 9 was true. But we would be much less doubtful of argument 10: Nobody *has proved* that marijuana is harmful. This makes it seem like argument 10 is firmer ground on which to build an argument than argument 9 is. We are at least much surer that the premise in argument 10 is true.

But look again. Both arguments 9 and 10 are making assumptions, just as argument 8 was. They all have *missing premises*. (Most arguments, in fact, have missing premises.) Argument 9 says that marijuana should be legal because it is harmless. The assumption behind this is:

PREMISE 2 (missing).   Things that are harmless should be legal.

This assumption seems obviously true. If a thing is harmless (actually does no harm of any kind), then it should be legal. In fact the assumption is so obviously true that it might seem like a waste of time to write it out. Still, it needs to be stated to fill in the gap in the argument. Unless you take premise 2 for granted (that is, unless you *assume* it), argument 9 will not make much sense. Argument 10 also involves a missing premise, but quite a different one; it says that marijuana should be legal because it has not been *proved* to be harmful. The assumption in argument 10, therefore, is:

PREMISE 2 (missing).   Things that haven't been proved harmful should be legal.

Now that assumption is not nearly so obviously true as the previous missing premise was. In fact the missing premise in argument 10 does not seem true at all. There are a lot of drugs and chemicals and plants that have not been proved harmful — a lot of them have not even been tested yet. Surely they shouldn't automatically be legal. (For instance, just because you've found some mushrooms (toadstools?) in your backyard that nobody has proved harmful, it doesn't mean that you can legally feed them to your rich uncle.)

11. You shouldn't have legislation against a thing that the majority of the population does. And today the majority smokes marijuana. So marijuana should be legalized.

Argument 11 can be evaluated more quickly. It is different from arguments 1–10 in that it is a complete argument. It has no gaps in it that need to be filled in with assumptions. In arguments 8, 9, and 10, for instance, unless you believe something that is not stated but *assumed* — the missing premises — you can believe the reasons given and yet not believe the conclusion. Argument 11 is different. It does not rely on any unstated reasons; everything necessary for the argument is stated outright. If the reasons actually given are true, then the conclusion is also true. This (as we shall see in Section 2 of this *Validity* chapter) is the property of *validity*. If you believe the reasons given, then you must also believe the conclusion. That is, if you believe that there should be no legislation against things that the majority does, and if you believe that the majority uses marijuana, then you automatically believe that there should be no legislation against marijuana (i.e., marijuana should be legalized). Argument 11 is complete and needs no additional premises. But just as needing missing premises did not automatically make arguments 8, 9, and 10 unsound, not needing missing premises does not automatically make argument 11 sound. In fact it is not a sound argument because everything it says is false. Sometimes you *should* have legislation against a thing that the majority of the population does. Racial discrimination is an example. The fact that a majority does something doesn't mean it should be legal. And despite the way it seems in some circles, the majority of Americans do not smoke marijuana. According to studies, a sizable percentage of the population has never even tried it.

False premise

The Basic Kernel of a Good Argument

To argue effectively for a conclusion, any reasons you start with must be plausible and relevant. If the premises you begin an argument with are not at least plausible and relevant, it is no use going on.

A *plausible* premise is one that is reasonable, believable at least on the surface, and not silly or obviously wrong. Plausible statements may turn out to be false on closer inspection later on, but they are the kinds of statements that are credible enough to *need* closer inspection later on.

Plausible

A *relevant* premise is one that helps establish a conclusion; it furnishes evidence in favor of the conclusion; it is not beside the point or *irrelevant*. ("Relevant" here means relevant to the *conclusion*, not relevant to your life.)

Relevant

The reasons why an argument's initial premises have to be plausible and relevant are easy to see and are mostly negative. If your opening premises are not at least plausible, they certainly cannot be used to establish something *else*. You would first have to give other reasons why your premises are right, and those other reasons would then have to be plausible.

The same kind of objection applies to giving premises that are irrelevant. "What you're saying may be right," your audience will think, "but it's beside the point of what you're trying to prove." You would first have to show the connection between your premises and the conclusion you're arguing for, and that would require another argument that would itself have to be relevant.

There is no hard and fast way to tell if premises are plausible or relevant. It is more a matter of being as reasonable as you can in studying some of the more precise tools in reasoning, and in practicing building and criticizing arguments.

Suppose you were trying to come up with an argument for the legalization of marijuana and your mind ran along the paths of arguments 1–11. Which ones would be good starts for an argument?

The first two arguments consist of premises that are plausible: A little bit of marijuana doesn't seem to merit prison, and marijuana has been used to treat glaucoma. But in neither argument is the premise relevant. Neither one has to do with legalizing marijuana for general adult use (and that's what the argument was supposed to be showing). So neither argument, nor both together, would be a very good start.

The premises in arguments 3 and 4 are plausible also. You might not be *sure* that organized crime would stop making so much money out of marijuana if it were legalized, but it is a reasonable thing to believe. You are willing to entertain the possibility realistically. That's what it means to say it's plausible. In these arguments, however, the premises are again irrelevant. Not so irrelevant as in the first two, though: Hurting organized crime and generating tax money do count *somewhat* in favor of legalization, but only very slightly. Neither one deals with the important issues. So neither of them is a good place to begin arguing either.

Argument 5, we have seen, is also not relevant. Jimmy Carter is not an expert, after all, and we have no reason to believe his statement is based on expert advice. And if it were, we would certainly want to know what the expert's advice was.

Skip down to argument 9. It's a different case altogether. Here the premise in the argument is not plausible. It is simply not reasonable to maintain that marijuana is harmless. After all, ordinary foods like bacon, milk, eggs (even drinking water in many places) are not harmless. It is difficult to believe that inhaling a foreign substance deep into one's lungs repeatedly is harmless. Before accepting such a premise, a great deal of evidence would have to be produced in its favor. So much for plausibility. Is the premise relevant? Notice first how answering this question doesn't seem to matter much. If the premise is so implausible, it couldn't be a very effective way of proving the conclusion, whether it is relevant or not. Still, a mental exercise shows that it is relevant in this sense: If it *were* true, it would certainly go a long way toward proving the conclusion.

Arguments 7, 8, and 10 consist of premises that are plausible; there is nothing initially unbelievable about them. And in each case the premises seem relevant, though less in arguments 7 and 8 than in 10. Though arguments 7 and 8 are not conclusive by any means, and they may not even be geared to the central issue in the debate, they do *contribute* to a defense of legalization. So they are moderately good starts for arguments. Argument 10 is the best place to start, however; its premise is both relevant to the central issue and plausible.

2. Soundness, Validity, Truth

The criticism leveled against these eleven arguments is primarily intended not to settle the issue of the legislation of marijuana, but to show how reasons and arguments can be criticized and evaluated logically.

The issue of legalization is by no means settled. First, there are undoubtedly other arguments besides arguments 1–11 for legalizing marijuana. You can probably think of some yourself. Some people, for example, have given an argument like this:

> 12. Even if marijuana is harmful, even if it is addictive, even if it leads to harder drugs, your body is your own. Smoking marijuana doesn't interfere with the rights of others. *You* have the right to decide for yourself if you want to smoke it.

Second, though none of the arguments as they stand seem to prove the conclusion, no arguments *against* the conclusion have even been examined. So we cannot conclude that marijuana should not be legalized. All we can conclude legitimately is that none of the eleven arguments has *shown* that marijuana should be legalized. Third, the criticism leveled against some of the arguments may not be fatal. For example, argument 10 was criticized because its missing premise looked false. And so it does: Things should not be made legal simply because they haven't been *proved* harmful. But maybe that isn't precisely the assumption of the argument. Marijuana is different from the untested mushrooms you found in the yard. It's not just that marijuana hasn't been proved harmful; it's that it still hasn't been proved harmful even though a lot of tests *have* been performed on it. If this statement is added to argument 10, that argument becomes a considerably better one for legalization.

The criticism of these eleven arguments shows that there are certain ways to analyze arguments and reasons logically. When you think up an argument for a conclusion, you should ask yourself a number of questions: "Are the reasons I give relevant? Are they true? Have I left any gaps in the argument? What assumptions am I making?"

The same holds true of reasons and arguments given by you or anyone else for believing anything. All arguments can be analyzed logically and are subject to rational criticism. You should ask essentially the same questions when you evaluate someone else's argument as when you evaluate your own: "Are the statements relevant?" That is, are the statements — the premises — relevant to proving that conclusion? "Are the statements true?" That is, do they describe the way things actually are or only the way the arguer thinks they are? "Are all the gaps in the argument filled in?" That is, have any required premises been left out? "If there are gaps, what missing premises need to be filled in? And are those missing premises in turn true?"

Learning how to answer each of these questions well requires both practice and a knowledge of some concepts and methods of reasoning. Fundamentally, there are two questions that have to be answered about any argument.

1. Are the premises true?

2. Even if the premises are true, do they prove the conclusion?

These two questions correspond to the two basic conditions of a sound argument: *truth* and *validity*. For an argument to be *sound* — to prove its conclusion — both conditions must be met: (1) all its premises must be true, and (2) it must be valid.

The Need for True Premises

Definition of "true"

It is easier at first to see the requirement of truth. *A statement is true when it describes the way things actually are*. To have a sound argument, one that really proves its conclusion, you need true premises. That is, your reasons for believing the conclusion must be true. If your premises are not true, you won't be able to prove that your conclusion is true by means of them.

Suppose your parents are trying to convince you that in the "good old days" people lived a better life than they do today. Now a statement like this is so vague that it is hard to tell whether it is true or false. "When we were young," they might say, "there wasn't any drug addiction or organized crime or disrespect for the law. And it stands to reason that life is better when these things aren't around." If the premises were true, they probably would be good reasons for believing the conclusion. Life probably would be better, at least somewhat, if there were no organized crime, drug addiction, and disrespect for the law. They are indeed relevant, but a little reflection will show you that the first premise is false, not plausible. Drug addiction, organized crime, and disrespect for the law have all been here for many generations, including your parents' generation. The claim that these things did not exist in the "good old days" won't help to prove the conclusion because it is a false claim; it doesn't state something factual. Now suppose your parents retreat a little and say, "OK, those have been around for a long time. But there certainly was a lot less organized crime then, and a lot less drug addiction too." This is a weaker claim than their first one, but you still have to figure out if it is true. You might contend that there was just as much organized crime then as now, that the difference between then and now is not the amount of organized crime, but the publicity it receives. And you might think much the same kind of thing about drug addiction too. If alcohol, nicotine, and caffeine, for example, count as drugs, it may be that the major difference in addiction between thirty years ago and now is not the percentage of hooked people, but the drugs those people are hooked on.

Now which side is right about organized crime and drug addiction? The best answer is that it's not clear. Unless your parents can come up with some solid, unbiased information to support their side, there is little reason to believe that their claim is true. Of course the same thing holds for your side, but your parents' position is more vulnerable. They are the ones who wanted to prove their conclusion, so the burden of proof is on them. Unless they can give some evidence that their claim about organized crime and drug addiction is *true*, their argument has not been shown to be *sound*. They haven't proved their conclusion.

The other concept that is central to good reasoning is *validity*. *An argument is valid when the conclusion follows logically from the premises.* Validity is roughly what people mean when they say an argument is *logical*. They mean that the premises bear a certain logical relation to the conclusion. A group of premises can lead you to believe a conclusion; they can take you closer and closer to it. But validity is one step stronger than this. A valid argument not only leads you to the conclusion, but leaves you no way out but to accept it. Probably, though, the best way to get a feeling for validity is by seeing the way it works in examples.

Definition of "valid"

Suppose your economics teacher says that the free-enterprise system produces less expensive consumer goods than any other system and that because the United States has a free-enterprise system, American consumer goods are less expensive than the goods produced in socialist countries. There are three distinct statements contained in this argument. Two of them are premises, and one is the conclusion. We can formulate the argument this way:

PREMISE 1.   The free-enterprise system produces less-expensive consumer goods than any other system.

PREMISE 2.   The United States has a free-enterprise system.

∴ CONCLUSION 1.   The United States produces less-expensive consumer goods than socialist countries.

One way to question the argument's soundness would be to ask if the premises are true. But whether they are or not, the argument is valid; the conclusion follows logically from the premises. To see this, disregard for the moment the question of whether the premises are actually true or false. Consider them only as *suppositions*. That is, *suppose,* for the sake of argument, that free-enterprise systems do produce less-expensive goods (as premise 1 says), and *suppose* that the United States has a free-enterprise system (as premise 2 says). Given these suppositions, we *have to* conclude that the goods the United States produces are less expensive than those produced in socialist (i.e., non-free-enterprise) economies. A socialist would be very likely to disagree with premise 1; some conservative Americans would disagree with premise 2. Thus both socialists and conservatives would maintain that the argument's premises were not true, and they would disagree violently with one another about where it failed. But both socialists and conservatives would have to agree that the argument was valid. The reason is that, whether the premises are true or not, the conclusion follows logically from them.

That is a distinguishing mark of validity: No matter which side people in an argument take, no matter how much they disagree about what is true, they always should be able to agree about the argument's validity.

You can get a better idea of why this argument is valid by contrasting it to an invalid argument containing the same premises. Suppose your economics teacher draws a different conclusion from the same two premises:

> CONCLUSION 2.   American goods are better made than the goods produced in socialistic countries.

Now it did follow from premises 1 and 2 that American goods are less expensive. But it does not follow from premises 1 and 2 that American goods are better made. To see this, again consider the premises only as suppositions. Suppose that indeed free-enterprise systems do produce less-expensive goods (premise 1) and that the United States does have a free-enterprise system (premise 2). But supposing that these premises are true does not tell us anything at all about how well made any goods are — free enterprise or socialist, American or whatever. The premises tell us only about the *prices* of goods, not about their *quality*. So if we try to draw the conclusion from these premises that American goods are better made (conclusion 2), we will have an invalid argument.

This example is in many ways an obvious one. Once you get the feel of the argument, you'll see that the premises here are actually irrelevant to the conclusion. This doesn't happen in all invalid arguments, however. Sometimes an argument will be invalid even though the premises are relevant to the conclusion: for example, when the premises cover only part, not all, of the conclusion. But when the premises *are* irrelevant to the conclusion, the argument will be blatantly invalid. Look at this argument offered by a student to a teacher.

*Irrelevance
and
invalidity*

> You should give me a good grade in the course because if I don't get a B, my father will be very angry with me.

What's wrong with this argument is not truth. The premise — that if the student does not get a B, his father will be very angry with him — may very well be true. What's wrong is that the premise gives you no reason to believe the conclusion that the teacher should give the student a better grade. The conclusion does not follow. The two statements seem unrelated. The argument is invalid.

The argument about American goods being better made is invalid in the same way. The premises are concerned with relative prices, the conclusion is concerned with relative quality, and nothing in the premises links price and quality. Of course we can add another premise that does link the two, and then that enriched argument might turn out to be valid. But this argument as it stands, with only the two premises it has, is *invalid*; the conclusion does not follow from the premises.

Consider a few more examples. Suppose someone is trying to prove that everyone should always obey the law. The person argues for it by saying, "Being a good citizen means always obeying the law, and everyone should be a good citizen." This argument is *valid*. It is valid because *if* we assume the premises, we have to believe the conclusion. To say it is valid doesn't mean that you think the premises *are* true. It doesn't mean that you think the conclusion is true either. It means that *if* you accept the premises, you have to accept the conclusion also.

This example can be varied a little so that it becomes a slightly trickier example of invalidity than the one we have just considered. Suppose someone else argues for the same conclusion by saying, "Man is an animal who lives in society. And people become full-fledged members of this society only if they obey all the laws of the society and obey them all the time. And everyone who lives in a great, free society like ours should become a full-fledged member of it. And that is why I say that everyone should always obey the law." This argument sounds a lot like a politician's speech because it uses a great many words to try to sound profound, but it says almost the same thing the previous argument said. Almost, but not quite. In spite of its length, the argument is invalid. If we disregard some fine points, the first two sentences say pretty much the same thing as the first premise of the previous argument:

PREMISE 1.   Being a good citizen means always obeying the law.

The rhetoric of the words is beside the point, and we can leave it out of our formulation. The third sentence, however, says something slightly different from "everyone should be a good citizen." Instead, it says something like this:

PREMISE 2.   Everyone who lives in a free society should be a good citizen.

Now the argument is invalid because we cannot prove from premises 1 and 2 that *everyone* should always obey the law. Part of the conclusion cannot be proved by the premises. All that the premises can prove is that everyone *in a free society* should always obey the law.

The other argument, if its premises were true, would show that everyone should obey the law, no matter what kind of society the person lives in. This argument, though, if its premises were true, can only show what people in a free society should do. If you draw a more general conclusion than that from the premises (as this arguer has done), the argument will be invalid.

Truth and validity are the two basic concepts in logical analysis because, for an argument to be sound (to prove its conclusion), it must be both valid and have true premises. Moreover, if you have a valid argument and all of its premises are true, you *have* proved the conclusion. When it comes right down to it, validity and truth of the premises are all there is to a good argument. The premises are true. Validity guarantees that the conclusion follows from those premises. Therefore, the conclusion must be true.

Definition of "sound"

The Combinations of Truth and Validity

Summary

You should realize from the beginning that the two concepts are independent of one another. It is possible for an argument to be both valid and have true premises (i.e., sound), or to be valid with *false* premises, or to be *in*valid with true premises, or to be neither valid nor have true premises. That is, arguments can be valid, or have true premises, or both, or neither; any combination of the two is possible. Only one of these combinations, though, produces an argument that is sound. Having true premises and being valid is the only way an argument proves its conclusion.

We can illustrate these combinations by means of some examples that are a little simpler than the ones we have been using. Their artificiality will help to illustrate the points about validity and soundness.

An argument that is valid and has true premises   "The 'tail' of a comet always points away from the sun. Therefore, when a comet is traveling away from the sun, it is preceded by its tail."

This is a sound argument; the single premise in it is true. (The less-dense gases in the tail are blown farther by the solar wind, and there is no air resistance to make them lag behind.) The argument is valid because the conclusion does nothing more than draw out a surprising logical consequence of the premises in more forceful language.

An argument that is valid and has false premises   "People should have the right to risk their lives as long as they do not endanger the lives or property of others. Motorcyclists who do not wear helmets or goggles do not endanger any lives or property but their own. Therefore, motorcyclists should not have to wear helmets and goggles."

This is a valid argument because if we supposed for the sake of argument that the premises were true, we would be forced to accept the conclusion. If we grant that people should have the right to risk their lives under these conditions, and that motorcyclists who do not wear helmets or goggles do fulfill those conditions, then to be consistent we have to accept that motorcyclists should have the right to go without helmets and goggles. That is what it means for an argument to be valid. Unfortunately, as the premises stand, at least one of them is not true. Not wearing goggles does seriously endanger the lives of others. So the second premise is false, and the argument is unsound. Whether the first premise is true is another interesting question. But no matter how we answer it, this argument is still unsound because premise 2 is false.

An argument that has true premises and is not valid   "Over 75% of the heroin addicts in the United States started out by smoking marijuana. Therefore, over 75% of the time smoking marijuana does lead to taking heroin."

The premise in this argument is true. At least the evidence of interviews, questionnaires, police reports, and records of penal and nonpenal drug-addiction centers strongly supports the premise. But the argument is nevertheless invalid. From the fact that a high percentage of heroin addicts began by smoking marijuana, it does not follow logically that smoking marijuana leads to taking heroin. Even if every single heroin taker began with marijuana, it would not follow that marijuana use leads to heroin use. By the same logic we could prove that breathing air leads to taking heroin, since 100% of those on heroin began by breathing air. The only statistics that would be relevant (i.e., logically connected) to whether marijuana use leads to heroin use are statistics on how many marijuana smokers end up taking heroin, not vice versa.

An argument that is neither valid nor has true premises   "More traffic accidents are caused by drunk driving than by all other factors combined. So if you drink (excessively), don't drive."

The argument is not sound; the premise is simply a falsehood. Drunk driving *is* a major cause of traffic accidents, but it doesn't outweigh all of the other causes, e.g., negligence, fatigue, speeding, etc. Nor is the argument valid. Even if drunk driving did outweigh all the other factors, it would not *follow* that you shouldn't drive if you've been drinking excessively. Notice that the conclusion of this argument — if you drink excessively, you shouldn't drive — is true. That, however, doesn't mean that the argument is valid. To be valid, it is not enough that the conclusion be true (for that matter, it is not enough that the premises *and* the conclusion be true). To be valid, the premises must *prove* the conclusion, and the premise of this argument does not do that.

Ask yourself how the premise is relevant to the conclusion. Strictly, to prove the conclusion, we would have to add two more premises:

PREMISE 2 (missing).   Drunk driving increases the likelihood of having an accident.

PREMISE 3 (missing).   You shouldn't do things that increase the likelihood of having an accident.

From these three premises together we can deduce the conclusion, but the conclusion is not deducible from the first premise alone. Moreover, once we have added the other two premises, the original premise is no longer needed to prove the conclusion. It follows from premises 2 and 3 alone.

We can now see that the original premise is actually quite irrelevant to the conclusion. The fact that more traffic accidents are caused by liquor consumption than by all other factors *does not show* that the likelihood of a traffic accident increases when you drink (of course the likelihood *does* increase, but the premise doesn't show this). It doesn't show this for much the same reason that what heroin addicts do doesn't prove anything about what marijuana smokers do. To find out if driving while drunk increases the chances of having an accident, we have to investigate drunk drivers and see how many of *them* get into accidents. It won't help to investigate the people who get into accidents and find out how many of them were drunk. So the missing premises 2 and 3 are independent of the stated premise 1; the conclusion follows from premises 2 and 3, but not from premise 1. So the original argument is not valid.

Judging Validity and Truth in Practice

Validity and truth are concepts to be used *both* when constructing an argument of your own *and* when criticizing someone else's arguments. They are the central concepts in reasoning about *any* argument.

Applying them in practice in either situation requires more than a merely theoretical understanding. If you find that a premise in an argument, considered fairly, is false, that is a fatal criticism. If it is someone else's argument, you have refuted it; you have found it to be unsound. If it is an argument that you are thinking of presenting, you should drop it and find another, or maybe reevaluate the point you were trying to prove. Similarly, finding that a premise is true is finding something favorable about the argument.

Reasons needed to judge truth

Remember that merely *saying* a premise is true or false isn't enough. That won't convince others, and it shouldn't convince you. You have to support your judgment with *reasons,* good reasons, plausible and relevant reasons.

Argument 3, for example, said that organized crime would stop making so much money out of selling marijuana if it were legalized. That is true. The reason is that organized crime makes so much money out of it partly *because* it is illegal. They can get it across the border, make payoffs to police, etc. If it were legalized, legitimate companies (tobacco companies, probably, as they already have trademarks on names like "Acapulco Gold") could bring it across the border and distribute and sell it more cheaply than organized crime could.

You might feel like objecting: "But organized crime *might not* lose money." But that's not a good objection at all. The mere *possibility* of its being false doesn't show it *is* false. If you think the premise is false, you have to maintain that organized crime *would not* (not just *might not*) lose money. And to maintain this you need reasons to back up what you say.

The reasons you give have to be real reasons; they cannot, for example, simply repeat the premise or be more doubtful than what you are using them to support. But they don't have to involve hard data or statistics. You know many things without being able to produce statistics to support them. Thus argument 6 has a premise that "almost everybody nowadays agrees that there's nothing wrong with marijuana." You know that is false. How? Well, if you just think about the varied population of the United States and how controversial an issue marijuana still is, you will have concrete reasons against the premise. If you happen to have statistics, so much the better, but they are certainly not always needed. What is needed is a plausible reason.

Validity is the other key way to object to an argument, your own or someone else's. If you find an argument invalid, you haven't refuted it, but you have shown that it is incomplete, that there are steps missing, that the conclusion does not follow from the premises. This will be a fatal criticism if the missing steps are illegitimate. If it is your own argument that you have found invalid, you should formulate the missing steps to guard yourself against assuming something illegitimate.

As with truth, you have to produce a *reason* to back up your judgment that an argument is invalid. Saying "The premises do not force you to believe the conclusion " is a reason in a sense, but it really just *repeats* your claim that the argument is invalid. After all, that is what the word "validity" means.

Reasons needed to judge validity

You have to show *how* the conclusion fails to follow from the premises, *how* you can accept the premises for the sake of argument and still not accept the conclusion. Thus, in argument 10 we showed that the alleged fact that marijuana has not been proved harmful (the premise) does not *all by itself* show that it should be legal. The premise does not even mention the idea of legalization, so it cannot prove anything about it. Another premise must be added to link legalization to proving something harmful: "Substances that have not been proved harmful should be legal."

Besides giving an explanation of how a premise is false or an argument is invalid, you can produce concrete examples that actually show the falseness or invalidity. An example that accomplishes this is called a *counterexample*.

Problems

Answer each question and give an original example or a brief explanation.

1. Can an *invalid* argument have true premises and a false conclusion?

2. Can an *invalid* argument have false premises and a true conclusion?

3. Can a *valid* argument have false premises and a true conclusion?

4. Can a *valid* argument have true premises and a false conclusion?

5. Can you have a valid argument in which you don't accept the premises at all and don't accept the conclusion either?

6. Must you believe the conclusion of a valid argument?

7. Must you refrain from believing the conclusion of an invalid argument?

8. Suppose you determine that an argument is valid, and then you discover that you believe the premises. Do you have to believe the conclusion too?

3. *Counterexamples*

Giving counterexamples is a particularly effective tool of criticism whether you are constructing your own argument or evaluating someone else's. Exercising self-criticism while constructing your argument makes you less subject to criticism by others afterwards.

Definition of "counter-example"

A counterexample is an example that goes *counter* to what is being claimed or argued. In the comments on arguments 1–11 about marijuana we brought up numerous counterexamples without calling them that. There can be counterexamples to the truth of a premise or to the validity of an argument.

Counterexamples to Truth

If someone says, "It doesn't snow in the tropics," you can reply, "Yes, it does. On many mountaintops, for example, it snows regularly." That is a counterexample. Someone has made a general claim and your example shows that it isn't true.

Counterexamples are often used this way in everyday life. We used one in talking about argument 11, which said, "You should not have legislation against a thing that the majority of the population does." We brought up racism. That's a counterexample because it is something you *should* have legislation against despite the majority's view. You should be able to think of many other counterexamples to this premise. Usually, the first counterexample is the hardest to develop.

It is important to be fair in giving counterexamples. Take the claim: "It doesn't snow in Miami." Now it did snow in Miami in 1977; a few snowflakes fell and melted as they hit the ground. This is not much of a counterexample, though, because it interprets the claim more strictly than it was meant. Reasonably interpreted the claim doesn't mean, "It absolutely *never* snows in Miami"; rather, it more nearly says, "It virtually never snows in Miami." In New Orleans, by contrast, there is very light snow on one or two days every couple of years, and a heavy enough snowfall to stay on the ground for an hour every ten years or so. Under these conditions it is false to say, "It doesn't snow in New Orleans." It does. There is a regularity in the exceptions (unlike Miami's once).

A single exception is not usually enough

When you're trying to show a claim false, you need a counterexample that's not merely a fluke. It should usually be a real and regular case.

Counterexamples to Validity

Counterexamples are even more useful in criticizing arguments for validity. We used one when evaluating the very first argument for legalizing marijuana: You shouldn't have to go to prison for possessing marijuana; therefore, marijuana should be legal. This argument is invalid; the conclusion doesn't follow from the premise. The same reasoning would show that going through a red light also should be legal. "Going through a red light" is a *counterexample to the validity* of argument 1.

Similarly, argument 2 can be shown invalid by means of a counter-example. It says that marijuana is useful in treating certain diseases. But that premise will not validly get you to the conclusion that marijuana should be legalized. "Morphine" is a good counterexample. Morphine too is useful in treating certain diseases; therefore, the same pattern of reasoning would show that morphine should be legal also. But that's not so. Therefore, something must be wrong with the pattern of reasoning used. The reasoning is not valid.

That is exactly how counterexamples to validity work in general. You find an example the premises are true of but which the conclusion is not true of. That is a counterexample because it shows that the same reasoning will lead you from true premises to a false conclusion. Because a valid argument is one that always leads you from true premises to a *true* conclusion, your example has shown that the reasoning in the original argument is not valid.

How counter-examples work

Therefore, one good way to test for validity is to search actively for counterexamples. You do this by supposing (for the sake of argument) that the premises are true. Then you examine other unmentioned examples the premises are also true of. Finally, you look to see if the conclusion is false for any of those examples. If it is, then the example is a counterexample. You're most likely to find counterexamples, then, by examining examples that the arguer did not have in mind.

Testing for validity

Rebutting Counterexamples to Validity

When you give a counterexample to an argument's validity, you rely on the arguer's agreeing with you that the counterexample makes the conclusion false. Thus the counterexample to argument 1 works only because the arguer agrees with you that going through red lights should not be legal. That is fine in this case because it would be clearly unreasonable to disagree with such an obvious truth.

But all counterexamples are not so obvious. Consider argument 3 again.

3. If marijuana is legalized, organized crime will stop making so much money out of it. Therefore, marijuana should be legalized.

We gave "prostitution" and "hit men" as counterexamples. The premise is true of them; if they were legalized, organized crime would stop making so much money out of them too. But the conclusion is not true of them. Prostitution and hit men should not be legal.

But now suppose the arguer replies, "Prostitution *should* be legal."
The arguer has *accepted* the example; he or she has refused to admit
that it is a *counter*example.

And that isn't so implausible here. You can't respond by saying,
"Look, it's clearly unreasonable to maintain that prostitution should
be legal." Many reasonable persons have maintained and do maintain
that position. It is not an *obvious* truth.

At this point there are really only two responses you can make: (1)
you can try to show (by giving other reasons) that accepting the
example *is* unreasonable, or (2) you can try to think of a stronger,
more obvious counterexample. In this argument "hit men" does this.
The arguer cannot reasonably accept that hit men should be legalized.

There is a give and take to arguing by means of counterexamples.
It offers a pure instance of strategy in reasoning, and it sometimes
opens up new areas for rational examination. Look at argument 2
again. "Morphine," as we have just seen, is a counterexample because
it too is used to treat diseases. So if argument 2 were valid, it would
show that morphine ought to be legal too. That is a good counterexample in this case because the mere fact that something has been
used to treat specific diseases is not a sufficient reason for thinking it
should be legalized. And "morphine" shows this.

But contrast this account with argument 12.

12. Even if marijuana is harmful, even if it is addictive, even if it
     leads to harder drugs, your body is your own. Smoking
     marijuana doesn't interfere with the rights of others. *You*
     have the right to decide for yourself if you want to smoke it.

"Morphine" is *not* a good counterexample to this argument. Someone who believed the premises in argument 12 would probably add,
"Of course, that goes for morphine too." Searching for a stronger
counterexample, you might arrive at "heroin." The arguer in this
case, however, might accept this example too by maintaining, "The
reasons I've given show that heroin, like marijuana and morphine,
should also be legalized. They are all aspects of personal freedom that
don't interfere with the rights of others."

Now your strategy in responding to the arguer will still have the
same two options. You can try to show that accepting the legalization
of heroin is unreasonable, or you can try to find an even stronger
counterexample ("suicide," maybe). The temptation (maybe justifiable) is to dismiss the person's views as unreasonable: "We should *not*
legalize heroin. Period. He or she is merely being stubborn."

But remember that the point of reasoning is not just to debate or to
win arguments. It is also to open up ideas that you have never
considered closely. If a seemingly reasonable person says in response
to your alleged counterexample, "Well then, heroin too should be
legalized," you shouldn't automatically leap to the conclusion that the
person is being irrational. Nor should you automatically jump to a

stronger counterexample. You should first *consider* the person's claim: What can be said *in favor of* legalizing heroin?

Let's try for a second to do just that. Notice that it is the sort of claim you might never consider closely. "Heroin" is a word that *sounds* scary. Your initial response is probably, "It's crazy to think heroin should be legalized." But a belief is only as good as the reasons it rests on. And many of the bad effects of heroin may be due not to the heroin itself, but to its being illegal. Many crimes are committed by addicts, for example, but that may be because illegality makes heroin so expensive. If heroin were given out cheaply in tightly controlled government centers, that might very well *reduce* the crime rate and thus save the lives of many innocent people who are victims of crimes committed by addicts desperately in need of money.

This is not a defense of the legalization of heroin; it is part of an examination of whether legalization is wildly irrational. Before you condemn such a view, you should think about it, and think about it hard. That is one of the best ways to open up new ideas for yourself. It is one of the ways scientists have made exciting discoveries, by considering a claim that has been taken for granted and asking, "But is it true?" That is a fundamental part of creative reasoning.

A Scheme for Rational Argument

This account of arguing and rebutting by means of counterexamples yields a diagram of how an ideal rational argument should run between two people.

A presents an argument.

B either accepts it as sound or criticizes it by producing a counterexample.

A either withdraws the argument or accepts the example.

Either B shows that accepting the example is unreasonable, or B comes up with a stronger counterexample, one which A cannot accept.

This is a scheme of the progress of an argument between two people. But it also diagrams a dialogue you can have with yourself while constructing an argument on your own. A useful procedure is to search for counterexamples to your own claims and reasoning. Being self-critical in this way will help you anticipate other people's counterexamples and be better prepared to rebut them.

Problems

1. Find two more counterexamples to the claim, "You shouldn't have legislation against a thing the majority does."

2. On page 27 there is a statement that says, "Being a good citizen means always obeying the law." Find a convincing counterexample (not just a fluke) to the truth of this claim.

3. On page 28 there is an argument that says, "Over 75% of the heroin addicts in the United States started out by smoking marijuana. Therefore, over 75% of the time smoking marijuana does lead to taking heroin." Find another counterexample to the validity of this argument.

4. Find a counterexample to the validity of the argument on page 29, "More traffic accidents are caused by drunk driving than by all other factors combined. So if you drink (excessively), don't drive."

5. Can you have a counterexample to a sound argument?

6. Describe a clear counterexample to the truth of the claim, "Anyone who commits suicide is insane."

7. Describe a clear counterexample to the validity of the argument, "Rockefeller must be a smart man. Otherwise he couldn't have become so rich."

8. "My grandfather smokes two packs of cigarettes a day, and he is eighty-seven. That shows that cigarettes are not so harmful." Is this a counterexample?

4.   The Three Steps for Constructing an Argument

Learning how to figure out whether arguments are valid and have true premises requires both that you have a clear understanding of each concept and that you are able to apply those concepts in practice. Understanding the concepts involves seeing that they are really completely independent of one another. Validity means that the premises — whether they are true or false — logically imply the conclusion. And you may have an argument in which the premises are true, whether they logically imply the conclusion or not.

Summary: soundness

Validity means that a certain relationship holds between the premises and the conclusion: In a valid argument, believing the premises *forces* you to believe the conclusion, assuming the premises *forces* you to assume the conclusion, and imagining that the premises are true *forces* you to imagine that the conclusion is true. In each case it is this force, a force of logic, that is the key to validity. Nothing forces you to believe the premises in a valid argument, but *if* you believe them, then you automatically believe the conclusion also. Similarly, the premises in a valid argument may or may not actually be true, but *if* they are true, then the conclusion is also. The truth of the premises, on the other hand, relates only to the "if" part of this formulation. A *sound argument* is simply a valid one with true premises. Putting truth and validity together is what makes an argument unbeatable. For then the premises are true, and the premises imply the conclusion. So the conclusion has been proved.

Learning how to apply the concepts in practice, however, involves more than being familiar with their definitions. The arguments one usually comes across in newspapers, books, and television, for example, are usually harder to figure out than those given here. Actual arguments are often more confused; important parts of them are left out or assumed; and irrelevancies, repetitions, and catchy language often make premises look more convincing than they are. Much of the time it will be up to you to sort out the argument. You will have to figure out exactly what conclusion the arguer is trying to prove. From what the arguer says, you will have to piece together the premises. You will have to fill in the assumptions that the arguer has omitted. Only at this point will you be in a position to criticize the argument in an informative, logical way and to see clearly what is right and what is wrong about it.

One of the best ways of learning how to reason is to learn how to construct an argument on your own. Having a grasp of the definitions of validity and soundness is not the same thing as being able to make up a sound argument for a conclusion you believe. Many questions arise almost immediately. How, for example, do you begin? What is the first thing you should do? There should be some orderly, logical way to start assembling premises to prove the conclusion. And once you have started, other questions will arise. How can you tell if a particular reason you have is relevant to proving the conclusion? Furthermore, how can you tell if the reasons you have given are true?

Validity can be questioned in the same way. Does your conclusion follow from your premises? How do you know that you haven't left out some required premise? How do you know that you haven't left a loophole somewhere, a way for your conclusion to be false even though your premises are true? How do you know when your argument is finished?

Logic cannot give full answers to all these questions. It can, though, give full answers to some, and partial, helpful, and informative answers to the others. To argue for a conclusion, the first thing you *Three steps* have to do is understand clearly what it says. You should be able to *in arguing* state its meaning. The second thing you have to do is understand how many different claims are being made in the conclusion. Conclusions often have more than one part or aspect. And isolating these parts carefully will virtually dictate what you have to establish to prove the conclusion. Third, once you have broken the conclusion down into its component parts, you have to think of a reason for believing each one. These reasons should, of course, be as plausible as possible, and each one should be stated in a separate premise.

There are three steps, then, involved in proving a conclusion.

STEP 1. State clearly the meaning of the conclusion.

STEP 2.   Isolate the component parts of the conclusion.

STEP 3.   Formulate the most plausible reason you can to cover each part and put each reason in a separate premise.

Much will be said about all three of these steps in later chapters. Following these steps conscientiously, we shall see, enables you to construct an argument that is valid. It does not guarantee that the argument will be sound because it does not guarantee that all the premises are true. But it can give you a deeper insight into the reasons for believing that it is sound.

Step 1. State the Meaning

The rationale for step 1 is straightforward. To prove something, you have to understand what it means. If two people are arguing about whether socialism is an unjust economic system, the first thing they have to do is get clear on what they mean by socialism. This does not always mean that they should be able to come up with a definition. But they should be able to agree at least on the important earmarks of socialism. Without this their disagreement cannot even begin to be resolved.

Similarly, you might ask about the statement, "All men are created equal." Is this true or false? Some people argue vehemently that it is true and become enraged even at the suggestion that it is false. Other people think that it is not only false, but that it is *obviously* false. In support of the statement it is sometimes claimed, "Nobody has the right to tell other people what to do. There is a basic dignity that every person possesses, and sex or color or religion has nothing to do with what rights a person has." Against that statement people sometimes say, "Not only is everyone not equal, there are not even *two* people who are equal. People have extremely different amounts of intelligence, ability, strength, and desire. All the qualities most basic to success in life are distributed unequally."

Before you can even hope to find out if all men are created equal, though, you have to know what kind of equality is meant. In this case some answers about the truth of the statement are forthcoming as soon as the meaning is clarified. If intellectual or physical equality (or even equality in the ability to succeed) is what is meant, then it is pretty obvious that all people are not created equal, at least not in that sense of "equal" anyhow. If legal equality, on the other hand, is what is meant — that every person should be subject to the law in precisely the same respects as every other person — then it is probably true that all men are created equal, in this sense of "equal."

Paraphrasing can resolve disagreements

Sometimes paraphrasing a key term or two will be of great help in resolving a disagreement about the truth of a conclusion. Two people who seem to be disagreeing about whether "All men are created equal" is true might merely have different kinds of equality in mind.

If the kind of equality meant is spelled out, their disagreements about what is true may vanish.

Step 1 requires that you at least question the meaning of all the words in a conclusion. Often the words that conceal the most slippery issues are the words that are usually taken for granted or overlooked. Some of them may be hiding something important; others may be not. It will help to paraphrase the whole statement by putting it into other words. You have to know exactly what the conclusion says before passing any judgment on its truth.

Question the meaning of all parts

It is important to realize from the beginning that step 1 does not say that you should "define your terms." Most terms, even our common everyday terms, are too hard to define for this to be a realistic requirement. It is almost impossible, for example, to think up an adequate definition for the word "table." Tables need not be flat (they can be warped) nor must they have four legs or three legs (they can have one leg or six legs; they can have no legs and be suspended by wire from the ceiling). They need not be of any particular shape or be intended to support objects (they can be too delicate and intended only for decoration). There is an exception to almost every trait that tables possess. Yet we all know what tables are. We agree about which things are tables and which things are not. We can name traits that tables *generally* possess. There is no reason then to require that we give a definition of the word "table." Instead, step 1 requires simply that we understand clearly what is being said.

Clarifying ≠ defining your terms

There is a close relationship between steps 1 and 2, and it points up the pitfalls of simple definition. Not all the terms in a sentence are equally important. The importance of a term depends on what the conclusion *asserts*. Take the sentence, "All men are created equal," again. In a modern context this asserts something about equality. It does *not* also assert something about creation. The meaning of the term "created" is thus not nearly as important to explicate as the meaning of the term "equal." "To create" means "to make" or, more precisely, "to make out of nothing," and it has theological overtones. When Jefferson said, "All men are created equal," he probably did mean that God made men equal. But that is not what the statement means when we use it today, and even in Jefferson's time that was not the *point* of the statement. Anyone who insists on the divine aspect of the word "created" is missing the point. The atheistic objection that men were not created at all is irrelevant.

Step 2. Isolate the Component Parts

Step 2 deals with figuring out the points a conclusion is making. Before you can give an argument for a conclusion, you must have a clear idea of what claims are implicitly contained in it. These subsidiary claims can be thought of as parts or aspects of the conclusion. To give an argument for a whole conclusion, you give a reason for each of the claims that make it up. So, before arguing for the whole, step 2 directs you to break the conclusion up into its component parts.

For example, Amendment VIII to the Constitution of the United States prohibits "cruel and unusual punishments." On this basis some people maintain that capital punishment is unconstitutional. But to argue that capital punishment is prohibited by Amendment VIII, you have to argue both that it is a *cruel* punishment and that it is an *unusual* punishment. Therefore, even if being electrocuted, say, is in fact a cruel way to die, this still does not mean that the Constitution prohibits it as a punishment. In many states it *is* the usual method of punishment for certain crimes. Thus, breaking down Amendment VIII into its component parts shows that it was designed not to eliminate cruelty primarily but to eliminate unfairness. It requires that the punishment for a particular offense be standardized so that the worst — the most "cruel" — punishment that anyone can receive for that offense is the standard — the "usual" — one.

An example of step 2 worked out

Consider a more elaborate example of breaking a conclusion down into its component parts. A common practical belief is that the head of a family should own life insurance. Suppose you wonder whether or not that is a smart way to spend your money. A good way to find out is to construct an argument. So the conclusion to be argued for is

The head of a family should own life insurance.

Underlining the important words in the sentence will bring out the claims in it.

First, the most straightforward claim in the conclusion is

The head of a family should <u>own life insurance</u>.

That is, the conclusion implies that there is some reason for owning life insurance, that it accomplishes something. Emphasizing this part of the sentence does not tell you what the reason is; that's what you will have to think up in step 3. It only tells you that this is one of the claims you will have to argue for on the way to arguing for the whole conclusion. It tells you what you have to think up a reason *for*. In step 3 you would probably arrive at premises like these:

PREMISE 1.   Owning life insurance furnishes money for funeral expenses.

PREMISE 2.   Owning life insurance furnishes money to help the family out of its debts.

PREMISE 3.   Some life-insurance policies pay off mortgages and send children through college.

These are the kinds of reasons that people naturally tend to give for the conclusion, but they are not enough to be an adequate argument for it. You can list all the benefits you want, and that still will not show that the conclusion is true. Though life insurance furnishes these things, nothing in the argument says that owning life insurance is a *good* way of furnishing these things. You have not yet singled out life insurance as *the* way to achieve these results. After all, robbing banks will pay for funeral expenses, help pay off debts, and, in some cases, even pay off mortgages and send children through college. (So will many less extreme methods.) But it does not follow that the head of a family should go around robbing banks. What you need to cover the underlined part is a premise that says

> PREMISE 4.   Owning life insurance is the best way to furnish these results.

Without premise 4 your argument cannot be valid because it will not show that the head of a family should *own life insurance* rather than use some other method for gaining those results, for example, robbing banks.

The argument, though, still is not valid. The other parts of the conclusion are not covered at all. Another claim contained in the conclusion is

> The head of a family <u>should</u> own life insurance.

That is, you have to show not only that owning life insurance furnishes certain results best, but also that these results <u>should</u> be furnished. Again, actually coming up with a premise to cover this part is done in step 3 rather than in step 2. Step 2 directs you toward finding a suitable premise by specifying what that premise must be about: It must say roughly that the family <u>should</u> be provided with those benefits that life insurance gives.

Finally, there is another important part of the conclusion that has not yet been covered.

> <u>The head of a family</u> should own life insurance.

Clearly, you cannot prove the whole conclusion without saying something about the head of the family. Why is <u>that person</u> the one who should own life insurance? To be valid, the argument must have a premise to cover this part. (Underlining this phrase also emphasizes that it needs clarification in step 1. Just who is the head of the family? The one who makes the decisions? The major wage earner? The one who contributes the most actual support to the family?)

Thus the statement that the head of a family should own life insurance can be broken down into three subsidiary claims. To argue for it, a person would have to say (1) that there is something that <u>owning life insurance</u> provides best, (2) that this something <u>should</u> be provided, and (3) that <u>the head of the family</u> is the one who should provide it. Realizing that these three claims underlie the conclusion is the basis for the entire argument. Now all that is left is to think up a reason for each claim and put each reason in a premise. Done correctly, this will automatically make the argument valid. If the premises are true, then the argument will be sound, and the conclusion will be proved.

In this example the parts are clearly differentiated within the conclusion itself, and isolating each one virtually dictates where you will have to look for a reason. Quite a few conclusions, especially those with many parts, will resemble this. In these cases most of the work of constructing the argument will be finished by the end of step 2.

Step 2 can generate premises

Sometimes, though, breaking the conclusion down into its component parts will be much less informative than it is here. Step 2 will still tell you which claims you will have to give reasons for, but it will not give you much of a clue about what those reasons are. This is especially true of conclusions that are worded most simply. Suppose you believe that math should be a required course, and you are trying to construct an argument to prove it. This conclusion has two component parts. They can be isolated by emphasizing certain words: first, "Math should be a <u>required course</u>," and, second, "<u>Math</u> should be a required course." To argue effectively for the conclusion then, you will need a premise about required courses and a premise about math. In practice this means you will have to give a reason for believing, first, that a course should be required if it possesses certain properties or characteristics, and, second, that math possesses those properties or characteristics.

Now this does isolate the two subsidiary claims involved. But it is considerably different from the life-insurance example because here the properties or characteristics needed are left completely open. If *you* think that math should be a required course, *you* will have to come up with reasons (in step 3) that state what those properties or characteristics are. Many properties and characteristics, perhaps, will fit into this role, and therefore many different arguments may be given for this same conclusion. All such arguments, though, will give reasons for believing both subsidiary claims.

Step 2 requires thinking

Underlining words in the conclusion to break it down into its component parts should never become just a mechanical task. It is not something you can do without keeping in mind what the conclusion actually says, what it means. You cannot emphasize just *any* word in a conclusion and expect to come up with a subsidiary claim. The statement,

The head of a family should own life <u>insurance</u>,

does not capture anything. The statement as a whole means that he or she should own life insurance in contrast to using another method. But underlining "insurance" does not point up any contrasting position, and so it does not contribute to understanding the argument. Only slightly less preposterous is the claim:

The head of a family should <u>own</u> life insurance.

It is too farfetched to say that <u>owning</u> life insurance contrasts with some other way of getting it (renting it?), so this is not a contrast implied in the conclusion. (Chapter 4 has more to say about how to decide if something is actually a component part of the conclusion.) Even underlining unimportant words, however, can sometimes help you not to overlook certain claims that you might just take for granted. It makes you at least ask yourself: "Is *this* a claim that's implicitly contained in the conclusion?"

Step 3. Formulate a
Premise to Cover Each Part

Once you have broken a conclusion down into its subsidiary claims, all that remains is to support each claim with a good reason. There is a sense in which step 3 is often the easiest step, and there is another sense in which it is often the most difficult. It is the easiest step from the point of view of pure logic. Once you fully understand the meaning of a sentence (step 1), and you know which claims you have to advance to prove the sentence (step 2), all you have left to do is to state your reasons for believing those claims. From the point of view of constructing a logical argument for that conclusion, no more analysis is needed. From a factual point of view, on the other hand, coming up with a defensible reason for many claims is quite difficult. Again, not from a logical point of view (you know what has to be proved), but from a factual point of view (you may not know of any facts that prove it).

Take life insurance again. The conclusion has been broken down into three claims in step 2.

<u>The head of a family</u> <u>should</u> <u>own life insurance</u>.

Now step 3 directs you to think up a reason to cover each of these parts. You do this by rephrasing each claim as a question and then answering each one with a premise.

An example of step 3 worked out

QUESTION 1.   What does <u>owning life insurance</u> provide best?

QUESTION 2.   Why <u>should</u> a family be provided with that?

QUESTION 3.   Why should it be the <u>head of the family</u> who provides that?

To answer one of these questions is to give a reason for believing the conclusion. To answer all of them in the correct way will yield a valid argument for the conclusion.

In this case, we will come up with an argument like this:

PREMISE 1.   Owning life insurance furnishes money for funeral expenses.

PREMISE 2.   Owning life insurance furnishes money to help the family out of its debts.

PREMISE 3.   Some life-insurance policies pay off mortgages and send children through college.

PREMISE 4.   Owning life insurance is the best way to furnish these results.

PREMISE 5.   When the head of the family dies, the family needs money for funeral expenses, debts, and, in some cases, to pay off mortgages and send children through college.

PREMISE 6.   The head of the family has the responsibility to provide for these family needs even after her or his death.

In this argument premises 1–4 answer question 1; premise 5 answers question 2; and premise 6 answers question 3. From these premises together you can validly draw the conclusion, "The head of a family should own life insurance."

When giving one or more reasons for believing a subsidiary claim, you have to be careful to make sure that the reasons you state cover the whole claim and do not leave any loopholes. (This will be explained in detail in later chapters.) To give a reason of this sort for each of the subsidiary claims in a conclusion automatically yields a valid argument for that conclusion.

The conclusion is only as probable as the premise   The argument, of course, may not be sound. That will depend on whether the premises you have given are true or not. Logically, the conclusion will be as probable as the reasons behind it. Your reasons for some of the claims in a conclusion will be more plausible than others. In fact sometimes your reasons for believing certain things will seem so clearly false to you once you make them explicit that you will end up changing some of the beliefs you started out trying to prove. (Premise 4 of the life-insurance argument, for example, is at least quite doubtful. Questioning it will lead you to search for other better, more practical ways of getting what life insurance gives you.)

Constructing valid arguments in the proper way requires that you make explicit the underlying reasons for believing the conclusion and that you state not only the superficial reasons, but also the more general reasons you *assume* to be true without ever really having thought about them. Once you actually have the argument constructed, you'll be in a much better position to evaluate your reasons, your assumptions, and your conclusions.

A great deal more needs to be said about each of the three steps. It may not be clear yet how to apply them in concrete circumstances. Nevertheless, you should be beginning to see how analyzing your beliefs logically by means of the three steps can help you in a very basic way. You will be in a better position to say exactly what a statement means, what claims are involved in the statement, and what reasons there are for believing those claims.

Exercises to Chapter Two

The questions in part A, part B, and part C of these exercises correspond to one another (thus question 1 is on the same topic in each of the three parts; so is question 2; and so forth).

In part A do each question on your own.

In part B various possible answers (some right, some wrong) are offered to the questions in part A. Evaluate each of these possible answers in accord with the instructions to that particular question.

Part C contains the correct answers to many of these questions, together with analyses, explanations, and further reasoning techniques. Part C also contains some additional questions. (They are in parentheses and are printed in italic type.) Be sure to answer these additional questions before proceeding.

For best results in reasoning, do not look ahead to part B until you have finished part A, and do not look ahead to part C until you have finished both part A and part B.

Part D contains additional similar exercises, but without comments or answers.

Part A

Construct the best argument you can for each of these two conclusions.

1. You shouldn't smoke.

2. Young men should not be charged higher rates for auto insurance.

Tell whether each of the following arguments is sound. Do this by taking each premise and saying whether it is true or false, and then by taking each argument as a whole and saying whether it is valid or invalid. Give a brief but good reason to support *each* answer.

3.   PREMISE 1.   You should treat others as you would like them to treat you.

PREMISE 2.   You don't want anybody to take advantage of you.

∴ CONCLUSION 1.   You shouldn't take advantage of anybody.

4.   PREMISE 1.   One of the things you want from a new car is good gas mileage.

PREMISE 2.   Toyota gives you good gas mileage.

∴ CONCLUSION 1.   You should buy a Toyota.

5.   PREMISE 1.   Our laws are written in language that is next to impossible for the common man to understand.

PREMISE 2.   The rich can hire lawyers who can get around the law because of the language.

PREMISE 3.   The common man cannot afford such lawyers.

∴ CONCLUSION 1.   Our laws should be written in language that the common man can understand.

6.   PREMISE 1.   Laws are supposed to protect everyone equally.

∴ CONCLUSION 1.   The laws should be written so that ordinary people can understand them.

7.   PREMISE 1.   Smoking in enclosed public places causes serious harm even in nonsmokers.

PREMISE 2.   The laws should not permit people to do serious harm to others.

∴ CONCLUSION 1.   Smoking in enclosed public places should be illegal.

Part B

1. Here is an argument with eight premises for the first conclusion in part A. Evaluate the argument. That is, take each of the premises and tell whether it is true or false and why. Then say how good a reason each is for believing the conclusion. Then decide which of the premises are needed to form a valid argument for the conclusion. Which can be left out?

    PREMISE 1.   Cigarette smokers have a higher risk of lung cancer and emphysema.

    PREMISE 2.   The Surgeon General says that cigarette smoking is dangerous to your health.

    PREMISE 3.   Cigarettes are very expensive.

    PREMISE 4.   Smoking cigarettes makes you look ugly.

    PREMISE 5.   Breathing cigarette smoke makes nonsmokers run a higher risk of lung cancer and emphysema.

    PREMISE 6.   Lung cancer and emphysema kill people.

    PREMISE 7.   To avoid the higher risk of lung cancer and emphysema, you shouldn't smoke.

    PREMISE 8.   No one should run the higher risk of lung cancer and emphysema.

    ∴ CONCLUSION 1.   You shouldn't smoke.

2. Here is an argument with six premises for the second conclusion in part A. Evaluate the argument. Are the premises true or false? Why? Which of the premises can be fitted together to form arguments that are valid? Support whatever you say with reasons.

    PREMISE 1.   Many young men are good drivers.

    PREMISE 2.   Some young men cannot afford the high insurance rates.

    PREMISE 3.   High insurance rates cause many young men to drive without insurance.

    PREMISE 4.   Good drivers shouldn't be charged high insurance rates.

    PREMISE 5.   People shouldn't be charged higher insurance rates than they can afford.

    PREMISE 6.   Insurance rates shouldn't be based exclusively on age or sex.

    ∴ CONCLUSION 1.   Young men shouldn't be charged higher rates for auto insurance.

In questions 3–7 write out specific criticisms for or against each of the comments below. Don't just agree or disagree, but say *why* the comment is right or wrong.

3. Evaluate each of the following comments on the argument in part A, question 3.

   PREMISE 1.   You should treat others as you would like them to treat you

   PREMISE 2.   You don't want anybody to take advantage of you.

   ∴ CONCLUSION 1.   You shouldn't take advantage of anybody.

   Comments:

   (a) Premise 1 is true because it is the golden rule.

   (b) Premise 1 is false. What if you are a masochist? You still should not go around inflicting pain on others.

   (c) Premise 1 is false. You punish your children for doing certain things, but you wouldn't want your children to punish you for doing those things.

   (d) Premise 1 is false. Suppose someone beats you up. That doesn't give you the right to beat that person up in return.

   (e) Premise 1 is true. If you would like others to treat you a certain way, you should treat them that way.

   (f) Premise 1 is true. If you treat others nicely, they will treat you the same. If you take advantage of other people, they will take advantage of you too when they get the chance.

   (g) The argument as a whole is valid because *if* you should treat others as you would like them to treat you and *if* you don't want to be taken advantage of, then *it follows* that you shouldn't take advantage of anyone.

4. Evaluate each of the following comments on the argument in part A, question 4.

   PREMISE 1.   One of the things you want from a new car is good gas mileage.

   PREMISE 2.   Toyota give you good gas mileage.

   ∴ CONCLUSION 1.   You should buy a Toyota.

   Comments:

   (a) Premise 1 is false. Not everybody wants good gas mileage. Some people want luxury or good handling.

   (b) Premise 1 is true. Even if other factors are important to you, *one* of the things you want from a new car is good gas mileage. It helps your pocketbook.

   (c) Premise 2 is true. Common knowledge.

(d) Premise 2 is true. Toyotas score among the best cars in their class on mileage tests.

(e) The argument is valid.

(f) The argument is valid because if you want good gas mileage and Toyota gives it to you, then a Toyota is what you should get.

(g) The argument is invalid because though you may want good gas mileage, it may not be the *only* thing you want from a new car; it may not even be a very *important* thing for you. So despite the fact that the premises are true, maybe you still should not buy a Toyota.

(h) The argument is invalid because the premises do not say that Toyota gives you the *best* gas mileage.

5. Evaluate each of the following comments on the argument in part A, question 5.

PREMISE 1.   Our laws are written in language that is next to impossible for the common man to understand.

PREMISE 2.   The rich can hire lawyers who can get around the law because of the language.

PREMISE 3.   The common man cannot afford such lawyers.

∴ CONCLUSION 1.   Our laws should be written in language that the common man can understand.

Comments:

(a) Premise 1 is false. It applies mostly to civil law, not to criminal law.

(b) Premise 3 is false. Lawyers are available to all. If you can't afford a lawyer, the court will appoint one for you.

(c) The argument is invalid. All this argument says is that the common man doesn't understand the laws, that other people can get around the law but the common man can't. None of this shows that the common man *should* be able to understand the language of the law. Maybe the complex language is necessary. Maybe we shouldn't care about the common man's understanding. Maybe we shouldn't even care about the common man's rights. All these are possibilities *other* than the conclusion. So the conclusion has not been proved.

6. Evaluate each of the following comments on the argument in part A, question 6.

PREMISE 1.   Laws are supposed to protect everyone equally.

∴ CONCLUSION 1.   The laws should be written so that ordinary people can understand them.

Comments:

(a) Premise 1 is true. The Constitution guarantees everyone equal protection.

(b) The argument is invalid. Just because the law is supposed to protect everyone equally, that doesn't show that they should be written in any particular way.

7. Evaluate each of the following comments on the argument in part A, question 7.

> PREMISE 1. Smoking in enclosed public places causes serious harm even in nonsmokers.
>
> PREMISE 2. The laws should not permit people to do serious harm to others.
>
> ∴ CONCLUSION 1. Smoking in enclosed public places should be illegal.

Comments:

(a) Premise 1 is false. It has not been proved that smoking causes serious harm in nonsmokers.

(b) Premise 1? I don't know.

(c) Premise 2 is true. One of the major functions of the law is preventing people from harming one another.

(d) Premise 2 is false. It would prohibit any number of things we do ordinarily, like driving a car, for example, or even breathing when you have a bad cold.

(e) The argument is valid. If smoking in enclosed public places causes serious harm and if the laws should not permit serious harm to be caused, then smoking in enclosed public places should be illegal.

Part C

Here are some comments, criticism, and further questions on the arguments in part B. Try to see how the comments and criticism apply to the arguments you have constructed in part A as well as to the criticism you gave in part B.

1. ∴ CONCLUSION 1. You shouldn't smoke.

The first thing you should do with this conclusion is to state clearly what it means. It is probably clear that what is meant by *smoking* is smoking *tobacco*, specifically smoking tobacco cigarettes. That much is clear. But who is meant by "you"? One plausible reading is that the conclusion means, "No one should smoke cigarettes." That is evidently what the arguer in part B, question 1 took it to mean. (*How can you tell that this is how the arguer took it?*) Another plausible reading is that it means, "People in general shouldn't smoke." (*Could it mean, "You, _____, should not smoke"? Fill your name in the blank.*)

Now let's consider the premises briefly.

> PREMISE 1. Cigarette smokers have a higher risk of lung cancer and emphysema.

The evidence of research certainly supports premise 1. We can say pretty confidently that it is true. Premise 1 also seems to be a very important reason for believing the conclusion.

PREMISE 2.   The Surgeon General says that cigarette smoking is dangerous to your health.

This is true. He did say this. But premise 2 is not nearly as good a reason for believing the conclusion as premise 1 was. It is another argument from authority. What we want to know is not what the Surgeon General *says* is dangerous, but what *is* dangerous. It is much better to think of premise 2 not as a reason for believing the conclusion directly, but as a reason for believing premise 1. We take the Surgeon General's word here because he knows about the tests that have been done on cigarette smoking and is reporting the results.

PREMISE 3.   Cigarettes are very expensive.

This is also true, though it depends on how much you value cigarettes. But in any case it is not much of a reason for believing the conclusion. It would be only if you think you shouldn't do things that are very expensive. (That is the missing premise needed to connect premise 3 to conclusion 1.)

PREMISE 4.   Smoking cigarettes makes you look ugly.

People's opinions vary on this quite a bit, and there seems to be no general truth or falsity to the matter. It is not much of a reason for believing the conclusion either. (*What missing premise would you need to fill in to connect premise 4 to the conclusion?*)

PREMISE 5.   Breathing cigarette smoke makes nonsmokers run a higher risk of lung cancer and emphysema.

This also seems to be supported by research, but how *high* the risk is is not so clear. Premise 5 would be a good reason for believing conclusion 1, though; it would be even better if it were combined with premise 1.

PREMISE 6.   Emphysema and lung cancer kill people.

True. Common knowledge. (*How does it help support the conclusion?*)

PREMISE 7.   To avoid the higher risk of lung cancer and emphysema, you shouldn't smoke.

(*Is this true or false? How can you tell? How does it fit in with the other premises?*)

PREMISE 8.   No one should run the higher risk of lung cancer and emphysema.

(*This might look true at first, but you should examine it again. Why shouldn't you run the higher risk? Doesn't the answer depend very heavily on how much higher the risk really is and on how much you like to smoke?*)

The only premises that fit together to form a valid argument for conclusion 1 are premises 1 and 8. It would be a better argument if premise 5 could somehow be related to the conclusion. This could be done in either of two ways. First, another premise could be added which says

PREMISE 9 (missing). You shouldn't do things that make others run a higher risk of lung cancer and emphysema.

Second, you could modify premise 8 so that it takes account of what premise 5 says.

PREMISE 8 (revised). No one should run the higher risk and cause others to run a higher risk of lung cancer and emphysema.

Premise 7 is not a good premise to have in the argument because it is not properly a *premise* at all. What it is is an *argument* written out as a statement. What you were trying to prove was "you should not smoke." You cannot prove that by saying "to avoid the higher risk, you should not smoke." That isn't a reason; it's a reason *plus* the conclusion.

2. ∴ CONCLUSION 1. Young men should not be charged higher rates for auto insurance.

Here again the conclusion needs to be paraphrased. There are two problems with its meaning: First, *which* young men are being talked about, and second, higher rates than *who*? It is implausible to take the conclusion to be saying that *no* young men should be charged higher rates. Surely that's too sweeping (and false) a claim to be a likely interpretation of what the statement means. More reasonably, it means that young men *in general* should not be charged higher rates, or that they should not be charged higher rates simply because they are young men. (*What is the rest of the paraphrase? Higher rates than who?*)

Now consider the premises:

PREMISE 1. Many young men are good drivers.

Surely it is true. They have very good reflexes and vision for example. And it is true even if they do lack driving experience.

PREMISE 2. Some young men cannot afford the higher insurance rates.

Obviously true.

PREMISE 3. High insurance rates cause some young men to drive without insurance.

Also obviously true, especially because it only says *some* young men. It also looks like it might be a good reason for believing conclusion 1. (*But how good a reason is it? Note that premise 3 says "high insurance rates," whereas conclusion 1 says "higher rates." Does this make any difference about how good a reason it is?*)

PREMISE 4. Good drivers shouldn't be charged higher insurance rates.

There are many good reasons for believing that premise 4 is true. Good drivers have fewer accidents than other people. There is thus less likelihood that the good driver's insurance company will have to pay off, and so it shouldn't charge such drivers high rates. In addition if premise 4 is true, then you have an argument that is pretty close to being *sound*. Premise 4 fits together nicely with premise 1. Together they do not quite prove conclusion 1, but they do prove a conclusion that is very nearly the same as conclusion 1. They prove that *many* young men should not be charged higher rates for automobile insurance. *(How would you beef up this argument – either by adding another premise or by changing premise 1 or premise 4 – to prove conclusion 1 itself?)*

PREMISE 5.   People shouldn't be charged higher rates than they can afford.

This statement is clearly false. Insurance rates should be linked to the amount of damages a driver causes, or is likely to cause, or some such thing. They should not be linked to what people can afford because that would, in effect, be underwriting bad drivers. Premise 5 does have one virtue as a premise, however. When coupled with premise 2, it makes a *valid* argument for the conclusion. This argument is not (as we have just seen) sound, but it is valid: If we were to accept those premises, we would *have* to accept the conclusion. The fact that premise 5 is false, incidentally, shows that premise 2 is a bad reason for believing the conclusion. The only way premise 2 could be a good reason is if premise 5 were true, because premise 5 is needed to "connect" premise 2 to the conclusion. So, the fact that premise 5 is so clearly false shows exactly what is wrong with premise 2 as a reason.

PREMISE 6.   Insurance rates shouldn't be based exclusively on age or sex.

There is a way in which premise 6 is the best premise given so far. In the first place it looks true. Insurance rates should be based on things (like good driving — premise 1) that are geared to the amount of money the insurance company will have to pay out for an individual driver. In the second place premise 5 is a fertile premise. It points to many other areas where hard thinking needs to be done on the problem: Are insurance rates for young men based on their age and sex exclusively? Is charging higher rates, then, discriminatory? Is it unconstitutional? Is there a basis for a class action suit against the insurance companies? Is a company justified in basing its rates on age and sex exclusively if that age and sex group has a higher accident rate? Shouldn't rates be geared to what an *individual* is likely to do rather than to what the *group* is likely to do? Premise 6 is a good premise because it brings these questions to mind and so links the problem to other farther-reaching issues. If premise 1 is added to premise 6, we have indeed the basis of an interesting and rich argument for the conclusion. It is not valid though, at least not yet. A missing premise, or more than one, needs to be filled in to make it valid. *(What missing premises need to be added to premise 1 and premise 6 to have a valid argument for the conclusion? These missing premises should link* both *premise 1 and premise 6 to conclusion 1. Fill in the missing premises. Is the argument you have come up with* sound?*)*

For questions 3–7, be sure to apply the answers given here both to the criticism you gave in part B and to the answers you gave on your own in part A.

3.   PREMISE 1.   You should treat others as you would like them to treat you.

PREMISE 2.   You don't want anybody to take advantage of you.

∴ CONCLUSION 1.   You shouldn't take advantage of anybody.

(a) Premise 1 is true because it is the golden rule.

Not a good reason at all. Calling premise 1 the golden rule gives you no evidence that it is true.

(b) Premise 1 is false. What if you are a masochist? . . .

This is a legitimate objection to premise 1 if "you" there means "everyone." Masochists are a *counterexample* to premise 1.

(c) Premise 1 is false. You punish your children even though you wouldn't want them to punish you.

Another counterexample. It is a counterexample provided you think you *should* punish your children. (*Why is this provision necessary?*)

(d) Premise 1 is false. Suppose someone beats you up. That doesn't give you the right to beat that person up in return.

This is not an objection. It is *not* a counterexample. Premise 1 doesn't say that if people treat you badly, you can treat them badly in return. It says you should treat people as you would like them to treat you. Those are entirely different things.

(e) Premise 1 is true. If you would like others to treat you a certain way, you should treat them that way.

This "reason" is not a reason at all. It merely repeats what premise 1 says. You cannot support a statement by repeating it.

(f) Premise 1 is true. People will reciprocate the way you treat them.

This is a good reason because it bases belief in premise 1 on what people will do. The reason, then, for treating others as you would like them to treat you is that this will get you treated the way you would like to be treated. Given this reason, premise 1 becomes a selfish principle. (*But is the reason true? Do people generally treat you as you treat them?*)

(g) The argument is valid because the conclusion follows.

Exactly so.

4.   PREMISE 1.   One of the things you want from a new car is good gas mileage.

PREMISE 2.   Toyota gives you good gas mileage.

∴ CONCLUSION 1.   You should buy a Toyota.

(a) Premise 1 is false. Not everyone wants good gas mileage. Some people want luxury or good handling.

(b) Premise 1 is true. Even if other factors are important, *one* of the things you want from a new car is good gas mileage. It helps your pocketbook.

(Does (a) answer (b)? How?)

(c) Premise 2 is true. Common knowledge.

This is a fair answer in this case, though usually it isn't.

(d) Toyotas score among the best on mileage tests.

This is a better answer than (c).

(e) The argument is valid.

You need to spell out *why* you think it is valid.

(f) The argument is valid because if you want good gas mileage and Toyota gives it to you, then a Toyota is what you should get.

No. The same reasoning would "prove" that you should buy a Datsun, or a horse, or a new pair of shoes. There are many counterexamples. The premises do not force you to believe that a Toyota is what you should buy.

(g) The argument is invalid because good mileage may not be the most important thing. So the premises might be true and the conclusion false.

Right. (*Think about ads for other products. They seldom give you reasons to buy their product rather than their competitor's. They usually give you at most a reason for buying their kind of product. Tide, Cheer, Oxydol, Biz, etc., all clean your clothes. What reasons do laundry-detergent commercials give you for buying their particular brand? Are the reasons they give convincing ones?*)

5.   PREMISE 1.   Our laws are written in language that is next to impossible for the common man to understand.

PREMISE 2.   The rich can hire lawyers who can get around the law because of its language.

PREMISE 3.   The common man cannot afford such lawyers.

∴ CONCLUSION 1.   Our laws should be written in language that the common man can understand.

(a) Premise 1 is false. It applies mostly to civil law, not to criminal law.

This is a good and relevant distinction. But it doesn't show that premise 1 is false exactly. It does show that premise 1 should restrict itself to talking about civil law. It would probably be a good idea simply to interpret the argument as talking about civil law whenever it talks about "our laws."

(b) Premise 3 is false. Lawyers are available to all. If you can't afford a lawyer, the court will appoint one for you.

Although this is no doubt true, it does not have much to do with premise 3. Premise 3 does not say that the common man cannot afford to hire a lawyer, it says the common man cannot afford to hire *such* lawyers, namely, the kind of lawyer the rich can hire, one who will help you get around the law. Court-appointed lawyers aren't likely to do this. Neither are the lawyers the "common man" (whoever that is) *can* afford.

(c) The argument is invalid because . . .

It *is* invalid. (*Does the long reason given in part B prove that the argument is invalid? How?*)

6.   PREMISE 1.   Laws are supposed to protect everyone equally.

∴ CONCLUSION 1.   The laws should be written so that ordinary people can understand them.

(a) Premise 1 is true. The Constitution guarantees everyone equal protection.

This is a good reason only within a limited context in which the truth of the United States Constitution is accepted by all parties as a given. Outside that context (for example, anywhere else in the world) it is not much of a reason. It is an argument from authority. What makes you think that what the Constitution says in this regard is right?

(b) The argument is invalid, Equal protection (premise 1) doesn't show that the laws should be understandable to all (the conclusion).

Right. The argument is invalid, and that's why.

7.   PREMISE 1.   Smoking in enclosed public places causes serious harm even in nonsmokers.

PREMISE 2.   The laws should not permit people to do serious harm to others.

∴ CONCLUSION 1.   Smoking in enclosed public places should be illegal.

(a) Premise 1 is false. It has not been proved that smoking causes serious harm to nonsmokers.

The fact that it has not been proved is *not* a reason to say that premise 1 is *false*. To say premise 1 is false is to assert that smoking in enclosed public places *does not cause* serious harm to nonsmokers. But this has not been proved either. If it hasn't been proved one way or the other, is premise 1 true or false? The correct answer is the one given in (b):

(b) Premise 1? I don't know.

Exactly right. If it hasn't been proved either way, then the best answer you can give is "I don't know." However, you cannot just *say* "I don't know." You have to give a reason why that's the best answer. That reason is given in the criticism of (a) above.

(c) Premise 2 is true. One of the major functions of the law is preventing people from harming one another.

(d) Premise 2 is false. It would prohibit things like driving a car and breathing when you have a bad cold.

(Which answer is right, (c) or (d)? Is one of the major functions of the law to prevent people from harming one another? Does this show that premise 2 is true? Are driving a car and breathing when you have a cold counterexamples to premise 2? If so, which is better as a counterexample? Why?)

(e) The argument is valid. If smoking in enclosed public places causes serious harm and if the laws should not permit serious harm to be caused, then the laws should not permit smoking in enclosed places; that is, smoking in enclosed public places should be illegal.

Exactly.
(In arguments 3–7 above, which of them are sound? Why?)

Part D

Construct the best argument you can for the conclusions in numbers 1, 2, and 3. Afterwards, criticize your arguments. Is each of the premises true? Why do you think so? Is the argument valid? Why?

1. Medical care should be made affordable for everyone.

2. To get a good job, get a good education.

3. Life, liberty, and the pursuit of happiness are inalienable rights.

Carefully evaluate each of the arguments in numbers 4–8. Say whether each of the premises is true or false and why. Then say whether the argument as a whole is valid or invalid and why.

4.   PREMISE 1.   Each species of plant or animal occupies a unique place in the environment.

PREMISE 2.   If one becomes extinct, there is no telling what impact that will have on the rest of the environment.

PREMISE 3.   The loss will be irreplaceable.

∴ CONCLUSION 1.   We cannot allow any species to become extinct if we can help it.

5.   PREMISE 1.   If gasoline prices keep going up, inflation will become even more burdensome.

PREMISE 2.   Regulation by the government is the only effective way to keep gasoline prices down.

∴ CONCLUSION 1.   The government should regulate gasoline prices.

6.   PREMISE 1.   In the United States guns are easy to buy.

PREMISE 2.   In European countries it is much harder to get a gun.

PREMISE 3.   There are far fewer shootings per capita in European countries than in the United States.

∴ CONCLUSION 1.   Guns should be controlled more closely in the United States.

7.   PREMISE 1.   We shouldn't inflict pain, especially if we can easily avoid it.

PREMISE 2.   Cows, pigs, chickens, etc., feel pain when they are butchered.

PREMISE 3.   Eating vegetable matter will feed us more efficiently, cheaply, and nutritiously than eating meat.

∴ CONCLUSION 1.   The only moral choice is vegetarianism.

8.   PREMISE 1.   A sound argument is one that leads you from true premises to true conclusions.

PREMISE 2.   But you cannot ever tell for sure if anything is true.

∴ CONCLUSION 1.   The idea of a sound argument is useless.

Answer each of the questions in numbers 9–16.

9.   What if all the premises in an argument are true? Does that show that the conclusion is true also?

10.   In a valid argument if you accept the premises you have to accept the conclusion. But what if you don't accept the premises? Won't that show that the argument is not valid? Explain.

11.   Suppose someone gives you an argument in favor of a conclusion. You inspect the argument and find it is valid. Moreover, you already know that the conclusion is true. What do you therefore know about the arguer's premises? Explain.

12.   Suppose that someone gives you an argument, but you think its conclusion is false. You inspect the argument and find it is valid. Moreover, suppose you show that one of the arguer's premises is false. What have you therefore shown about the arguer's conclusion? Explain.

13.   Suppose someone gives you an argument in favor of a conclusion. You inspect the argument and find it is valid. Then you inspect the premises and find that you believe all of them. Then you look at the conclusion and find that you do not believe it; you think it is false. What are you going to do?

14.   "It is worth noting that over the past fifteen years — a period during which American women began using the pill regularly — life expectancy among American women has *increased* significantly. That fact alone should make it obvious that the pill is not a *major* health hazard." (Michael

H. Hart, *The 100: A Ranking of the Most Influential Persons in History (New York: 1980), p. 421.)*

Find a counterexample to this argument. If Hart's reasoning is correct, what other actions would not be "a *major* health hazard"?

15. Can you think up a counterexample to the reasoning in this argument, or do you think it requires a physical experiment? Why?

> Contrary to popular belief, it doesn't do any good to run fast when it is raining — you'll get just as wet. The faster you run, the more drops hit you per second because you run "into" drops that would have missed you if you were walking. So what you make up by going fast you lose by being hit by more drops per second.

16. Sometimes people try to disprove a position by giving attempted counterexamples that don't work. The following is a genuine chain letter. Identify the attempted counterexamples, explain how they are supposed to work, and then tell how they fail.

> "TRUST IN THE LORD WITH ALL YOUR HEART AND HE WILL ACKNOWLEDGE AND HE WILL LIGHT THE WAY."
>
> This prayer was sent to you for luck. The original copy is from the Netherlands, it has been around the world ten times. The luck has been brought to you. You're to receive good luck within four days of receiving this letter. "This is no joke." You will receive it in the mail.
>
> Send copies of this letter to people you think need good luck. Do not send money, do not keep this letter. It must leave you within ninety-six hours after you receive it.
>
> Please send twenty copies and see what happens to you on the fourth day.
>
> This chain comes from Venezuela and was written by St. Anthany De Calif, a missionary from South America.
>
> Since this chain must make a tour of this world, you must send twenty copies, identical to this one photostated. Either to one of your friends, parents or acquaintances.
>
> An officer received $70,000. Don Colbert received $30,000 but lost it because he broke the chain. While in the Phillipines General Welch lost his life six days after he received this letter, he failed to circumstance the prayer. However, before he died he received $775,000.
>
> After a few days you will receive a surprise. "This is true even if you are not superstitious."
>
> Take note of the following:
>
> Constantine Black received the chain in 1933. He asked his secretary to make twenty copies and send them. A few days later he won a lottery in his country for two million dollars.
>
> Carlos Crocbrite an office employee received the chain, he forgot it. A few days later he lost his job. He found the chain and

sent it to twenty people and five days later he received a better job.

Doris Merchild received the chain and did not believe in it. Nine days later she died.

FOR NO REASON WHATSOEVER SHOULD THIS CHAIN BE BROKEN.

Chapter Three

Clarifying
Meaning

1. The Need for Clarifying Meaning

*Truth
presupposes
meaning*

Before you can even begin to figure out if a statement is true or false, you have to know what it means. Unless you know the meaning of a statement, it is literally impossible to make even a reasonable guess about whether it is true or false.

You can convince yourself of this by considering an extreme case. Take the statement:

Snijeg je bijel.

Is it true? Is it even plausible? Does it state a fact? You cannot give a rational answer to any of these questions. Unless you know that this is a sentence in Croatian that means "snow is white," you will have no idea whether it is true or false.

The same holds for statements in English. If you do not know what a statement means, then it is as if it was written in Croatian as far as you are concerned. If someone says,

The Rockefeller Foundation is eleemosynary,

you cannot even give a reasonable guess about whether it is true or false unless you know the meaning of the last word. It does not follow from this that if you do know the meaning of a statement, you will know automatically whether it is true or false. But it does follow that the first step in judging a statement as true is to understand its meaning.

This chapter will explain this first step (introduced in Chapter Two) of constructing arguments: State the meaning. Chapter Four will concentrate on steps 2 and 3. Both chapters also, of course, aim at developing critical and logical patterns of thinking about your beliefs and the reasons that back them up.

An Example of Clarifying Meaning

Take natural foods as an example. In the last fifteen years or so there have been many claims about things that are natural. Organically grown vegetables are said to be natural, as are meats and cereals that have no "chemical preservatives" added. Other things besides foods are often called natural: certain kinds of clothing, housing, transportation, detergents, furniture. There is even a brand of cigarettes that is advertised as "natural" ("nothing artificial added"). These claims all imply that natural things are better than things that are not natural, foods in particular, and this is a claim you might wonder about. One good way to approach it is to think up the best argument you can for the conclusion, "Natural foods are better for you than foods that are not natural."

The first step in constructing an argument is to state the meaning of the sentence to be argued for. To say that one food (or one kind of food) is better for you than another means that it is healthier, that it contributes more to your well-being. That part of the conclusion is easy enough. But what does it mean to call some foods "natural"? The question is not an easy one.

Your first try at clarifying the meaning might be that something is natural if it "comes from nature," that is, from plants and animals and rocks and so forth. This is a fair answer in a way, but a little reflection will show that it won't do at all. "Nature" also contains the minerals from which we process our most lethal chemicals. Besides, one of the animals is man himself, and so everything that is man-made will be natural too. In short, if "natural" means "comes from nature," then *everything* without exception is natural. This can't be right, then, because the point of calling certain things natural was to contrast them to other things that aren't natural, i.e., things that are artificial.

Your next interpretation of "natural" might be that "natural" means "nothing artificial added," and what "artificial" means is "man-made." This clarification does capture some of what is meant by the word "natural," but it raises at least two problems. First, there is not a very clear-cut distinction between what is man-made and what is not. We get both organically grown vegetables and artificial foods by taking carefully selected things that are found in nature and combining and recombining them, so being natural is only different in degree from being artificial. The second problem is that this clarification shows that the conclusion is false. The fact that something is natural, with nothing artificial added, does not imply that it is healthier. (Toadstools are natural; the most lethal poisons known are those found naturally in certain animals; organic meat becomes toxic within days.) There is no reason to think that a natural thing is automatically better for you than a man-made thing. So if all "natural" means is "nothing man-made added," the claim, which seemed true at the outset, now seems clearly false.

But nonnatural foods are often made of chemicals or have chemicals added to them. Many of them contain preservatives, and some even contain drugs. Surely these are reasons for preferring natural foods.

Inspecting the reasons closely, however, you'll find that they are not reasons at all. They are ways of just resaying the same slippery and false thing, that natural foods are better. It may *sound* like a condemnation to say that some foods are made of chemicals or have chemicals added to them, but it really isn't. *All* things are made of chemicals, organically grown tomatoes as much as plastic or sodium chloride. To say that a product has chemical preservatives added just means that something has been put in it to keep it from spoiling. (Some preservatives may indeed be bad for you; that's not what is at issue here. But realizing a preservative is chemical is not a *reason* for believing that it is bad for you.) Similarly, to say that a product has drugs in it is not to say anything particularly bad. A "drug" is just a "substance used as a medicine." If you take organically grown willow leaves for your headache, you are taking a drug just as truly as if you take the aspirin (acetylsalicylic acid to use the *chemical* name) that the willow leaf contains.

The statement, "Natural foods are better for you," if it says anything at all, says something that is clearly false. It *seems* true initially because we attach positive subjective feelings to the word "natural"; it *sounds* reassuring. The statement is supported by other words (like "chemicals" and "drugs") that call up strong negative feelings. To find out if the statement actually is true, however, you have to disregard those feelings and get down to what the statement really means. A good way to do this is to *paraphrase* the statement: to restate it in different, clearer words.

The meaning of a statement may give you difficulty in two different ways. First, it may contain words that you do not understand. Second, you may know what each word in the statement means by itself and yet not know the meaning of the whole statement.

The Meaning of Individual Words

Using a dictionary

If you come across a word whose meaning you do not entirely understand, the first thing to do is to look it up in a dictionary. To tell whether the Rockefeller Foundation is indeed eleemosynary, obviously you have to look up the meaning of "eleemosynary". If you hear that your favorite teacher was fired for nepotism, you should look up "nepotism" even if you have a vague idea that it involves people hiring their relatives.

Although using a dictionary is very important for reasoning well, it will not automatically solve all the problems with word meanings. For example, you frequently hear that objective exams (those with true-or-false or multiple-choice questions) are fairer than subjective exams (those with essay questions). Is it true that objective exams are fair? You might start to answer it by looking up the word "objective" to get a more precise idea of its meaning.

But this is a case in which using a dictionary uncritically can actually lead you astray. *Webster's New Collegiate Dictionary*, eighth edition, contains many different definitions of "objective". Just picking out the appropriate one requires reasoning. The most relevant is

> Expressing or involving the use of facts without distortion by personal feelings or prejudices.

You might conclude from this that objective exams are fair because, by definition, they are unprejudiced. The dictionary even goes further: One of the synonyms listed for the word "objective" is "fair." So *obviously* objective exams are fair.

But that reasoning is incorrect. The term "objective exam" is being used here in two different ways:

1. True-or-false or multiple-choice exam.

2. Unprejudiced test.

It is cheating to think that you have proved anything by using the same words, "objective exam," to cover both uses. What you needed to prove was whether "objective exams" in *meaning 1* were also "objective exams" in *meaning 2*. This question is best asked by entirely leaving out the misleading word "objective":

> Are true-or-false or multiple-choice tests unprejudiced?

Phrased this way, the claim looks quite doubtful. Many standardized tests, for example, have been geared to the backgrounds of white, middle-class Americans. Moreover, you can take a prejudiced question and put it easily in either a true-or-false or an essay form; the form of a test is not what makes it fair.

A dictionary does not help in a case like this. The original question was slanted because the two different meanings of "objective exam" were not clearly distinguished, and the dictionary only corroborated this slant.

The moral of this is that a dictionary, like any other tool, has to be used intelligently and critically. It cannot ever be used as a *substitute* for reasoning out a problem, even though it is an excellent tool for explaining words with unknown or uncertain meanings. If you do not use a dictionary in your reading and writing, your knowledge is likely to be too impoverished for you to reason things out well in practice.

The Meaning of
the Whole Sentence: Paraphrasing

Sometimes you may know the meanings of all the words in a sentence, yet the meaning of the whole sentence will still be unclear to you. What step 1 directs you to do then is to *paraphrase* the sentence; to restate it carefully and accurately in different words. Both the paraphrase itself and the activity of thinking up the paraphrase will make you better able to figure out if the sentence is true.

If you plan to travel to some exotic country, someone will inevitably tell you, "People are the same the world over." This may *sound* true, but is it? It needs paraphrasing. The meaning of the sentence relevant to this context of traveling is

People (cultures) are the same everywhere.

One quick paraphrase shows you that the statement is obviously false. Cultures are not the same. The behavior, thoughts, attitudes, and approaches to life of different cultural groups vary dramatically.

Capturing the sense in that context

You might ask, "How do you know for sure that this is the correct paraphrase? The sentence doesn't mention anything about *cultures.*" The answer is that we are not sure; it just seems to capture the sense that is relevant to traveling to an exotic country — that's the *context.* There might be another sense in which people *are* the same the world over. In another context it might possibly mean

Individuals everywhere are basically the same from a physical point of view.

People everywhere do have two arms, two legs, etc., but that is not relevant here. You were not traveling to an exotic country to count people's arms and legs; you were going to see an exotic culture. The ring of truth that the statement had at the beginning, however, probably stemmed from this irrelevant meaning. Once you have paraphrased the statement relevantly, it is hard to see how you could ever have thought it was plausible.

Paraphrase is widely needed

It is amazing how often paraphrasing is needed, and how many problems it solves quickly. It is valuable when you are analyzing someone else's argument (discussed in Chapter Five) or when you are just wondering about the ordinary things you hear. Most general beliefs that people have require a clarification of meaning. This is especially true for those slogans and cliches that people say so often, believe, and sometimes even try to live their lives by. Take the expression, "Life is what you make it." No matter how reassuring this statement sounds when people say it to one another, it means, roughly, "In general a person has the ability to make his or her life happy or unhappy." This is false. Prolonged lack of food, water, and housing, severe physical disability, hormonal imbalances, glandular secretions — all of these, if prolonged and serious enough, can defeat even the strongest determination to be happy. Even when they are less serious, there is no denying that these conditions do *make* people unhappy. The fact that a few people can be happy in the face of these does not at all show that life is what you make it. It shows at most that those few people have abilities that most people don't. The same kind of paraphrase will show that "you should always give a person the benefit of the doubt," that "money is the root of all evil," that "children are our greatest natural resource," and a hundred other statements like them are either false or quite doubtful. Sometimes they are even harmful if taken seriously. Why would people ever sincerely say, "Don't knock it till you've tried it"? Does that apply to suicide? Child molesting? To heroin? It must if it means "Don't criticize *anything* until you've tried it." Partly because they were not clear about what they meant, the speakers did not bother to look for the thousands of actions that you *should* criticize without first trying. Some common phrases and statements are almost entirely devoid of meaning. Try to figure out what "positive thinking" really means. And once you realize that "Coke adds life" is an utterly empty slogan, it stops even looking like a reason to buy a Coke.

Problems

Clarify the meaning in problems 1–4; use a dictionary wherever it is helpful.

1. What does "primitive" mean when anthropologists talk about "primitive people"?

2. "Religion is the opiate of the masses."

3. "He's an idealist, but I'm a realist." According to your clarification, would he agree to your characterization of his position?

4. "JEEP. Jeep wrote the book on four-wheel drive."

5. Here are the definitions of "natural" and "nature" contained in *Webster's New Collegiate Dictionary*, eighth edition. Which of the meanings, if any, clarifies the statement, "Natural foods are better for you"?

   nat-u-ral   adj.
   1. based on an inherent sense of right and wrong
   2a: being in accordance with or determined by nature
   3b: illegitimate
   4: having an essential relation with someone or something
   5: implanted or being as if implanted by nature
   6: of or relating to nature as an object of study and research
   7: having a specified character by nature
   8a: occurring in conformity with the ordinary course of nature
   9: possessing or exhibiting the higher qualities of human nature
   10a: growing without human care
   10b: existing in or produced by nature
   11b: living in or as if in a state of nature untouched by the influences of civilization and society
   12a: having a physical or real existence as contrasted with one that is spiritual, intellectual, or fictitious
   13b: marked by easy simplicity and freedom from artificiality, affectation, or constraint
   14a: having neither flats nor sharps

   na-ture   n.
   1a: the inherent character or basic constitution of a person or thing: essence

2a: a creative and controlling force in the universe
2b: an inner force or the sum of such forces in an individual
3:   a kind of class usually distinguished by fundamental or essential characteristics
4:   the physical constitution or drives of an organism
5:   a spontaneous attitude
6:   the external world in its entirety
7a: a man's original or natural condition
7b: a simplified mode of life resembling this condition
8:   natural scenery

6. The *American College Dictionary* defines "witch" as

A person, usually a woman, who professes or is supposed to practice magic, especially black magic or the black art.

Is this a good definition? According to this definition, can anyone be falsely condemned as a witch?

7. "That's true in theory, but false in practice."

Suppose this is paraphrased as

PARAPHRASE 1.   On paper that looks good, but in reality there are just too many variables.

Why is paraphrase 1 not a good paraphrase?

8. Evaluate this ad[1] on the grounds of meaning.

Ever compare what's inside?

A Box of Stuffing.
Enriched bromated wheat flour; sugar; dried onion; salt; hydrogenated cotton-seed, soybean and palm kernel oils; hydrolyzed vegetable protein (for flavor); dried celery with sulfur dioxide added as a preservative; yeast; defatted soy flour; modified wheat starch; dried parsley; spices; caramel color; whey; chicken fat; calcium propionate (added to retard spoilage); onion powder; natural flavor; turmeric; dehydrated chicken meat; monosodium glutamate (flavor enhancer); artificial flavor; citric acid, BHA, TBHQ and propyl gallate (preservatives).

A Potato.
Potato.

Now which would you choose?

*Contents based on ingredients list found on side panel of Stovetop® Chicken Flavor Stuffing Mix box. © 1979 The Potato Board

[1]© 1979. The Potato Board. Reprinted by Permission.

2. *Ambiguity*

There are many different problems with clarifying the meaning of a statement, and there are many fallacies connected with meaning. Listing these specific problems and fallacies, however, would probably not be very helpful: There are too many of them, and there is no general solution to all of them. Or rather, the only general solution is to *paraphrase* — rewriting the sentence in different words, paying close attention to what could reasonably be meant by it.

But there is one special problem with meaning that is worth taking up explicitly: ambiguity. It is *the* key problem in paraphrasing and lies at the root of most fallacies of meaning.

How Ambiguity Functions in Language

Literally, a term is *ambiguous* if it is capable of being understood in more than one sense. For example, the noun "orange" is ambiguous because it can refer to the fruit or to a particular color — the color of oranges. Sometimes the various meanings of a word differ only in shading or emotional overtones. The term "poet," for instance, is often used to mean "one who writes verse." In that sense being a poet is contrasted to being someone who writes in prose or does not write anything. But the term "poet" can also mean "one who writes *good* poems." In that sense a poet is contrasted to a mere versifier. The former use of the word is a neutral one; the latter use of the word carries positive overtones. Though the two meanings are close, the word is still ambiguous.

Definition of "ambiguous"

So, ambiguity is common. There is probably a lot of truth in the contention that almost all words in natural languages like English are ambiguous. Ambiguity, in fact, may even be necessary to the way a language works. Skillful playing on ambiguities in language is one of the characteristics of good writing.

Unobjection-able ambiguity

The same thing holds for vagueness. Vagueness can be thought of as a type of ambiguity. A term is vague when it does not clearly either apply to or fail to apply to a given case. The term "happy" is vague because, though there are times when you are clearly happy and other times when you are clearly not happy, there are still other times when it is not clear which (if either) you are. You might even express this vagueness by saying that there are times when you are *both* happy and unhappy. What you mean if you express it that way is that in one sense of the ambiguous term you are happy and in another sense of the term you are not. It is not a criticism of a word to say that it is vague or ambiguous: That is simply a description of the way it functions in the language.

Vagueness

Ambiguity is objectionable on logical grounds only if it makes a statement misleading with regard to truth or falsity. It is objectionable when it leads a person to have a mistaken idea about the truth of the statement.

Objectionable ambiguity

This happens most generally in the following way. An ambiguous word is used in a statement. Interpreting the word in one way, the statement in question seems to be true; interpreting the word in another way, the statement in question seems to be false. If the two interpretations are not distinguished openly, the fact that there are two different meanings involved may not be noticed. Then the statement can appear to be simply true or simply false, without any question of interpretation. When this happens, the ambiguity is objectionable on logical grounds.

For example, parents sometimes say things like, "We're worried about little Billy. It's not normal for a six-year-old to enjoy playing the piano so much." All the second sentence means literally is

> Most children don't enjoy playing the piano as much as little Billy does.

This is no reason to worry about little Billy. After all, the same thing was true of Beethoven. Why are the parents worrying then? Probably because they have the idea that "not normal" means "*below* average development." Speakers often use the word "normal" in this sense, as when they say that insane or retarded people "are not normal." Confusing this negative meaning with the first neutral one is what makes people so concerned about being "normal," when in fact there is no reason to be.

Paraphrasing reduces confusion

Paraphrasing the sentence first — and distinguishing the two meanings of "normal" — reduces considerably the possibility of such confusion. Being different from the statistical norm can be a positive indication as easily as it can be a negative one. Though ugly or retarded people are not normal, neither are beautiful or intelligent people. Not being normal (in the first sense) is, in itself, nothing to worry about.

Two Signs of Ambiguous Language

Obvious falsity

One very common sign of ambiguous language is obvious falsity. When a statement a person makes is obviously false — so obviously false that it sounds like something only an imbecile would say — that may be because the statement is ambiguous in some respect, and you are interpreting it incorrectly. And the probability of ambiguity is increased when you know that the speaker is *not* an imbecile, that he does otherwise seem to know what he is talking about. This, of course, does not mean that people never say things that are obviously false. They do. But when you interpret a person's statement in such a way that it is obviously false, you may be shortchanging the person by interpreting what he says in a way that was not meant.

For example, nearly all professional biologists would agree that the theory of evolution is a well-founded and verified scientific explanation for the differences among living creatures. But opponents of evolution sometimes claim, "The theory of evolution is not based on fact. By its very title it is just a *theory*."

Here the opponents understand the word "theory" to mean "a mere guess" or "a conjecture." But their interpretation makes the biologists' claim *obviously* false: According to this interpretation, biologists are saying, "A mere guess about evolution is a well-founded and verified scientific explanation." They would be contradicting themselves.

But this obvious falsity is evidence that the interpretation, rather than the statement itself, is incorrect. And in this case it is; the term "theory" is ambiguous. According to *Webster's New Collegiate Dictionary*, eighth edition, "theory" also means

> A plausible or scientifically acceptable general principle or body of principles offered to explain phenomena.

Biologists are using the term in this sense, not in the sense of "a mere guess."

Obvious truth

The same kind of thing occurs when a person says something obviously *true*, so obviously true that it seems a waste of time to say it. If the person who says it is otherwise a fairly thoughtful person and not given to making trivial statements, your judgment that the statement is an obvious truism is likely to be founded on a misinterpretation of what he or she meant. Not necessarily, of course — the speaker may this time be saying something absolutely trivial. But you should at least double-check the statement to see if there may not be some ambiguity that you missed. If the Stanford-Binet people say, "Objective IQ tests are fair," they are not making the trivially true claim that "fair IQ tests are fair." They are claiming that standardized IQ tests are in fact free from prejudice.

Both the biologists and the Stanford-Binet people are making *interesting* claims, ones that can be confirmed or disconfirmed only on the basis of evidence. In each case one interpretation makes the claims merely obvious and *un*interesting. And this in turn is a good reason to think that that interpretation is incorrect.

Using the signs

A general rule of thumb, then, is to use the signs, obvious truth or obvious falsity, as a way of recognizing ambiguities. The presence of either should alert you to recheck your interpretation for accuracy. There is a good chance you are distorting what the person meant.

A number of practical problems with paraphrase still need solutions. For example, to give a good paraphrase you must recognize beforehand that something there *needs* paraphrase; once you have decided to paraphrase a statement, you have to know how *deeply* to look into its meaning; and you have to be able to tell if your paraphrase is the correct one.

To help with these problems, the rest of the chapter examines some methods for giving accurate paraphrases and some of the tests for the correctness of a paraphrase.

Problems

1. "Only the fittest survive." How many different aspects of this sentence are ambiguous?

2. "Thou shalt not kill." Does this mean that war is forbidden by the Bible? Why? What does the commandment mean?

3. "There are exceptions to every rule." Consider this principle and its paraphrase:

    PARAPHRASE 1.   There are situations in which any law or general principle does not hold true.

    Is Paraphrase 1 an accurate paraphrase? Does it make the original come out obviously false?

4. "If you do it, you dig it." This is a slogan in transactional analysis therapy. Two possible paraphrases are

    PARAPHRASE 1.   You only do things you like to do.

    PARAPHRASE 2.   If you spend time doing something, you are finding it interesting or enjoyable.

    Aren't these paraphrases obviously false? (Give a few good counter-examples.) Is the slogan then also obviously false? What does it mean?

5. "Any action is permissible between two consenting adults." Give a paraphrase that makes the statement not obviously false.

6. Is it sometimes reasonable to act unreasonably? Before you answer the question, paraphrase it.

3.   How to Give a Paraphrase

What a Paraphrase Is

Paraphrase requires sensitivity to what could reasonably be meant by a statement or phrase. It also requires a critical attitude that does not interpret a statement to mean *just anything*, but limits it intelligently to a certain range of possibilities. Most statements assert that something is true by describing a particular state of affairs. The statement will be true if that state of affairs exists; it will be false if another, different state of affairs exists. For such a statement, then, a correct paraphrase portrays clearly that certain specifiable events would make it true and certain specifiable events would make it false. The goal in writing out a paraphrase is always to make the statement clearer with respect to truth and falsity.

Steering a middle course   In practice, when you paraphrase something, you must steer a middle course between two extremes. You have to avoid paraphrasing statements so strictly and narrowly that almost any state of affairs will make them false. But you also have to avoid paraphrasing them so loosely that almost anything will make them true.

Habitually and unconsciously you *interpret* every sentence you are able to understand. *Paraphrase* is doing the same kind of task, only in a more conscious and precise way. In a paraphrase you actually write out what you interpret the sentence to mean.

Para-phrasing and interpreting

You interpret statements all the time, not just in reasoning courses or when thinking hard. You do not *call* it "interpreting," but you do have an idea of what people mean when they say things to you. This *is* interpreting what they say. If the weatherman says, "It will be in the middle 90s tomorrow," you know what this statement means and implies. You interpret the words, "the middle 90s," to mean temperatures roughly between 93° and 97° (not necessarily 95°); you interpret "tomorrow" to mean not one minute after midnight, but for some hours during the afternoon.

Notice that this natural interpretation does steer a middle course; it is neither too loose nor too narrow. Under certain weather conditions the sentence will be clearly true; under certain other weather conditions the statement will be clearly false; and under still other weather conditions (since "the middle 90s" is vague) the sentence will be neither clearly true nor clearly false. Being able to imagine these conditions *is* knowing the meaning of the sentence. Your paraphrase will be a good one if you capture these conditions in words.

Loose vs. narrow inter-pretations

There is an interplay between the interpretation of a sentence and its truth. Suppose someone stubbornly (and incorrectly) interprets the weatherman's statement in a very narrow way and writes out

Interplay between truth and meaning

PARAPHRASE 1.   Tomorrow at every second of the day the temperature will be exactly 95° F.

Under paraphrase 1, the weatherman's statement is asserting something so precise, delimited, and free from vagueness that it will almost certainly turn out to be false. In fact, under this paraphrase very few days in history have ever been "in the middle 90s." On the other hand suppose someone gives an extremely loose paraphrase:

PARAPHRASE 2.   At some moment tomorrow the temperature will touch anywhere between 93° F and 97° F.

Under paraphrase 2 the weatherman's statement is much more likely to be true, but it tells us very little about what the weather will be like tomorrow. Paraphrase 2 would be true even on Mars, where every day the temperature passes through the 90s (for a few seconds) on the way from boiling to freezing. Now we know that this is not going to happen on Earth tomorrow, but the point is that the weatherman's statement under paraphrase 2 does not even rule this out.

Narrowing a paraphrase makes a statement say something more precise (narrow) at the expense of making the statement true under fewer (narrower) circumstances. Loosening the paraphrase makes a statement true under a wider (looser) set of circumstances, but at the expense of making what the statement says vague (loose). Just as in everyday interpretations, you have to guard against distorting a statement with a paraphrase that is either too loose or too narrow. You have to keep in mind what the speaker could have *plausibly* or *reasonably* meant by the statement in that situation.

What a Reasonable Paraphrase Is

The primary rule to follow is to be *reasonable* when giving a paraphrase. That involves paying attention to the speaker and the context, and it begins with a *strict* understanding of the words. After considera-

The strict *meaning* tion you may decide that the speaker did not mean the sentence so strictly. Yet the strict meaning — the precise, literal meaning of the words — is something that should still be kept in mind.

Usually, the best paraphrase of a statement is one that is fairly, though not extremely, strict. This is especially true when paraphrasing individual words within a sentence. Say you are wondering about whether God exists or not. Before you can even hope to figure out an answer, you have to figure out, at least roughly, what the word "God" means. Otherwise you do not know *what* you are questioning the existence of. Now, the word "God" is one that is generally used to refer to a being who has certain attributes — absolute power, knowledge, goodness, etc. Within the limits of this meaning the question of whether God exists or not makes perfectly good sense; it asks: "Is there such a being?" You cannot, however, legitimately interpret the word "God" to mean "whatever has the highest value in a person's life" because it makes a mockery of the question. Of course if *all* you mean by the word "God" is whatever has the highest value in a person's life, then *obviously* God (in this trivial sense) exists. People do have values, and one of them is bound to be the highest. Thus for one person God might be money, for another God might be his family, and for another what God is might fluctuate from day to day. This sort of thing is often said, and, if you are not paying close attention to what is happening, it can even sound profound. In fact it is not profound at all. It is merely a play on the word "God." None of this answers the original question. You were not wondering whether there were things that people value highest (you already knew that!); you were wondering if a being with absolute power, knowledge, goodness, etc., exists. Paraphrasing the word "God" loosely here would simply confuse the two different issues.

On the other hand no rule says a sentence should *always* be paraphrased strictly. In some cases a loose paraphrase reflects more accurately what the statement means. Suppose that at a trial a detective is asked point-blank, "Did A kill B?" and he replies, "Well, he did and he didn't." The strict paraphrase is

> PARAPHRASE 1.   A actually did kill B and A actually did not kill B.

But this could not *possibly* be true. Because paraphrase 1 would make his statement obviously false (a sign of an incorrect paraphrase), we would be sure that this is not what the detective means; for example, a perjury conviction would be certain under this paraphrase. In this context his answer means

> PARAPHRASE 2.   In one sense of the word "kill," A did kill B, but in another sense of the word "kill," A did not kill B.

We can't tell what circumstances the detective has in mind that caused him to say this. We can imagine some, though. He might mean that A did perform an action that started the chain of events that resulted in B's death (so A *did* kill B in that sense), but the action was such an innocent one and the chain of events was so improbable that A can be said to have no responsibility for B's death (so in that sense A did not kill B). Or the detective might mean that A's finger did pull the trigger, but that someone else pulled A's finger. There are many possibilities (you can think up your own candidates), but they all hinge on the looser interpretation of paraphrase 2.

Now it may be that if the detective meant paraphrase 2, he should have said so. What he did say was misleading. This is a just criticism of *how* the detective said it. But criticism should not be confused with paraphrase. It is implausible to take him to mean something self-contradictory. There are many cases where people say things that, interpreted strictly, would be self-contradictory or incoherent or obviously false.

> Can a person be dead even though his heart is still beating? Well, yes and no.

> Are you happy with your job? I'm happy and yet I'm unhappy.

> Everyone knows that 2 + 2 = 4. (Everyone, that is, absolutely everyone without a single exception, does not know this — new-born infants, for example.)

> Is a transsexual male or female? Both.

In each of these cases an ambiguous word is used ("dead," "happy," "everyone," "male," "female"), and in each case a loose paraphrase is required to capture what the speaker meant. Thus in the first case the speaker might be contrasting heart death (the usual legal sense of the word "dead") to, say, brain death, or to some other sense of the word "death." In the second case you can probably think up any number of senses of the word "happy" (pleasure, long-term fulfillment, security, and so forth) that the speaker might be contrasting. But without more information the paraphrase you give has to leave the actual details as unspecified as they were in the original. In the third and fourth cases you can probably assume a fairly standard context and so can make a more detailed guess about what was meant. The following are plausible paraphrases:

In the legal sense of the word "dead" the person is not dead because his heart is still beating, but in some other (unspecified) sense of the word "dead" the person is indeed dead.

I'm happy with my job in one sense of the word "happy," but I'm unhappy with it in another sense.

Everyone, in the sense of every rational adult, knows that 2 + 2 = 4.

A transsexual is a male in the sense of having an X and a Y chromosome but a female in the sense of having female genital organs.

It should be clear from all this that there is no general rule that will tell you if your paraphrase is correct. In each individual case you have to pay close attention to what could reasonably be meant by the statement and choose the best paraphrase on the basis of this plus the literal meaning. Sometimes this will call for a strict paraphrase, one that puts narrow limits on the conditions for the truth of the statement. At other times a loose paraphrase will be best. This is especially so when it is needed to avoid thinking that the speaker is just talking nonsense.

4. How to Test a Paraphrase

Primary Test: Matching Applications

Matching

Although there is no way to guarantee that a paraphrase you give is correct, there are ways to test it. The major test is that *the paraphrase and the original statement must match*. That is, because the paraphrase is supposed to state the meaning of a sentence, the paraphrase should turn out to be applicable in all of the situations where the sentence itself would apply. The paraphrase should also be inapplicable in all of those situations where the sentence itself would be inapplicable. The applications of the paraphrase, then, should match the applications of the sentence itself. If they do not match, that is good evidence that the paraphrase is incorrect.

Take a familiar sentence as an example: "The Surgeon General has determined that cigarette smoking is dangerous to your health." Let's concentrate only on the Surgeon General's statement:

Cigarette smoking is dangerous to your health.

Suppose that initially you take that statement to mean

PARAPHRASE 1.   Smoking cigarettes will invariably do physical damage to the smoker.

This is not a correct paraphrase because a few people who smoke and remain undamaged physically will count against paraphrase 1 but will not count against the statement by the Surgeon General. That is, if a few people smoke (heavily and for a long time) and are not damaged by it, this will show that "smoking cigarettes *will* do damage to the smoker" is false; for these people, at least, smoking cigarettes will not do damage to them. However, these people do not show that "cigarette smoking is dangerous to your health" is false. Cigarette smoking is still dangerous to your health even though some people's health remains undamaged by smoking. The Surgeon General's statement is not so strong as to mean that smoking cigarettes *will* invariably damage you.

On the other hand, he did not mean merely that

PARAPHRASE 2.   Smoking cigarettes may do physical damage to the smoker.

His statement is stronger than that. After all, almost anything *may* do physical damage to you. Crossing streets *may* get you hit by a car; living in New York City *may* get you mugged. Yet neither crossing streets nor living in New York City could be described correctly as "dangerous to your health." Thus the phrase "may damage you" applies to a lot more things than the phrase "is dangerous to your health." Therefore, the former is not a correct paraphrase of the latter.

Neither of these interpretations matches the original. Paraphrase 1 is too strong; paraphrase 2 is too weak. The Surgeon General's statement means this:

PARAPHRASE 3.   It is highly likely that a person who smokes cigarettes will be physically damaged by it.

What would make the Surgeon General's statement false is not a few smokers who remain undamaged but a *large percentage* of smokers who remain undamaged. The statement would not be true if cigarette smoking was merely as likely to cause damage as crossing streets or living in New York City: It takes a *high* likelihood of damage to make the Surgeon General's statement true.

Thus paraphrase 3 is much better than paraphrase 1 or 2. It does match the original statement in that it seems to apply to the same situations the original applied to; that is, the cases where a *large number* of people (though not necessarily everyone as in paraphrase 1) have a high *probability* (not just a possibility as in paraphrase 2) of being damaged physically if they smoke cigarettes. Of course, even interpretation 3 may not be adequate. There may be situations we haven't considered in which the interpretation applies and the original statement does not. The thing to do, then, is to test the paraphrase further by thinking up new situations and seeing if one applies and the other doesn't. Whenever they both apply or neither applies —

whenever they match — it is further corroboration of the correctness of the paraphrase. But one clear case of failure to match will be very good evidence of the incorrectness of the interpretation.

You always have to test a paraphrase against the original. Try to think up test cases, cases that prove the paraphrase false, for example; these cases must also prove the original statement false. Think up cases that would prove the paraphrase true; if the paraphrase is correct, these cases will also prove the original true. Even fuzzy cases are helpful (though, because they are fuzzy, you cannot put much reliance on them). The fuzziness of paraphrase and original should also match. If, for example, half the population of heavy smokers are damaged physically by cigarette smoking, it will not be clear whether that is a high-enough percentage to show a significant likelihood, and so the truth of the paraphrase would be fuzzy. But the original would be fuzzy in this case too. Half the population of smokers does not show clearly that cigarette smoking is dangerous to your health.

True, false, even fuzzy cases should match

The paraphrase and the original should match in their application even to imaginary cases. If you can imagine a situation in which the paraphrase would be true (or false), in that situation the original statement must also be true (or false); otherwise the paraphrase will not match the original and so will not be correct. Thus "objective test," as we saw, does not mean the same as "test that is true or false, or multiple choice." But we could have figured out this by seeing that the phrases do not match. You can image tests that are true or false or multiple choice that you would not be tempted to call "objective." (For example: "Steak tastes better than lobster: true or false" or "Circle the best religion: Judaism, Catholicism, Protestantism, Islam.") You can also imagine essay tests that are about as objective as a test can be. ("Write an essay on your 106 favorite chemical elements.") Such examples of "objective" and "subjective" tests, even though they are only imaginary cases, show that the two phrases do not match. One would be true of a certain set of circumstances, whereas the other would be false; therefore, the one is not an accurate interpretation of the other.

Imaginary cases should also match

Matching Is a Test for Meaning, Not Truth

It is important not to be confused about what is going on when you compare a paraphrase and an original statement to see if they match. At the stage of clarifying meaning, step 1, you are not trying particularly to find out whether either of the statements in question *is* true or false — not yet. You are doing something preliminary to that: finding out what it means. And this involves not determining whether either statement *is* true or false in reality but determining if there is a match between the conditions under which they *would be* true or false. To figure out conditions under which a statement *would be* true is to think up a situation and decide whether the statement would apply in that situation. To figure out if a statement *is* true, on the other hand, you

Matching what would be true or false

have to decide, in addition, if what the statement says actually describes something about the world.

The cigarette-smoking case, for example, shows that *if* a few people were undamaged by smoking, paraphrase 1 *would be* false, whereas the Surgeon General's statement *would be* true. So the statements do not match. But this does not show that the Surgeon General's statement *is* in fact true. That is a matter for empirical testing, and you can not find out the answer by merely reasoning. Of course, matching conditions often does give you a good insight into the truth of the statement (as in the example of objective tests). That is one of the main reasons why accurate paraphrase is so beneficial. But after paraphrasing you always have to take at least one additional step to find out if the statement is true: You must discover if the statement describes the way things actually are.

Secondary Test:
Obvious Truth or Obvious Falsehood

Aside from matching applications there is another test for the correctness of a paraphrase, and it was used all along in the discussion of step 1. You can test the correctness of a paraphrase by seeing if it makes a statement come out to be *obviously* true or *obviously* false. The degree of obviousness is the key here. If a paraphrase makes the sentence look so obviously true that no one would think it was worth saying, or so obviously false that no one could possibly believe it, there is a very good chance that the paraphrase is incorrect.

Being at least a little bit doubtful of the accuracy of your paraphrase is a matter of justice as well as logic. You can't tell whether a person's statement is true or false until you interpret it. But once you do interpret it and write out the paraphrase, the possibility of your error enters the picture. If you judge that the statement under your paraphrase is false or silly or true but not worth saying, this judgment *may* be an accurate assessment of the person's statement. But it may show instead that you have misunderstood what the person was saying. The only fair thing to do under these circumstances, since the paraphrased statement is in a way a joint enterprise, is to hold the paraphrase doubtful.

Justice in paraphrasing

The likelihood that the paraphrase is inaccurate is increased by two factors: how obvious the faultiness is and how knowledgeable the person is in that area. The two factors are closely linked.

First, the more obviously false or obviously trivial a paraphrased statement is, the less you should be willing to attribute it to people who seem otherwise sane, moderately intelligent, and knowledgeable. Similarly, the emptier and more trivial a paraphrased statement looks, the slower you should be to attribute it to people who otherwise act like they are saying something informative.

The second factor is simply the opposite side of the first. The more highly you think of a person's intelligence and knowledge in an area, the less likely it will seem that he or she is saying something obviously false or trivial.

This test for the accuracy of a paraphrase is, in a sense, another version of the matching test. For if a statement is reasonable (though perhaps false), the paraphrase should not be outlandish. The reasonableness of original statement and paraphrase should match.

Summary of tests

Thus there are two ways (or two different aspects of the same way) to test the accuracy of a paraphrase: (1) the original statement and the paraphrase must match in all of their applications, and (2) the more obviously false or trivial a statement is under a paraphrase, the less likely it is that the paraphrase is accurate. Of course, the fact that a particular paraphrase seems to pass these tests does not guarantee that it is accurate. Even if a paraphrase and another statement match in all of the situations that you have considered, they may fail to match in some situation you have not thought of. And the fact that a paraphrase is not obviously false or trivial will not in the slightest show that it is accurate. The tests furnish evidence, not a guarantee, that a particular paraphrase is a good one.

Problems

1. "The punishment should suit the crime."

   PARAPHRASE 1. Criminals should have done to them the same thing they have done to their victims.

   PARAPHRASE 2. Criminals should suffer to the same degree that they have made their victims suffer.

   Apply *bank robbery* to the original quotation and both paraphrases to see how they match. Are the paraphrases accurate? Are they reasonable?

Criticize the following paraphrases by showing how they fail to match the originals.

Original: "That's true in theory but false in practice" (for questions 2 and 3).

2. PARAPHRASE 1. Knowledge taught in the classroom is no substitute for experience.

3. PARAPHRASE 2. The evidence shows that to be true, but in reality it is false.

Original: "Only the fittest survive" (for questions 4, 5, and 6).

4. PARAPHRASE 1. Only the physically strongest will continue to exist.

5. PARAPHRASE 2. Only the best-adapted people live the longest.

6. PARAPHRASE 3. Only organisms that adjust to their environments are able to succeed in their goals.

7. Give a paraphrase of "That's true in theory but false in practice" that *does* match the original. Is it a reasonable statement?

8. Give a paraphrase of "Only the fittest survive" that *does* match the original. Then evaluate it for truth.

5. Giving Multiple Paraphrases

For some statements it is not possible to write a paraphrase, at least not a single paraphrase, that matches in all important aspects. If the sentence contains serious ambiguities, no single paraphrase will be entirely adequate. A seriously ambiguous statement is one with two separate senses, and so two separate paraphrases will be required to capture them. To take account of serious ambiguities, then, it is best to write out *both* versions of what might have been meant by the original. (It is usually not necessary to have more than two if the pair of them is chosen to capture a contrast.) If this is done well, it can be the single most-helpful aspect of paraphrasing.

Serious ambiguity requires multiple paraphrases

   Take a claim that has been made and used as a basis for action for nearly two thousand years: "The Jews killed Christ." If the Biblical evidence is accepted on the whole, the sentence does appear to be true. Yet asserting that it is true leaves one with an uneasy feeling that something about the statement is quite incorrect, that it should not be accepted at face value. The problem is that the sentence is ambiguous. In reality it requires two distinct paraphrases: one to capture why many people have thought it was true and another to capture how it has been applied in practice. Think about what makes the sentence appear true. According to the Biblical account, some Jews — perhaps about ten — were more or less directly responsible for Jesus's death by passing judgment. More doubtfully, a number of other Jews — perhaps a hundred or so — may also have been responsible by shouting and influencing the proceedings. Still more doubtfully, it might be claimed that many other citizens of Jerusalem were indirectly responsible for Christ's death because they allowed an unjust trial to go on without trying to stop it. This last claim is, of course, much more doubtful than the first two for several reasons: To make it stick you would have to prove at least that these people *knew* about the trial, that they knew it was *unjust,* and that there was some reason to believe that they had the *ability* to stop it. And the Biblical record gives very little evidence that these conditions were met. In any event, what makes the sentence, "The Jews killed Christ," appear true is that it is being interpreted to mean that "some individual Jews killed Christ." Paraphrased this way, the sentence seems defensibly true; *some* — a few, somewhere between ten and a few thousand — Jews were indirectly responsible for Jesus's death and so could be cited perhaps as people who "killed Christ."

However, this interpretation does not really seem to capture what is meant by the statement. After all, the statement would not have continued in general use for two thousand years if all it meant was that a bunch of people who have been dead for 1900 years killed Christ. And why is it that people say that the Jews killed Christ when they do not say that some Near Easterners or some Caucasians or some Romans killed Christ? The answer is that "*the* Jews" does not typically mean "some individual Jews." It more typically means "the Jewish people." So another interpretation of "The Jews killed Christ" is "The Jewish people killed Christ." It is under this interpretation that the sentence has been used to justify a lot of actions taken against Jews. But under this interpretation the sentence is *false*. The Jewish people did not kill Christ. Most members of the Jewish people were not even alive then. Moreover, it does not really seem to make sense to say that a *people*, rather than some individuals, killed somebody.

In this sentence, then, the ambiguity of the phrase, "the Jews," is exploited in such a way as to make some actions taken against the Jewish people appear justified when they are not. Let's give both paraphrases of the statement, "The Jews killed Christ":

PARAPHRASE 1.   Some Jews killed Christ.

PARAPHRASE 2.   The Jewish people killed Christ.

Now, it seems reasonable to suppose that if A killed B, then A can legitimately be *held responsible* for the death of B, and if killing B was unjust, then it may very well be right to *punish* A for killing B. So if paraphrase 1 is true, some Jews can legitimately be held responsible for the death of Christ, and, because Jesus's conviction seems to have been unjust, those Jews perhaps should be punished. But the Jews in question have been dead for close to two thousand years, of course, so there are no actions people could take against them even if they wanted to. If paraphrase 2 were true, on the other hand, the whole Jewish people could legitimately be held responsible for the death of Christ and punished consequently. There are plenty of Jews in question here to take action against. However, paraphrase 2 clearly *is not* true.

For any actions to be based legitimately on the sentence, "The Jews killed Christ," the sentence must *both* be true *and* justify the actions. What has happened throughout history is that people have based their judgments about the *truth* of the sentence on paraphrase 1, but they have based their *actions* taken against Jews on paraphrase 2. And that is clearly fallacious.

A great deal of discriminatory behavior is based on this kind of fallacy, sometimes even by well-intentioned people who are taken in by the ambiguity. Certain members of a group perform an action that certain people do not like; instead of blaming only the individuals actually involved, these people sometimes feel justified in punishing other individuals of that group who had nothing to do with the action.

They could not feel justified, though, if they first paraphrased their own beliefs.

What is the correct answer, then, to the question, "Did the Jews kill Christ?" Is the sentence, "The Jews killed Christ," true or false? The answer cannot be either true or false by itself. The *only* correct answer has two parts: "Well, if you mean that *some* individual Jews killed Christ, then it is true" (and it is a harmless enough statement). If, on the other hand, you mean that the Jewish people killed Christ, then it is patently false." The only correct answer, then, is one that mentions both paraphrases and says whether the sentence is true or false under each.

The same kind of account holds for any sentence that contains serious ambiguities. More than one interpretation will be necessary, and a judgment must be given about the truth or falsity of the statement under each paraphrase. If you are clarifying the meaning of a statement and you cannot clearly decide which of two para- *When in* phrases is more accurate, the reasonable thing to do is to give both. *doubt,* You can say: "*If* paraphrase 1 is what is meant, then the statement is *give two* true; *if* paraphrase 2 is meant, however, then the statement is false." *paraphrases* This does not commit you to giving a final judgment about what a particular sentence or person means (maybe no final judgment here is even possible), but it allows you to take account of the alternative meanings and make a reasoned judgment about the truth or falsity of each.

Exercises to Chapter Three

The questions in part A, part B, and part C of these exercises correspond to one another (thus question 1 is on the same topic in each of the three parts; so is question 2; and so forth).

In part A do each question on your own.

In part B various possible answers (some right, some wrong) are offered to the questions in part A. Evaluate each of these possible answers in accord with the instructions to that particular question.

Part C contains correct answers to many of these questions, together with analyses, explanations, and further reasoning techniques. Part C also contains some additional questions. (They are contained in parentheses and printed in italic type.) Be sure to answer these additional questions before proceeding.

For best results in reasoning do not look ahead to part B until you have finished part A, and do not look ahead to part C until you have finished both part A and part B.

Part D contains additional similar exercises, but without comments or answers.

Part A

Carefully paraphrase statements 1–8. If more than one interpretation is needed to capture a statement, give them all. Then briefly say whether the statements are true or false under your interpretation, and why. (Often you will have to test your paraphrase against the original by thinking up test cases or by seeing if your interpretation makes the statement too obviously true or obviously false.)

1. An advertisement for an oil company: "Our business is people helping people."

2. A person should always be given the benefit of the doubt.

3. Lenin was a dirty communist.

4. If you believe something, it is true for you.

5. An advertisement for buying diamonds: "Every diamond is unique because no two in the world are exactly alike." (*Reader's Digest.* October, 1979. p. 52.)

6. Set off in a box on the editorial page of a newspaper: "Quote of the week: 'Over the long term we will either bring inflation down or it will assuredly get worse.' " — Jimmy Carter.

7. Morality is just a matter of opinion.

8. An argument against gun-control legislation: "It's not the gun that kills, it's the man who holds the gun."

Part B

Evaluate each of the following paraphrases by taking each one in turn and judging whether it captures accurately the meaning of the original. For each, explain why it is accurate or exactly how it is not accurate.

If more than one of the interpretations are needed to capture different senses of the original, say which ones are necessary and why.

Then take each interpretation and say whether it makes the statement come out true or false; give reasons to support your answer. Sometimes a comment is given about the truth of the interpretation. Evaluate that also. In short, evaluate each of the paraphrases thoroughly.

1. An oil company ad: "Our business is people helping people."

   PARAPHRASE 1.   Our main concern is to assist people.

   PARAPHRASE 2.   The main concern of the stockholders and employees of this company is to help people.

   PARAPHRASE 3.   Our company discovers, processes, and sells oil products for profit, and that helps people.

   PARAPHRASE 4.   The people who work for the company are helping to better living conditions for the population.

Comment on Paraphrase 4:

   True. It is through their efforts that natural resources are made available to the consuming population for their betterment and comfort.

PARAPHRASE 5.   Our business is people working together for their own benefit as well as the benefit of others.

Comment on Paraphrase 5:

True. This is how businesses are run.

2. A person should always be given the benefit of the doubt.

PARAPHRASE 1.   You should always have trust in people.

PARAPHRASE 2.   If you are not sure whether a person is right or wrong, you should assume he or she is right.

PARAPHRASE 3.   When you do not know for sure whether someone is telling the truth or lying, you should act on the supposition that it is the truth.

Comment on Paraphrase 3:

False. If a woman is walking down a dark street at night, she should not accept an invitation to get into a stranger's car.

PARAPHRASE 4.   A person is innocent until proven guilty.

PARAPHRASE 5.   If there is any question about a person's actions or character, you should never make a final judgment against that person.

Comment on Paraphrase 5:

False. There is nothing wrong with being fair and open-minded in your relationships with people, nor with occasionally overriding your reservations and giving someone your complete trust. But, if the "doubt" exists, there may be a reason for it. It does not make sense to routinely trust or distrust people. It is more reasonable to give people the benefit of the doubt *sometimes,* based on your best information and instincts.

3. Lenin was a dirty communist.

PARAPHRASE 1.   Lenin was a communist who did not wash enough.

PARAPHRASE 2.   Lenin was a communist and being a communist is bad.

PARAPHRASE 3.   Lenin was a corrupt communist.

PARAPHRASE 4.   Lenin founded communism in Russia. Under communism all private property was seized and is now under state control. Russia is our archenemy; it threatens our way of life. Therefore, Lenin, who began communism in Russia, is a threatening figure to most people in the United States.

4. If you believe something, it's true for you.

PARAPHRASE 1.   If you think something is true, then it is.

Comment on Paraphrase 1:

Obviously false. Believing something doesn't make it so.

PARAPHRASE 2.   If you think something is true, then you think it is true.

Comment on Paraphrase 2:
Obviously true. It is merely repeating itself.

PARAPHRASE 3.   If you accept something as true, then as far as you are concerned, it *is* true.

5. An advertisement for diamonds: "Every diamond is unique because no two in the world are exactly alike."

PARAPHRASE 1.   No two diamonds are exactly alike because no two are exactly alike.

PARAPHRASE 2.   Every diamond is special and valuable because no two are exactly alike.

Comment on Paraphrases 1 and 2:
 Either trivial or false.

6. Set off in a box on the editorial page of a newspaper (New Orleans *States-Item*. February 2, 1980): "Quote of the week: 'Over the long term, we will either bring inflation down or it will assuredly get worse.'" — Jimmy Carter.

Comment:
Jimmy Carter's statement is trivial.

7. Morality is just a matter of opinion.

PARAPHRASE 1.   If someone believes something is right, then it is right.

Comment on Paraphrase 1:
False. Something can be wrong even though a particular person feels it is right. For example, murder.

PARAPHRASE 2.   Individuals have their own personal opinions about what is moral and what is not.

Comment on Paraphrase 2:
True. People do have different views, about morality as well as other topics.

PARAPHRASE 3.   Right and wrong are determined only by the individual's judgment.

Comment on Paraphrase 3:
True. A person can believe that it is OK to commit murder. Nintey-nine percent of society can believe murder is wrong or immoral, but the person is still entitled to his or her opinion.

PARAPHRASE 4.   If you believe in your own mind that your beliefs about morality are true, then they are true for you.

Comment on Paraphrase 4:
True. If in your own mind you think that certain things about morality are true, then obviously these things are true for you.

8. An argument against gun-control legislation: "It's not the gun that kills, it's the man who holds the gun."

> PARAPHRASE 1.   It does not need to be paraphrased. The statement is true and means just what it says.

> PARAPHRASE 2.   A gun alone cannot kill anybody, but a man can use a gun to kill somebody.

Comment on Paraphrase 2:
True. A gun alone cannot kill; it is an instrument to kill with. If guns were outlawed, something else would be used.

> PARAPHRASE 3.   Guns don't kill; it is the person who commits the crime with it.

Comment on Paraphrase 3:
True. Weapons are innocent; the people who use them to commit crimes are guilty.

> PARAPHRASE 4.   Guns are not responsible for the death of a person; it is the person who causes the gun to fire who is responsible.

> PARAPHRASE 5.   For a gun to terminate life, someone must pull the trigger.

> PARAPHRASE 6.   Guns are will-less, brainless instruments that require a being of will, intelligence, and the physical capability of pulling the trigger to be fired.

Comment on Paraphrases 4, 5, and 6:
All these paraphrases are true. A gun is a device that can cause harm when triggered by someone, but only when triggered by someone. It cannot do it by itself.

Part C

Here are some correct answers to part B. They contain explanations and criticism of the paraphrases, together with some further questions (in parentheses and italic type). Try to see how the criticisms apply also to the paraphrases you gave on your own in part A.

If your answers in part A do not agree with those given here, it may be for a number of reasons. First, yours is wrong; second, your answer says the same thing as the one given here, only in different words (the explanation will help you decide if this is so); third, your paraphrase concentrates on different aspects of the original (in which case you should figure out why the interpretations given here concentrate on these aspects). The answers given here are never intentionally incorrect, but there is a fourth possibility as well — that your answer is right and the one given here is wrong.

1. An oil company ad: "Our business is people helping people."

> PARAPHRASE 1.   Our main concern is to help people.

A good interpretation. It is one of the things that the original statement means. The original is also pretty clearly false under this interpretation. The *main concern* of the oil company is not to assist people; it's to make money.

> PARAPHRASE 2.   The main concern of the stockholders and employees of this company is to help people.

Better. It clarifies the meaning of "our." Paraphrase 2, like 1, makes the original false.

> PARAPHRASE 3.   Our company discovers, processes, and sells oil products for profit, and that helps people.

Also a good interpretation, but it captures a different sense than paraphrase 1 or 2. Notice that paraphrase 3 stands a fair chance of being true. That *is* the company's business, and those activities presumably do help people. *(This last claim is debatable, though. How might you argue that it is false?)*

To paraphrase the original well, you need *both* 2 and 3. That's because the word "business" is ambiguous in this statement; it can mean "main concern" or "what you do to make a profit." Paraphrase 2, if true, would imply that the oil company is concerned about people's welfare, but 2, as we have seen, is false. Paraphrase 3, on the other hand, is true, but it does not at all imply that the company is concerned about people's welfare. Any kind of company could describe its business that way. The *mafia* could maintain that they help people satisfy their desires for drugs and illegal gambling and sex; the mafia's business, too, is "people helping people."

The original advertisement is misleading because you might judge its truth with paraphrase 3 in mind and draw its implications on the basis of paraphrase 2. Only noticing both interpretations will prevent the deception.

> PARAPHRASE 4.   The people who work for the company are helping to better living conditions for the population.

Comment on Paraphrase 4:
   True. They bring resources to consumers.

The paraphrase does not capture the original. It misses the word "business." The original does not just say that the company helps others; it says that that is their *business*. This is what makes the statement false, and misleading, in spite of the true things said in the comment.

> PARAPHRASE 5.   Our business is people working together for their own benefit as well as the benefit of others.

Comment on Paraphrase 5:
   True. That is how businesses are run.

This paraphrase is just as ambiguous as the original; it leaves the two senses of "business" undifferentiated. It restates, but does not *clarify*, the original.

2. A person should always be given the benefit of the doubt.

PARAPHRASE 1.   You should always have trust in people.

Not a good paraphrase. It leaves out the idea of "the doubt."

PARAPHRASE 2.   If you are not sure whether a person is right or wrong, you should assume he or she is right.

Does not quite capture it. Giving the benefit of the doubt is not about being right or wrong so much as about whether the person is lying or not. Hence:

PARAPHRASE 3.   When you do not know for sure whether someone is telling the truth or lying, you should act on the supposition that it is the truth.

Comment on Paraphrase 3:
False. A woman at night should not get into a stranger's car.

Best paraphrase yet. *(Is the case of the lone woman late at night just an exception or is it a key counterexample?)* Paraphrase 3, however, leaves out the idea of "always." *(If "always" were not in the original, would the counterexample still apply?)*

PARAPHRASE 4.   A person is innocent until proved guilty.

A bad paraphrase for at least four reasons. It is restricted to guilt and innocence, whereas the original applies more broadly. It is a cliche. It is at least as unclear and as much in need of paraphrase as the original. It seems obviously false in its own right; aren't you guilty if you murder someone even though you die before it can be proved? Or if it is true, it is only in a narrow courtroom area. *(Would 4 be a good paraphrase if we substituted "should be considered innocent" for "is innocent"? Would it then be true?)*

PARAPHRASE 5.   If there is any question about a person's actions or character, you should never make a final judgment against that person.

Comment on Paraphrase 5:
False. Giving someone your complete trust is OK sometimes . . . , but your judgment should be based on your best information and instincts.

A good paraphrase, but what is especially good is how reasonable the full comment is.

3. Lenin was a dirty communist.

PARAPHRASE 1.   Lenin was a communist who did not wash enough.

Though this is a *literal* paraphrase, it is not accurate. It is not something a person would mean by the original statement. Thus in some cases a straight, word-for-word paraphrase will not be right.

PARAPHRASE 2.   Lenin was a communist and being a communist is bad.

PARAPHRASE 3.   Lenin was a corrupt communist.

Paraphrase 2 is the best, and far better than 3. Derogatory terms like "dirty" are best paraphrased as in 2. Notice that 2 is something that would be held by a strong anticommunist, and that is exactly the sort of person who would say the original. Paraphrase 3 would be said more likely by a communist, or at least someone who was neutral with respect to communism. Such people are unlikely to use the phrase "dirty communist," and that shows that 3 is not accurate. *(Can you describe a situation, a context, in which someone* could *say the original and mean it in the sense of 3?)*

> PARAPHRASE 4.   Lenin founded communism in Russia. Under communism all private property was seized and is now under state control. Russia is our archenemy; it threatens our way of life. Therefore, Lenin, who began communism in Russia, is a threatening figure to most people in the United States.

This is an argument or an explanation, *not* a paraphrase at all. *(The last sentence all by itself would not be a good paraphrase either. Why not?)*

4. If you believe something, it's true for you.

> PARAPHRASE 1.   If you think something is true, then it is.

Comment on Paraphrase 1:
Obviously false. Believing something doesn't make it so.

> PARAPHRASE 2.   If you think something is true, then you think it is true.

Comment on Paraphrase 2:
Obviously true. It is merely repeating itself.

These two paraphrases together are excellent. One makes it come out obviously false; the other makes it come out obviously true. Notice that 2, though true, doesn't *say* anything; it's *trivial,* redundant, and uncontroversial, and has no application in practice. What makes 2 such a good paraphrase is the actual repetition of the words; there is no danger of taking the original seriously under this interpretation. Together, then, the two paraphrases show the original statement is useless. It either says nothing or says something false.

There are many statements that are like this. They sound plausible on the surface, but when you look into them a little more deeply, they turn out to be trivial under one interpretation and false under the other. They are especially tricky because as long as they are not paraphrased, it is easy to mix the two separate senses together so that the statement appears *both* true and applicable. To repeat, in one sense (2) it is true but inapplicable, in the other sense (1) it is applicable but false. To judge a statement "either trivial or false" is to make a powerful criticism.

> PARAPHRASE 3.   If you accept something as true, then as far as you are concerned, it *is* true.

This has exactly the same ambiguity as the original. What does "as far as you are concerned" mean? Does it mean only that "you accept it"? If that is what is meant, that should be the paraphrase: "If you accept something, then you accept it." Again, it is trivial. Or does it mean something more than merely that you accept it? If so, then you have to spell out exactly what more is meant. Paraphrase 3, just like the original, is either trivial or false.

5. Diamond ad: "Every diamond is unique because no two are exactly alike."

> PARAPHRASE 1.   No two diamonds are exactly alike because no two are exactly alike.

> PARAPHRASE 2.   Every diamond is special and valuable because no two are exactly alike.

Comment on Paraphrases 1 and 2:
Either trivial or false.

> Exactly. It is trivial in sense 1 and false in sense 2. Paraphrase 1 is the primary meaning (from the dictionary). The diamond company is really taking its customers for fools here. Being unique does not make a thing valuable: No two cockroaches are exactly alike either.

6. In a newspaper: "Quote of the week: 'Over the long term, we will either bring inflation down or it will assuredly get worse.' " — Jimmy Carter.

Comment:
Jimmy Carter's statement is trivial.

> The newspaper pretty clearly thinks Carter's statement is trivial. They have set it off in a box and called it the "Quote of the week" to point out how trivial it is. *(By giving a careful paraphrase of Carter's statement, show how it is* not *trivial.)*

7. Morality is just a matter of opinion.

> PARAPHRASE 1.   If someone believes something is right, then it is right.

Comment on Paraphrase 1:
False. Something can be wrong even though a particular person feels it is right. For example, murder.

> This captures well the primary meaning of the original, and it is a correct evaluation. For some reason murder is not a very convincing counter-example to people. A more convincing one is child molesting. If a child molester thinks that it is all right to molest children, that will not *make it* all right. So the original statement is false; morality is not just a matter of opinion. *(If morality is not a matter of opinion, what* is *it a matter of?)*

> PARAPHRASE 2.   Individuals have their own personal opinions about what is moral and what is not.

Comment on Paraphrase 2:
True. People do have different views, about morality as well as other topics.

> This is a secondary meaning of the original statement, and the comment that it is true seems correct. Notice that nothing follows from 2 about whether the individual's opinions *are* right, only that he or she *has* them.

> PARAPHRASE 3.   Right and wrong are determined only by the individual's judgment.

Comment on Paraphrase 3:

True. A person can believe that it is OK to commit murder. Ninety-nine percent of society can believe murder is wrong or immoral, but the person is still entitled to his or her opinion.

> Another accurate paraphrase but the comment is no good at all. The critic has misunderstood his own paraphrase. You can tell because the evaluation does not apply to what is said in the paraphrase. The criticism offered is in favor of something like 2, but the paraphrase given is another version of *1*.
>
> Paraphrases are intended to clarify the meaning of an unclear statement. It is essential then that you take the meaning of your *paraphrase* literally and seriously. Be sure to evaluate the truth of *it*, and not of something else with which you confuse it. If there are two senses to a statement, you need two paraphrases.
>
> *(All three of these paraphrases are in terms of an* individual's *opinion. What other plausible interpretations can you give regarding* whose *opinions? Is the original still false under these other readings?)*

> PARAPHRASE 4. If you believe in your own mind that your beliefs about morality are true, then they are true for you.

Comment on Paraphrase 4:

True. If in your own mind you think certain things about morality are true, then obviously these things are true for you.

> See the answer to the fourth question in part C. *(Explain why this is an unacceptable paraphrase.)*

8. An argument against gun-control legislation: "It's not the gun that kills, it's the man who holds the gun."

> PARAPHRASE 1. It does not need paraphrase. The statement is true and means just what it says.

> The statement does need paraphrase because in a literal sense guns *do* kill. If a policeman at a murder trial is asked, "Which gun did the killing?" he will answer without hesitation. Guns kill in the same way hammers pound nails. So you can't just take the original literally. The argument must mean: There is a *sense* in which guns do not kill. The paraphrase has to capture that sense.

> PARAPHRASE 2. A gun alone cannot kill anybody, but a man can use a gun to kill somebody.

Comment on Paraphrase 2:

True. A gun alone cannot kill; it is an instrument to kill with. If guns were outlawed something else would be used.

> The last sentence of the comment obviously has not been thought out. Guns make it much *easier* to kill people. (It would be hard to assassinate a president with a knife.)

PARAPHRASE 3.   Guns do not kill; it is the person who commits the crime with it.

Comment on Paraphrase 3:

True. Weapons are innocent; the people who use them to commit crimes are guilty.

"Crime" is not in the original. So it shouldn't be in the paraphrase.

PARAPHRASE 4.   Guns are not responsible for the death of a person; it is the person who causes the gun to fire who is responsible.

PARAPHRASE 5.   For a gun to terminate life, someone must pull the trigger.

PARAPHRASE 6.   Guns are will-less, brainless instruments that require a being of will, of intelligence, and with the physical capability of pulling its trigger to be fired.

Comment on Paraphrases 4, 5, and 6:

All these paraphrases are true. A gun is a device that can cause harm when triggered by someone, but only when triggered by someone. It cannot do it by itself.

Paraphrases 2, 5, and 6 are good and say essentially the same thing. Paraphrase 4 is all right, but the word "responsible" is ambiguous here and needs to be paraphrased itself. *(How is "responsible" ambiguous here? Give paraphrases that capture the ambiguity.)*

What is wrong about all these answers, though, are the comments. One of the purposes of paraphrasing is to bring out issues that are hidden beneath the surface meaning. That requires that you evaluate the paraphrases carefully. If you thought the original statement was true under any of these paraphrases, you didn't think it out enough. Guns are sometimes responsible for deaths; guns do sometimes terminate lives without anyone's pulling the trigger; guns do not always require an intelligent being who wills to pull the trigger. There are *accidents.* Guns fall off shelves and go off; children drop them and are killed; hunters are killed accidentally while cleaning their guns. In all these cases the gun does kill and there is no person holding it.

One main reason for gun control is the existence of gun accidents like these. The original covers this up, however, by making it look like the only issue is killing done on purpose. Whether you are for or against gun control is irrelevant here. By inspecting the paraphrases you should have noticed (when you were searching for counterexamples) that they were *false* because of accidents, and this would have brought the hidden issue to light.

Part D

Paraphrase statements 1–6. If more than one interpretation is necessary, give them all. Then say briefly whether each statement is true or false, and why.

1. Vitamin C prevents colds.

2. Buy nationally advertised brands.

3. You should do what you think is right.

4. Criminals in this country generally receive light sentences.

5. There are exceptions to every rule.

6. Money is the root of all evil.

The paraphrases of statements 7-24 are more difficult.

7. You can't make up for sleep that you have lost.

8. Alcoholism is a disease.

9. Rape is not an act of lust; it is an act of violence.

10. Anyone who commits suicide is insane.

11. History repeats itself.

12. It's my country, right or wrong.

13. So-and-so isn't well adjusted.

14. When people commit crimes, they must pay their debt to society.

15. Man is the highest animal.

16. There is a 20 percent chance of rain in the city tomorrow. (One out of five *what?*)

17. Women reach their sexual peak at around 35 years of age; men reach theirs at around 18.

18. Laughter results from an interrupted defense mechanism.

19. A historian's primary job is to state the facts, just as they happened.

20. Life is absurd.

21. What's so good about impressionist artists is that they try so hard to interpret reality.

22. Answer these questions by means of a paraphrase: What is the difference between defining "atheist" as "someone who does not believe in God" and defining it as "someone who does not believe that there is a God"? Which is a better definition?

23. If the law of causality is true, then there is no free will.

24. Which (if any) of the following statements *disagrees* with what 23 means?
    (a) Some human acts aren't caused by anything before them.
    (b) We do have free will.
    (c) Even though every action of mine is caused by external circumstances, my will is still free.
    (d) People can *choose* to do or not do an action.

Chapter Four

Component Parts
and Premises

1. The Component Parts of a Statement

As we saw in Chapter Two, the three steps for constructing an argument for a conclusion are

STEP 1. State clearly the meaning of the conclusion.

STEP 2. Isolate the component parts of the conclusion.

STEP 3. Formulate the most plausible reason you can to cover each part, and put each reason in a premise.

Step 1 is paraphrasing — understanding the meaning of what you have to prove. Step 2 is recognizing the subsidiary claims that you have to establish to prove the whole conclusion. And step 3 is giving the reasons to cover those claims; that is, proving the conclusion.

Isolating the Claims
Needed to Prove a Conclusion

Step 1 is completed when you have a good understanding of what the conclusion is saying. You begin the second step by asking yourself, "What would I be believing if I believed this conclusion?" or, "Which implicit assertions do I make when I assert this conclusion?" That is, before you can effectively prove the conclusion, you have to know what subsidiary claims are involved in it, what its component parts are.

Suppose you are trying to construct an argument for the following statement:

The United States has a free-enterprise system.

There are two distinct component parts of this conclusion, and you will need at least two premises in the argument. One will say what a free-enterprise system consists of, and the other will say that the United States has *that*. The component parts of the statement, then, are

PART 1.   The United States has a <u>free-enterprise system</u>.

PART 2.   <u>The United States</u> has a free-enterprise system.

These two parts of the statement can also be represented as two subsidiary claims:

CLAIM 1.   Certain characteristics make a system a free-enterprise system.

CLAIM 2.   The United States has those characteristics.

Or you can ask yourself about the conclusion in the form of a question: How can a person tell if the United States has a free-enterprise system? To answer this you have to answer two subsidiary questions:

QUESTION 1.   Under what conditions is something a free-enterprise system?

QUESTION 2.   Do these conditions hold in the United States?

These two questions correspond to the two component parts of the statement as well as to the two subsidiary claims involved in the statement.

It is important to see that these are just various ways of doing one thing: figuring out what claims you will have to make to argue effectively for the conclusion. Whether you do this by underlining words and phrases in the conclusion, by writing out the statements involved, by asking the appropriate questions, or by some other method, the important thing is to isolate the claims.

Subsidiary claims are open-ended

It is also important to notice that the subsidiary claims involved in the conclusion are open-ended. They state only that certain un-<u>specified characteristics</u> make something a free-enterprise system and that the United States has <u>those characteristics</u>. Nothing tells you specifically what those certain characteristics are; that's what is left open-ended. And the claims are open-ended for a very good reason: The conclusion is not committed to any specific characteristics. (At least it is not committed to any that go beyond the meanings of the terms.) So a good way of isolating the subsidiary claims, and emphasizing their open-endedness, is to substitute the symbol X for the unspecified characteristics:

CLAIM 1.   What makes something a free-enterprise system is X.

CLAIM 2.   The United States has X.

Once you have figured out what things you would have to prove in order to prove the conclusion, step 2 is literally over. You are now ready to begin step 3, which is actually proving them (or at least giving the best reasons you can for them). You are ready to decide what X is, — to specify the characteristics that make something a free-enterprise system and that the United States has.

The "Connectedness"
of Premises: Yields Validity

Steps 2 and 3 are so closely related that they are often discussed together in this chapter. They do, however, perform different functions in constructing an argument.

There is something very pretty — logically pretty — about the way that step 2 and step 3 fit together with the two basic concepts of reasoning, validity and truth. To have a sound argument (remember, one that actually proves its conclusion) the argument must be *valid* and its premises must be *true*. It will be valid, again, if believing its premises *forces* you to believe its conclusion. Its premises will be true if what they say describes the way things are. The argument will be sound if it has validity and truth.

Now look at what step 2 accomplishes. Earlier we broke the conclusion

The United States has a free-enterprise system

down into the claims:

CLAIM 1. Certain characteristics make a system a free-enterprise system.

CLAIM 2. The United States has those characteristics.

These two claims together constitute a *valid* argument for the conclusion. That is, you can fill in any characteristic (any X), no matter whether it is true or false or outlandish or silly, and the conclusion will follow logically from the two claims. The argument will be valid because if a free-enterprise system is made by having characteristic X (whatever it is) and if the United States has that same X, then it will follow logically, validly, and unavoidably that the United States has a free-enterprise system. Thus step 2, if done correctly, yields a valid argument. It does not, however, tell you anything at all about *truth*.

Step 2 yields validity

If we consider the two claims as they stand as premises, the argument, as we saw, is valid, and soundness then is just a matter of having both premises be true. Are the premises in this argument true? If you think about it for a minute, you'll see that you can't possibly tell. Nothing informs you what the characteristics in question are. It is only in step 3 that you specify these characteristics and so put yourself in a position to judge if the premises are true or false; truth depends on step 3, on how *plausible* the thing you substitute for X is. In step 3 you have to fill in X so that both premises look as true as you can possibly make them. You think up the best reason you can for each of the component parts, and put each in a separate premise. If those reasons are true, then the argument you have built is sound: It is valid, and it has true premises. Because it is valid, the more plausible the premises are, the more likely the argument is to be sound.

Suppose you choose a characteristic like "laissez faire, completely unrestricted capitalism." You will have an argument like this:

PREMISE 1.   Laissez faire, completely unrestricted capitalism makes a system a free-enterprise system.

PREMISE 2.   The United States has laissez faire, completely unrestricted capitalism.

∴ CONCLUSION 1.   The United States has a free-enterprise system.

This argument is still valid, but now you can see that it isn't sound: Premise 2 is clearly false. If, on the other hand, you choose a different characteristic — say, "private ownership of competitive businesses" — you will have the following argument:

PREMISE 1.   Private ownership of competitive businesses makes a system a free-enterprise system.

PREMISE 2.   The United States has private ownership of competitive businesses.

∴ CONCLUSION 1.   The United States has a free-enterprise system.

This argument, too, is valid, and it has a much better chance of being sound. Both the premises look plausible; they seem true. To the extent that you believe they are true, you will believe the argument is sound. To that extent also, you will be justified in believing that you have proved the conclusion.

How the three steps work together

So, following the three steps will give you the best chance that you have at a sound argument. Step 1 clarifies the meaning so that ambiguities and distortions don't get in the way of either validity or truth. Step 2 breaks the conclusion down into its component parts or subsidiary claims; doing this correctly makes the argument valid automatically. All that's left to making the argument sound is that its premises are true. And you will have good reason to believe that they are true according to how well you are able to perform step 3.

Truth isn't certain; validity often is

You can see from this that there is an important asymmetry about validity and truth, the two qualities necessary for soundness. Doing step 2 correctly *guarantees* with *certainty* that you will have a valid argument. Nothing can give you a guarantee like that for truth.

Validity is a tool of logic. However, truth is, in a way, harder to determine. To find out the truth of statements in biology, you have to study biology. To find out about validity in biology, you don't have to know much about biology at all, but you have to know how to reason. In an argument about ethics an enormous amount of complicated thinking may be required to find out if the premises are true or false, but any rational human being should be able to tell in a short while if the argument is valid.

Finding and Connecting
Multiple Component Parts

Before examining how steps 2 and 3 work together in practice, let's consider a few technical details of step 2.

One of the hardest things about constructing an argument is picking out the component parts of the conclusion. It looks easy, especially when you do it by underlining words or phrases in the conclusion. But you can't ever let underlining become a merely mechanical task. You have to *understand* what claims are being made. (Emphasizing certain parts by underlining them is just a way of discovering those claims, of not overlooking any.) You also have to understand how those claims fit together, how they "connect." And you have to make your premises fit together or connect in the same way, so that, when taken all together, they make a valid argument for the conclusion.

Connectedness is what ensures validity. If your first subsidiary claim is, "What characterizes a free-enterprise system is X," then your second subsidiary claim is already dictated. It *has* to be, "The United States has X." The argument is automatically valid because you are using X (that is, the same thing) in *both* subsidiary claims. Obviously it won't work to say, "What characterizes a free-enterprise system is X," and, "The United States has Y." This would hardly be an argument at all (unless some other premise linked X and Y in a certain way). It wouldn't prove the conclusion. (Nor, of course, would it disprove it.)

Connectedness ensures validity

Of course, connecting the premises to make a valid argument becomes more difficult when the conclusion to be argued for is more complicated than this one. But there are certain ways that all valid arguments hang together. Take the following statement as the conclusion:

> CONCLUSION 1.   All men are endowed by the Creator with the inalienable rights to life, liberty, and the pursuit of happiness.

Deciding how many main component parts there are in the conclusion may be difficult. You might try initially to divide it up into only two (one is underlined once and the other is underlined twice):

<u>All men are endowed by the Creator with</u> <u>the inalienable rights to life, liberty, and the pursuit of happiness</u>.

You might, that is, try to say what characteristics someone must have in order to have the inalienable rights to life, liberty, and the pursuit of happiness, and whether all men are endowed by the Creator with those characteristics.

Now, say you think about those two parts for a while. It will probably be very hard to think up a good reason to cover either one. You really have to ask yourself, "What characteristics *do* give you these rights?" The answer to this won't be easy, and it will require some careful figuring out. But say you come up with the following premise:

> PREMISE 1.   Someone has the inalienable rights to life, liberty, and the pursuit of happiness if he or she has the ability to reason out goals and can take steps toward achieving them.

Now, that is a long and complicated premise, one that will be hard to evaluate in any wholesale way. But once you have chosen premise 1 as the reason to cover the double-underlined part of the conclusion, the premise you choose to cover the single-underlined part must be:

> PREMISE 2.   All men are endowed by the Creator with the ability to reason out goals and take steps toward achieving them.

Premise 2 is dictated because "the ability to reason out goals and take steps toward achieving them" is being used as the characteristic X. And you will be able to see readily that the argument from premises 1 and 2 to conclusion 1 is a valid one.

A more complicated breakdown

But in another sense this argument hardly does justice to such a complicated conclusion. Premise 1, in particular, groups a lot of different characteristics together without explaining them. To construct a really well-thought-out argument for the conclusion, you need a premise about what makes a right inalienable, and premises about why life, liberty, and the pursuit of happiness (whatever that is) are such rights. Then, instead of breaking the conclusion down into two parts, you might break it down into six:

1. What characteristics must someone have in order to have rights?

2. Are all men endowed by the Creator with these characteristics?

3. What characteristics make a right inalienable?

4. How does life have those characteristics?

5. How does liberty have those characteristics?

6. How does the pursuit of happiness have those characteristics?

Using these questions to divide the conclusion into six component parts, you can make up a more detailed and more explanatory argument based on the earlier one. Thus we have argument 2:

> PREMISE 1.   Someone has rights if he or she has the ability to reason out goals and can take steps toward achieving them.

> PREMISE 2.   All men are endowed by the Creator with the ability to reason out goals and take steps toward achieving them.

(From these two it follows logically that all men are endowed by the Creator with rights.)

> PREMISE 3.   A right is inalienable if it cannot be taken away without depriving the person of the ability to reason out goals and take steps toward achieving them.

PREMISE 4.   Without life a person does not have the ability to reason out goals and cannot take steps toward achieving them.

PREMISE 5.   Without liberty a person cannot take steps toward achieving his or her goals.

PREMISE 6.   The pursuit of happiness is the ability to take steps toward achieving one's goals.

(From premises 3, 4, 5, and 6 it follows logically that life, liberty, and the pursuit of happiness are inalienable rights. And if you add premises 1 and 2, the whole conclusion follows logically.)

Notice that whether you break the conclusion down into two parts or into six, essentially the same techniques are used to ensure validity. Certain phrases (or at least their gist) are repeated to make the premises connect. Thus in argument 2, "the ability to reason out goals and take steps toward achieving them" (or a portion of it) is carried throughout the argument and ties all the premises together. (It thus functions like X in the earlier examples.) Also, in both arguments for conclusion 1 the phrase "all men are endowed by the Creator with" is treated as a single part, so it is written out as a single phrase in the premises and is not broken down further (though of course it could be).

How to connect premises

Whether you break this conclusion down into two parts or six, every part is covered by a premise. Thus premises 1, 3, 4, 5, and 6 together cover the same ground as premise 1 of the first argument. So if you began by breaking conclusion 1 down into only two parts, you might continue by breaking down its premise 1 into subsidiary claims.

There is an architectural beauty in the way these parts fit together. It is much the same kind of beauty that one often encounters with validity. Parts are engineered to fit together to support a conclusion; then other parts are constructed to support the first parts; and so forth until a solid structure is attained. In the end you hope to come up with an argument like a well-built building: All the statements are supported by others, and at the foundation are statements that you feel you can trust to stand on their own.

The Value of Isolating
Component Parts: Two Hard Examples

Breaking a conclusion down into its component parts is a harder task than you might at first imagine. It is difficult to pick out only the key subsidiary claims and leave out the unimportant ones.

Why a good breakdown is hard

There's no general formula that tells you which words and phrases (and which aspects of those words and phrases) constitute important subsidiary claims. You may miss some even if you carefully emphasize each word. Another thing that makes this process hard is that even the simplest statements, when broken down far enough, will reveal issues, usually philosophic issues, of great complexity. (Even such a claim as "you should brush your teeth three times a day" involves questions about whether you should do what you want, what it's reasonable to want, and whether other people are entitled to tell you what to do "for your own good.")

Why a good breakdown is fruitful

But breaking a conclusion down into parts is also fruitful. Seeing that simple statements contain much deeper issues — philosophic, moral, political, psychological — will make you understand those statements in a much fuller way. You won't be so tempted to accept them without question; you'll be prompted to look for alternatives; you'll have a new appreciation for how statements fit together into patterns.

Emphasizing the component parts of a conclusion is fruitful also because it forces you to approach the conclusion in novel ways. Trying to understand the significance of a word that you have underlined will often open up fresh points of view that you've never considered before.

An example will illustrate both the difficulties and rewards of a careful breakdown. In Chapter Two we considered the sentence, "All men are created equal." It is clear from the beginning that the sentence has at least two important parts. One part will say what kind of equality is in question — here the equality involved, we saw, is being entitled to the same treatment under the law. And the other will say why all men have that kind of equality. The problem arises when you consider the word "created." Is this an important part of the conclusion? Do you need a premise that covers the claim, "All men are created equal"?

Your first answer might be Yes. So you underline the word "created" and try to give reasons for believing that human beings were created (and created equal at that). This would probably involve talking about the reasons for thinking God exists, for thinking God created everyone to be entitled to the same treatment under the law — a truly formidable undertaking.

On the other hand, after thinking about the conclusion for a while, your answer might change to No. This is the answer that was argued for in Chapter Two. It was said there that the point is not God or creation, it is *equality* and how all human beings have it. If you choose this answer, then you decide not to underline the word "created"; you might say that "all men are created equal" was just Jefferson's old-fashioned and misleading way of saying "all men are equal."

But there is a third level to this reasoning. Notice that "all men are equal," if it means "all men are entitled to the same treatment under the law," is pretty clearly false. Convicted murderers, for example, are excluded from public office, and they don't get the same treatment under gun laws as other people. (They also lose the liberty to walk down the street and pursue happiness; this might lead you to wonder about how a right is "inalienable.") A natural way to think about this is to say that criminals *lose* some of their rights because they have committed a crime. But if all men *are* entitled to the same treatment under the law, this explanation won't work. If they *are* equal, then they haven't lost any rights; if they have lost some rights, then they *are not* equal. But Jefferson very carefully did not say that all men *are* equal. He said that all men are *created* equal. Now you can appreciate more easily the significance of the sentence with that word underlined. It means that all men *begin* with equal rights, that they are all *born* entitled to the same treatment under the law. By their actions afterward they may lose some of their rights and thereby no longer be entitled to the same treatment under the law.

By struggling through various levels of reasoning, you can see that there is indeed a point in underlining the word "created." What you find is that "all men begin equal" *is* a subsidiary claim in "all men are created equal," and "all men are equal" is *not*. Breaking the conclusion down into its component parts by underlining words and phrases focuses your thoughts on these claims.

Underlining helps you search deeper

So, isolating important claims, even with the focus of an underlined word, is not always an easy task. If you were deceived by what was said about "all men are created equal" in Chapter Two, then you should realize that sometimes the claim you are looking for will evade you. Of course, isolating claims is often easier than this. Just emphasizing a word and thinking about it will often reveal the claims you will need to argue for the conclusion.

Sometimes, however, it's much harder. Take the simple sentence: Two flashes of lightning are occurring at the same time. If you break this down into its component parts, there are several phrases you might rationally emphasize: "How could you tell there are <u>two flashes</u>?" "Under what conditions would there be flashes of <u>lightning</u>?" "Under what conditions are two events <u>occurring at the same time</u>?"

Try to answer the last question. A plausible answer is

Two events occur at the same time if an observer standing halfway between them would see both of them at the same instant.

Thinking about this, though, will involve further subsidiary claims; among them is a claim about <u>seeing</u>: Someone would see both events at the same time only if what lets people see things (namely, light) moves just as fast from either direction, that is, only if the speed of light is constant. Also, to underline another component part, <u>an observer</u> will see those same two flashes of lightning at different instants if he happens to be traveling very fast toward one and away from the other. Thus whether two events take place at the same time is relative to an observer, how fast he is going, and in what direction.

This, roughly, is the theory of relativity. And reasoning like this, according to Einstein himself, lies at the foundation of the theory of relativity. He examined what it is for events to take place <u>at the same time</u> (to be <u>simultaneous</u>), tried to isolate the various claims involved in this, and came up with the subsidiary claims about the speed of light and the relativity of simultaneity to an observer. The rest of the theory emerged from the same kind of mental investigation. Einstein developed the theory not by experimenting (though he was familiar with some experiments done), but by reasoning, by isolating the claims involved in a statement (step 2) and thinking up a premise to cover each claim (step 3).

When you think about these results for a while, they actually seem simple. The difficult part was realizing in the first place that there were some claims to isolate, that the statement about simultaneity needed breaking down into its component parts. Almost everything you discover by reasoning will seem simple enough *afterward*.

Constructing an argument by the three steps is not likely to inspire you to think up another theory of relativity, of course. But step 2 does force you to concentrate on parts of a sentence you might ordinarily neglect. Formulating the actual premises of the argument, the best reasons you can to cover each of those parts, is done in step 3.

Problems

Treat each of these statements as a conclusion you plan to argue for. Break each one down into its component parts. Tell what you would have to establish to prove the whole conclusion.

1. Lie-detector tests fight employee crime.

2. Prospective employees should be given a lie-detector test.

3. The family is dying out.

4. Women should not be drafted.

5. You should keep your promises.

6. Labor unions are a major cause of inflation in America.

2.   *Arriving at Premises: Two Methods*

Subdividing a conclusion (step 2) and supporting it with premises (step 3) interact when an argument is constructed. So the order in which you do them can vary. It will depend, to a large extent, on your starting point. You may start with just the conclusion or you may start with the conclusion, plus one or more premises. In the first case you will have to come up with the whole set of premises; in the second case you will have to come up with the missing premises, the unstated ones necessary to go from the premises you have to the conclusion you want.

The two
methods

Thus there will be two methods for arriving at the premises. In the first, you start from the conclusion alone. You begin by breaking the conclusion down into its component parts, and then you think of a reason to cover each. This is "working backward." In the second method, you start from the conclusion plus some supporting premises. Usually, you begin in this method by filling in the missing premises, and then you check your answer by breaking the conclusion down into its component parts and making sure each is covered by a premise. This is "working from the middle."

Method 1: Working Backward

Let's consider a down-to-earth example in an extended way. Suppose you have heard that poll taxes, which have been used in several Southern states, are unjust; you decide to prove it by constructing an argument with that as its conclusion:

CONCLUSION 1.   Poll taxes are unjust.

You need to get clear on the meaning. According to *Webster's New Collegiate Dictionary*, eighth edition, a poll tax is "a tax of a fixed amount per person levied on adults and often payable as a requirement for voting." That is enough for step 1.

Now in step 2, a good breakdown into subsidiary component parts is

PART 1.   Poll <u>taxes are unjust</u>.

PART 2.   <u>Poll taxes</u> are unjust.

That is, to construct an argument for conclusion 1, you will need to answer these two questions:

QUESTION 1.   Under what conditions is a tax unjust?

QUESTION 2.   In what way do these conditions hold for poll taxes?

There are many possible answers to question 1. Some will be true, some false, and only a limited number will be relevant. Which of them should you choose to make into your premise? The answer depends on two considerations: First, you want to choose a reason that is *true*; second, you want to choose a reason that will *connect* with the answer you will give to question 2 in such a way as to make it true also.

The rationale for the first consideration is straightforward. The point is to construct a sound argument, so it's no use choosing as a premise a statement that looks false. Thus you couldn't use a premise like

Chosen premise must be true

A tax is unjust if it puts limitations on the exercise of people's rights.

This is false. *All* taxes, in effect, limit what would otherwise be unrestricted rights. Income taxes take away a right to the unlimited use of the money you have earned; luxury taxes take away the right to buy luxuries at the simple retail price. But taxes in some form, with the consequent limitations on rights, are necessary for people to live together at all. They are not therefore unjust.

The rationale for the second consideration is that you cannot construct the various premises for an argument in isolation from one another. Now you are trying to build a valid argument; its premises, therefore, must fit together (connect) validly. So the premise you choose to answer question 1 will automatically determine the premise you choose to answer question 2. In thinking up premise 1, then, it is important to keep in mind what the result in premise 2 will be. Thus, say we chose as the first premise:

Chosen premise must connect to other premises

A tax is unjust if people of only one race or sex must pay it.

That seems undoubtedly true. But using it as premise 1 would require the following as our premise 2:

People of only one race or sex must pay poll taxes.

To have premises that connect to form a valid argument forces us to use an obviously false premise 2. So the full argument would again be unsound.

When you answer question 1 by saying which conditions make a tax unjust, you must keep in mind that you will have to say that those conditions hold for poll taxes when you answer question 2. Only by using the same conditions in both premises will the argument be valid, and your task is to build a valid argument with premises that are true.

It is better to answer question 1 with a premise that is both plausible and relevant:

PREMISE 1.   A tax is unjust if it makes it harder for poor people to exercise their basic rights than for rich people.

This premise looks true because basic rights are those that everyone has to the same degree; making the exercise of them dependent on one's income is, in effect, to deny that they are basic to everyone.

This premise also dictates that the second premise will be plausible:

PREMISE 2.   Poll taxes make it harder for the poor than for the rich to exercise the basic right to vote.

Voting is a basic adult right, according to the Constitution; because a poll tax is a fixed amount rather than a percentage of income, it will be harder for a poor person to pay than for a rich one.

By isolating component parts and choosing a premise to cover each, we have constructed what looks like a sound argument. It is valid because the premises "connect," and all the evidence examined points to the truth of the premises.

Method 2: Working from the Middle

Suppose you think that your college bookstore overcharges for its textbooks, and you decide to prove it by constructing an argument. By using method 1 you have come up with this argument:

PREMISE 1.   A store overcharges for an item when it makes an excessive profit on it.

PREMISE 2.   The college bookstore makes an excessive profit on its textbooks.

∴ CONCLUSION 1.   The college bookstore charges too much for its textbooks.

This looks like a good start for an argument. It is valid because both component parts are covered: <u>The college bookstore</u> <u>charges too much</u> <u>for its textbooks</u>. Moreover, premise 1 seems true. The problem is premise 2: What reasons do you have in its favor?

Let's suppose you attack this problem by constructing a further argument for *it*, i.e., an argument with premise 2 as its conclusion. This further argument will then act as additional support for the main conclusion 1.

One way to begin arguing for premise 2 is to break *it* down into *its* component parts, which is method 1 again. You would figure out, first, what percentage of profit is excessive, and, second, if the college bookstore makes that percentage of profit on its textbooks. These would correspond to the underlining in

<u>The college bookstore</u> <u>makes an excessive profit</u> on its textbooks.

Once you get to this point, though, you will realize that you've reached a dead end. Answering the first question — what percentage of profit is excessive — involves complicated and variable economics. And you are probably not in a position to examine the bookstore's accounts to see what profit it does make on its textbooks. So you couldn't answer the second question very easily anyway. Using these premises, then, is not going to be very fruitful.

It is important not to construct premises for a given conclusion by considering that conclusion only in the abstract. Sometimes it is just not realistic simply to look at the statement as it appears on the page, underline, and construct premises directly from the underlined parts. Remember that underlining is supposed to be an aid in isolating the reasons that can be used to support the conclusion.

What reason, then, might you have for *actually* believing premise 2 for *your* college bookstore? Consider it not as an exercise in a textbook on reasoning, but as an actual concrete case. One good, realistic reason you might have is that other bookstores charge significantly lower prices for similar books. In this case one of the premises you should use to support premise 2 is

PREMISE 3.   Other bookstores charge significantly lower prices than the college bookstore for comparable textbooks.

Now the problem of building a plausible argument for premise 2 becomes more intricate than merely thinking about it in the abstract.

Premise 3 is one of your reasons for believing premise 2. But premise 3 by itself is not a valid argument for premise 2. Something has been left out. Perhaps something so obvious that it is difficult to see, but still something that is needed to make the argument valid.

Notice that premise 3 says that other bookstores charge lower prices, but what you need to show is that your bookstore makes an <u>excessive profit</u>. In giving premise 3 as a reason for believing premise 2, you are *concluding* that your college bookstore makes an excessive profit *from* the fact that it charges more than other bookstores. You must therefore be *assuming* that the higher the prices a bookstore charges, the greater are its profits. A premise saying that, then, is missing from the argument. Let's state it this way:

Filling in a missing premise

> PREMISE 4.   The profit a bookstore makes is related directly to the prices it charges for its books.

Notice that it is necessary to *state* premise 4 to have a valid argument from premise 3 to premise 2. You assumed premise 4 (or something very much like it) when you thought that premise 3 was a good reason for believing premise 2. But the process of constructing a valid argument requires that you state the assumptions outright. These assumptions are missing as premises in the argument, and they are needed to draw the conclusion from the reasons given for believing the conclusion. Also, by writing the assumption out, you become much better able to evaluate it.

Now, do premises 3 and 4, taken together, constitute a valid argument for premise 2? They say that other bookstores charge less than yours and that profits are linked directly to those charges. Together, then, they prove that your bookstore makes *more* profit than the others, but not that your bookstore's profits are *excessive*. That is still missing from the argument. You are *assuming* that the other bookstores are making at least a fair profit themselves — that, for example, they are not operating at a loss — and that making more profit than that would be excessive. So we need one last premise to have a valid argument for premise 2:

> PREMISE 5.   A profit that is significantly greater than the other, similar bookstores make is excessive.

Premises 3, 4, and 5 constitute a valid argument for premise 2. They would do nicely if you were trying to prove premise 2 (either as a stage on the way to proving conclusion 1 or not). They do not, as we have already seen, constitute the *only* valid argument for premise 2. And it is unlikely that you would have come up with these three particular premises if you began constructing the argument by underlining key words in premise 2.

Nevertheless, premises 3, 4, and 5 *do* correspond to key words in premise 2, only not in a very obvious way. One of the subsidiary claims involved in premise 2 is

The college bookstore makes <u>an excessive</u> profit on its textbooks.

How can you tell if a bookstore's profit is <u>excessive</u>? One way is given by premise 5: A bookstore's profits are excessive if they are greater than the profits of other, similar bookstores. But how do you tell what its profits are? The answer to this is given by premise 4: You can tell about its profits by looking at the prices of its textbooks. Thus premise 4 corresponds to the following part of premise 2:

Premises in method 2 also cover component parts

The college bookstore <u>makes</u> an excessive <u>profit</u> on its textbooks.

Finally, premise 2 says

<u>The college bookstore</u> makes an excessive profit <u>on its textbooks</u>.

How can you know this about the college bookstore? By comparing its prices to those in other bookstores. And premise 3 tells you how the college bookstore compares.

Thus premises 3, 4, and 5 do correspond to the subsidiary claims involved in premise 2 that we isolated on page 105. Premise 4 and premise 5 together give the reasons for believing that the college bookstore <u>makes an excessive profit</u>; premise 3 gives the reason for believing that <u>the college bookstore</u> makes an excessive profit <u>on its textbooks</u>. No matter which way you go about trying to think up an argument for a conclusion, then, there must be one or more premises to cover each of the component parts of that conclusion.

Deciding Which Method to Use

The two methods differ only in the way you go about beginning the construction of an argument; they do not differ at all in their net result. Method 2 is preferable when you already have a solid reason for believing a conclusion. You work from the middle by stating your reason in a premise and then filling in the missing premises. (The second method will be even more important, and it will be explained in much greater detail, when we analyze arguments given by someone else. For a person's argument consists usually of a stated conclusion and some stated reasons for believing it; it is up to you to figure out the hidden, unstated premises in the person's argument.)

Method 1 is preferable when you are trying to build an argument for a conclusion from scratch. It is especially useful when you have never thought hard about the conclusion before, or when you want to approach the conclusion in a fresh way and do not want to let preconceived reasons influence you. You may also try to build an argument using the first method because you *disagree* with the conclusion. This will not only give you an advantage in arguing against it later, but it also may enable you to see some good in a view that you opposed blindly earlier.

When to use method 1

Both methods are ways of building a valid argument. The argument, to repeat, may not be sound — its premises may not be true — but it has to be valid. Nothing essential may be left unstated; there must be no gaps or loopholes between the stated premises and the stated conclusion. Making sure that each of the component parts is covered by the premises is a way of making sure that everything required is in fact stated.

Both methods of constructing arguments may still be unclear in your mind. Filling in unstated premises is crucially important in reasoning, and it is one of the most difficult tasks to do well. There will be a good deal of further explanation of both methods.

Problems

In each of the problems below there is a conclusion to be argued for plus a premise you might naturally use to support it.

First, break the conclusion down into its component parts. Then tell which part of the conclusion is covered by the stated premise.

Finally, construct an argument for the conclusion, either by using the stated premise (method 2) or by working backward from the subdivided conclusion alone (method 1).

1. CONCLUSION: A good grade is not the most important goal in a course.

PREMISE: Grades don't have a long-term significance in your life.

2. CONCLUSION: Atheists lead unhappy lives.

PREMISE: To lead a happy life, people must be able to look forward to something after death.

3. CONCLUSION: Life imprisonment is more humane than capital punishment.

PREMISE: A person who is in prison for life at least always has tomorrow to look forward to.

4. CONCLUSION: Wiretapping is an infringement of liberties.

PREMISE: The right to private conversation without fear of prosecution is a fundamental personal liberty.

5. CONCLUSION: Poverty breeds crime.

PREMISE: If people are so poor that they cannot afford the necessities of life, they will try to get more money any way they can.

6. CONCLUSION: The best child-care center is one that is unstructured.

PREMISE: Preschool children need time to develop interests and abilities at their own pace.

3. *The Logical Arrangement of an Argument*

Diagraming the Levels of an Argument

Let's return to the argument about your college bookstore. That argument all together looks like this:

PREMISE 1.   A store overcharges for an item when it makes an excessive profit on it.

PREMISE 2.   The college bookstore makes an excessive profit on its textbooks.

PREMISE 3.   Other bookstores charge significantly lower prices than the college bookstore for comparable textbooks.

PREMISE 4.   The profit a bookstore makes is related directly to the prices it charges for its books.

PREMISE 5.   A profit that is significantly greater than other, similar bookstores make is excessive.

∴ CONCLUSION 1.   The college bookstore overcharges for its textbooks.

If you dwell on this argument for a while, you will realize that all the premises are not on the same level. The argument has a logical arrangement or logical order to it, which might be diagramed this way:

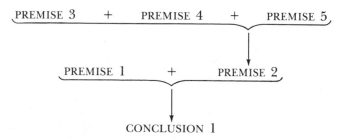

At the bottom level is conclusion 1. Because conclusion 1 needed support by an argument, we came up with the original argument, which consists of premises 1 and 2. These two premises constitute the next level, and we use brackets to show that they fit together and an arrow to show that they support conclusion 1. Finally, premise 2 was also seen to be weak and in need of support. The argument consisting of premises 3, 4, and 5, then, constitutes yet another level, and the brackets show that these three premises support premise 2. In each case the brackets contain an argument that is *valid*, and the arrow points to the *conclusion* of that valid argument.

This portrays the logical arrangement of the whole argument in the sense that it shows the relationships of validity that hold between all the statements in the argument. At each stage we are *deducing* or *inferring* a particular conclusion from the supporting premises. On the top level, premises 3, 4, and 5 are not backed up by anything; on the second level, premise 1 is also not backed up by anything. The diagram shows that no reasons or arguments have been produced to support them; they are considered plausible enough not to need further supporting arguments. Because premise 2 was considered doubtful by itself, it is supported by premises 3, 4, and 5. This means that we can *deduce* premise 2 as a conclusion from these three premises. So the doubtful question of whether premise 2 is true reduces to the three simpler questions of whether premises 3, 4, and 5 are true. If they are, it follows logically and necessarily that premise 2 is true. If one of these premises is false, we have failed to prove premise 2. (This would *not* show that premise 2 is false; it would show only that this is not a sound argument for believing it.) Conclusion 1, the main conclusion of the argument, is in fact supported by all the premises in the argument. It is deduced directly from premises 1 and 2, and through premise 2 it is based indirectly on premises 3, 4, and 5. Therefore, if premises 1, 3, 4, and 5 are all true, we *have proved* conclusion 1. If one of them is false, we have failed to prove conclusion 1. (Again, if one or more of the premises is false, it does not follow that conclusion 1 is false; it shows only that it has not been proved.)

*Logical
arrangement
shows where
further
support is
needed*

Arranging premises and conclusions in their logical order displays the argument's strong and weak points. The diagram reminds you that the arguments in brackets should be valid, and so it alerts you to fill in the missing premises. More importantly, though, it helps you to correct the argument in the places where it needs correcting. Once you have constructed a valid argument for a conclusion, any doubts that you may have about the truth of the conclusion should be shifted to doubts about one or more of the premises that logically supports that conclusion. If the premises in that argument are true, then the conclusion (no matter how doubtful it may appear) has been *proved*: it too is true. So any doubts you still have about the conclusion should be focused on the premises instead. As long as you are unable to find anything wrong with these, the reasonable attitude is to believe the conclusion. The whole weight of an argument depends finally on those premises that are not supported by any further reasons. And the diagram shows clearly which premises these are.

The Technique for
Supporting Doubtful Premises

The logical arrangement of an argument will show you where the argument needs additional support. When you have completed the argument (or think you have) and arranged its premises and conclusion in their logical order, you will be left in one of three positions: Either all the unsupported premises will be true, or one or more of the unsupported premises will be false, or else one or more of the unsupported premises will be doubtful (neither clearly true nor clearly false). In the first case the argument is sound and you are finished with it; you can justly say that you have proved the conclusion. In the second case you are also finished with the argument. If even one of the premises is false, the argument is unsound; it has failed to prove the conclusion.

It is in the third case, however, that showing the logical arrangement helps the most. To the extent that one of the unsupported premises is doubtful (neither clearly true nor clearly false) you are justified in doubting the conclusion. But this is an uncomfortable position to be in. You have not proved the conclusion because not all of the premises really look true, but you cannot dismiss the argument either because none of the premises looks quite false.

Doubtful, unsupported premises

What do you do about a doubtful premise? You think up an additional argument to support *it*. You do this in one of the two usual ways: by breaking the premise (now a conclusion) down into its component parts and thinking up a premise to cover each part, or by taking the best reason you have for believing the doubtful conclusion and filling in the missing connecting premises.

Once you have constructed this additional argument and showed its place in the logical arrangement, you no longer have to worry about the doubtful premise. It has been supported by a valid argument, and your attention can shift to the premises that support it. If these additional premises look clearly true, the previously doubtful premise will have been proved and the whole argument will be sound. Failing this, if one of the additional premises is pretty clearly false, you will be able to judge that the argument is unsound and be able to say why. In either case you will be justified in thinking that you are done with the argument. But if one of the additional premises that you have come up with is doubtful, it will be necessary to construct yet *another* argument to support *it*. And the same three possible positions will be open at *this* stage of the argument also: Either all the premises will be true, or at least one will be false, or, once again, one may be doubtful.

Producing an argument shifts focus from conclusion to premises

This process could go on indefinitely, but in practice it soon comes to an end, either in true premises or a false premise, or else in a realization of exactly what makes you doubtful of the whole line of argument, including the main conclusion. This last position may not be as satisfying psychologically as the first two, but there are some issues that simply are doubtful, where it is not likely that you will come up with hard and fast answers. In these cases, getting a good hold on what it is that makes the issue questionable not only is the best you can do, but also is quite informative.

Diagraming the logical arrangement of your argument, then, not only displays for you the interrelationships between the various premises and conclusions, but also furnishes you with a technique for locating the weak spots where additional argumentation is needed. (It also lets you see more clearly when your argument is completed.)

The technique can be summarized as follows. The logical arrangement of the argument is shown after each stage in the reasoning.

1. You begin with a conclusion that you are trying to prove.

CONCLUSION 1

2. You construct the best argument you can for conclusion 1 (by either method). You have to make sure that the argument is *valid*, that the premises cover the whole conclusion without leaving any gaps. (Let's suppose this argument has three premises.)

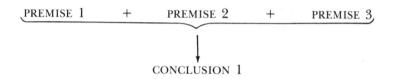

3. You examine each of the premises individually for *truth*.

   (a) If the premise being considered is true, it needs no further argumentation.

   (b) If the premise being considered is false, then the argument is unsound; it fails to prove conclusion 1. You can now try to construct a different argument for conclusion 1, or you can try to construct an argument against conclusion 1. But *this* argument (premises 1–3) is finished.

   (c) If the premise being considered is doubtful, you begin again with (1), taking the premise being considered as the conclusion. (Let's suppose that premises 1 and 2 have been found to be true, but that you have serious doubts about premise 3.)

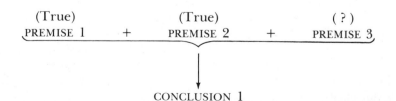

1. Premise 3 is the conclusion to be proved.

2. You construct the best valid argument you can think of for premise 3. (Suppose this argument has two premises.)

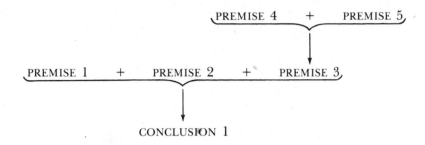

3. You examine premises 4 and 5 for *truth*.

   (a) If the premise being considered is true, it needs no further support.

   (b) If the premise being considered is false, then *this* argument (from premises 4 and 5 to premise 3) is unsound. So is the whole argument (from premise 1 through premise 5 to conclusion 1). You can now try to construct a different argument for premise 3, or you can try to think of an argument against premise 3. But the argument from premise 1 to premise 5 is finished.

   (c) If the premise being considered is doubtful, you begin again with (1), taking the doubtful premise as the conclusion. (Let's suppose premise 5 has been found to be true but that premise 4 is doubtful.)

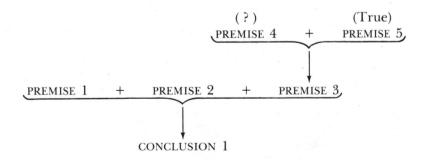

1. You think up the best valid argument you can for premise 4 and examine each of the premises in it for truth. (Suppose there are three of these.)

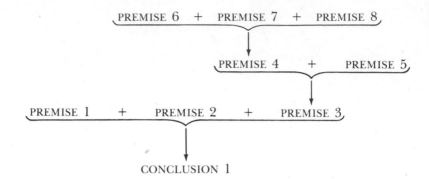

PREMISE 6   +   PREMISE 7   +   PREMISE 8

PREMISE 4   +   PREMISE 5

PREMISE 1   +   PREMISE 2   +   PREMISE 3

CONCLUSION 1

Logical Arrangement: Reasoning Deeper

One major effect of using this technique may be that you will begin examining unsupported premises more carefully. If you think hard about the unsupported premises in the college bookstore argument, for example, you might bring yourself to question any one of them (premise 1, 3, 4, or 5). You can plausibly ask, "What reason do I have for believing *that*?" And you can then, by filling in the missing premises, turn that reason into a valid argument to support the premise you wondered about.

For example:

> PREMISE 5.   A profit that is significantly greater than other, similar bookstores make is excessive.

Questioning premises you believe

What reason is there for thinking that premise 5 is true? Probably the reason that will come into your mind first is that other bookstores are certainly *not* operating at a loss. They are making a profit themselves. So for the college bookstore to exceed this profit is excessive. You formulate this first reason as

> PREMISE 6.   The other, similar bookstores are making a fair profit (or better).

Then the connecting premise you need to link premise 6 with the conclusion (premise 5) will be

> PREMISE 7.   A profit that is more than a fair one is excessive.

This part of the structure would look like

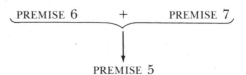

PREMISE 6   +   PREMISE 7

PREMISE 5

Now these two premises look genuinely true, and that should calm any doubts you have about the truth of premise 5. If in spite of this you now question premises 6 and 7 in their turn, you may be led to raise some very interesting and deep questions. What makes a profit a *fair* one? Should *bookstores* make any profit at all? Should *stores* generally make a profit? Why should there be *any* profits? These philosophic and ethical questions lie at the root of the question about your college bookstore.

It is important to see that you do not have to answer these questions for the practical matter at hand. The unsupported premises in the argument look true, and because the argument is also valid, you can say justifiably that you have proved that your college bookstore overcharges for its textbooks. Still, it is also important to see that underneath that practical matter is a deeper and harder set of questions and that you take certain answers to these questions for granted when you give your argument. That is, you accept certain positions uncritically. If you portray the logical arrangement of the argument and persist in questioning the reasons behind the premises, you will soon find yourself in a position to question old dogmas and maybe formulate some truly innovative and exciting alternatives to the standard position.

Philosophic positions underlie practical matters

Reasoning deeper can reveal new insights

Maybe college bookstores should not make any profit. Why? Because maybe the costs should be paid out of taxes. Why? Because everyone in the state benefits (at least a little and indirectly) by good education, and so everyone should pay (at least a little and indirectly) in taxes for education, including textbooks. Maybe the students should get them at cost, or even free. Now that position may be wrong, but just formulating it as a possibility in the background of the practical issue opens up any number of new insights.

Problems

In the last set of problems (on p. 108) you constructed arguments for six conclusions. Take each of those arguments and diagram its logical arrangement. Which is the weakest premise in the argument? Suppose that premise with an additional argument and diagram the result.

4.   A Realistic Example

Unlike most subjects in school, reasoning is a skill rather than a body of knowledge. The ability to apply reasoning techniques correctly will therefore depend very heavily on practicing those techniques rather than merely hearing instructions in the abstract.

Let's consider a realistic example. It will have many more vaguenesses and uncertainties than a neat specification of the rules might lead you to expect. But it will be much more like the actual problems that you will run into when you try to construct arguments for points of your own. The example will serve to illustrate the main tasks in constructing an argument as they often occur in practice: breaking a statement down into its component parts, thinking up good reasons, filling in the missing premises, and arranging the premises and conclusion in their logical order. The example will also illustrate some of the finer points of constructing an argument: how to phrase premises, how to get the most-informative missing premise, how to fix up an argument, and how to think your way beneath the surface of what is being said. During the discussion of the example, you should pay attention to the *general* manner in which problems are overcome or lessened as well as to the specific devices used.

An ordinary, noncontroversial example is better for illustrating the method than a controversial one would be. In the exercises, however, there are a number of controversial examples.

Constructing the Argument

Suppose your history teacher says:

> Alexander of Macedon was one of the greatest generals who ever lived.

When you ask, "Is that true?" you are taking the statement as a conclusion and asking for reasons that support it. The kind of reason you might be given is that

> Alexander conquered Persian armies of more than 100,000 men with only 20,000 Greeks.

You can take this statement to be a premise in the argument. And it looks on the whole like a good reason for believing the conclusion.

You are beginning to construct an argument with a conclusion plus a premise. So to make the argument valid, you need a connecting premise, one that states why the premise is a convincing reason for believing what the conclusion says. Why does conquering enemy armies with only 20,000 men make Alexander one of the greatest generals who ever lived?

A missing premise you might come up with by thinking about validity is

> Conquering 100,000-man Persian armies with only 20,000 Greeks is something that only one of the greatest generals could do.

This premise links the feats of conquering that Alexander accomplished (mentioned in the first premise) with being a great general (mentioned in the conclusion). But in spite of this it is not the best way to state the missing premise because the information it contains is too specific to Alexander. It is not *broad* or *general* enough to qualify as a good statement of the missing premise. A better missing premise is

> Only a great general could win victories against five-to-one odds.

This premise is better because it does not talk so specifically about Persians and Greeks. What makes a general great is not conquering *Persians* with *Greeks*, but conquering enemy armies, whatever the nationalities involved. (Napoleon, another great general, could not conquer Persians with Greeks because he was not *fighting* the Persians and was not *commanding* Greeks.) Similarly, the specific numbers do not seem to matter particularly. It is conquering against such heavy odds that shows someone to be a great general. The "five-to-one" just specifies how heavy the odds were. (Maybe even that is a little too specific. Maybe it would be better to have the connecting premise just say "against heavy odds," leaving it vague.) The second formulation of the missing premise, then, is better than the first: It tells in broad, unspecific terms one of the things that makes someone a great general, regardless of nationality or the specific numbers involved. Then the premise stated earlier tells how Alexander did *that*.

We must return now to the question, "Is the argument valid?" Will the two premises we now have prove the conclusion? The answer is no. There is still something missing from the argument. The initial premise says that Alexander conquered Persian armies of more than 100,000 men with only 20,000 Greeks, and the premise we filled in says that conquering at five-to-one odds is something only a great general could do. But the conclusion does not follow from these. What does follow is that Alexander was a great general. What you started out to prove, however, was more than that — namely, that he was one of the greatest. So you need to fill in another premise:

> Very few generals could have accomplished feats of generalship as great as that.

(You could have gotten by with having only one missing premise if you had said earlier, "Only one of the greatest generals could win victories at five-to-one odds." But the scheme with two missing premises seems slightly preferable to this because it separates what it takes to be a *great* general from what it takes to be one of the *greatest*. But this preference is a matter of judgment.)

The argument, with all its premises assembled, is

PREMISE 1.   Alexander conquered Persian armies of more than 100,000 men with only 20,000 Greeks.

PREMISE 2.   Only a great general could win victories against five-to-one odds.

PREMISE 3.   Very few generals could have accomplished feats of generalship as great as that.

∴ CONCLUSION 1.   Alexander of Macedon was one of the greatest generals who ever lived.

Now this looks like a good argument; its premises seem plausible and it also looks valid. You could make sure that it was valid by rephrasing the premises slightly to repeat the appropriate words where needed. Thus someone might be very picky and say that the conclusion talks about Alexander of Macedon, whereas premise 1 only talks about Alexander. Because the same name (Alexander of Macedon) is not used, nothing in the argument says that both Alexanders are the same person. An objection like this, though, is too picky to be taken seriously; it is obvious that both names refer to the same person. Besides, you could simply add "of Macedon" to premise 1 if you wanted to. A similar objection (although not quite so picky) is that the phrase, "one of the greatest generals who ever lived," is not contained in the premises at all; so how could you prove it in the conclusion? Sometimes this *is* a good objection to an argument, but in this case it is not. The *idea* of "one of the greatest" seems to be contained in premise 3: Very few generals, it says, could have accomplished such a thing. Which generals? It is clear that premise 3 means only the greatest. But if you think that this is not clear, then you can reformulate premise 3 to include the phrase "one of the greatest" explicitly. For example:

PREMISE 3a.   Only one of the greatest generals could accomplish such a feat.

The validity of the argument can be checked more closely by seeing whether the whole conclusion is proved by the premises. That involves going through steps 2 and 3 for constructing arguments. Once you examine it closely, you will find that the conclusion has four main component parts, and each of these parts is covered in a premise. Think about the conclusion: Alexander of Macedon was one of the greatest generals who ever lived. What reasons might there be for believing this? Well, pretty clearly it has something to do with (1) what Alexander did. Other parts of the conclusion are the claims (2) that Alexander was a general and (3) that he was a great general. Parts (2) and (3) are summed up with an additional claim (4) that he was in the class of the greatest generals. Thus, to give an adequate argument for the conclusion, you have to say at least four separate things:

1. What Alexander did.

2. What makes someone a general.

3. What makes someone a great general.

4. What puts someone in the class of the greatest generals.

Each of the four parts is covered in a premise. Part 1 is contained straightforwardly in premise 1. Part 2 is also contained in premise 1 because it says that Alexander (a single person) conquered the Persian armies. We only say things like this if the single person is the general in actual command. So premise 1 really already includes the claim that Alexander was a general. Part 3 is contained in premise 2, and part 4 is contained in premise 3.

Now, there are many other arguments you might have given for the conclusion. Because you began with your teacher's statement as premise 1, though, that much of the argument is settled from the start, leaving only a few correct ways to fill in the missing premises. These differ mostly in phrasing: You could rephrase premise 3 as we did above to make premise 3a; you could combine premises 2 and 3 into a single premise ("Only one of the greatest generals could win victories at five-to-one odds"); you could make premise 2 more or less generalized; but that's about it. It is almost as if you are not really constructing an argument of your own, but *analyzing* and filling in the missing premises in your teacher's argument.

Thus, the argument illustrates a further point about reasoning: You couldn't have constructed this argument about Alexander on your own, from scratch, unless you had read a biography or had already known something about him. You couldn't construct the argument by logic or reasoning alone. Logic can't tell you what Alexander did. No amount of reasoning about the conclusion will tell you that Alexander conquered Persian armies with 20,000 Greeks. *Given* the conclusion and premise 1, logic (plus some common knowledge) will enable you to construct premises 2 and 3, but it will not give you premise 1 itself. There is a strong sense in which reasoning does not give you new information; instead it gives you the ability to understand and deal with information you already have.

Diagraming the Logical Arrangement and Checking for Truth

The logical arrangement of the premises in this argument is straightforward. You started with premise 1 as a reason for believing conclusion 1, and then you added premises 2 and 3 to make the argument valid. So the logical order is

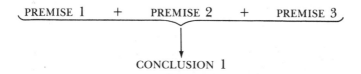

All that remains, then, is to see if the premises are true. Is premise 1 true? The answer to that seems to be yes: Your history teacher said so; it is unlikely that he or she is lying or mistaken about such a thing; and you have no special reason to doubt it. If you are still skeptical about the truth of premise 1, looking up the exploits of

Alexander in some history books should settle the matter. (There is not much use, in this context, in questioning historians' sources. You might question them profitably, though, if you were thinking hard about Greek history: On how many independent sources is our knowledge of Alexander's wars based? Were these sources eyewitnesses? How reliable are their reports in other areas where we can check their accuracy? How were such large numbers of men counted? But in this reasoning context you have a good bit of evidence in favor of premise 1 and no evidence specifically against it, so you can conclude that premise 1 is true.)

How about premise 2? Is it true that only a great general could win victories against five-to-one odds? Notice that premise 2 is not specifically about Alexander or his victories; it has to be evaluated as a statement that would apply to any general. You might see some counterexamples to it: A general with an air force can easily win victories against five-to-one odds if the enemy consists wholly of ground forces. This would not make him a great general, however; vast superiority in war equipment does not make a general great. So a legitimate objection to premise 2 might be: "Premise 2 as it stands is false; it would be true only if both armies had approximately the same

war equipment." If this objection holds up (and it looks as if it does), your argument has been refuted. As it stands, premise 2 is false; the argument is unsound. What can you do now? You probably would not give up the whole argument because of this objection. After all, Alexander did not have an air force, and checking the history books will show that he did not have superiority in war equipment either. So the objection to premise 2 in general does not apply to Alexander in particular. The thing to do, then, is to amend the argument by changing premise 2 to something like

> PREMISE 2a.   Unless he has a vast superiority in war equipment, only a great general could win victories against five-to-one odds.

This patches up premise 2 so that the objection no longer applies to it.

But changing premise 2 to premise 2a has ramifications for the rest of the argument. To keep the argument valid, you now have to add another premise:

> PREMISE 4.   Alexander did not have a vast superiority in war equipment.

You added a qualification to premise 2 about what it takes to be a great general (component part 3), so you have to add the same qualification to what Alexander did (component part 1); otherwise you will not have proved that Alexander was a great general. Without premise 4 there would be a gap between the premises and the conclusion, and the argument would not be valid. Almost always, when you change one part of an argument to meet an objection, you have to change another part also to keep the argument valid.

The logical arrangement of the reworked argument is now

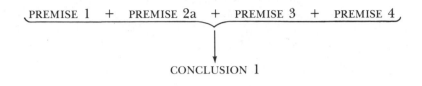

PREMISE 1   +   PREMISE 2a   +   PREMISE 3   +   PREMISE 4

CONCLUSION 1

We saw already that premise 1 is true, and we rejected premise 2. So we next have to evaluate the truth of premise 2a.

Premise 2a looks more plausible than premise 2 did. You might be able to think up more objections to it, though, and they would center around ways a person could win victories against five-to-one odds and yet fail to be a great general. Pure luck might be such a way, but that is not very believable against odds as heavy as five-to-one. Instead of thinking up more objections to premise 2a, however, you might simply wonder what makes it true. Provided both armies have approximately the same war equipment, *why* does it take a great general to win victories against heavy odds? If you wonder about premise 2a, you may want to break it down into its component parts and think up an argument to support it. If we put aside the question of war equipment for the moment, there are two component parts to premise 2a. First, what does it take to be able to win victories against five-to-one odds? Second, how is that characteristic of only a great general? The answers you come up with may give you deeper reasons for thinking that premise 2a is true. To win victories against great odds, one essential ingredient is strategy — to nullify the opposing army's numerical superiority. And strategy in turn requires both intelligent planning and troops who are disciplined enough to carry out those plans. And the ability to accomplish things like these are among the most crucial characteristics of being a good general.

Backing up a doubtful premise

Answers like these are not usually easy to find, but once you have them, they furnish the basis of a strong and informative argument for premise 2a. What you have to do is phrase them so that they correspond to the component parts isolated above. (You also have to bring back the qualification about superiority of war equipment, but this will not cause a problem.) The answers will yield the following premises:

> PREMISE 5.   Unless there is a vast superiority of war equipment, winning victories against odds as great as five-to-one requires strategy, intelligent planning, and well-disciplined troops.

> PREMISE 6.   The earmarks of a great general are his strategic ability, the intelligence of his planning, and his ability to discipline his troops.

Premises 5 and 6 constitute a valid argument for premise 2a. Moreover, each of them upon examination looks true. If that's so, then you can legitimately claim to have proved premise 2a. The structure of the argument now is

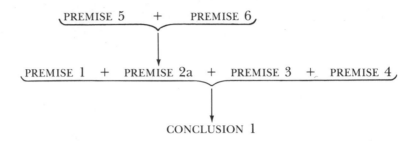

Premises 3 and 4 still must be examined. Premise 3 looks true, but a fair knowledge of history is needed to be sure about it. Premise 4 has evidence for it in much the same way that premise 1 had: To find out if it is true, you have to check what the historians of Alexander's Greece had to say. In fact, both premise 3 and premise 4 seem to be true on the basis of historical evidence.

The argument, we can be reasonably assured, is sound.

Exercises to Chapter Four

The questions in part A, part B, and part C of these exercises correspond to one another (thus question 1 is on the same topic in each of the three parts; so is question 2; and so forth).

In part A do each question on your own.

In part B various possible answers (some right, some wrong) are offered to the questions in part A. Evaluate each of these possible answers in accord with the instructions to that particular question.

Part C contains correct answers to many of these questions, together with analyses, explanations, and further reasoning techniques. Part C also contains some additional questions. (They are in parentheses and printed in italic type.) Be sure to answer these additional questions before proceeding.

For best results in reasoning do not look ahead to part B until you have finished part A, and do not look ahead to part C until you have finished both part A and part B.

Part D contains additional similar exercises, but without comments or answers.

Part A

Construct an argument for conclusions 1–6. (Be sure to paraphrase any conclusions that need it.) Break each down into its component parts by formulating the appropriate questions or subsidiary claims to isolate each part. To test the correctness of the breakdown, remember that the result of filling in the claims or

answering the questions should yield a *valid* argument for the conclusion.
Sample conclusion:

> If the Reign of Terror had lasted ten years, Napoleon would not have risen
> to power in France.

In part A you break this down into component parts. Suppose you think there are
three of them: (1) covering <u>the Reign of Terror lasting ten years</u>, (2) covering
<u>Napoleon rising to power</u>, and (3) the relation between those two occurrences —
<u>if</u> ... <u>not</u>. You do part A by asking three *questions* that isolate each part or by
formulating *subsidiary claims* that capture each part.

For example, questions:

> QUESTION 1.   What would be the effects of the Reign of Terror's lasting
> ten years?

> QUESTION 2.   What factors did Napoleon's rise to power in France depend
> on?

> QUESTION 3.   How would those effects have ruled out those factors?

Or, by subsidiary claims:

> CLAIM 1.   The Reign of Terror's lasting ten years would have produced
> certain effects.

> CLAIM 2.   Napoleon's rise to power depended on certain factors.

> CLAIM 3.   Those factors would not have been present if those effects had
> not occurred.

This is a good breakdown because it yields a valid argument when you answer the
questions or when you fill in the effects and factors in the subsidiary claims.

1. To get a good job, get a good education.

2. Eighteen-year-olds should be allowed to vote.

3. The law should be written in language that the common man can understand.

4. Computers are smarter than humans.

5. It is important to keep up with current events.

6. ESP and other supernatural phenomena are beyond the scope of science.

Construct an argument for conclusions 7–10 by breaking them down into their
component parts and thinking up a premise to cover each part. The argument you
come up with in each case must be *valid*. In addition, its premises should be as
plausible as you can make them. (Again, be sure to paraphrase.)

7. You should vote for X.

8. University students should be required to take a foreign language.

9. America: Love it or leave it.

10. There isn't anything really so bad about shoplifting.

Part B

The following (1–6) are various attempts to do part A. Evaluate each attempt by saying which component part of the conclusion each question or subsidiary claim covers, and which component parts are left uncovered. For any parts left uncovered, formulate the additional questions or claims needed to cover them.

This section can also be done as a single multiple-choice test, but it is much more beneficial to evaluate each breakdown on its own merits.

1. To get a good job, get a good education.

PARAPHRASE 1.   To get a high-paying job, one needs a college degree or professional training.

PARAPHRASE 2.   A good education increases your chances of getting a good job.

PARAPHRASE 3.   The best way of attaining desired employment is by first attending a school that provides high-quality teaching and training.

Breakdowns:

(a) QUESTION 1.   What is a good job?

QUESTION 2.   What is a good education?

(b) QUESTION 1.   What are the characteristics of a good job?

QUESTION 2.   What are the effects of a good education?

QUESTION 3.   Does a good education help you get a good job?

(c) CLAIM 1.   Certain skills and knowledge are helpful in increasing your chances on the job market.

CLAIM 2.   A good education gives you those skills and knowledge.

(d) CLAIM 1.   There are certain requirements for getting a good job.

CLAIM 2.   There are certain characteristics only a good education gives.

CLAIM 3.   Those characteristics are needed to meet the requirements for getting a good job.

(e) QUESTION 1.   Are there certain prerequisites for getting a good job?

QUESTION 2.   Can these prerequisites be obtained by getting a good education?

(f) CLAIM 1.   A person must have certain qualifications to get a good job.

CLAIM 2. A good education is needed for a person to acquire these qualifications.

(g) QUESTION 1.   What qualities are provided best by a good education?

QUESTION 2.   Why are these qualities important for getting a good job?

(h) QUESTION 1.   How do you get a good job?

QUESTION 2.   What conditions must be met to get a good job?

QUESTION 3.   What is the result of a good education?

QUESTION 4.   How is the result of a good education linked to getting a good job?

2. Eighteen-year-olds should be allowed to vote.

PARAPHRASE 1.   People who are eighteen are just as qualified to vote as people who are over twenty-one.

Breakdowns:

(a) CLAIM 1.   People who are allowed to vote should have certain qualifications.

CLAIM 2.   Eighteen-year-olds have those qualifications.

(b) QUESTION 1.   What requisites are necessary to vote?

QUESTION 2.   Do eighteen-year-olds possess those requirements in the same quantity as people over twenty-one?

(c) QUESTION 1.   What makes an eighteen-year-old acceptable for serving in the armed forces?

QUESTION 2.   Won't these same attributes suffice for allowing an eighteen-year-old to vote?

(d) CLAIM 1.   There are certain characteristics of people twenty-one years and older who are allowed to vote.

CLAIM 2.   Eighteen-year-olds have those characteristics.

3. The law should be written in language that the common man can understand.

PARAPHRASE 1.   The law should be written in a way that people without legal training can understand.

PARAPHRASE 2.   Laws should be written in a way so that most people will know what they mean.

(a) QUESTION 1.   What is the purpose of the law?

QUESTION 2.   Can that purpose be fulfilled if the common man does not understand the law?

(b) QUESTION 1.   What characteristics should the language that laws are written in have so that the common man can understand them?

QUESTION 2.   Should the laws be written in language that has these characteristics?

(c) CLAIM 1.   There are certain characteristics of a language that the common man can understand.

CLAIM 2.   The law should be written in language with those characteristics.

(d) CLAIM 1.   There are certain conditions under which something should be written in language that the common man can understand.

CLAIM 2.   These conditions apply to the law.

4. Computers are smarter than humans.

(a) QUESTION 1.   What are the characteristics of computers?

QUESTION 2.   What are the characteristics of humans?

(b) QUESTION 1.   What are the characteristics of computers?

QUESTION 2.   What are the characteristics of humans?

QUESTION 3.   What are the characteristics of being smarter?

(c) CLAIM 1.   There are certain characteristics of being smart.

CLAIM 2.   Humans have those characteristics to a greater degree than computers have.

(d) QUESTION 1.   What tasks can computers perform?

QUESTION 2.   What tasks can humans perform?

QUESTION 3.   Why is performing the first set of tasks more indicative of intelligence than performing the second?

5. It is important to keep up with current events.

(a) CLAIM 1.   Current events affect people's lives.

CLAIM 2.   The knowledge of these events is important to an individual.

(b) QUESTION 1.   What effects do current events have?

QUESTION 2.   Why are those effects important?

6. ESP and other supernatural phenomena are beyond the scope of science.

(a) QUESTION 1.   Which qualities put a thing beyond the scope of science?

QUESTION 2.   In what way do ESP and other supernatural phenomena possess those qualities?

(b) CLAIM 1.   ESP and other supernatural phenomena have certain qualities.

CLAIM 2.   These qualities put something beyond the scope of science.

The only real way to correct part A and test the main material in the chapter is to criticize the arguments that you personally have constructed. Because that is not possible in a textbook, this section contains some uncomplicated arguments for the conclusions, and these will be criticized in part C. While going through part B, then, be sure to compare your argument as well as you can to the ones given here.

Questions 7–10 contain arguments for the conclusions listed in 7–10 in part A. Take each premise in the arguments and underline the component part it covers. Then say which parts are left uncovered and what missing premises would be needed for them. Finally, say which premises are most in need of further support and why.

7. ∴ You should vote for X.

(a) PREMISE 1.   You should vote for the candidate with the best qualifications.

PREMISE 2.   X has the best qualifications of any candidate.

(b) PREMISE 1.   You should vote for a candidate who has a clean political record and who has had constant involvement with the public.

PREMISE 2.   Candidate X has had a clean record and constant public involvement.

8. ∴ University students should be required to take a foreign language.

(a) PREMISE 1.   Taking a foreign language helps the college student become a well-rounded person.

PREMISE 2.   College students will be striving to compete in the business world.

PREMISE 3.   The business world needs well-rounded people.

(b) PREMISE 1.   University students should get the broadest education possible.

PREMISE 2.   They would be more broadly educated if they had knowledge of a foreign language.

PREMISE 3.   The best way to accomplish this is to require them to take a foreign language.

(c) PREMISE 1.   Taking a foreign language is the most convenient and practical way to be exposed to a culture other than your own.

PREMISE 2.   University students should be required to be exposed to other cultures.

PREMISE 3.   Exposure should take place in the most convenient and practical way.

9. ∴ America: Love it or leave it.

PARAPHRASE 1.   American citizens should have strong feelings of affection for America, or they should not live in America.

PARAPHRASE 2.   If the people in the United States do not like or approve of what the government is doing or stands for, then these people should move to another place.

(a) PREMISE 1.   People aren't forced to stay in America if they don't like it.

PREMISE 2.   People who don't find the country to their liking should leave it.

(b) PREMISE 1.   America should be unified.

PREMISE 2.   People who do not love America produce disunity.

PREMISE 3.   The best way to eliminate this disunity is to have these people leave the country.

∴ CONCLUSION 1.   People who don't love America should leave it.

10. ∴ There isn't anything really so bad about shoplifting.

(a) PREMISE 1.   The intentional destruction of property and the causing of physical harm to others are the only crimes that are really bad.

PREMISE 2.   Shoplifting doesn't destroy property or physically harm people.

PREMISE 3.   Shoplifting is simply taking, without violence, items of value from places of business without paying for them.

(b) PREMISE 1.   The only bad effects of shoplifting are the minimal costs to store owners.

PREMISE 2.   Store owners have a lot of money and can easily withstand the added expense shoplifting puts on their business.

PREMISE 3.   There isn't anything really so bad about acts that affect only those who can easily withstand their effects.

Part C

Here are some comments, explanations, and criticisms of the answers in part B. Try to see how they apply also to the answers you gave on your own in part A. (Also, be sure to compare the paraphrases you have given to the ones given here.)

In addition, part C contains further questions to answer. (They are in parentheses and are printed in italics.)

1. To get a good job, get a good education.

(a) QUESTION 1.   What is a good job?

QUESTION 2.   What is a good education?

The main thing left out in this breakdown is the *link* between a good education and getting a good job. If you have formulated the questions correctly, the conclusion should follow once you answer them. Here it won't; you will merely have two unrelated statements.

(b) QUESTION 1.   What are the characteristics of a good job?

QUESTION 2.   What are the effects of a good education?

QUESTION 3.   Does a good education help you get a good job?

Question 3 is an attempt to link getting a job with getting an education, but it fails to do this adequately because it merely *repeats* the conclusion. The answer to question 3 would be the *whole* conclusion, not one component part. The conclusion of an argument cannot also be one of the premises (as it would be in this case) because the conclusion is what you are trying to prove, not one of the *reasons*. Otherwise you would be trying to "prove" the conclusion merely by saying it twice. *(Suppose you answered question 3. That would make the answers to questions 1 and 2 not needed as premises. Explain why.)*

(c) CLAIM 1.   Certain skills and knowledge are helpful in increasing your chances on the job market.

CLAIM 2.   A good education gives you those skills and knowledge.

This is a good breakdown. The conclusion is being understood in the sense of paraphrase 2: "A good education increases your chances of getting a good job." Claim 1 covers (in the paraphrase) "increases your chances of getting a good job," and claim 2 covers "a good education." All you have to do is fill in the particular skills and knowledge (the same in both parts), and you will have a valid argument for the conclusion. *(Will it be sound?)* What makes the breakdown so simple here is the simplicity of the paraphrase. *(When you break a conclusion down into its component parts, is it better to break down the paraphrase of the conclusion or the conclusion as originally stated?)*

(d) CLAIM 1.   There are certain requirements for getting a good job.

CLAIM 2.   There are certain characteristics only a good education gives.

CLAIM 3.   Those characteristics are needed to meet the requirements for getting a good job.

An excellent breakdown, and of a more difficult version of the conclusion than in (c). *(Compare the three paraphrases. What exactly is the difference in emphasis among them? Which one matches more accurately the original?)* The three claims in this breakdown cover the conclusion in this way:

<u>To get a good job</u>, <u>get</u> <u>a good education</u>.

(e) QUESTION 1.   Are there certain prerequisites for getting a good job?

QUESTION 2.   Can these prerequisites be obtained by getting a better education?

Question 1 is phrased incorrectly. It should ask, "What are the prerequisites for getting a good job?" That way you have to think up the specific prerequisites to answer the question, and this will furnish you with a key premise in your argument.

Question 2 is not quite right either. It has to be a little stronger. It should ask something like: "Can these prerequisites *easily* (or *better* or *only*) be obtained by getting a good education?" You need a premise this strong because you have to show that <u>a good education</u> is what you should get rather than trying another method for getting a good job. Thus you have to show that getting a good education is at least a pretty good way of meeting the prerequisites.

The next two breakdowns accomplish this by using words like "must," "needed," "best," and "necessary." Both of them will yield valid arguments.

(f) CLAIM 1.   A person must have certain qualifications to get a good job.

   CLAIM 2.   A good education is needed for a person to acquire those qualifications.

(g) QUESTION 1.   What qualities are provided best by a good education?

   QUESTION 2.   Why are these qualities important for getting a good job?

There is something important about (g) in addition to its yielding a valid argument. Question 2 asks, "*Why* are these qualities important? . . . " Strictly, all that is needed for validity is, "*Are* these qualities important?" By asking *why*, you will in effect get two separate premises in reply: one that they *are* important (premise 2), and then a reason *why* they are (premise 3). And premise 3 will support premise 2. The logical arrangement of the argument will look like this:

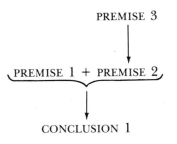

(h) QUESTION 1.   How do you get a good job?

   QUESTION 2.   What conditions must be met to get a good job?

   QUESTION 3.   What is the result of a good education?

   QUESTION 4.   How is the result of a good education linked to getting a good job?

(There are at least three things wrong with this breakdown. What are they? Evaluate this breakdown completely in the light of the analyses just presented.)

2. Eighteen-year-olds should be allowed to vote.

   (a) CLAIM 1.   People who are allowed to vote should have certain qualifications.

   CLAIM 2.   Eighteen-year-olds have those qualifications.

A good breakdown. Claims 1 and 2 cover the conclusions like this:

<u>Eighteen-year-olds</u> <u>should be allowed to vote</u>.

(b) QUESTION 1.   What requisites are necessary to vote?

  QUESTION 2.   Do eighteen-year-olds possess those requirements in the same quantity as people over twenty-one?

This is also a good breakdown and will yield a valid argument for the conclusion. Notice that the premises cover the component parts not of the conclusion as it stands, but of paraphrase 1: "People who are eighteen are just as qualified to vote as people who are over twenty-one." If the paraphrase succeeds in capturing the exact meaning of the original, then theoretically it should make no difference which you break down. In practice you have to maintain a reasonable attitude. The less certain you are of the accuracy of your paraphrase, the more you should be inclined to break down the original; on the other hand, the more misleading the original is, the more you should break down the clearer paraphrase.

The way the premises cover the component parts of the paraphrased conclusion is a little bit complicated:

<u>People who are eighteen</u> <u>are just as</u> <u>qualified to vote</u> <u>as people who are over twenty-one</u>.

Thus the first question asks about the necessary requisites — asking when people <u>are qualified to vote</u>. Question 2 asks about <u>people who are eighteen</u> and compares them with <u>people who are over twenty-one</u> with respect to having <u>just</u> the same qualities.

(c) QUESTION 1.   What makes an eighteen-year-old acceptable for serving in the armed forces?

  QUESTION 2.   Won't these same attributes suffice for allowing an eighteen-year-old to vote?

This breakdown will produce a valid argument, but mentioning the armed forces probably should not be included in the breakdown. It is not part of the conclusion either explicitly or implicitly. There might be more things relevant to the question besides service in the armed forces. So question 1 should be a little less specific:

  What relevant attributes does an eighteen-year-old possess?

This way you can fill in the attributes in many different ways: service in the armed forces, responsibility for one's loans, the ability to marry without parental approval, and so forth. Ideally, the breakdown is supposed to limit the possibilities as little as possible; then, when you think up the premises in step 3, you have a broader range to choose from.

(d) CLAIM 1.   There are certain characteristics of people twenty-one years and older who are allowed to vote.

  CLAIM 2.   Eighteen-year-olds have those characteristics.

This breakdown will not yield a valid argument. *(Which component part of the conclusion is not covered by either claim?)*

3. The law should be written in language that the common man can understand.

Paraphrase 1 is a shrewd paraphrase that focuses on one clear, relevant interpretation of "the common man." In this case this "legal" sense is more accurate than an economic sense or an intellectual sense. *(What is inaccurate about paraphrase 2?)*

(a) QUESTION 1.   What is the purpose of the law?

QUESTION 2.   Can that purpose be fulfilled if the common man does not understand the law?

Question 1 is a good foundation for a premise. It covers, "The law should." The "should" is implied in the word "purpose." Question 2, however, does not cover the remainder of the conclusion, but only, "the common man can understand." It does not cover the "language that the law is written in." When you answer the two questions, you will not prove that laws should be written in language that lets untrained people understand them; you will only prove that "untrained people should understand the law." You still need to say that we should get people to understand the law by having it written in a certain kind of language (rather than, say, by hiring lawyers). So you need another question to cover these parts:

QUESTION 3.   Is writing the law in nontechnical language the best way to get people to understand it?

These three questions now cover the whole conclusion.

Note that it is not necessary to have three separate parts isolated. You could have phrased question 2 in a way that also covered what question 3 asks:

QUESTION 2 (revised).   Can this purpose be met if the common man cannot understand the language that the law is written in?

The revised question 2 covers "be written in language the common man can understand." With question 1 it will yield a valid argument.

(b) QUESTION 1.   What characteristics should the language that laws are written in have so that the common man can understand them?

QUESTION 2.   Should the laws be written in language that has these characteristics?

The breakdown here is wrong because question 1 does not cover a component part; it covers the whole conclusion. Look carefully. It covers:

the language in which the laws are written

and

so that the common man can understand them

and even the word "should" in

what characteristics <u>should</u>.

Thus answering question 1 would give you a premise that restates the whole conclusion. It would say, for instance:

PREMISE 1.   The laws should be written in a language with such-and-such characteristics so that the common man can understand them.

But this already says the conclusion; it isn't an *argument* for it. It doesn't give you any reasons *why* the law should be written this way.

It is easy to fall into the trap of repeating the conclusion in one of the component parts and thus in a premise. That won't ever yield a good argument: You can't prove a point by saying it twice.

(c) CLAIM 1.   There are certain characteristics of a language that the common man can understand.

CLAIM 2.   The law should be written in language with those characteristics.

(d) CLAIM 1.   There are certain conditions under which something should be written in language the common man can understand.

CLAIM 2.   These conditions apply to the law.

Both (c) and (d) are legitimate breakdowns that cover all the component parts of the conclusion. *(By underlining show which parts are covered by the breakdown in (c), and then which parts are covered by the breakdown in (d).)* But there is a subtle yet important difference between them. Breakdown (e) is not likely to be a very fruitful way of thinking up premises. All the weight rests on claim 2 and that's most of what you had to prove in the first place. You cannot justify claim 2 except by providing an argument that should have been used to prove the original conclusion. So this breakdown doesn't do much work for you.

Contrast this with (d). It is fruitful because claim 1 gets to the heart of what you have to prove in order to prove the conclusion: Under what conditions *should* something be written in language that untrained people can understand? When they cannot live prosperously without it? When its language is something that they encounter as an important part of their lives? Answering these questions well goes far toward constructing a good argument for the conclusion: one that is valid *and* has plausible, justifiable premises.

4. Computers are smarter than humans.

(a) QUESTION 1.   What are the characteristics of computers?

QUESTION 2.   What are the characteristics of humans?

This doesn't work: "Are smarter than" isn't covered.

(b) QUESTION 1 and 2 above, plus

QUESTION 3.   What are the characteristics of being smart?

This doesn't work either: Nothing in the breakdown points out the comparison being made, that is, nothing covers the "er" in "smart<u>er</u>."

(c) CLAIM 1.   There are certain characteristics of being smart.

    CLAIM 2.   Humans have those characteristics to a greater degree than computers have.

A good breakdown that requires you to come to grips with the central problem that you have to settle before proving the conclusion: the characteristics of being smart. Establishing that is necessary before you can compare such different things with respect to smartness.

(d) QUESTION 1.   What tasks can computers perform?

    QUESTION 2.   What tasks can humans perform?

    QUESTION 3.   Why is performing the first set of tasks more indicative of intelligence than performing the second?

A more detailed breakdown that will also yield a valid argument. Question 3, because it begins with the word "why," will again furnish two premises: (1) a simple statement that the first set of tasks *is* more indicative of intelligence than the second; and (2) a statement, answering the "why," that gives a reason in favor of (1). Statement (2) will then support (1) in the logical arrangement.

You don't have to believe a conclusion to construct an argument for it. *(What subsidiary claims would you have to prove if you wanted to argue against the conclusion?)*

5. It is important to keep up with current events.

(a) CLAIM 1.   Current events affect people's lives.

    CLAIM 2.   The knowledge of these events is important to an individual.

Claim 2 is not a component part, but the whole conclusion. It is what has to be proved, not a premise or a reason.

(b) QUESTION 1.   What effects do current events have?

    QUESTION 2.   Why are those effects important?

This needs another subsidiary claim because "keep up with" is not covered. We could change question 2 to

QUESTION 2 (revised).   Why are those effects important to keep up with?

or we could isolate that part in a third question:

QUESTION 3.   Is it necessary to keep up with those events to do something about those effects?

(Try to fill in the premises to cover the component parts isolated by these questions. Clearly, the hard question is our revised one: How is <u>knowing</u> about current events important? What proportion of them can you realistically do anything about?)

6. ESP and other supernatural phenomena are beyond the scope of science.

(a) QUESTION 1. Which qualities put a thing beyond the scope of science?

QUESTION 2. In what way do ESP and other supernatural phenomena possess those qualities?

This breakdown *does* cover all parts of the conclusion. Question 1 covers "beyond the scope of science," and question 2 covers "ESP and other supernatural phenomena." However . . .

(b) CLAIM 1. ESP and other supernatural phenomena have certain qualities.

CLAIM 2. These qualities put something beyond the scope of science.

This breakdown also covers all parts of the conclusion:

<u>ESP and other supernatural phenomena</u> <u>are beyond the scope of science</u>.

However . . .

Both (a) and (b) will get you to trick yourself, even though both will yield a valid argument. There is a trick word in claim 2 of (a) and in claim 1 of (b). (It is beneficial here to try to find the trick word before proceeding.)

The trick word is not "ESP" or "phenomena" or even "supernatural"; it is "other." The conclusion takes it for granted that ESP *is* a supernatural phenomenon (not a natural one). And you will take it for granted too if you argue on the pattern of (a) or (b). But that is a subsidiary claim of the conclusion — an important claim, too — that is not brought out by either of the breakdowns given.

The conclusions should have been broken down into smaller parts:

CLAIM 1. ESP has certain characteristics.

CLAIM 2. Certain characteristics make something a supernatural phenomenon.

CLAIM 3. ESP has the characteristics that make something supernatural.

CLAIM 4. Possession of all those characteristics puts something beyond the scope of science.

Here, claim 1 covers "ESP," claim 2 covers "supernatural phenomena," and claim 3 covers the tricky words "and other" because it asserts straightforwardly that ESP *is* a supernatural phenomenon. Claim 4 covers the rest.

And claim 3, the hidden claim, is the one that is most likely to yield a premise that is false. There doesn't seem to be much evidence at all that ESP is supernatural, only that it is hard to explain.

Breaking a conclusion down into its component parts serves two functions: One, it is supposed to guarantee you a valid argument if you do it correctly. But, two, it is supposed to get you to notice claims that you would otherwise overlook. That is what was needed here.

Note that in answering 7–10 in part B, you have been *analyzing* arguments rather than constructing them. This calls for skills that will be developed much more fully in Chapters Five and Six.

7. ∴ You should vote for X.

(a) Perfect: <u>You should vote for X</u>. The component part underlined once corresponds with premise 1; the part underlined twice corresponds with premise 2 (and so forth for examples with more than two premises).

(b) Premise 1 covers, "You should vote for," but premise 2 does not really cover "X." The conclusion means you should vote for X *rather than* X's opponents. Maybe X's opponents also have had clean political records and a constant involvement with the public. So the argument is invalid. *(How would you revise premise 2 to make it cover "X" adequately?)*

8. ∴ University students should be required to take a foreign language.

(a) <u>University students</u> <u><u>should</u></u> be required to <u>take a foreign language</u>.

"Required" is not covered by any of the premises. So the argument is invalid. *(Formulate a missing premise to cover this part.)* *(What in the argument is most in need of paraphrase?)*

(b) All parts are covered: <u>University students should</u> <u><u>be required to take</u></u> <u>a foreign language</u>.

So the argument is valid. Premise 1 is not very plausible because of "broad*est possible*." At least it needs some reasons to support it. *(How would you break premise 1 down into its component parts to make an argument for it? Diagram the resulting logical arrangement.)*

(c) Premise 1 covers, "to take a foreign language"; premise 2 covers, "University students should be required"; and premise 3 connects "convenient and practical" in premise 1 to what "should be required" in premise 2, thus making the argument valid. If this is confusing, notice that premise 2 could have been written with premise 3 attached to it: "University students should be exposed to other cultures in the most convenient and practical way." The ending is written as a separate premise simply to make it easier to evaluate.

Notice also that restricting the argument to "the most convenient and practical" makes the premises here much more plausible than the unrestricted ones in the previous argument (b).

9. ∴ America: Love it or leave it.

(What is the difference between the two paraphrases given in part B? What does "America" mean in paraphrase 1?)

(a) Hardly an "argument" at all. Premise 1 is irrelevant, and premise 2 merely repeats the conclusion to be proved.

(b) This is a valid argument for the conclusion: <u>People who don't love America</u> <u><u>should</u></u> <u>leave it</u>.

Alternatively, you can say that premise 2 and premise 3 overlap, and that premise 3 covers everything except the word "should." The good thing about this argument (as far as validity goes) is that it captures the *relation* between not loving America and leaving it. For the original statement does not *say* exactly that you should love America; it only says that if you do not, you should leave. *(Does the statement* imply *that you should love America?) (The argument is valid. Is it sound? Why or why not?)*

10. ∴ There isn't anything really so bad about shoplifting.

(a) A valid argument. The premises answer these questions:

QUESTION 1.   What characteristics make something really bad?

QUESTION 2.   Why doesn't shoplifting have these characteristics?

Premises 2 and 3 answer question 2. *(How? Diagram the logical arrangement of the premises.)* In addition to being valid, the premises look surprisingly plausible. *(If you think premise 1 is false, try to think of a good counterexample.)* Is the argument sound?

(b) This argument is valid also: <u>There isn't really anything so bad about shoplifting</u>.

Premise 2 "connects" premise 1 to premise 3 and is necessary for the argument to be valid. *(Explain how this connecting takes place, that is, why premise 2 is necessary for validity.)*
   The argument here is definitely not sound though, because premise 1 is false: Shoplifting also has negative effects on consumers. We could make premise 1 more plausible by changing it:

PREMISE 1 (revised).   The only bad effects of shoplifting are the minimal costs to store owners and a tiny increase in prices to consumers.

(If we changed the argument this way, what other *changes in the argument would we have to make?)*

Part D

In 1–10 break each statement down into its component parts. (Be sure to paraphrase the conclusions first.)

1. Anyone who really wants a job can find one.

2. Nuclear energy is too risky.

3. Deep down inside, everyone believes in God.

4. Shakespeare is the greatest English playwright.

5. Most lawyers are more interested in winning their cases than in justice.

6. Abortion should be illegal.

7. Human beings are a product of heredity and environment.

8. Russia does not want to rule the world.

9. Medical science works in the interest of mankind.

10. Personal success or failure is best judged by material possessions.

Conclusions 11–20 are to be proved or disproved. Construct the best argument you can, either for or against each one. (Your argument must be valid, and it should contain premises that are as plausible as you can make them.) Be sure to paraphrase each one.

11. You should have the right to kill a robber who breaks into your home.

12. Love is a necessary ingredient of a happy marriage.

13. In elections your vote will not matter in the long run.

14. Kindness is a weakness.

15. Prostitution should be legalized.

16. A couple should be married before they live together.

17. Bilingualism will be a destructive factor in American society.

18. Humanity is basically good.

19. Women are intellectually inferior to men.

20. Athletics hinders one's ability to get a good education.

21. As you probably noticed, a number of the conclusions to be argued for in part A are doubtful, maybe false. Take this a step further. In the exercises to Chapter One you had to think up three statements that many people believe but that seem to you to be false. You had to give the best argument you could to show they were false.

   Now take those three conclusions and try to construct the best argument you can that they are *true*. Really try to put yourself in your opponent's place and defend that point of view.

22. In the example about the flashes of lightning on page 101, what is *another* way you could tell that two events were taking place at the same time? Einstein said that all such ways are really equivalent. How does your way come down to approximately the same thing as standing in the middle and seeing them both?

23. In many states it is not enough to *possess* a valid driver's license: It is illegal to drive without having the license with you in your car. Give an argument for and against this practice.

Additional conclusions (to be broken down into component parts or argued for or against):

24. Progress is on the whole a good thing.

25. In general, parents know best.

26. Sales taxes discriminate against the poor.

27. It is bad for the children when both parents work and the child must be placed in a child-care center.

28. A woman should dress like a woman and not try to look like a man.

29. Mankind is the most important thing there is.

30. Christians have a right to save savages.

31. Homosexuality is a clinical disorder that is as treatable as other maladies (for example, kleptomania).

32. Taking prescription medicine without your doctor's advice is usually dangerous.

33. A liberal arts education is not as necessary as other practical studies, such as business and engineering.

34. People who earn A's in school are smarter than those who don't.

35. Religion has a useful purpose in society.

36. Historians should always try to be objective.

Chapter Five

Analyzing Arguments

1. Five Steps for Analyzing Arguments

The Importance of Analyzing Arguments

Not being fooled

It is probably clear to you why an ability to analyze arguments is important. Many times people have a stake in convincing you of something, even in fooling you. When you look around you critically, you will find misleading, tricky arguments everywhere. Many advertisements contain arguments that attempt to convince you of something, namely, that you should buy the product. Politicians often try to give you reasons to vote for them (at least they hope you will take them to be reasons). If you cannot analyze those reasons — figure out if they are true or false and whether they actually prove what they are trying to prove — you are much more likely to be taken in by bad arguments.

Under-standing

But the ability to analyze arguments is useful for more than just avoiding being fooled. Sometimes you simply want to *understand* what someone is arguing for and how the argument is supposed to work. An explanation in geology class, a new economic plan, the feasibility of toxic-waste disposal in the oceans, an argument that chiropractic is medically unsound — all are hard but important topics, and understanding them requires some careful analysis.

Constructing vs. Analyzing Arguments: Similarities and Differences

Similarities

Analyzing someone else's argument is very much like constructing an argument on your own. In either case you have to understand the point of the argument; think clearly about the issues, those covered explicitly and those only implied; and evaluate reasons. Paraphrasing, covering all the parts of a conclusion, arranging the argument logically, and assessing validity and truth are tasks that are essential to both constructing and analyzing arguments. Reasoning is thinking your way clearly and cogently through a thing, and this remains the same whether the thing is your own argument or someone else's.

But in other ways analyzing an argument is quite different from constructing one. After all, you usually know pretty much what you are trying to prove, and once you have made up the premises, you know how you *think* they support the conclusion. You can be wrong, *Differences* of course, even about the functioning of your own arguments. But you have an insight into your own argument that you usually do not have into someone else's. People do not break their arguments into premises and conclusions. They write them oat in regular paragraphs: the sort you find in books, newspapers, and the things people say. If you want these arguments broken down into premises and conclusions (to analyze them), *you* have to do the breaking down. Similarly, *you* have to paraphrase the other person's argument, figure out the argument's logical arrangement, and fill in the missing premises.

These may sound the same as what you did when constructing your own argument, but in analyzing someone else's argument there is another factor that comes into play. That factor is *fidelity*. That means *Fidelity* that whenever you perform any of the steps in reasoning, you have to do it in such a way as to remain *faithful* to what the arguer was arguing. When you paraphrase, you have to capture the *arguer's* meaning; you have to pick out the *arguer's* conclusion and fill in the premises the *arguer* would have to hold and so forth.

The Five Steps

There is a five-step method for analyzing arguments:

STEP 1.   Paraphrase the argument.

STEP 2.   Break the argument down into premises and conclusion.

STEP 3.   Arrange the premises and conclusion in their logical order.

STEP 4.   Fill in the missing premises needed to make the argument valid.

STEP 5.   Criticize the argument for validity and the premises for truth.

Following these five steps will not guarantee that your analysis of an argument is correct, but doing them conscientiously will enable you to understand, analyze, and criticize an argument on rational grounds.

The first three steps deal with the analysis of an argument, whereas step 5 deals with criticism of the argument. Step 4 stands halfway between analysis and criticism because it is there that the argument has to be completed.

Explanation of the Steps

Let's consider each step separately.

STEP 1.   Paraphrase.

Paraphrase

Before you can evaluate an argument's soundness, you have to understand it. The best way to understand it is to paraphrase it: read the argument carefully and restate it in your own words. Paraphrasing arguments is often difficult, but it gives you a much better understanding of them.

STEP 2.   Break the argument down into premises and conclusion.

Conclusion

The *conclusion* is what the arguer is trying to prove; the *premises* are the statements presented to support the conclusion. It should be clear why this step is important. If you identify the conclusion incorrectly, the focus of your analysis will be wrong. If you do not recognize which statements are given as reasons, you won't realize how the argument is intended to work.

STEP 3.   Arrange the premises and conclusion in their logical order.

*Logical ar-
rangement*

The logical order of an argument is the arrangement that shows how premises support conclusions. Diagraming these relationships is the best way to assess the logical order of the statements making up an argument. Diagrams reveal unsupported statements and gaps in the argument where missing premises need to be filled in.

STEP 4.   Fill in the missing premises needed to make the argument valid.

*Missing
premises*

For an argument to be sound, for it really to prove its conclusion, it must have true premises and also be valid. If there are gaps or missing steps in the reasoning, they must be filled in with premises. The mere fact that there *are* unstated premises in an argument does not automatically make the argument bad. Sometimes, an obviously true premise is left unstated. But sometimes a false or doubtful premise is omitted intentionally because its presence would reveal bad reasoning. Finally, a premise may be left out because the arguer has not thought the matter out and does not realize that a premise is missing. Once you fill in the missing premises, you will be in the best position possible to *evaluate* the argument.

STEP 5.   Criticize the argument for validity and the premises for truth.

Criticism

People sometimes say that it is enough to understand a person's position or point of view. But that is just not so; you also have to evaluate that position. And, to be fully rational, you have to be able to give reasons to back up your evaluation.

The same point can (and should) be made about things other than arguments and positions: about artworks, like paintings, poems, and novels; about people's actions, like suicide or giving money to beggars; about political and economic systems; about social institutions, like monogamy or trial by jury. Certainly it is important to understand why a poet said this or that, what a person's motivations were, how trial by jury evolved, and so forth. But it is also important to evaluate such things: Are they right or wrong or somewhere in between or neither? Are they good or bad, helpful or harmful? Is the painting put together *well*? Did the person do *right*? Does trial by jury *work*?

In step 5 you evaluate an argument on two grounds: the truth of   *Truth*
the premises and validity. If the premises (the ones stated or the ones filled in by you in step 4) are false, you will judge the argument to be unsound. If the stated premises do not cover all component parts and   *Validity*
it is impossible to come up with any plausible missing premises to cover the rest, you will judge the argument to be invalid, hence unsound. You will judge the argument to be *sound*, on the other hand, only if you find that all the component parts are covered by stated or unstated premises and that *all* the premises, stated as well as filled in, are true.

After performing the five steps, you'll know an argument inside and out. You'll understand what it means (step 1); you'll understand what it is trying to prove and what reasons are being given to prove it (step 2); you'll understand how those reasons fit together and support one another (step 3); you'll understand what has been left unsaid in the argument (step 4); and, finally, you'll be able to say exactly what is right and wrong about the argument (step 5).

Now this looks like a great amount of work to do to analyze an argument. But as you progress, you'll find that much of the technique will become second nature; you'll acquire the *habit* of reasoning well.   *The habit of*
You'll think about what people mean when they say things, whether   *reasoning*
they have given good reasons, reasons that actually prove the conclusion they are trying to prove. You'll find yourself keying in on the missing premises, where the weaknesses often lie.

You'll usually find that even when the reasoning is quite hard, it will be worthwhile. You'll have the satisfaction of understanding fully   *The value of*
and thinking critically. You won't be fooled. And besides the satisfac-   *the method*
tion, the ability to reason carefully through hard issues will be extremely useful in other aspects of your life: in writing term papers and essay tests, listening to lectures, understanding political and economic issues, even figuring out possible solutions to personal problems.

Problems

1. Why is it necessary to fill in the missing premises of an argument? Why isn't it enough just to evaluate the stated ones?

2. How can an argument still be good if there are missing steps in it?

3. Suppose you find that one of the premises in an argument is false. What reasons might there be for examining the other premises?

4. Why isn't it enough to understand a person's position? Why is it also necessary to evaluate it?

2. *Using the Method*

Let's analyze a couple of examples, and afterward we can take up the shortcuts, rules of thumb, and finer points in the individual steps. It is important to have a grasp of how the method as a whole works in practice before you can appreciate the finer points of the steps.

EXAMPLE 1

Consider the following advertisement:

> *Handcrafting Makes the Difference:* If you are in the market for a television, you should buy Brand Z. Other televisions have printed electrical circuits that are stamped out by a machine. But in Brand Z televisions the connections are entirely handmade.

Step 1. Paraphrase   What the argument says is clear:

> PARAPHRASE 1.   If you intend to buy a television, Brand Z is the one you should buy. The main difference between Brand Z and other brands is that the electrical connections in other brands are effected by means of machine-made printed circuits, whereas the electrical circuits in Brand Z televisions are made by hand.

There does not seem anything problematic in the meaning of this argument, although you might think it is a little bit misleading. "Handcrafted" has strong positive connotations of a "craftsman" making something by hand, from scratch. That is not the same as a factory worker who merely connects parts (which themselves are made by machines).

Step 2. Break the argument down into premises and conclusion   The second sentence of the ad is clearly the conclusion. The advertising people are trying to prove that if you are in the market for a television, you should buy Brand Z (rather than another brand). The next two sentences are given as reasons for the conclusion; hence, they are premises. The first sentence (in italics) really doesn't say anything more than what is spelled out in the premises, so it's not needed. The argument, thus, is

> PREMISE 1.   Other televisions have printed electrical circuits that are stamped out by a machine.

PREMISE 2.   In Brand Z televisions the connections are entirely handmade.

∴ CONCLUSION 1.   If you are in the market for a television, you should buy Brand Z.

Step 3. Logical arrangement   Both premises are given as independent reasons for believing the conclusion. That is, premise 1 does not support premise 2, and premise 2 does not support premise 1. But each of them does support the conclusion. Thus the logical order of the argument is a simple one:

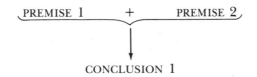

CONCLUSION 1

Step 4. Fill in the missing premises needed to make the argument valid   The argument as stated so far is not valid; the conclusion does not follow from the premises. If we believe for the sake of argument that other televisions have machine-made connections (premise 1) and that Brand Z televisions have handmade connections (premise 2), it still is not *proved* that if we are in the market for a television, we should buy Brand Z. There is a missing step between the premises and conclusion here, an *assumption* that the arguers are making:

PREMISE 3 (missing).   Televisions with hand-connected parts are better than televisions with machine-made electrical circuits.

If this were not taken for granted, the stated premises could not have been given as reasons for believing the conclusion.

(Why, you might ask, didn't the arguers *state* this as a premise instead of assuming it? Maybe because they thought it was too *obvious* to need stating, but maybe for a more suspicious reason.)

There is another missing premise in this argument. All we can legitimately prove given these three premises is that Brand Z televisions are *better* than other brands, not that you should *buy* a Brand Z television if you are in the market for a television set. To reach this main conclusion, we need another missing premise, which says

PREMISE 4 (missing).   If you are in the market for a television you should buy the better brand.

Now the whole argument *is* valid: On the basis of the first three premises we can prove that Brand Z is better, and if we add premise 4 we can prove conclusion 1.

Step 5. Criticize the argument for validity and the premises for truth   Without the missing premises filled in, the argument would be invalid; but with the missing premises filled in, it is valid because there are no missing steps between the premises and the main conclusion. All the component parts of the conclusion are covered by one or more premises: The first three tell you what distinguishes <u>Brand Z televisions</u> from other brands; premise 4 tells you that <u>if you are in the market for a television, you should buy</u> a brand with those distinguishing features.

Are the premises — stated as well as filled in — true or false?

Of course, because Brand Z is not an actual company, we cannot really judge premise 1 or premise 2. If there were such a company, these claims would more than likely be true: The Federal Communications Commission — probably — wouldn't let Brand Z advertise an outright lie. (If you were still doubtful, you could check out the claims yourself.)

The missing premise 3, however, is false. There seems little reason to believe that hand-connected televisions are better than machine-connected ones, and there seems much reason to believe the opposite: Machine-printed circuits are virtually identical, whereas handmade connections vary a lot; machines do not daydream or get tired or bored; machines are capable of far more precision; and so forth.

Missing premise 4 is true: You want value for your money, so (other things being equal) you should buy the better television.

The truth of premise 4, however, hardly matters because premise 3 is an essential part of the argument, and it is false. So the whole argument is unsound.

EXAMPLE 2

Consider an argument that appears on street signs in Manhattan:

Littering is filthy and selfish. So don't do it.

Step 1. Paraphrase   The argument says that littering — throwing things like paper, beer cans, and the remains of food on the ground — is offensive, dirty, and ugly and only benefits yourself. So you shouldn't do it.

Step 2. Break it into premises and conclusion   The argument is trying to make you believe that you shouldn't litter. And two reasons are given for this conclusion: that it is filthy and that it is selfish.

PREMISE 1.   Littering is filthy.

PREMISE 2.   Littering is selfish.

∴ CONCLUSION 1.   You shouldn't litter.

Step 3. Logical arrangement　　The logical arrangement of this argument is straightforward. Because neither premise is a reason for believing the other, they are independent of one another. But both fit together to support the conclusion:

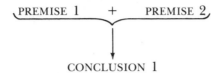

Step 4. Fill in the missing premises needed to make the argument valid　　The two premises inside the brackets do not *force* you to believe the conclusion. They cover the word "<u>litter</u>" in the conclusion, but there is no premise to cover the component part "<u>you shouldn't</u>." The argument is not valid as it stands. A missing premise is needed:

> PREMISE 3 (missing).　　You shouldn't do things that are both filthy and selfish.

Adding premise 3 makes the argument valid. All the component parts of the conclusion are now covered, and if you accept the three premises (for the sake of argument), you have no option but to accept the conclusion also.

Step 5. Criticize the argument for validity and the premises for truth　　The argument with premise 3 added, as we just saw, is valid; it was not valid before premise 3 was added.

Now we come to truth. Consider premise 1 first. Littering certainly does seem "filthy." Though of course opinions may differ, most people would say that paper, beer cans, and food remains on the street are dirty and ugly.

Premise 2 also is true. In general, people throw litter on the ground to save themselves the trouble of taking it to a garbage can, and they do it despite the fact that other people dislike it. That's a good reason for believing premise 2.

Finally, consider premise 3, the missing premise. It is important to realize that premise 3 does not oppose filthy things or selfish things; it opposes only things that are *both* filthy and selfish. And it certainly looks true. Filthy things are often unhealthy, even directly harmful. It is a good working principle of day-to-day morality that you shouldn't do things that are bad for others without good justification, and selfishness is hardly a good justification.

The overall evaluation we get from this reasoning about the argument is that it is a good one. It is sound. And that's an uncommon occurrence.

Problems

1. The argument about Brand Z televisions is initially persuasive because we tend to think of handmade things as better. Under what conditions *are* handmade objects of better quality than machine-made ones?

2. In the analysis of that argument it was said that we could believe premises 1 and 2 because the FCC would probably not permit an outright lie. But consider the following announcements:

   > Sign on newspaper dispenser boxes in a large city: "This vending machine is operated by a small-business man who has to buy the papers offered for sale in this machine. When papers are taken without being paid for, I am the one who suffers the entire loss, as I have to pay for every paper.
   > "So please ... please do not take any papers from this machine unless you pay for them."

   The vending machines are owned and stocked by the newspaper.

   > A flyer sent out by Hibernia National Bank: "*NEW BANKING HOURS* ... for your convenience.
   > "On February 23 your banking becomes more convenient than ever before."

   The new "more convenient" hours are six hours shorter per week than the old, and no new times are offered.

   Are these announcements bold-faced lies or are they merely misleading? How do you think the newspaper and Hibernia would defend themselves against a charge of lying? Would the defense be adequate?

   Problems 3–7 apply to the argument about littering.

3. Paraphrase: "Filthy" typically means something stronger than "dirty and ugly." It sometimes means "foul, putrid, disgustingly dirty."

   Is throwing newspapers onto the ground in Manhattan *filthy* in this stronger sense? Does this affect the analysis of the argument?

4. Premises and conclusion: We broke the first sentence of the argument into two premises. Why is that better than making it a single premise: "Littering is filthy and selfish"?

5. Logical arrangement: Diagram the argument after premise 3 (missing) has been added.

6. Evaluation: The argument, we said, was not committed to opposing either selfish or filthy actions, only actions that are *both* filthy *and* selfish. Find an example of a selfish action that's acceptable because it is not filthy. Find an example of a filthy action that's acceptable because it is unselfish.

7. Suppose that you like the way an area looks when it has litter on it. (Is that possible?) Should you then litter?

3. Paraphrasing

Paraphrasing is the first step in analyzing arguments, just as it was the first step in constructing arguments, because paraphrasing is a way of making explicit what you understand the argument to mean. You cannot really do any analysis at all without understanding what is meant, and understanding is the first step in any rational appraisal. An argument cannot even be broken down into premises and conclusions unless you have some understanding of what it means.

Of course, people often understand things without actually putting them into other words. Anyone who can use English to get along in life understands much of what is said. But people also *misunderstand* often. They are fooled by a twist of meaning, or unintentionally distort someone else's position, or simply fail to understand a complicated argument. *Paraphrase aids understanding*

Paraphrasing, putting someone's argument into different, more familiar words, is usually a matter not of translating a passage word for word, but rather of grasping and writing down the *gist* of what is being said. In the ideal case to paraphrase correctly is to say *exactly* the same thing the other person says, but in different words. In practice you have to come as close as you reasonably can to what the person means. *Capturing the gist*

There are three distinct purposes of paraphrasing an argument: *Purposes of paraphrasing*

1. To understand it better, in more depth.

2. To be better able to judge whether the statements in it are true or false.

3. To make sure that the terms in the argument do not shift meaning between premises and conclusion, that is, to help judge validity.

The first purpose, understanding something in depth, can be an end in itself. This is the function of paraphrase in reading literature, for example. "Sunday Morning," a poem by Wallace Stevens, ends *Understanding*

> And, in the isolation of the sky,
> At evening, casual flocks of pigeons make
> Ambiguous undulations as they sink,
> Downward to darkness, on extended wings.[1]

It is necessary to understand what is being said literally in a poem before you can appreciate it fully. What Stevens's poem says is

> PARAPHRASE 1.   Flocks of pigeons can be seen flying against the sky as night is coming on; they move so easily and rhythmically that it is difficult to tell at any moment whether they are going up or down, but gradually they glide down with their wings spread into the darkness below the horizon.

---

[1]Copyright Wallace Stevens. Used by permission of Alfred A. Knopf, Inc.

There are greater depths of meaning in the poem than this (for example, the darkness refers literally to the night coming on, but on a symbolic level it also means that the birds are gliding toward death), and further paraphrase would bring out many other meanings. Any explication of the poem must be built on a clear understanding of what the lines describe literally.

The second and third purposes of paraphrase, however, are the ones related most directly to reasoning as such. Paraphrasing makes statements clearer and therefore enables you to give a more accurate judgment of their truth. Finally, in paraphrasing you pin down the terms in the argument to specific meanings, and that rules out shifts of meaning that may make the argument invalid.

Truth

Validity

As far as analyzing arguments goes, in contrast to explicating literature or understanding things for their own sake, you do not have to go deeper into the meaning of the argument than is necessary for judging truth and validity.

Fidelity in Paraphrase

Paraphrasing someone else's argument is in many ways the same kind of task as paraphrasing a conclusion. Thus almost all of what was said in Chapter Three applies directly here. The major difference in the two tasks is that when you paraphrase someone else's argument, you have to be very careful to be *faithful* to what *that person* is saying. *Fidelity* is the single most important characteristic of a good paraphrase. Fidelity consists of reproducing the meaning of the arguer's argument accurately, in being true to what the person means.

Fidelity

Because much of your subsequent analysis is based on your initial paraphrase, you want to be certain that you are analyzing the *arguer's* argument and not some other argument you may wish to foist on the arguer. There is a fallacy, known as the "straw-man argument," in which you misinterpret a person's argument (consciously or unconsciously) in such a way as to make it look easily refutable. It is called a "straw-man argument" because a man made out of straw is easier to knock down than a man made out of flesh and blood. So in the fallacy you misinterpret a flesh-and-blood argument in such a way that it looks as if it is made of straw; that way you can knock it down (refute it) more easily.

Straw-man argument

For example, suppose someone gives the argument,

> No government can place restrictions on what a person does with his or her own body. Abortion: it is a woman's right to choose.

A good paraphrase would be something like this:

> PARAPHRASE 1.   The law cannot justifiably regulate actions a person performs on his or her own body (as long as the action concerns only that person's body). A woman has the right to abort a fetus at will.

Contrast this accurate paraphrase to the straw-man argument:

PARAPHRASE 2.   A woman has the right to kill a baby at will.

This statement is easy to refute, but it is not at all what the arguer said (or meant). The question of whether or not it is a woman's right to abort a fetus is a harder question than whether or not it is her right to kill a baby. Interpreting the argument in this way sets up a position (made of straw) in which the person's real argument does not have to be confronted. *You* may think that aborting a fetus is the same as killing a baby. But if you do think this (and if you have some reasons to back up that belief), it should form part of your criticism of the person's argument (in step 5); it should not be part of the paraphrase. In paraphrasing someone's argument, you are not concerned especially with what *you* think is true or false, or right or wrong. All you are really concerned with is capturing what the arguer's argument means.

How Can You Tell What the Argument Means?

If the arguer is not around to tell you, how do you know what he or she meant? And if the argument can be understood in more than one sense, how can you tell which is the most faithful sense?

There is no completely satisfactory general answer to these questions, although there are some good partial answers. Fortunately, by using multiple paraphrases, we can sidestep the problem in a genuinely satisfactory way.

The best approach is to ask yourself: "What could reasonably be meant by that argument in this context?"

The important words here are "reasonably" and "in this context." People do not generally mean to say things that are completely unreasonable or completely implausible (though sometimes they do), so when in doubt it will generally be more accurate to paraphrase the person's argument into something that could be meant *reasonably*. (This is more fully discussed in Chapter Three, Section Three.)

Reasonable paraphrase

Context

The same statement can mean vastly different things depending on various external circumstances: who said it, when and where it was said, what was going on while it was being said, the tone of voice of the person who said it. All of these are part of the *context* of the statement.

Contexts

Einstein reportedly once said that he was "only a *student* of mathematics"; a lot of college freshmen in introductory mathematics courses might say the same words. But the meaning of "student of mathematics" would be very different indeed. An argument using the word "democracy" will have to be paraphrased in very different ways depending on whether it was given in ancient Athens, contemporary Switzerland, the United States, or the USSR. When people say, "Oh, yeah, she was unhappy. She cried all the way to the bank," they mean she was *happy* and *didn't* cry. And that will have to be in the paraphrase.

For day-to-day arguments you have to pay close attention to the context in which they are given. If they are advertisements or neutral reports, that has to be taken into account. If the arguer is being ironic, the meaning will be just the opposite of what you would ordinarily take it to be. In practice you already do this much of the time without giving it much thought. To paraphrase well, though, it is necessary to consider such external circumstances explicitly whenever they might affect what is meant. When you are not aware of the circumstances in which an argument was stated, or when the context is not given (as, for example, with most of the arguments in this book), the most reasonable approach is to assume a standard context, that is, to assume that they are not being given in a *special* situation that might warp the meaning of the argument.

A standard context

Multiple Paraphrases

Even taking strict account of the context, or assuming a standard one, will often not dictate a single, sure paraphrase. But there is a satisfactory way of capturing what the arguer means. If more than one paraphrase of an argument seems reasonable in that context, give *both*. Very often, the *only* way to do justice to an argument, especially a potentially misleading argument, is to make a note of the various possible (reasonable) things that could be meant by it. Sometimes the argument will be sound if one thing is meant and unsound if another thing is meant. A premise might be true in one of its meanings and false in another. It is important, then, to have noted both. A word or phrase may shift meaning between premises and conclusion, making the argument invalid. And you won't be likely to catch this shift unless you have noted the two meanings *explicitly*.

Why multiple paraphrases are necessary

Giving more than one paraphrase of ambiguous expressions certainly makes the rest of the job of argument analysis and criticism easier. Once the paraphrasing is done well, it is a straightforward matter to judge the argument as valid or invalid; it is also easier to distinguish premises from conclusions and judge premises to be true or false.

Paraphrase simplifies analysis

In addition, giving more than one paraphrase is about your only defense against really deceptive arguments. One of the hardest arguments to deal with — one that often tricks even good reasoners — is the kind in which the premises are true in one sense of the terms and the argument is valid in another, different sense of the terms. ("The Jews killed Christ. So they should be punished" is an example of this; see p. 79.) An argument of this sort is especially deceptive because, though the premises *are* true and the argument *is* valid, it is *not* sound. There is no *single* meaning under which the argument *both* is valid *and* has true premises.

It is important not to be too rule-bound in this (or any other) step in reasoning. Writing out entire arguments in alternative paraphrases can be laborious. For longer arguments you can simply write out an adequate paraphrase and at the end take note of variant readings of potentially misleading parts. For example:

Inhaling tobacco smoke causes lung cancer.

> PARAPHRASE. Inhaling "tobacco smoke" over a long period of time (say, over ten years) increases significantly the chances that you will get lung cancer.

Alternatives:

> PARAPHRASE 1. Tobacco smoke = large quantities (say, more than a pack a day).

> PARAPHRASE 2. Tobacco smoke = small quantities (say, one or two cigarettes a day).

If the context showed that the arguer was discussing smokers, paraphrase 1 would be more reasonable. If the context showed that the arguer was discussing the effects of smoke on nonsmokers in the vicinity, paraphrase 2 might be more reasonable. In the absence of context it is good to note both.

Paraphrase is often difficult and complicated (though it quickly gets easier and more simplified with practice). But a good case can be made for the position that giving multiple paraphrases actually makes the job of paraphrasing easier. Once you recognize multiple paraphrases as a real possibility, it no longer is necessary to decide exactly which of various possible alternatives the arguer *really* meant. You can instead simply list the reasonable alternatives. Your evaluation of the argument will be *conditional*: You will say, "*If* the arguer meant X, then the argument works this way; *if* the arguer meant Y, then the argument works this other way." That is an impressive way to be able to argue, and you will have covered the person's argument no matter which alternative was meant. *Multiple paraphrases make para-phrasing easier*

Two Special Problems in
Paraphrase: Connotations and Scope

Recognizing serious ambiguities   Perhaps *the* major problem in step 1 is not paraphrasing unclarities as such, but learning to *recognize* which unclarities and ambiguities are seriously misleading. Ambiguities are everywhere, but not all of them are serious or occur in key places.

The only general strategy is to paraphrase the whole argument carefully. The hope is that this will draw your attention to serious unclarities that you might otherwise have missed. The other thing that will help is practice. By getting used to explicating meaning, especially the meaning of expressions with which you are already familiar, you can come to have a "feeling" for tricky places in arguments. *General strategy*

Practice

There are two special kinds of meaning problems, connotation and scope, that are frequent, important, and easier to recognize than most.

Denotation

Expressions with strong connotations   Nearly all words and phrases have a neutral, literal meaning. That literal meaning, divorced from any emotional overtones the word may have, is called the word's *"denotation."*

Connotations

In addition to denotation, though, most words also possess emotional overtones, either positive or negative. These emotional overtones, expressed in language, are the "connotations" of the word.

Political examples

Important legal issues are sometimes heavily influenced by connotations. Opponents of unions practically won the battle beforehand by getting their legislation labeled the Right-to-Work Law. Actually, the law simply means that employers can hire workers who do not belong to a union. (That is the *denotation*.) You can understand reasons for or against this, but it is hard to be against something *called* "the right to work." The connotations, not reasons, are the persuasive force. A similar case is whether stores should "fair trade" items. Should they? The automatic response is yes: "Fair trade" *sounds* good. All it means here, though, is that stores must sell items at a pre-established price rather than compete by offering lower prices. That hardly seems to promote fair trade. Still another case: Lenin won many adherents by calling his party the Bolsheviks (which means "majority"), even though his party was nearly always in the *minority*.

Advertising examples

But it is in advertisements that strongly connotative words figure most prominently. Here is a sample selection of ads, from a single issue of *Cosmopolitan*, that have strong connotations as the major part of their persuasive power.

Nuance. An exquisitely delicate fragrance that lasts and lasts. And like a whisper is almost impossible to resist. Nuance by Coty.

Instant Styling Perm. With Exclusive Predict-A-Curl. The perm you want is the perm you get.

Isn't it time you knew an exciting drink to order? — instead of taking a man's suggestion. I used to skirt the issue of what cocktail to order — deferring to my male companion. Imagine how happy I was to discover Drambuie Over Ice for myself — and break with tradition. Cool and unruffled, it seems lighter and subtler than the drinks a man might suggest. Next time you're asked, why not order a Drambuie Over Ice. Not just because it's an exciting drink. Because it's also a slightly courageous move. DRAMBUIE OVER ICE.

Le Sport is more than a fragrance. It's a way of life . . . Day and night, you play with style. *Le Sport*. Le fragrance with style.

The end of fat lipstick. 'The Slim One' is here. 'The Slim One' by Flame Glo.

Now, what nature didn't give you Natural Lilt can!

MG Midget. Waves of excitement with a price that's a breeze.

Benson & Hedges Lights. "B & H, I like your style."

The new Free Spirit Bra/from the new Playtex . . . Look natural. Not naked.

TANDEM GIRL. She's fresh. She's free. She's career. She's confident. She's karat gold by Tandem. Tandem Jewelry.

When your taste grows up, Winston 100's out-tastes them all. Only Winston 100's Sun-Rich™ Blend of the choicest richest tobaccos tastes this smooth and satisfying.

All these advertisements are built on connotations; they are encouraging you to buy their products by playing on your emotional reaction to certain words. The literal reasons for buying the products seem flimsy and slippery when you try to figure out the *denotations* of the words. Doesn't an "exquisitely delicate fragrance" mean a perfume that smells only *slightly*? Is that *good*? To say that a product has an "exclusive" process just means that it's the *only* product with it; it says nothing *in favor* of the process. It's possible, I guess, for a drink to be "exciting," though it's hard to understand why. They also say it's "cool and unruffled." Of course it is "cool"; it has *ice* in it. But "unruffled"? Does that mean that the drink isn't blushing? Literally, that seems pretty silly. What literally *is* "style"? And how does it apply to both perfumes and cigarettes? The difference between a "fat" lipstick and a "slim" one is merely the size of the tube (the denotation), not a difference in the size of the wearer's waist (a connotation). The words "nature" and "natural," we saw earlier, were ambiguous and vague, but what little literal meaning they do have seems to make the permanent ad and the bra ad self-contradictory.

Literal meaning

Once you get the hang of it, recognizing and handling words with strong connotations becomes fairly easy. It's best to give two paraphrases: one spelling out the literal meaning of the word, its denotation; the other spelling out the word's emotional overtones, its connotation.

Capturing the connotations in words exposes how the argument is tricky; it shows how it is *supposed* to work. But the denotation is more important to the logic of the argument. Validity and truth depend usually on what the argument says *literally*. So it is more important in analysis to specify the denotation than the connotations.

Denotation more important

Some words and phrases don't have any denotation at all; some have only a little. If they have none at all, they cannot really be *reasons* for anything. "Boo" and "hurrah" are such words. They don't *say* anything; they merely *express* emotion. Calling someone a "twerp" says a little, but it is mostly connotative. Consider again the advertisements from *Cosmopolitan*. They were for products as different as cosmetics and liquor, cars and cigarettes. But the words are so empty of

Words without denotation

denotation that most of them could be used in a snappy ad for a reasoning text:

> *Reasons and Arguments.* Isn't it time you bought an exciting reasoning text? *Reasons and Arguments* brings you waves of excitement at a breezy price. Be courageous and break with the tradition of those fat old symbolic logic texts.
>
> *Reasons and Arguments* is a slim, elegant book. A book with style. Cool and unruffled, yet with exquisitely delicate arguments so valid that they're impossible to resist.
>
> It's time your reasoning power grows up. Learn to reason naturally.
>
> A good reasoner is fresh! Free! Confident!
>
> *R & A*, I like your style.

Scope   Take the statement:

People get better-paying jobs when they have a college degree.

Before you decide if it is true, you have to understand what it means. All the words in it look understandable enough, but *which* people is the speaker discussing?

You might make at least three hypotheses:

1. Every single college graduate . . .

2. Some college graduates . . .

3. Nearly all college graduates . . .

The phrases that begin each of these paraphrases are called "quantifying words" or simply "quantifiers" because they tell *how much, how many,* or *what quantity* of a group is being discussed.

The problem of scope   The problem of scope is specifying to which individuals or things a statement is meant to apply. Frequently, this is simply a problem of supplying the appropriate quantifying word to specify what quantity the arguer meant.

QUANTIFYING TERMS

Absolutely all without exception

All, every (including everything, everybody, always, everywhere)

*The vast majority, almost all, nearly all, a very high percentage of, in general, almost always

The majority, most, a high percentage of, usually

Many

Some[1] (including something, somebody, sometimes, somewhere)

---

[1] It is questionable where exactly the word "some" should go on the list. That is because it is probably the vaguest quantifying word; in different circumstances it can be used to mean anything from "at least one" all the way to "the vast majority."

A few, at least one or two, not very many

*Very few, almost none, a very small percentage of, in general . . .
not, almost never

None (including nothing, nobody, never, nowhere)

Absolutely none without exception

If a statement to be paraphrased does not mention a specific quantity, you can usually find one on this list that captures the intended scope of the statement. This, again, amounts to deciding which of the quantifying terms expresses best what the statement could *reasonably* be taken to mean.

The two categories of quantifying terms marked with asterisks in the list are the most usually correct paraphrases of general statements. One fits positive statements; the other fits negative statements. When a statement says that an indefinite group has a certain characteristic, it is often most reasonable to interpret it to mean that the group *in general* possesses that characteristic. And this is roughly equivalent to saying that the members of the group *almost all* have that characteristic or that the *vast majority* of them have it. *The most usual accurate quantifying terms*

There are two things to keep in mind when trying to choose the right word from the list. The first is that problems of determining scope are like all other problems of paraphrasing in that you will sometimes need more than one paraphrase to capture the meaning or meanings of the original. Scope can be as ambiguous as any other aspect of meaning. *Scope and multiple paraphrases*

Second, you have to test your paraphrase against the original in the same way you do for other aspects of paraphrase: You make sure the original and the paraphrase *match*. The conditions under which you would say the paraphrase was true have to be the same as the conditions under which you would say the original was true, and the conditions that would show the paraphrase to be false have to show the original to be false, too. *Scope and matching*

Let's try a few examples.

People get better-paying jobs when they have a college degree.

> PARAPHRASE 1.   Every single college graduate will get a better-paying job than he or she would get without a college degree.
>
> PARAPHRASE 2.   Some college graduates will . . .
>
> PARAPHRASE 3.   Nearly all college graduates will . . .

Neither paraphrase 1 nor 2 is accurate. They *don't match* the original. Only a few exceptions will show paraphrase 1 to be false, but more than a few exceptions are needed to show the original to be false. Paraphrase 2 is so weak that it is certainly true: *Some* college graduates of course get better-paying jobs. But that quantity does not match the quantity needed to show the original to be true. The best paraphrase, paraphrase 3, lies between the extremes and matches the original well.

Similarly,

Thou shalt not kill.

is probably paraphrased best by using the asterisked category:

> PARAPHRASE 1.   Killing should almost never be done.[1]

The asterisked category is not adequate for all questions of scope, though:

Stealing is wrong.

> PARAPHRASE 1.   In general, the unjustified taking of someone else's property is wrong.

> PARAPHRASE 2.   The unjustified taking of someone else's property is always wrong.

In this case paraphrase 2 captures the speaker's meaning better.

Sometimes you will have to restrict the scope by using more than a mere quantifying word from the list. For example, consider the ad:

The Marine Corps builds men. Join the Marines.

Restricted scope   The Marines are not saying exactly that "the vast majority" or even "a few" should join the Marines. The vast majority of *whom*? A few of *whom*? The answer here is dictated by the premise; it is not intended to apply to *women*, for example. The scope of the conclusion *is restricted* to those who want to be built into men. Leaving aside the thorny paraphrase of "builds men," a good paraphrase of the argument is

> PARAPHRASE 1.   The Marine Corps "builds men." Anyone who wants to become a man should join the Marines.

It should not worry you too much, but it will not always be possible to come up with a paraphrase that really matches. With meaning (and especially scope) there are sometimes so many variables entering in as part of the context that you just cannot take all of them into account. (The paraphrase of the Marines' advertisement, for example, *is* a good paraphrase. But you cannot push even it *too* far: What about Russians who want to become men? Or four-year-olds? Or sophisticated computers? Are *they* being told to join the Marines? We *assume* that these don't fall within the scope of the statement, but it would be very difficult — and pretty pointless as well — to rule them out explicitly in the paraphrase.)

---

[1]Because this statement from the Bible is both controversial and important, it would probably be wise to include a quite different alternate paraphrase as well:
PARAPHRASE 2.   People should never kill.

This sort of complication (and there are others like it) is seldom very crucial in argument analysis. What it does, once more, is underline the need for keeping a reasonable attitude toward paraphrase. The main point of paraphrasing an argument is to be able to analyze and evaluate it, not to be fixed on solving all the possible complications. If the many fine shades of meaning and interpretation are not important in analyzing and evaluating *that* argument, then they don't need any special mention. They need mention only if they are important as part of how the argument works.

Keeping a reasonable attitude toward paraphrase

Problems

Paraphrase each statement, concentrating on connotations and scope. Then tell whether the statement is true or false, and why.

1. Rational people are cold-blooded and unemotional.

2. Jocks are dumb.

3. Here is a unique collection of records by the legendary Otis Redding. At a fabulous price. But you better hurry — the offer is limited.

4. Explicit sex and violence don't belong on television.

5. Exercise is good for you.

6. A & P cares about you.

7. What *is* the denotation of "twerp"?

4. Premises and Conclusions

STEP 1.   Paraphrase.

STEP 2.   *Break the argument down into premises and conclusion.*

STEP 3.   Arrange the premises and conclusion in their logical order.

STEP 4.   Fill in the missing premises needed to make the argument valid.

STEP 5.   Criticize the argument.

In comparison with paraphrasing, breaking an argument down into premises and conclusions is easy. In fact, we have been breaking arguments down into premises and conclusions since Chapter One without any special instructions about how to do it. Still, there are a few finer points of technique that need to be explained.

Remember while reading this section not to get too caught up in the details. If you do not always get the finer points right, you will often still be able to analyze an argument successfully by keeping in

*Goal of
step 2*

mind that the whole purpose of step 2 is to understand the argument
better and to figure out if it is sound.

How to Pick Out Premises

You are already familiar with the words "premise" and "conclusion,"
but more precise definitions are often helpful. Precisely,

*Definition of
"premise"*

A premise is a reason given for believing a conclusion. You may
have reasons "in your head," but they are called *premises* only after
you have *given* them, by writing them out (or saying them) in the
form of a statement.

*Stated
premises*

Premises may be "stated premises" or "missing premises." When
someone gives an argument for a conclusion, the arguer states certain
reasons for believing the conclusion. If the argument is *valid*, the
stated premises are the only ones needed to draw the conclusion. In
valid arguments there are no missing premises.

*Missing
premises*

If the argument is *invalid*, however, the conclusion does *not* follow
from the stated premises. There will then be certain further premises
that need to be added to the argument to make it valid. These are the
missing premises. After the missing premises are filled in (by you, not
the arguer), they function in the argument in the same way that stated
premises do.

You pick out the stated premises in an argument, then, by
enumerating the separate reasons given. (The order does not matter.)
You weed out irrelevant comments, repetitions, empty verbiage or
rhetoric — anything that is not being given as a *reason* for *believing* the
conclusion.

How to Pick Out the Conclusion

We can give a similar definition for the familiar term, "conclusion":

*Definition of
"conclusion"*

The conclusion of an argument is the statement the arguer is trying
to prove by means of the reasons he or she is giving.

It follows from this that you cannot pick out the conclusion on the
basis of the content of the statement; you can only pick it out by
examining the way the statement fits into the argument. If it is what
the arguer is trying to prove, it's the conclusion; if the arguer is using
it to prove something else, it's a premise. For example, one person
may give an argument that capital punishment should be abolished
because it is inhuman; another person may argue that because capital
punishment should be abolished, our whole penal code needs to be
changed. In the first case

Capital punishment should be abolished

is the *conclusion*; it is what the arguer is trying to prove. In the second
case it is a *premise* (and not a conclusion at all); the arguer is using it to
try to prove something else.

To pick out the conclusion correctly, it is important that you pay attention to three things: what the argument *actually* says, what could *reasonably* be the conclusion of what it says, and what is the *context* in which it was said.

You should notice that in the definition of "conclusion" there is a tension between what the arguer actually *says* and what the arguer *intends* to prove. Both aspects are needed to identify the conclusion. The correct conclusion is usually one that makes the stated reasons as relevant as possible. That's giving the speaker the benefit of the doubt; it guards against saddling the arguer with an easily refutable conclusion (a straw-man argument). Yet practical reasoning is not the same as pure logic. In practice you have to consider the argument in the context in which it occurs — who said it; where, how, when, and why it was said. You also have to take into account background knowledge that is relevant to the argument.

If a billboard says that McDonald's hamburgers are 100 percent pure beef or that Brand X removes women's facial hair fast, we will know (from the fact that they appear in the general context of American society) that these are arguments in favor of eating at McDonald's and buying Brand X. But if the signs appear in societies where cows are considered sacred or where women's facial hair is considered attractive, the conclusions to be drawn reasonably in *these* contexts would be ones *against* eating at McDonald's or buying Brand X.

Do not let the fine points of context intimidate you. Remaining reasonable is the best way to identify what the arguer is trying to get you to believe. Most of us share a large body of common background knowledge, and this enables us to agree so often about what the conclusion of an argument is. Even when we disagree about the conclusion, our common culture enables us to argue for our choice rationally. It is only when an argument deals with points of view that are far from this common background knowledge that we have to be very careful about picking out the conclusion. *Our common background*

If no special context of an argument is apparent, assume a standard context (as with paraphrase) and a standard knowledge of events and issues; choose the most reasonable conclusion in the light of these. This will not always give you the right answer, but it will give you a reasonable answer. And in most cases, it will enable you in fact to pick out the correct conclusion. *Assuming a standard context*

Rules of Thumb
for Identifying Conclusions

The ability to pick out conclusions correctly is probably learned best by going through examples with explanations, but a few rules of thumb may be helpful.

A conclusion may be stated or unstated. If it is unstated, you have to exercise a little more caution in identifying it. You also have to take *Unstated conclusions* more pains to formulate it well because you don't have the arguer's exact wording as a guide. With unstated conclusions you are more heavily reliant on context, and so a greater element of uncertainty enters.

An argument can have more than one conclusion. In some cases these can be independent, but more usually one conclusion is a preliminary step on the way to another. The important conclusion is the main one, the major statement the arguer is trying to establish.

The main conclusion

There are certain words in arguments that often indicate the conclusion. The most important of these words is "therefore." It keys you in on the conclusion because when you use it typically, what you are doing is *drawing a conclusion*. So the sentence that follows the "therefore" is almost always a conclusion, frequently the main conclusion. The word "so" is another important conclusion-indicating word that occurs often in everyday arguments. There are some other words that sometimes help to identify the conclusion:

Conclusion-indicating words

it follows that	hence
accordingly	consequently
we can conclude that	thus

It is important that you not put too much reliance on such words, however. English is used in too many diverse ways to peg its words down to only one function. Conclusion-indicating words are merely clues; they can help, but they can also mislead.

Another misleading indicator is the position of the sentence in the argument. You tend to think of conclusions as coming at the end of the argument, and a good deal of the time, of course, they do. But they do not always or even in general. A conclusion can occur just as easily anywhere in an argument.

The position of the conclusion

Better than relying on either position or indicator words is to *think* the word "therefore" into the argument. When people give arguments, they are saying in effect:

Thinking "therefore"

These reasons (premises) are true, *therefore,* this (conclusion) is true.

And they are saying this in effect whether or not they actually use the word "therefore." What you have to do is think of the argument in this form and put the "therefore" in where it belongs. We've been doing this since Chapter One by using the symbol, "∴", before the conclusion of the arguments we've written out in premises-and-conclusion form.

Examples   The best way to go through the examples is to identify the conclusion of each argument on your own before reading the comments that follow them.

1. Absence makes the heart grow fonder. Therefore, one good way to remain happily married is to take separate vacations occasionally.

Comment:

   The conclusion is the sentence following the word "therefore."

2. Violence on television should be banned because it teaches
   youngsters to commit crime.

Comment:

   The conclusion is that violence in television should be banned.
   That's what the arguer is trying to convince you of. The *reason* for
   banning it is that it teaches youngsters to commit crime. That's
   premise 1.

3. Courvoisier VSOP. The brandy of Napoleon.

Comment:

   If you don't know who Napoleon was, and if you don't assume (a
   missing premise) that he had good taste in brandy (actually, he
   didn't), the only thing that lets you guess the conclusion is your
   knowledge that it's an *advertisement*. Because advertisements are
   designed to sell a product, this context tells you that the unstated
   conclusion is "You should buy Courvoisier VSOP."

4. The Fiat Brava may be the best value in European performance
   sedans on the market today, all facts considered.

   Its performance stats compare with cars costing thousands of
   dollars more.

   Its EPA estimated MPG is the equal or better . . .

   Its styling appointments, room, and ride make it one of the
   Continent's best-looking and most comfortable cars.

   And Brava gives you a number of other things most other European performance sedans don't. An engine-relaxing, gas-saving
   5th gear, standard, for one. And, for another, a 24 month/24,000
   mile limited power-train warranty. One twice as long as most cars
   in its class.

   So before you make your ultimate decision, test-drive the Fiat
   Brava.

Comment:

   The first sentence is a conclusion based on the specific claims that
   follow. But it's only a preliminary conclusion on the way to the
   main one, which is the last sentence. (Because (4) is an advertis-
   ment, you could also make out a case for saying its *real* main
   conclusion is "You should buy a Fiat Brava.")

5. See Colorado. There is snow in the beautiful Rockies. Skiing.
   Winter Sports. Colorado is the answer. And Continental has *direct*
   flights to Denver. Daily.

Comment:

The conclusion depends on the context. If it's a sign at the Continental office, the conclusion is "You should fly Continental to Colorado," or even "You should fly Continental." It would be perfectly acceptable to the arguer that you fly somewhere other than Colorado as long as you fly Continental. If it's an advertisement in a Colorado Tourism Office, its conclusion is "You should visit Colorado." In this context the statements about Continental's daily flights are *premises* about how easy it is to get to Colorado.

6. The Communists disdain to conceal their views and aims. They openly declare that their ends can be attained only by the forcible overthrow of all existing social conditions. Let the ruling classes tremble at a Communistic revolution. The proletarians have nothing to lose but their chains. They have a world to win. Workers of all countries, unite!

Comment::

This is the last paragraph of Marx and Engels' *Communist Manifesto,* but even if you didn't know that, you should have seen that it's obviously *for* rather than against a Communistic revolution.

PREMISE 1.   The Communists' ends can be attained only by the forcible overthrow of all existing social conditions.

PREMISE 2.   The proletarians have nothing to lose but their chains.

PREMISE 3.   The proletarians have a world to win.

∴ CONCLUSION 1.   Workers of all countries should unite to overthrow the ruling classes.

The other sentences have been left out of the breakdown because, though they may look like premises on first glance, they are not being given as *reasons* for believing the conclusion.

7. She saw that the man had a knife. Therefore, she began to be afraid.

Comment:

Here what follows the "therefore" is *not* a conclusion. That she saw that the man had a knife is not being given as a reason *to make you believe* that she began to be afraid. What she saw *caused* her to be afraid. But the speaker is simply making two claims. The speaker is not trying to get you to conclude one from the other. In fact the speaker is not trying to get you to conclude anything. For that reason, (7) is not an argument at all.

How to Pick Out Arguments

As the last example illustrates, it is sometimes difficult to tell when a group of statements is an argument. A definition may help:

An argument is a set of reasons given for believing a conclusion.

Definition of "argument"

When people merely list a group of alleged facts (whether true or false), or opinions, or interesting details, they are not making an argument. If they are giving those facts or opinions or details *in order to* convince you of something else, then they *are* giving an argument. The distinction is a subtle one and making it requires some judgment. Identifying something as an argument depends partly on figuring out the writer's intentions and partly on whether the writer's statements can plausibly be taken as reasons. In practice, because the writer usually is not available for questioning, the whole burden falls on a reasonable understanding of the writer's words plus the context.

There are two questions to ask:

1. Is the writer trying to convince me of something, stated or un-stated?

2. Is the writer trying to convince me of it by giving me reasons to believe it?

It is an argument only if the answer to both questions is yes.

The Relationship Between Rational Argument and Other Forms of Persuasion

You have probably noticed that when writing out some arguments in premises and conclusion, the wording has sometimes been changed. For example, when the Communist Manifesto actually said, "Workers of all countries, unite!" The conclusion was written out to say

Workers of all countries should unite.

In the argument against litter the conclusion, "Don't litter," was changed to

You shouldn't litter.

In other instances as well the word "should" has been inserted into the conclusion or the premise.

The reason behind this is a subtle one, but it has important implications. Because an argument is an attempt to get you to believe that something is true, the conclusion of an argument should be a sentence you can evaluate as being true or false. That is, it should be a *statement*, not a command or a question. *Commands* are neither true nor false; they do not even claim to be true or false. If the lieutenant says, "Charge!" he or she is giving a command. You can either obey or

Commands are not true or false

disobey the command; you can respond by saying, "I will" or "I won't," but you cannot respond by saying true or false. It just doesn't make sense to say that commands are true or false. So when you have an argument that has commands in it, it is better to rewrite the commands so that you can view them as statements. This is not always possible, and there are some philosophic problems with it, but as a practical device it will often allow you to evaluate what the person says *as* an argument in terms of validity and *truth*. Frequently, the best all-around way to do this is to use the word "should"; that is, transform "Do X!" into "You should do X." This latter sentence can be approached as a statement: Saying "You should charge" is true or false brings the claim within the realm of argument analysis and reasoning because now what is relevant is wondering what *reasons* there are *for believing* that you should charge.

Rewriting commands as statements

The difference between a command and a statement is important because it goes to the heart of what rational argument is and what reasoning can and cannot do. Advertisements illustrate the difference well. Very many ads — maybe most of them — are not arguments at all. Many are not even close to being arguments.

Advertisements are often not arguments

If a billboard says

Drink COCA-COLA

and shows you a picture of someone drinking a bottle, it is *not* giving you an argument, not even a bad argument. Arguments are things that give you *reasons* to *believe* something. Saying "Drink Coca-Cola" is simply trying to get you to *do* something, namely, to buy and drink Coke. And it is not trying to get you to do that by giving you *reasons*, not the slightest reason is advanced. Rather, it is trying to operate on you psychologically, to *make* you buy Coke.

Very many advertisements are like this, especially ones that appear on billboards and the glossy full-page advertisements in magazines. They range from giving no argument at all to giving full-fledged arguments (like the one for Fiat Brava on p. 163). The United States recently enacted a stricter law regulating truth in advertising. The law, unfortunately, does not seem to have resulted in more advertisements with true premises; it has led to advertisements that do not give premises (or arguments) at all. When Fiat says that "Brava gives you . . . an engine-relaxing, gas-saving 5th gear, standard," it is making a true claim, one that is relevant to believing the conclusion. If it were not true, Fiat could be prosecuted. Coca-Cola could not be prosecuted for its advertisement; it doesn't *say* anything.

Though we take it for granted, it is disturbing that such advertisements should succeed at all. If advertising people cannot find a reason for you to buy Coke, they sing you a song, and the song sells the product! (It might be a better world if people refrained from buying a product unless they had a reason for believing they should buy it. But the world is not that way.) You can be caused to buy a product, even if

Persuasion is not necessarily argument

you are a good reasoner, by things that have almost nothing to do with reason: the appeal of certain colors, catchy photographs, plays on words, mindless repetition.

This might bring up in your mind some pessimistic doubts about the power of reasoning. You can be persuaded to *do* things — buy Coke, or charge the enemy, or refrain from littering — by all kinds of methods: threats, hypnotism, shouting, clever oratory, appeals to your conscious or unconscious desires. Or you can be persuaded by reason. Reasoning helps you at least to *see* loopholes and irrelevancies and falsehoods in advertisements. That is a solid advantage. It also helps you figure out that you may have *no* reasons at all for buying the product. The pessimistic doubts about the power of reasoning enter when you realize that sometimes the advertisements *still* make you want the product, *still* get you to buy it.

Doubts about reasoning

In spite of such doubts, reasoning is one of the best tools we have for dealing with such pressures. When you interpret the commands in an advertisement as statements, as real premises and conclusions, you are giving the advertisement the benefit of the doubt. "Let's suppose," you are saying, in effect, "Let's suppose that the advertiser is not just treating me like a rat in a laboratory, let's suppose that the advertiser is not just trying to make me buy the product whether I think I should or not, but let's interpret what the advertiser is saying as an argument, as a rational presentation of reasons why I *should* buy the product."

Problems

Decide whether each example is an argument. If it is, break it down into premises and conclusion. Give a reason to back up any doubtful cases.

1. Eggs are high in cholesterol. Deposits of cholesterol in arteries and veins often lead to strokes and heart attacks. So to live longer, do not eat eggs.

2. Greece has one of the lowest crime rates of any Western country. Its murder rate, for example, was less than 10 percent the murder rate in the United States.

3. "When supply of a commodity exceeds demand, the price of it on the open market drops. The U.S. dollar is no different. We have supplied other nations with more than 190 billion dollars in military assistance, economic and technical aid and loans since the end of World War II. Can the dollar be saved? You bet! Let's start by immediately cutting off aid to all countries where the value of the dollar is declining. Then watch the demand pick up!" (Letter to the editor, *U. S. News and World Report*, March 27, 1978.)

4. "I been rich and I been poor. Rich is better." — Ella Fitzgerald.

5. In Chapter Two we had the argument, "If mariruana is legalized, organized crime will stop making so much money out of it." The unstated

conclusion, we said, was that marijuana should be legalized. That was assuming a standard context.

Now describe a different context for the argument in which the un-stated conclusion would be, "We should *not* legalize marijuana."

Describe another context in which the original sentence would not be an argument at all.

6. Suppose a religious teacher says to you, "Socrates is a man, and all men are mortal; therefore, Socrates is mortal." What would you say the conclusion was?

But suppose the religious teacher is using the argument because he intends to convince you, without saying it, that you should pray to safeguard against your own mortality. What would you say the conclusion was now?

5. *Arranging the Premises and Conclusions in Their Logical Order*

STEP 1.   Paraphrase.

STEP 2.   Write the argument out in premises and conclusions.

STEP 3.   *Arrange the premises and conclusions in their logical order.*

STEP 4.   Fill in the missing premises needed to make the argument valid.

STEP 5.   Criticize the argument.

Step 3 is like steps 1 and 2 in that it is part of the clarification of an argument rather than part of the criticism or evaluation. The difference is that in clarifying an argument you prepare for criticism by taking the argument apart and understanding it. Doing the first two steps well requires that you not let your own points of view intrude and that you remain faithful to what the arguer is arguing. The same is true of step 3. To arrange the premises logically, you figure out the order in the arguer's argument. When doing step 3, you have to remain neutral about the validity of the argument and the truth of its premises. You are trying to determine how the arguer's premises fit together logically as reasons.

Keeping neutral

Simple Arguments

The logical arrangement of the premises and conclusion shows how the various statements in the argument support one another logically. In the simplest kind of argument there is one premise and one conclusion. For example,

You shouldn't give your money away to people you feel sorry for. You know that nobody would be giving it to you if you were on the bottom.

The argument is easily written out as a single premise and a single conclusion:

> PREMISE 1.   Nobody would give money to you if you were on the bottom.

> ∴ CONCLUSION 1.   You shouldn't give your money away to people you feel sorry for.

In a simple argument the logical arrangement is also simple:

> Premise 1 logically supports conclusion 1.

or

PREMISE 1

|

↓

CONCLUSION 1

The ⟶ just means "supports" or "logically supports"; it is easier in complex arguments to draw arrows than it is to write the word "supports" all the time.

This simple logical arrangement illustrates a couple of key points. Premise 1 *logically supports* conclusion 1, which means that premise 1 is being offered as a reason in favor of conclusion 1. This will serve, then, as a definition of the term "supports" in its logical sense:

Logically supports

> One statement supports another when the first is being given as a reason for believing the second.

Definition of "supports"

Notice that premise 1 does not have to be a *good* reason for believing conclusion 1. The important thing in the logical arrangement is whether the arguer *intended* the premise as a reason for believing conclusion 1. The "logic" in "logically supports" and "logical arrangement" is the logic the arguer *believes* is there. Whether the premise *is* a good reason will be evaluated in steps 4 and 5, but with step 3, as with steps 1 and 2, you have to keep your own judgments out of the analysis. You write down "premise 1 ⟶ conclusion 1" *not* because you think it is right, but because it is what the arguer thought was right. In step 3 (again as in steps 1 and 2) the primary requirement is that you be *faithful* to the person's argument.

Fidelity

Two Categories
of Logical Arrangement

In many cases the logical arrangement of an argument is fairly easy to diagram. That is because there are only two major varieties of logical arrangement, and diagraming becomes really complex only when both of them are used together in the same argument.

Horizontal arrangement   The first category can be called a horizontal arrangement. We have had many examples of it already. The argument about littering, for example, was broken down like this:

PREMISE 1.   Littering is filthy.

PREMISE 2.   Littering is selfish.

∴ CONCLUSION 1   You shouldn't litter.

The logical arrangement of the argument is

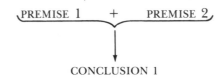

PREMISE 1   +   PREMISE 2

CONCLUSION 1

This is the correct logical arrangement because each of the premises is being given as a reason for believing the conclusion, and each is independent of the other. Premise 1 does not logically support premise 2, and premise 2 does not logically support premise 1. But *together* they logically support conclusion 1. This category can be

Horizontal   called "horizontal" because both premises are on the same stage or level in the argument.

Any argument that consists of a list of independent reasons for believing a conclusion has a horizontal arrangement. If an advertisement says

Here are four good reasons for buying Brand X,

the logical arrangement will be

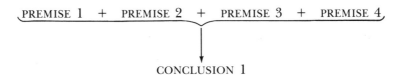

PREMISE 1   +   PREMISE 2   +   PREMISE 3   +   PREMISE 4

CONCLUSION 1

(Conclusion 1, of course, is that you should buy Brand X.)

It is not always easy to tell if an argument has a horizontal arrangement, however. Sometimes you have to think it out. For example,

We should not inflict pain, especially if we can easily avoid it. Cows, pigs, chickens, etc., feel pain when they are butchered. Eating vegetable matter will feed us more efficiently, cheaply, and nutritiously than eating meat. The only moral choice is vegetarianism.

Written out in premises-and-conclusion form:

PREMISE 1. We should not inflict pain, especially if we can easily avoid it.

PREMISE 2. Cows, pigs, chickens, etc. feel pain when they are butchered.

PREMISE 3. Eating vegetable matter will feed us more efficiently, cheaply, and nutritiously than eating meat.

∴ CONCLUSION 1 The only moral choice is vegetarianism.

This is a carefully constructed argument, and its premises are linked closely to one another. Nevertheless, each of the premises is independent of the others: The fact that we should not inflict pain (premise 1) does not give a reason for believing that animals feel pain when they are butchered (premise 2); neither do premises 1 and 2 give us a reason for believing that we can be fed sufficiently on vegetables alone (premise 3). Though the premises are about the same subject, any one of them could be false without affecting the others. That is what it means to say they are *independent* of one another. The correct diagram of the logical arrangement, therefore, is again a simple horizontal one:

Independent premises

PREMISE 1   +   PREMISE 2   +   PREMISE 3

CONCLUSION 1

Vertical arrangement The second category of logical arrangement occurs when an argument consists of one premise that supports another premise which in turn, supports another premise, and so forth, until the last premise in the series supports the conclusion. Thus, the arrangement, when diagramed, will look "vertical":

Vertical

One premise

Another premise

Another premise

Conclusion

An example of an argument with a vertical arrangement is

Violence on television teaches youngsters to commit crime. It should be closely regulated during early evening hours. Therefore television stations will have to find some alternative to all the police dramas broadcast between 7 and 9 P.M.

Written out in premises-and-conclusion form:

PREMISE 1.   Violence on television teaches youngsters to commit crime.

PREMISE 2.   Violence on television should be closely regulated during early evening hours.

∴ CONCLUSION 1.   Television stations will have to find some alternatives to all the police dramas broadcast between 7 and 9 P.M.

Premises not independent   Here premise 2 is not independent of premise 1. Rather, premise 1 is being given as a reason for believing premise 2: The (alleged) fact that violence on television teaches youngsters to commit crime (premise 1) is being given as a reason to support the contention that violence on television should be regulated during early evening hours (premise 2). And then premise 2 is used to support the conclusion.

The arrangement here, then, is

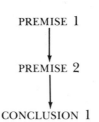

What makes this argument "vertical" rather than "horizontal" is that one of the premises supports another; they are not independent of each other as they are in horizontal arguments.

It is important not to be misled by an accidental feature of the example. Here premise 1 supports premise 2, which in turn supports the conclusion. But the order in which the premises and conclusions *Written order is not logical order*   were actually written is irrelevant to their logical order. People write down their premises in a certain order for any number of reasons; to do step 3 it is often necessary to rearrange them in their logical order. Take a longer and considerably more complex argument:

The arguments for changing the foreign-language requirement have been stated many times in the past. The basic reason for a change is that each student's plans and interests are not identical; therefore, each student's needs are not identical. A foreign-language requirement for each liberal-arts student is not a realistic approach to educational needs. For example, where a political-science major may best be benefited by computer science, an English major may need a foreign-language skill. The issue here is not whether or not foreign languages are inherently good, but whether a blanket requirement is in the interest of all students.

Disregarding the first sentence (which introduces the argument but is not a reason), the examples (I've put them in brackets because they are merely parenthetical), and a few other fine points, we can write out the argument in premises and conclusions in this way:

PREMISE 1.   Each student's plans and interests are not identical.

PREMISE 2.   Each student's needs are not identical.

PREMISE 3.   A foreign-language requirement for each liberal-arts student is not a realistic approach to educational needs.

[PREMISE 4.   A political-science major may best be benefited by computer science; an English major may need a foreign-language skill.]

PREMISE 5.   A blanket foreign-language requirement is not in the interest of all students.

∴ CONCLUSION 1.   There should be no foreign-language requirement for liberal-arts students.

This is the correct way to do step 2: Write out the premises in the order they actually occur. But this is not their logical order. Premise 2 is supported by premise 1: Students' needs are not identical, the arguer is saying, *because* their plans and interests are not identical. So part of the arrangement is

PREMISE 1

⟱

PREMISE 2

Now what does premise 2 support? In a way it supports premise 3. But in a much more direct way it supports premise 5: *Because* students' needs are not identical (premise 2), a blanket requirement is not in the interest of all students (premise 5). So the arrangement this far is

PREMISE 1

⟱

PREMISE 2

⟱

PREMISE 5

How about premise 3? Where does it fit in? Reading it carefully, you'll realize that it is the premise that is closest logically to the conclusion: If a foreign-language requirement for each liberal-arts student is not a realistic approach to educational needs (premise 3), then there should not be such a requirement (conclusion 1). More of the whole arrangement now comes to light:

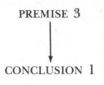

PREMISE 3

CONCLUSION 1

And now it is relatively easy to see that the logical support for premise 3 is contained in premise 5: If it is not in the interest of all students (premise 3), then it is not realistic as a requirement for all students (premise 5). The complete logical arrangement then is

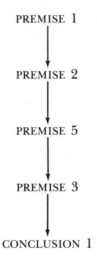

PREMISE 1

PREMISE 2

PREMISE 5

PREMISE 3

CONCLUSION 1

This diagram displays the skeleton of the argument, the logical arrangement of its premises and conclusion. (Remember again that we are not saying that a premise is *in reality* a good premise to support the next, only that it fits into the *design* of the argument that way: This diagramed arrangement depicts accurately and faithfully the way the person's argument fits together.)

Stages in an argument   Having a vertical arrangement produces *stages* in the argument. One statement is argued for on the basis of another, and then a third on the basis of the second, and so on. In effect, then, what a vertical argument produces is a series of subarguments, each having its own premise and conclusion. In this argument about foreign languages, for example, at the first stage premise 2 functions just like a conclusion we have drawn on the basis of premise 1. Then premise 5 is a conclusion of a small subargument with premise 2 as its main reason. In the end, each of the premises will directly support one other premise, and they will all indirectly support the conclusion.

Mixtures of the Two Categories

Most longer arguments are neither purely horizontal nor purely vertical, but some combination of both categories. It is easy to see why. If you give a list of independent reasons for a conclusion (and thus have a horizontal argument), some of those reasons may not seem strong enough to you on their own: They will look like they require another reason in turn to support *them*. Once you have produced a reason to back up one of your premises, the argument will become partly vertical.

We saw a detailed example of this in the last section of Chapter Four where we were trying to *construct* an argument for the conclusion, "Alexander of Macedon was one of the greatest generals who ever lived." When constructing that argument, we took a premise that seemed weak or doubtful and came up with an argument to support *it*, thus producing a second or backup stage in the argument. Then we found that there was a weak premise in that argument also and had to come up with still another argument, another stage further back, to support *it*. We did all this consciously, trying hard to give an argument that was reasoned out, was valid, and had premises that were not doubtful.

But people do much the same kind of thing without thinking it out so consciously. They do not always do it as well as if they had been trained to reason it out, but they do essentially the same task. They perceive certain parts of their argument as needing support, and they supply other reasons to support them.

When *analyzing* an argument, your job is to "sort out" the order of   *Sorting out* the person's argument. The job will be much easier if you always think of it as trying to prove a conclusion and then seeing which reasons are used to support other reasons. Here is an example of an argument with a mixed arrangement:

> The economy is failing. Our massive social programs are severely inflationary. We are threatened from the outside militarily. The Soviets are advancing into countries and menacing our allies. Therefore, the bleeding-heart liberals who want heavy domestic spending and a tight military budget are wrong.

The derogatory term "bleeding-heart" can be left out of the breakdown into premises and conclusion:

PREMISE 1.   The economy is failing.

PREMISE 2.   Our massive social programs are severely inflation-ary.

PREMISE 3.   We are threatened from the outside militarily.

PREMISE 4.   The Soviets are advancing into countries and menacing our allies.

∴ CONCLUSION 1.   The liberals who want heavy domestic spend-ing and a tight military budget are wrong.

The conclusion here is talking about two issues: The first two prem-ises deal with *domestic spending*, whereas the other two premises deal with *military spending*. Consider the first two. Either one is a reason for the other, or they are independent. But it is easy to see that they are not independent: That our social programs are inflationary is being offered as a reason for believing that our economy is failing. So premise 2 supports premise 1, and premise 1 supports the conclusion directly. The next two premises work the same way. The conclusion states that a tight military budget is wrong. Why is it wrong? Because we are being threatened militarily (premise 3). How do you know we are being threatened militarily? Because the Soviets are advancing and menacing our allies (premise 4). Thus, premise 4 logically sup-ports premise 3, which in turn logically supports the conclusion. The whole arrangement, put together, looks like this:

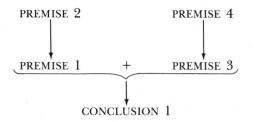

The diagram shows that premise 1 and premise 3 are independent premises in direct support of conclusion 1, that premise 2 supports premise 1, and that premise 4 supports premise 3.

The Purpose of
Diagraming the Logical Arrangement

One purpose of diagraming the arrangement is simply to see how a person's argument fits together logically. That is important because it shows which premises in an argument are supported by further premises and which are unsupported. That in turn will make you wonder whether those unsupported premises are true or false or doubtful. Doubt on one level will often carry down to give you grounds for doubt on a lower level.

But the main reason for diagraming the logical arrangement is that it shows precisely where missing premises need to be added to the argument. Filling in missing premises well is probably the single, hardest part of argument analysis, and knowing exactly where missing premises need to be filled in simplifies the task considerably.

How the logical arrangement does that will be explained in more detail in the next chapter, but briefly it works in four steps.

1. Wherever there is an arrow in the arrangement, you have a subargument.

2. If the subargument is *valid*, it requires no missing premises.

3. If the subargument is *invalid*, add the missing premises that are needed to *make* it valid. (Doing this for each of the subarguments will make the entire argument valid: Its conclusion will now follow logically from the premises.)

4. Evaluate each of the premises, stated as well as filled in, by judging whether it is true or false. (The argument will be *sound* if all the premises are true.)

How the logical arrangement shows location of missing premises

Take the last example. The diagram of the argument shows that the whole argument is composed of three subarguments, which are circled in the following:

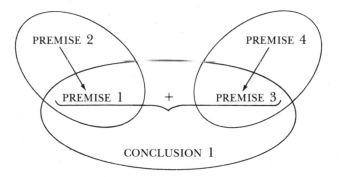

Each of the three subarguments here is invalid. (You can check this for yourself.) Though there are exceptions to the third rule, whenever you have an invalid subargument in the arrangement, you usually need to add at least one missing premise to make that subargument valid. That means that in this argument you will have to add at least three missing premises (call them "premise 5," "premise 6," and "premise 7"). You will have to formulate the missing premises in such a way as to make each of these arguments valid:

PREMISE 2	PREMISE 4	PREMISE 1
PREMISE 5 (missing)	PREMISE 6 (missing)	PREMISE 3
∴ PREMISE 1	∴ PREMISE 3	PREMISE 7 (missing)
		∴ CONCLUSION 1

The actual missing premises, to anticipate step 4, in this example are

PREMISE 2.   Our massive social programs are severely inflationary.

PREMISE 5 (missing).   Programs that are severely inflationary make economies fail.

∴ PREMISE 1.   The economy is failing.

PREMISE 4.   The Soviets are advancing into countries and menacing our allies.

PREMISE 6 (missing).   Soviet advances and their menacing our allies constitute a military threat to the United States.

∴ PREMISE 3.   We are threatened from the outside militarily.

PREMISE 1.   The economy is failing.

PREMISE 3.   We are threatened from the outside militarily.

PREMISE 7 (missing).   The only right policy is one that saves the economy and also stops outside military threat.

∴ CONCLUSION 1.   The liberals who want heavy domestic spending and a tight military budget are wrong.

We can further anticipate step 5 here and evaluate the premises. The logical place to begin is at the top of the arrangement.

Premise 2 seems true: Massive social programs are generally inflationary because they make money more plentiful and so increase the demand for (and the cost of) goods; though whether ours are "severely" inflationary is more doubtful. Still, the premise is plausible enough to judge it to be true.

Premise 5 (missing) is clearer: Inflation erases savings and decreases productivity, and those are parts of a failing economy. So, premise 5 is true.

Because premises 2 and 5 are true and the subargument is valid, it follows that premise 1 is true. There is no need to evaluate it independently.

Premise 4 also is true: There are many instances of Soviet aggression that could be cited. (It is much less clear, though, about the instances of "menacing" our allies.)

Premise 6 (missing) is a little more doubtful, but it still seems true. It is not obvious that Soviet advances and menacings are *military* threats, rather than economic ones. But advances into the oil-supplying Middle East by a country like the Soviet Union, which seems to seek control and is about America's equal, can readily be taken ultimately as a military threat. Because the subargument was valid, and the premises have been found to be true, we can conclude that premise 3 is true.

Because we have found that premises 1 and 3 are true, the only thing that remains to be considered is premise 7 (missing). If it is true, then the whole argument is sound, and the conclusion has been proved. Premise 7 is by far the weakest part of the argument; when examined, it seems to be clearly false. A policy that saves the economy and stops outside military threat does not seem the only right policy. There are other considerations involved in policy, too (domestic poverty, poor housing, malnutrition, crime — which the "massive social programs" were designed to reduce). Moreover, even if these were the only important issues, it is not at all clear that there would be *any* right policy. There just may not be any humane, reasonable way to stop inflation. It is unlikely that a higher military budget would have stopped the Soviet advances (in several cases — Czechoslovakia, Afghanistan — it is unlikely that anything but an unrealistic, actual intervention on our part would have deterred them, and then only at enormous risk of war), and they would surely still be "menacing" our allies. Finally, it is not clear that any "right" alternative policy is offered by the opponents of the liberals. Given the massive depletion of natural resources, simply cutting domestic spending is not a believable remedy for the economy.

The argument, thus, seems definitely unsound. The missing premise 7 is false, and it is needed for the arguer to go from premise 3 and premise 1 to the conclusion. The conclusion has not been proved.

You can see from this example that arranging the premises logically in a diagram for a complex argument is essential to filling in the missing premises and thus to evaluating the argument. Confronted by the whole argument in a block as it first appeared (on p. 175), it would have been much harder to come up with premise 7 as the missing premise. Taking the argument as it stands, in a big block, is just too complicated. Diagraming simplifies it, divides it into manageable subarguments, and shows you where missing premises are needed. *Step 3 simplifies complicated arguments*

Some Tips

Often, longer arguments have logical arrangements that are more complicated and harder to figure out than the ones we have considered. (Some examples are worked out in the exercises.) All you can do with an involved argument is examine it bit by bit: Look to see which premises are linked closely to others, and write down those more apparent subarguments. Look for the premises that are related most directly to the conclusion, and write these fragments down as subarguments. *General method*

Take premises that do not seem to fit and search for other parts of the argument they might support. Try to figure out how the sub-arguments fit together. That is the only general method. But a few tips may help.

One is that examples logically support the general statements they are examples of, not vice versa. The logical arrangement in such cases is:

*The arrange-
ment of
examples*

Example

↓

General Statement

Thus, part of the earlier argument about a foreign-language requirement said:

PREMISE 2.   Each student's needs are not identical. . . .

PREMISE 4.   A political-science major may best be benefited by computer science; an English major may need a foreign-language skill.

Here premise 4 is being offered as corroboration (or support) for what premise 2 says. So this part of the arrangement is

PREMISE 4

↓

PREMISE 2.

*Supports ≠
causes*

Another tip has to do with *causes*. If one event, A, causes another event, B, that does not mean that the statement describing A supports the statement describing B. (One of the statements *may* support the other, but it does not do so in all cases.) One statement *supports* another, again, only if it *gives you a reason to believe* the other. And that is not the same as events causing one another.

Consider this example:

Descartes said, "I think, therefore I am," but he had it backwards because he overestimated the importance of Thought. It should be, "I am, therefore I think"; that is, I could not think unless I *already* existed.

This objection confuses "causes" with "supports." Descartes's argument was

PREMISE 1. I think.
_____

∴ CONCLUSION 1.   I exist.

Descartes was saying that the mere fact that I think should lead me to believe that I exist; the premise is good evidence for the conclusion.

But turning Descartes around is *not* an argument:

PREMISE 1.   I exist.

∴ CONCLUSION 1.   I think.

The premise here could not be a reason for believing the conclusion; the fact that a thing exists (premise 1) gives no reason for believing it thinks. (A counterexample: Tape recorders both exist and can *say* "I exist"; but they do not think.) "I exist" is part of the *cause* that "I think," but it does not logically support it.

A related tip has to do with premises that *sound* like they support one another because they are closely linked. To repeat, before you say that one premise supports another, you have to make sure that what the first says gives you a *reason* for believing the second. And that means more than that they are talking about the same subject.

> Carrying a handgun makes you feel safer, and hence braver. When you feel brave, you are more likely to do rash, impulsive things. But doing things impulsively is one of the easiest ways to get yourself hurt. So in the end, carrying a handgun makes you more likely to get hurt.

Each one of the sentences in this argument can be taken to be a separate premise. It may look as if premise 1 supports premise 2, and that premise 2 supports premise 3, and that premise 3 supports the conclusion — thus a purely vertical arrangement. But that is not the correct arrangement at all. Each of the premises is independent of the others. Premises 1 and 2 are both talking about feeling brave, but premise 1 gives you no reason to believe premise 2: That carrying a gun makes you feel a certain way is one thing, and what you are likely to *do* when you feel that way is another thing entirely. The same is true of the relation between premises 2 and 3: They are independent also. The premises may be causally related, but they do not support one another.

You are apt to misread the relationship of the premises to one another because you are influenced by the presence of the conclusion. Because all three deal with related things and all are closely linked to the same conclusion, the impulse is to think of them as supporting one another. It may help, then, to disregard the conclusion temporarily and consider just the relationship of the premises to one another. You will find that they do not support one another any more than the following ones do:

PREMISE 1.   Paula is taller than Laverne.

PREMISE 2.   Laverne is taller than Lisette.

PREMISE 3.   Lisette is taller than Caroline.

∴ CONCLUSION 1.   Paula is taller than Caroline.

In spite of the fact that all four statements are talking about tallness, the relative heights of Paula, Laverne, Lisette, and Caroline are, of course, completely independent of one another.

The correct logical arrangement for both arguments (they are both valid, incidentally) is purely horizontal.

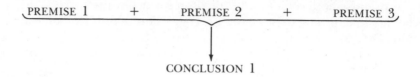

CONCLUSION 1

Exercises to Chapter Five

Again, the questions in parts A, B, and C correspond to one another. Part A consists of examples to do on your own. Part B consists of multiple-choice questions on the same examples. Part C contains answers, comments, and further questions.

For best results do not work ahead to part B until you have finished part A, and do not look at part C until you have finished both parts A and B.

Part D contains additional similar exercises, but without comments or answers.

Part A

Paraphrase the statements or arguments in 1–9. Pay special attention to scope and connotation (though, of course, don't neglect other aspects of paraphrase).

1. Southerners are bigots.

2. Blondes have more fun. (Buy Brand X hair coloring.)

3. Whales are mammals.

4. Said by a university teacher: "*Hamlet* is a great play. Everyone should read it."

5. Norman Mailer is a male chauvinist pig.

6. Capital punishment is wrong.

7. Women today are demanding that they be treated as equals.

8. Why are there so many diseases, tragedies, and natural catastrophes? I sometimes think it is because mankind is being punished for its sins.

9. Taking a course in reasoning will help students do better in their other courses in school. It would be a good idea to make reasoning a required course for all university students.

For 10–17: Break each down into premises and conclusions. (Be careful: Some may not be arguments.)

10. Singing Christmas carols in the public schools contradicts the separation

of church and state. The practice is unconstitutional and should be abolished.

11. The family that prays together, stays together.

12. Forty-seven Bibles are sold or distributed throughout the world every minute of the day.

13. "Inflation is hardest on the poor and pensioners. The rich find ways of adjusting to inflation. Businessmen make money out of it." — Arthur M. Schlesinger.

14. The number 1125 is divisible by 3. You can prove it because if you add up all the digits in it, you come up with a number that is divisible by 3. (1 + 1 + 2 + 5 = 9, and 9 is divisible by 3.)

15. According to studies at Northwestern University, men change their minds two to three times more often than women. Most women, the experiments found, take longer to make a decision than men do, but once they do, they are much more likely to stick to it.

16. Even though liberal-arts students are overwhelmingly in favor of doing away with the foreign-language repuirement, the faculty has decided to ignore student needs. They have voted to keep the requirement. We liberal-arts students therefore have no choice but to meet force with force. If we boycott all foreign-language courses next semester, the faculty will have to listen.

17. No-Doz. Safe as coffee.

Logical arrangement　For 18–25 arrange the premises and conclusion of each of the arguments in their logical order. (These same eight arguments will be used in the Exercises to Chapter Six as problems in filling in missing premises and in evaluating arguments.)

18. There are many religions, but they all believe in the same God. Therefore, religions should learn to live in peace with one another.

19. Singing Christmas carols in the public schools contradicts the separation of church and state. The practice is unconstitutional and should be abolished.

20. A sound argument is one that leads you from true premises to true conclusions. But you can't ever tell for sure if anything is true. Logic is useless.

21. Candidate X will reduce unemployment! Candidate X will improve the economy! Candidate X will lower taxes! Elect X.

22. Walt Disney always made such nice family movies. No violence or sex. You just know, when you see his movies, that he was a good man.

23. "Kellogg's MOST cereal is high in bran fiber, has wheat germ and a full day's allowance of ten vitamins and iron. These wholesome ingredients are woven into crunchy little biscuits with the taste of honest whole wheat.

With all that nutritional good taste, why settle for less than MOST?"

24. If you believe in gravity, you already believe that there are forces from the stars and planets that affect people on earth. That's just what astrology says: It says that the stars and planets exert forces on the people on earth, and that these forces are different according to the configuration of the stars and planets on the day you were born.

25. Judges are too easy on first offenders, and light sentences start the criminals down the road to more serious crime. It is unusual for a convicted robber who is a first offender to be given more than a couple of years in prison. When will we learn that a slap on the wrists is not enough?

Part B

Multiple Choice

In 1–9 circle the paraphrase that best captures the meaning of the original. If more than one is accurate, circle them all. If none of those given is correct, supply a paraphrase of your own. Give a brief reason to justify each answer.

1. Southerners are bigots.
   (a) All Southerners are bigots.
   (b) The vast majority of Southerners are bigots.
   (c) The vast majority of uneducated Southerners are bigots.
   (d) Some Southerners are bigots.
   (e) Other:

2. Blondes have more fun. (Buy Brand X hair coloring.)
   (a) Each blonde-haired person has more fun than any person with another color hair.
   (b) The vast majority of blondes have more fun.
   (c) The percentage of blonde women having fun is greater than the percentage of non-blonde women having fun.
   (d) Most women would increase the amount of fun they have by becoming blonde.
   (e) Other:

3. Whales are mammals.
   (a) Absolutely all whales without exception are mammals.
   (b) All whales are mammals.
   (c) The vast majority of whales are mammals.
   (d) Many whales are mammals.
   (e) Other:

4. Said by a university English teacher: "*Hamlet* is a great play. Everyone should read it."
   (a) *Hamlet* is a great play. Every person without exception should read it.
   (b) *Hamlet* is a great play. The vast majority of people should read it.
   (c) *Hamlet* is a great play. Every sufficiently literate, English-speaking person should read it.
   (d) Other:

5. Norman Mailer is a male chauvinist pig.
   (a) Norman Mailer is prejudiced against women.
   (b) Norman Mailer has traditional biased views about the relationship of men and women.
   (c) Norman Mailer unjustifiably thinks that women are not the equal of men.
   (d) Other:

6. Capital punishment is wrong.
   (a) Killing convicted criminals is always wrong.
   (b) Killing is always wrong.
   (c) In general, punishing people by executing them is not right.
   (d) Killing someone as a punishment is never right.
   (e) Other:

7. Women today are demanding that they be treated as equals.
   (a) All women today are demanding that they be treated as equal to men.
   (b) Most women today are demanding. . . .
   (c) Many more women today than in previous years are demanding. . . .
   (d) Many women today are demanding. . . .
   (e) Other:

8. Why are there so many diseases, tragedies, and natural catastrophes? I sometimes think it is because *mankind is being punished for its sins*. (The paraphrases below are of the italicized part only.)
   (a) Humanity is being chastised for its moral transgressions.
   (b) Individual human beings are punished for the sins they have committed.
   (c) Mankind as a whole is being punished for the sins mankind as a whole has committed.
   (d) Individual human beings are being punished for sins some human being has committed.
   (e) Other:

9. Taking a course in reasoning will help students do better in their other courses in school. It would be a good idea to make reasoning a required course for all university students
   (a) Taking a course in reasoning will help all university students do better in other courses.
   (b) It will help the vast majority of university students. . . .
   (c) Any university student who enrolls in and passes a course on rational thinking will be benefited by it in his or her comprehension of other university courses.
   (d) Other:

For examples 10–17 decide which of the answers is the best breakdown into premises and conclusion. If none of them is adequate, supply the correct answer yourself. When in doubt about an answer, give a brief reason to justify yours.

10. Singing Christmas carols in the public schools contradicts the separation of church and state. The practice is unconstitutional and should be abolished.

(a)   PREMISE 1.   Singing Christmas carols in the public schools contradicts the separation of church and state.

PREMISE 2.   The practice is unconstitutional.

PREMISE 3.   It should be abolished.

∴ CONCLUSION 1 (unstated).   You should not sing Christmas carols
in the public schools.

(b)   PREMISE 1.   Singing Christmas carols in the public schools contradicts the separation of church and state.

PREMISE 2.   The practice is unconstitutional.

∴ CONCLUSION 1.   It should be abolished.

(c)   PREMISE 1.   Singing Christmas carols in the public schools contradicts the separation of church and state.

∴ CONCLUSION 1.   The practice is unconstitutional and should be
abolished.

(d) Other:

11. The family that prays together, stays together.

(a)   PREMISE 1.   The family that prays together, stays together.

∴ CONCLUSION 1 (unstated).   If you want your family to stay together, pray together.

(b) It is not an argument. Just a matter of religious belief.

(c)   PREMISE 1.   The family that prays together, stays together.

∴ CONCLUSION 1 (unstated).   If you want your family to stay together, you should pray together.

(d)   PREMISE 1 (unstated).   Praying together helps people feel close to
one another.

∴ CONCLUSION 1.   The family that prays together, stays together.

(e) Other:

12. Forty-seven Bibles are sold or distributed throughout the world every
minute of the day.

(a)   PREMISE 1.   Forty-seven Bibles are sold or distributed throughout
the world every minute of the day.

∴ CONCLUSION 1 (unstated).   The Bible is very popular.

(b)   PREMISE 1.   Same as (a).

∴ CONCLUSION 1 (unstated).   Too many Bibles are being pushed on
people.

(c)   PREMISE 1.   Same as (a).

∴ CONCLUSION 1 (unstated).   More money is needed for even great-
    er Bible distribution.

(d) Not an argument. Just a simple statement of alleged fact.

(e) Other:

13. "Inflation is hardest on the poor and pensioners. The rich find ways of
adjusting to inflation. Businessmen make money out of it."

(a)   PREMISE 1.   Inflation is hardest on the poor and pensioners.

PREMISE 2.   The rich find ways of adjusting to inflation.

PREMISE 3.   Businessmen make money out of it.

∴ CONCLUSION 1 (unstated).   Inflation affects all of us.

(b)   PREMISE 1.   The rich find ways of adjusting to inflation.

PREMISE 2.   Businessmen make money out of it.

∴ CONCLUSION 1.   Inflation is hardest on the poor and pensioners.

(c)   PREMISE 1.   Inflation is hardest on the poor and pensioners.

PREMISE 2.   The rich find ways of adjusting to inflation.

PREMISE 3.   Businessmen make money out of it.

∴ CONCLUSION 1 (unstated).   Something should be done to help the
    poor and pensioners cope with inflation.

(d)   PREMISE 1.   Inflation is hardest on the poor and pensioners.

PREMISE 2.   The rich find ways of adjusting to inflation.

PREMISE 3.   Businessmen make money out of it.

∴ CONCLUSION 1 (unstated).   Inflation is good for the rich and
    businessmen, but it is bad for the poor and pensioners.

(e) Other:

14. The number 1125 is divisible by 3. You can prove it because if you add up
all the digits in it, you come up with a number that is divisible by 3. (1 + 1
+ 2 + 5 = 9, and 9 is divisible by 3.)

(a)   PREMISE 1.   If you add up all the digits in 1125, you come up with
    a number that is divisible by 3.

∴ CONCLUSION 1.   The number 1125 is divisible by 3.

(b)   PREMISE 1.   1125 is divisible by 3.

PREMISE 2.   If you add up all the digits in 1125, you come up with
    a number that is divisible by 3.

∴ CONCLUSION 1 (unstated).   Any number whose digits add up to a
    number divisible by 3 is itself divisible by 3.

(c) Not an argument. A mathematical statement that is undebatable.

(d) Other:

15. According to studies at Northwestern University, men change their minds two to three times more often than women. Most women, the experiments found, take longer to make a decision than men do, but once they do, they are much more likely to stick to it.

   (a)   PREMISE 1. According to studies at Northwestern University, men change their minds two to three times more often than women.

   PREMISE 2. Most women take longer to make decisions than men do.
   ———————————————————————————————
   ∴ CONCLUSION 1. Once women make a decision, they are more likely to stick to it than men are.

   (b)   PREMISE 1. According to studies at Northwestern University, men change their minds two to three times more often than women do.

   PREMISE 2. Most women take longer to make decisions than men do.

   PREMISE 3. Once women make a decision, they are more likely to stick to it than men are.
   ———————————————————————————————
   ∴ CONCLUSION 1 (unstated). Women are more stable in their decisions than men are.

   (c)   PREMISES 1, 2, and 3. Same as in (a).
   ———————————————————————————————
   ∴ CONCLUSION 1. Women are better decision-makers than men.

   (d)   PREMISES 1, 2, and 3. Same as in (a).
   ———————————————————————————————
   ∴ CONCLUSION 1. Most men make quicker but less lasting decisions than women.

   (e) Other:

16. Even though liberal-arts students are overwhelmingly in favor of doing away with the foreign-language requirement, the faculty has decided to ignore student needs. They have voted to keep the requirement. We liberal-arts students therefore have no choice but to meet force with force. If we boycott all foreign-language courses next semester, the faculty will have to listen.

   (a)   PREMISE 1. Liberal-arts students are overwhelmingly in favor of doing away with the foreign-language requirement.

   PREMISE 2. The faculty decided to ignore student needs.

   PREMISE 3. They have voted to keep the requirement.

   PREMISE 4. We liberal-arts students have no choice but to meet force with force.

PREMISE 5.   If we boycott all foreign-language courses next semester, the faculty will have to listen.

∴ CONCLUSION 1 (unstated). The faculty should pay attention to student needs.

(b)   PREMISES 1, 2, 3, 4, and 5.   Same as in (a).

∴ CONCLUSION 1 (unstated).   We liberal-arts students should boycott all foreign-language courses next semester.

(c)   PREMISES 1, 2, and 3.   Same as in (a).

PREMISE 4.   If we boycott all foreign-language courses next semester, the faculty will have to listen.

∴ CONCLUSION 1.   We liberal-arts students have no choice but to meet force with force.

(d) There is no argument here. Why do the students wish to do away with the foreign-language requirement? There could be many reasons why, but the students do not state any. So there is no argument.

(e) Other:

17. No-Doz. Safe as coffee.

(a)   PREMISE 1.   No-Doz.

∴ CONCLUSION 1.   Safe as coffee.

(b)   PREMISE 1.   Coffee is taken to keep a person awake.

PREMISE 2.   No-Doz can also be used to keep a person awake.

PREMISE 3.   Coffee is safe.

PREMISE 4.   No-Doz is as safe as coffee.

∴ CONCLUSION 1 (unstated).   You should take No-Doz to keep awake.

(c)   PREMISE 1.   No-Doz is as safe as coffee.

∴ CONCLUSION 1 (unstated).   You should buy No-Doz.

(d)   PREMISE 1.   No-Doz is as safe as coffee.

∴ CONCLUSION 1 (unstated).   You should buy No-Doz if you need something to help you stay awake.

(e) Other:

Logical arrangement In 18–25 the arguments from part A are first broken down into premises and conclusion, then several possible logical arrangements of the argument are given. Choose the correct logical arrangement for each. Back up your choice with a good reason.

18.   PREMISE 1.   There are many religions

PREMISE 2.   All the religions believe in the same God.

∴ CONCLUSION 1.   Religions should learn to live in peace with one another.

(a)
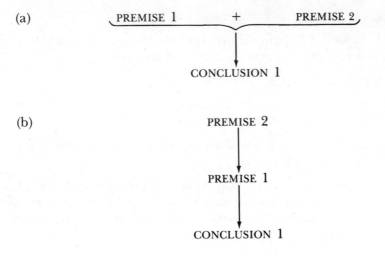

(b)

PREMISE 2

PREMISE 1

CONCLUSION 1

(c) Other:

19. PREMISE 1.   Singing Christmas carols in the public schools contradicts the separation of church and state.

PREMISE 2.   The practice is unconstitutional.

∴ CONCLUSION 1.   The practice should be abolished.

(a)
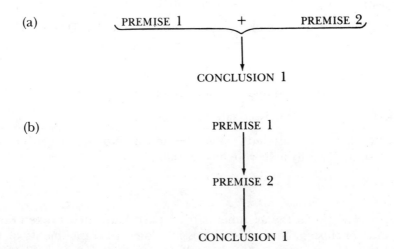

(b)

PREMISE 1

PREMISE 2

CONCLUSION 1

(c) Other:

20. PREMISE 1.   A sound argument is one that leads you from true premises to true conclusions.

PREMISE 2.   You can't ever tell for sure if anything is true.

∴ CONCLUSION 1.   Logic is useless.

(a)

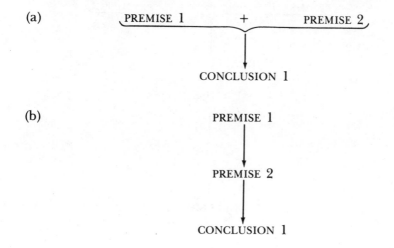

(b)

PREMISE 1

PREMISE 2

CONCLUSION 1

(c) Other:

21. PREMISE 1.   Candidate X will reduce unemployment.

PREMISE 2.   Candidate X will improve the economy.

PREMISE 3.   Candidate X will lower taxes.

∴ CONCLUSION 1.   You should vote for X.

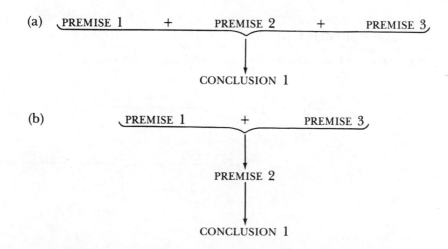

(c) Other:

22. PREMISE 1. Walt Disney always made such nice family movies.

PREMISE 2. His movies have no violence or sex in them.

∴ CONCLUSION 1. Walt Disney was a good man.

(a)

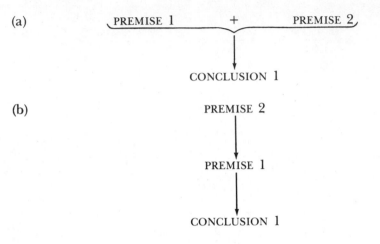

(b)

PREMISE 2
↓
PREMISE 1
↓
CONCLUSION 1

(c) Other:

23. PREMISE 1. Kellogg's MOST cereal is high in bran fiber, has wheat germ and a full day's allowance of ten vitamins and iron.

PREMISE 2. These wholesome ingredients are woven into crunchy little biscuits with the taste of honest whole wheat.

PREMISE 3. MOST has nutritional good taste.

PREMISE 4. You shouldn't settle for a cereal with less nutritional good taste than MOST has.

∴ CONCLUSION 1 (unstated). You should buy MOST cereal.

(a)

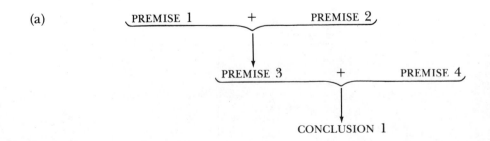

(b)

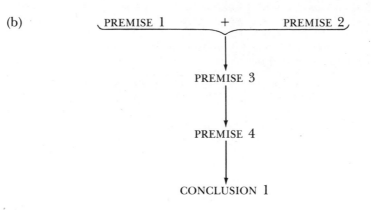

PREMISE 1   +   PREMISE 2

↓

PREMISE 3

↓

PREMISE 4

↓

CONCLUSION 1

(c) Other:

24. PREMISE 1.   If you believe in gravity, you already believe that there are forces from the stars and planets that affect people on earth.

PREMISE 2.   Astrology says the same thing as the laws of gravity. [Paraphrase of "That's just what astrology says."]

PREMISE 3.   Astrology says the stars and planets exert forces on the people on earth.

PREMISE 4.   Astrology says that the forces exerted are different according to the configuration of stars and planets on the day you were born.

∴ CONCLUSION 1 (unstated).   You should believe in astrology.

(a) PREMISE 1 + PREMISE 2 + PREMISE 3 + PREMISE 4

↓

CONCLUSION 1

(b) PREMISE 1   +   PREMISE 3   +   PREMISE 4

↓

PREMISE 2

↓

CONCLUSION 1

(c) Other:

25. PREMISE 1.   Judges are too easy on first offenders.

    PREMISE 2.   Giving light sentences starts criminals down the road to more serious crimes.

    PREMISE 3.   It is unusual for a convicted robber who is a first offender to be given more than two years in prison.

    PREMISE 4.   Light sentences are not enough.

    ∴ CONCLUSION 1 (unstated).   Judges should give harder sentences to first offenders.

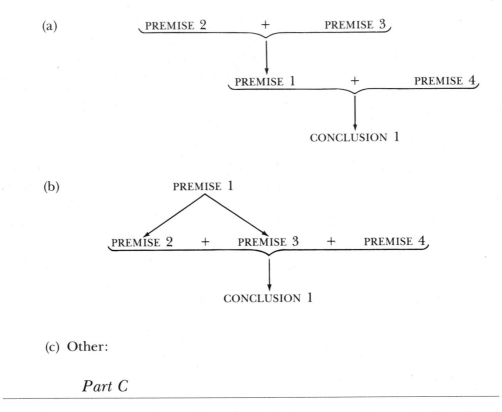

(a)

(b)

(c) Other:

Part C

Here are some comments on the multiple-choice answers in part B. Try also to apply the comments here to the answers you gave on your own in part A.

In addition, part C contains some further questions. They are in parentheses and printed in italics.

1. Southerners are bigots.

Comments:

The most accurate paraphrase is (b): The vast majority of Southerners are bigots. That matches the original. The original does not typically mean that *all*

(a) or *some* (d) Southerners are bigots. Finding a few unbigoted Southerners would not disprove the original, but it would disprove (a); finding a few bigoted Southerners would not prove the original, but it would prove (d). That is why neither (a) nor (d) matches the original. Choice (c), that the vast majority of *uneducated* Southerners are bigots, is also incorrect. It is more likely to be true than the original is, but no special context is given that would lead you to believe that the person had anything in mind about uneducated Southerners. In a standard context, (c) is wrong.

2. Blondes have more fun.

Comments:

Paraphrase (a) is not accurate because it talks about *persons*, whereas the original is used primarily of *women*. Paraphrase (b) is not a very good choice because it does not tell *who* blondes have more fun than. Paraphrase (c) is an accurate paraphrase. But even if it is true, it gives very little reason for dyeing your hair. A counterexample: The percentage of blonde women being Scandinavian is greater than the percentage of non-blonde women being Scandinavian, but dyeing your hair cannot help you become Scandinavian. What is missing in the argument is the *link* between having blonde hair and having fun. Paraphrase (d) captures this link. It (or it plus (c)) is the most accurate paraphrase given. (*Which is more likely to be true, (c) or (d)? Which would give a better reason for a woman to dye her hair?*)

3. Whales are mammals.

Comments·

The correct answer is (a). Choice (b) is correct only insofar as it means the same as (a). "Mammal" is a classificatory word, not a generalization. Either every single member of a species is a mammal, or none is.

4. Said by a university English teacher: "*Hamlet* is a great play. Everyone should read it."

Comments:

The paraphrase you gave before you saw the multiple choices should have some qualifications in it, like those in (c). Even though the teacher said "*everyone*" and did not mention any qualification, he or she did not *mean* "everyone without qualification or exception." So (a) is not accurate. The teacher did not mean, for example, that illiterate people (people who cannot read) should read *Hamlet*, nor that all literate Koreans should read it. Hence the qualifications in (c), which is the best answer given. You may have come up with a better answer as (d), though, or you might have concentrated on paraphrasing the word "great." (*Do the teacher's statements constitute an* argument?)

5. Norman Mailer is a male chauvinist pig.

Comments:

This does mean that Mailer is prejudiced and has traditional biased views and thinks that men and women are not equal. So (a), (b), or (c) does capture much of the literal meaning of the original. And each of them also captures some of the negative connotation in the original. (*Which words in (a), (b), and (c) spell out the negative aspect?*) But none of them manages to capture the intensity of the negative connotation. (*Try to spell out this intensely negative meaning in a paraphrase. What is the difference in denotation between calling Mailer a "male chauvinist pig" and calling him a "male chauvinist"?*)

6. Capital punishment is wrong.

Comments:

The only correct answer given is (d): Killing someone as a punishment is always wrong. Both (a) and (b) leave out the idea of *punishment*; killing a criminal in self-defense, for example, would be ruled out by (a) and (b), but it would not by the original or by (d). Choice (c) is also inaccurate because it leaves out the implication of *always*.

7. Women today are demanding that they be treated as equals.

Comments:

Paraphrase (a) is clearly wrong because it is not plausible and the original is; so they do not match. And (b), though closer, seems somewhat *less* plausible than the original. So it does not quite match either. On the other hand, (d) seems a little *more* plausible than the original: A lot of anti-feminists would admit (d) without admitting the original. Of the answers given, (c) comes closest.

8. Why are there so many diseases, tragedies, and natural catastrophes. I sometimes think it is because *mankind is being punished for its sins*.

Comments:

Paraphrase (a) is a word-for-word restatement, but it is not a good paraphrase. The aspect of the sentence that seriously needs paraphrase is its scope. *Who* is being punished for *whose* sins, according to the original? The sentence after analysis is misleading in just the way the sentence, "The Jews killed Christ," was found to be in Chapter Three. Notice that choice (c), though accurate in a way, does not make sense: Properly, sins — because they are actions or thoughts — can only be committed by individuals, and punishments can only be doled out to individuals. Therefore, (c) is ambiguous; it (like the original) means either (b) or (d). Each of these two captures a distinct sense of the original, and together they show exactly what is wrong with this "explanation" of human suffering. Paraphrase (b) says that individuals are being punished for the sins they themselves have committed. That certainly sounds like justice. The problem with it is that some people suffer diseases and catastrophes even though they seem not to have committed any sins personally (infants, for example). So if the original means (b), it is not very plausible. Paraphrase (d), on the other hand, says that individuals are punished for sins that *some* human being has committed, that is, not necessarily for their own sins. That might serve to explain why innocent infants suffer diseases and tragedies (because of other people's sins), but it certainly sounds *unjust*. How can you justly punish A for a sin B has committed? After analyzing the meaning, you can see that the original "explanation" does not hold water. Either it means (b) and is implausible, or it means (d) and the punishment is unjust.

9. Taking a course in reasoning will help students do better in their other courses in school. It would be a good idea to make reasoning a required course for all university students.

Comments:

The context of the argument itself makes (a) the best choice. The second sentence in the original argument says that reasoning should be made a required course for *all* university students. Since the only reason given for this is the first sentence, there too the arguer must mean the course will help *all* university students. That is what (a) says. Paraphrase (c) says pretty much the same thing; so it is also right. But it is not necessary to replace familiar words like "taking," "reasoning," and "help" with synonyms unless doing so genuinely increases your understanding of the argument. Paraphrase should be a help rather than a burden. The words do not look misleading here. Because (b) mentions "the vast majority" rather than "all," it is not as accurate a paraphrase, though it makes for a more plausible statement. If the arguer did mean (b), the missing premise would have to be:

> PREMISE 2 (missing).   Any course that would help the vast majority of students in their other courses should be required of all students.

This missing premise is not very plausible because of the difference in scope. *(What is the missing premise of the argument if the stated premise means (a)? Is it plausible?)*

Break down 10–17 into premises and conclusions.

10. Singing Christmas carols in the public schools contradicts the separation of church and state. The practice is unconstitutional and should be abolished.

Comments:

The best answer is (b) because the arguer is trying to show that singing Christmas carols in the public schools should be abolished, and the arguer gives two related reasons to support that conclusion. Answer (a) is wrong because the point of talking about constitutionality is to show that the practice should be abolished, not just that you should not do it. Answer (c) lumps together two separate points, constitutionality and abolishing the practice.

Actually, the argument requires a missing premise to connect those two points. (*Formulate the missing premise.*)

11. The family that prays together, stays together.

Comments:

Breakdowns (a) and (c) are identical except that the conclusion of (a) is a command. (*Explain what is wrong with having a command as a conclusion of an argument.*) Answer (d) is not only wrong, it is incoherent. Though you can have an argument with stated premises and an unstated conclusion (by guessing in a standard context what the arguer is trying to prove), you cannot really have an argument with a stated conclusion and *un*stated premises. Because an argument is reasoning from reasons, stated reasons, to a conclusion, if there are no stated premises, there is no argument. Answer (b) is wrong also. The fact that this is a religious belief is irrelevant to whether it is an argument. You can have arguments about religious beliefs, ethics, politics, opinions, or anything else. This *is* an argument because the speaker is saying this to convince you that if you want your family to stay together, you should pray together. That is the conclusion. So (c) is the best answer given. (*What is another plausible version of the conclusion?*)

12. Forty-seven Bibles are sold or distributed throughout the world every minute of the day.

Comments:

The breakdown in (a) looks reasonable. A person *could* use the statement to argue that the Bible is very popular. But there is no reason to believe that the arguer *is* trying to prove that. The arguer might just as easily be trying to prove that too many Bibles are being distributed, (b), or that not enough are, (c). You cannot tell, from the bare statement, on which side the speaker is or if the speaker is trying to prove *anything*. If you cannot tell what people are trying to prove, the reasonable thing is usually to take them as not giving an argument at all. So (d) is right. (*Describe three contexts that would make (a), (b), and then (c) the best breakdown.*)

13. "Inflation is hardest on the poor and pensioners. The rich find ways of adjusting to inflation. Businessmen make money out of it." — Arthur M. Schlesinger.

Comments:

Breakdown (a) makes the three statements look *neutral*. But Schlesinger is not merely listing three different effects of inflation. Both (b) and (c) are plausible. It is hard to tell for which of the two conclusions Schlesinger is arguing. When in doubt like this, it is safer and more faithful to the person's argument to take something that is *stated* as the conclusion. So (b) is better than (c). The "conclusion" to (d) is not a conclusion at all; it is a *summary* of the whole argument. Choosing (d) is really saying that the quotation is not an argument at all. But it is.

14. The number 1125 is divisible by 3. You can prove it because if you add up all the digits in it, you come up with a number that is divisible by 3. (1 + 1 + 2 + 5 = 9, and 9 is divisible by 3.)

Comments:

Breakdown (a) is right. The phrase, "you can prove it," shows you that the conclusion is "1125 is divisible by 3." The conclusion is what you are trying to prove. So it definitely is an argument. The fact that it is mathematical and undebatable, (c), is irrelevant to whether it is an argument. The conclusion to breakdown (b) is not a conclusion at all. Actually, it is the missing premise. It is the way you go *from* the premise *to* the conclusion. *If* adding up all the digits in 1125 gets you a number divisible by 3 (the stated premise), and *if* any number whose digits add up to a number divisible by 3 is itself divisible by 3 (the missing premise), then it follows that 1125 is divisible by 3 (the conclusion). It is easy to confuse the missing premise in an argument with its conclusion.

15. According to studies at Northwestern University, men change their minds two to three times more often than women. Most women, the experiments found, take longer to make a decision than men do, but once they do, they are much more likely to stick to it.

Comments:

Unless you have a very strong case for your choice, the statement that you decide is the conclusion of another person's argument should generally be one to which all the person's premises are relevant. Otherwise there is a danger that you are distorting the person's argument. This is especially true when the conclusion to the person's argument is not stated. If you cannot find a plausible candidate that does this, the person's remarks are probably not an argument at all. Irrelevance thus makes a useful test of a proposed breakdown.

    If the conclusion in (a) were right, both premises would be irrelevant. That men change their minds more often is no reason to think that women stick to their decisions longer; neither does the fact that women take longer to make a decision. So (a) is a distortion of the person's argument. Indeed, choosing any one of the statements as the conclusion makes a significant part of the rest irrelevant. So if there is a conclusion, it must be unstated. But (b) and (c) are no good either. In breakdown (b) premise 2 would be irrelevant: That women take longer to make a decision gives no reason to conclude that they are more stable in their decisions. And nothing in the argument indicates the arguer is trying to show that women are *better* decision-makers any more than that women are more stubborn than men. (*Why is that not the conclusion?*) The conclusion in (d) does make all the premises relevant, but it still is not what the arguer is trying to prove; it just *summarizes* the person's statements.

    Actually, the sentences are simply stating two independent facts. One is that men change their minds more often than women do (that is essentially what both premise 1 and premise 3 are saying); the other is that women take longer to make a decision (premise 2). They are independent of one another, and there is no argument involved. "Contrary to popular belief," the person seems to be saying, "men change their minds more often, and women stick to their decisions more." That is just a set of interesting facts, not an argument. (*Apply the test of irrelevance to the breakdowns in questions 14(b) and 13(c).*)

16. Even though liberal-arts students are overwhelmingly in favor of doing away with the foreign-language requirement, the faculty has decided to ignore student needs. They have voted to keep the requirement. We liberal-arts students therefore have no choice but to meet force with force. If we boycott all foreign-language courses next semester, the faculty will have to listen.

Comments:

The test of irrelevance shows that breakdown (a) is not the best. The arguers are not trying to prove that the faculty should pay attention to student needs, for if they were, they would not have given premises 4 and 5 as reasons. The fact that those premises are irrelevant to this supposed conclusion shows that it is probably not the actual conclusion. The conclusion in (b), that the students should boycott all foreign-language courses next semester, does make all the premises relevant. It's the best breakdown given. The conclusion in (c) is not the actual conclusion; it too would make one of the stated premises irrelevant. (*Which one?*) Answer (d) is wrong also. It's true that this is *not* an argument for doing away with the foreign-language requirement. No reason *is* given for that. But that does not mean it is not an argument, just that the critic has gotten the conclusion wrong. (*Analyze the meaning of meeting "force with force." How does it apply in the argument?*)

17. No-Doz. Safe as coffee.

Comments:

Both (a) and (b) are entirely wrong. There are no statements in (a), no claims, so these cannot be the premises or the conclusion. Words have to be filled in to make it coherent. Breakdown (b) goes wrong in the opposite way; it fills in far too much. Premises 1, 2, and 3 are not stated, so they are not premises. Both (c) and (d) are plausible. It is a question of whether the advertisement is arguing that people in general, without restrictions, should buy No-Doz, (c), or that people who need something to stay awake should buy it, (d). The conclusion of many advertisements is simply that you should buy the product, but that does not fit so well here because No-Doz has such a restricted audience. So (d) is better. The reason the difference is important is that stronger missing premises are needed to get to an unrestricted conclusion, like (a), than to a restricted one, like (b). (*What missing premise would you need in (a) that you would not need in (b)? Is the example really an argument? Give reasons to support your answer.*)

Logical Arrangement   Answers, comments, and further questions.

18. If you had to choose between answers (a) and (b), the horizontal arrangement (a) would be better. The two stated premises are independent of one another. Notice that premise 2 *could* be used to support premise 1 as in (b): That all religions believe in the same God *is* evidence that there are many religions. Still, (b) is wrong because the arguer pretty clearly did not intend to convince you of premise 1 by means of premise 2. The arguer intended them as separate statements.

    Thus the fact that one statement in an argument *could* be used as evidence for another does not show you that it *is* being used as evidence. Logical arrangement diagrams the actual *intended* use.

    The best answer, however, is (c) because premise 1 is merely an introductory statement and not really a reason for believing the conclusion at all. The fact that there are many religions gives no reason to think that religions should learn to live in peace with one another. The correct logical arrangement you should have filled in, then, is

PREMISE 2
|
↓
CONCLUSION 1.

19. This is a purely vertical argument. It is being concluded *from* premise 1 that the practice of singing Christmas carols is unconstitutional; the main conclusion 1 is then another step in the reasoning. So (b) is right.

20. Neither premise can be evidence for the other. They are independent. Therefore, (a) is the correct arrangement.

21. *You* may believe, as in (b), that if X reduces unemployment and lowers taxes she will improve the economy. But there is no reason to think this arguer is arguing that way. As far as you can tell, he is offering three independent reasons for voting for X. Arrangement (a) is a better choice. (*Why is "You should vote for X" the conclusion rather than "You should elect X," as stated?*)

22. This argument has a vertical arrangement, as in (a). That Disney's movies have no violence or sex (premise 2) is a good part of the arguer's reason for thinking Disney's movies are nice family movies (premise 1). The premises do not seem to be independent of one another as in (b). (*Could premise 1 be a support for premise 2 instead of vice versa? Why is that not the correct arrangement?*)

23. It is clear that premises 1 and 2 support premise 3: Premise 1 covers "nutritional," and premise 2 covers "good taste." The harder question is whether premise 3 is independent of premise 4 as in (a), or whether it supports premise 4 as in (b). If you pay careful attention to what premise

4 says, you see that there is really no question about it. Even if Most *is* nutritional and tasty, that gives you no reason to believe you should not settle for less: Premises 1–3 are about what Most has; premise 4 is about what you should not do. They are independent assertions.

24. The way premise 2 was stated originally in the argument can make it look completely independent of premise 1: The law of gravity says there are forces from the stars (premise 1), but that has nothing to do with what astrology says (premise 2). That is the reasoning behind arrangement (a). Paraphrasing premise 2, though, shows that (b) is the correct arrangement. Premise 2 clarified says that "<u>astrology</u> and <u>the law of gravity</u> say the same thing." "<u>The law of gravity</u>" is covered by premise 1; "<u>astrology</u>" is covered by premises 3 and 4. *(Why is the conclusion of this argument not "If you believe in gravity, you should believe in astrology"?)*

25. It is often difficult to follow the logical arrangement of a complex argument because the diagram looks so abstract on the page. It is much easier if you have mapped out the arrangement first on your own.

Here (a) is the better answer. Premise 1 cannot really support premise 2 as (b) says. A judge being too easy may *cause* criminals to go down the road to more serious crimes, but that is different from saying premise 1 *supports* premise 2. It does not make sense to say "judges are too easy; *therefore*, giving light sentences starts criminals down the road...." Rather, it is the reverse. Premise 2 gives you reason to think premise 1 is true: "Light sentences start the criminal down the road to more serious crimes; *therefore*, judges are too easy." Causing and supporting are completely different concepts. Similar reasoning will show that premise 3 supports premise 1 rather than vice versa. *(Explain.)*

Part D

Paraphrase the statements or arguments in 1-13. Note any variations in meaning that may be important in evaluating the statement or argument.

1. Body builders frequently look at themselves in the mirror. That kind of vanity is essentially feminine. Therefore, body builders are effeminate.

2. The Chicago Police Department is honest.

3. People who want to be in the know read *Newsweek*.

4. The Bible says, "Thou shalt not kill." Therefore, war is forbidden by the Bible.

5. A person should obey the law.

6. You should invest in America. Buy United States Savings Bonds.

7. I am the Lord thy God. Thou shalt not put strange gods before me.

8. "Child abuse is a major cause of death for children under two. Last year in America, an estimated one million children suffered physical, sexual or emotional abuse and neglect (many cases go unreported). At least 2000 died needless, painful deaths. And if you think child abuse is confined to any particular race, religion, income group or social stratum, you're wrong. It's everybody's problem." — National Committee for Prevention of Child Abuse.

9. America is a young country.

10. Schultz passed away.

11. Sign at a cleaners: "There is no charge for delivery. Customers who pick up their clothes will receive a 10% discount."

12. Sign on Interstate 55: "Visit Onandoga Cave, Missouri."

13. There are more murders in New York than in any other city. I wouldn't go there. It is too dangerous.

In 14–20 decide whether the example is an argument or not. If not, say why not. If it is an argument, break it down into premises and conclusions. Also, note any problems — of meaning, truth, or validity — that will be important in evaluating the argument.

14. It is questionable whether homosexuals should be allowed to teach in universities. But they should not be allowed to teach in secondary schools. And unquestionably they *must* not be allowed to teach children in the primary grades.

15. Every event has a cause. We know that from science. That is why the rain falls and why the murderer commits murder. Something causes the killer to kill just as much as something causes the rain to do what it does. The killer is no more "responsible" for the crime than the rain is "responsible" for the flood it causes.

16. "An improved voting machine is a good idea. But remember a voting device is only as good as the citizens who use it. Know the candidates. Study the issues. And vote — as if your freedom depends on it. It does." — Billy Graham.

17. Among the Mundugumoor, an angry wife may well attack her husband with a water-buffalo jaw. It would be inappropriate to call these women "shy" or "docile."

18. You have lied to me. Now I can never trust you.

19. "In the 10th century A.D. an Arab geographer states that the date palm flourished abundantly around the town of Sinjar, which lies at the foot of the hills of the same name which intersect the north Mesopotamian plain. At present, dates will not ripen north of Samarra, almost 200 miles to the southeast, and we must conclude that a thousand years ago both summer and winter temperatures were marginally higher than they are now." (Oates, *The Rise of Civilization*, New York: 1976, p. 18.)

20. She doesn't believe in God because she's just rebelling against the religion she was brought up in.

Analyze and evaluate arguments 21–28. Paraphrase where it is needed, and break them down into premises and conclusions. Then try to criticize the arguments as well. Try to key in on the *specific* thing that is wrong. Some clues are given in the questions that follow them.

21. "Gas is the most efficient of all the major energy systems. It's your least expensive way to heat. And today's gas heating equipment makes gas even more efficient, with new energy-saving features that can cut your gas use significantly.

"And for the future — America's underground gas deposits, plus new technologies, could provide economical gas energy for centuries to come. The Gas Advantage: A More Efficient Way to Heat." (*Reader's Digest,* October, 1979, p. 9.)

(*What does "efficient" mean in this argument? Look it up in a good dictionary. Which of the dictionary meanings are being implied here? How is it misleading? The sentence in the second paragraph looks a lot like an outright lie: We will be lucky if we still have usable gas by 2025 much less "for centuries to come." What cheating words in the sentence save it from being an outright lie?*)

22. Prostitution should definitely not be legalized. Not only would it hurt marriages, but if it were legalized, the prostitutes could sell their bodies to anybody, even children. And this is wrong. Children might be encouraged to pick up a hooker.

23. It is often assumed that college athletics hinders one's ability to get a good education, but there are good reasons to think the opposite. Many athletes come from poor backgrounds, and athletics are a way to obtain scholarships to good schools like Notre Dame or DePaul, which they would otherwise be unable to attend. Associations such as the N.C.A.A. require that athletes maintain a certain grade-point average to ensure that they get a good education from the schools they attend. A number of athletes have passed in their universities with very high grades in such difficult fields as pre-med and pre-law.

(*How are the arguments in 22 and 23 affected by problems of scope? What weight do the arguments carry for their conclusions?*)

24. It is ungrammatical to say that one thing is "more perfect" than another. Nothing can be *more* perfect: Either a thing *is* perfect, or it is not. There cannot be "degrees" of perfection. The same thing holds for certain other words like "unique" or "white." (*This argument is built on an analysis of meaning. Is it a correct analysis? How could you find out? Can you think of other words that might be counterexamples?*)

25. The first argument in Chapter Two for the legalization of marijuana said, "It just doesn't make sense that you should have to go to prison for having a little bit of marijuana." (*Is this argument vague? In how many ways? Is the vagueness in this case an important criticism of the argument?*)

26. The function of a college education should not be just to turn people into specialists. You are not well educated if all you know about is mathematics or chemistry or business. You should also know about your culture, your society, and your past. Yet many students will not take humanities courses voluntarily. It is necessary, therefore, that they be made degree requirements for all students. (*Are there problems of scope in this argument? How serious are they? Is this argument based, too, on a meaning analysis of the word "well educated"?*)

27. "When we cheat impersonal corporations, we indirectly cheat our friends — and ourselves. Department of Commerce data show that marketplace theft raises the cost of what we buy by more than two percent. We also pay for fraud against the government. According to federal estimates, doctors who collect Medicare and Medicaid money for unnecessary treatments, veterans who collect education money but who do not attend school, and other such chiselers cost the average taxpayer several hundred dollars a year." ("How Honest Are You?" *Reader's Digest*, October, 1979, pp. 32-36.) (*Who is "we" in this paragraph? If you cheat an impersonal corporation, how much do "you" cheat "you" and "your friends"?*)

28. "Intelligence" is often defined as "whatever IQ tests measure." There is no difference in the average IQ scores of men and women because, in the construction of the tests, questions that show a sex difference are deliberately eliminated. Nevertheless, by the definition above, men and women are equally intelligent. (*What is going on in this argument? What does "intelligent" mean? Could there be differences in the intelligence of women and men? Should questions that show a racial difference also be eliminated? Why or why not?*)

Chapter Six

Criticizing Arguments

1. Filling In the Missing Premises

STEP 1. Paraphrase the argument.

STEP 2. Write it out in premises and conclusions.

STEP 3. Arrange the premises and conclusions in their logical order.

STEP 4. *Fill in the missing premises needed to make the argument valid.*

STEP 5. Evaluate the argument.

Filling in missing premises is probably the most rewarding step in analyzing arguments. To do it well you need to be shrewd and clever, and it is in this process that you are most likely to ferret out weakpoints in the argument. For the things a person actually says in an argument, the stated premises, are often true; falsehoods will more likely lie in the premises the arguer has left *unsaid*. Finding these hidden weakpoints is often fun — like a detective finding the missing link in someone's alibi. Even when it is not fun, though, it is useful; it allows you to zero in on exactly what is wrong with a person's argument. Getting in the habit of looking for missing premises will make you an impressive and formidable critic.

The Basic Task

An argument consists of a certain number of stated premises and a conclusion. For the argument to be sound, for it to prove its conclusion, the argument must be both valid and have all true premises. The basic task of step 4 is to fill in those premises that are needed to make the person's argument valid.

If the stated premises by themselves already constitute a valid argument for the conclusion, then you are done with step 4. There are no missing premises in the argument; you can go directly on to

If the stated argument is valid

Basic task: completing invalid arguments

step 5 and begin evaluating whether the stated premises are true.

If, however, the stated argument is invalid as it stands (this is the more usual case), then you must formulate those additional premises needed to draw the conclusion.

So once you have finished the logical arrangement of premises and conclusions, there are three things to do:

1. Figure out if the argument is valid.

2. Fill in the premises needed to make it valid.

3. Determine whether each of the premises, stated as well as filled in, is true or false and give a reason to back up your judgment. (This is step 5.)

How to Determine an Argument's Validity

The concept of validity and many practical details of determining invalidity have already been covered. Chapter Two, Section 2 explained the concept, and the exercises to Chapter Two contained concrete cases on determining invalidity. Further, Chapter Four discussed two methods of *constructing* valid arguments, and the exercises to that chapter contained more problems in validity. The task of filling in the missing premises presupposes the ability to recognize invalid arguments. This section elaborates on the methods for determining the invalidity of arguments, primarily with an eye toward filling in the missing premises.

Symbolic logic

The surest methods for determining validity are contained in the field of symbolic logic. They are surest because they give exact, certain, and proved answers. The trouble with them is that they are not always very practical; they often do not "fit" arguments from everyday life very well, and thus they are not adapted to those situations in which people most often need the skill of reasoning. Besides, seeing the relevance of symbolic logic to practical reasoning takes a great deal of technical training, and it gives you little help in doing other tasks involved in good reasoning (like paraphrasing, or constructing arguments, or evaluating truth). The relationship is somewhat like the one between running and a knowledge of the muscular structure of the leg. Knowing the muscular structure allows you to understand the complexities involved in the simple act of running; a thorough knowledge might even help you become a better runner (if you were a fairly good one already), by suggesting new exercises, for example, or better ways of positioning your body. But it would not be a good way to *learn* how to run. The theoretical knowledge is just too far removed from the practical activity.

Still, it is important to know that validity can be defined and determined exactly, and symbolic logic does show this. You can appreciate the significance of this by contrasting validity with truth:

There is no way to know with certainty if most things are true; all you can reasonably do is go with the evidence. Symbolic logic shows that a much stronger case can be made for validity: Most arguments, when formulated in symbolic notation, can be known *for certain* to be valid or invalid.

Validity and certainty

The more practical methods for determining invalidity hinge on less-exact procedures. An argument is valid, remember, if accepting the premises (for the sake of argument) forces you to accept the conclusion also. The "force" here is obviously not physical force or moral force; it is the force of logic. If you accept the premises of a valid argument, the only way you can deny the conclusion is by contradicting what you have just accepted. So the "force" is one of impossibility: the impossibility of accepting the premises while denying the conclusion. Invalidity, then, is just the opposite:

Force of logic

> An argument is invalid if it is possible to accept the premises while *not* accepting the conclusion.

Definition of invalidity

The methods for proving an argument to be invalid revolve around your showing just *how* you *can* accept the premises and *not* accept the conclusion.

Here are two such methods, and afterward there are some examples using them.

First, the "scenario method." You test an argument by imagining a picture of the scene in which all the premises are accepted, and then you try to think of some way of not accepting the conclusion. That is, you try to imagine a loophole that will give you a way out of accepting the conclusion while still accepting the premises. What you are looking for, then, is a *counterexample* to the validity of the argument. The counterexample doesn't have to be a real-life one; it just has to be *imaginable*. Because a valid argument is one that rules out all alternatives to the conclusion — all loopholes, "ways out," counterexamples — as *impossible,* your ability to imagine a way out will prove the argument invalid.

The scenario method

In the scenario method, then, you say, "OK. Let's accept the premises. Suppose (for the sake of argument) that they are true: Isn't there *some* way I can get out of the conclusion?"

If you can't find a way out, it doesn't follow that the argument is valid. It may be that you haven't been inventive enough. But if you *do* find a way out, then you have shown that the argument *is* invalid. And that way out is exactly *where* it is invalid. And that, also, is exactly where a missing premise will be needed.

Second, the underlining method. This is essentially the same as the one used in constructing arguments. Underline the component parts of the conclusion that are covered by each of the premises. Then, any component parts that are left *un*covered have not been proved. Hence the conclusion as a whole will not follow logically from the stated premises, and the argument will not be valid. This method also will

The underlining method

tell you *where* the argument fails to be valid: in those component parts of the conclusion that are not covered. And it is precisely those parts, finally, that you will have to cover when you fill in the missing premises.

Underlining method schematized

This method needs a little more elaboration and detail before we go through some examples:

Take each premise and underline the component part of the conclusion it covers.

In general, a premise covers a part of the conclusion by using the same words or words that mean the same thing.

More than one premise may cover the same part (the arguer will then be giving more than one reason for that part).

It does not hurt the validity that some premises may not cover any part of the conclusion. (They may be on a higher level in the logical arrangement and not support the conclusion directly, or they may serve merely as links between premises, or — at worst — they may simply be irrelevant.)

Pay special attention to the important words in the conclusion (nouns and verbs mostly; watch especially for the word "should").

If at the end there is any component part that is not underlined, the argument is invalid (and you will know what the missing premise will have to cover).

Connecting

Once you have determined that an argument is invalid, you have to formulate the missing premises needed to make it valid. The missing premises must rule out all counterexamples to the reasoning. They fill in all the loopholes or gaps in the argument by "connecting" the stated premises to the conclusion.

You are already used to the idea of "connecting" premises because it was so important when constructing your own valid arguments. It is important in the same way when filling in missing premises. Both determining validity and the technique of connecting can be illustrated by some examples.

Let's analyze the following arguments about whether capital punishment should be the legal punishment for certain serious crimes. (The arguments are already broken down into premises and conclusions.) First we will analyze them for validity by the scenario and the underlining methods. Then we will fill in the missing premises and see how that remedies invalidity.

Analyzing Some Examples

1.   PREMISE 1.   Serious crimes should be punished with the most
          severe punishment possible.

   ∴ CONCLUSION 1.   Capital punishment should be the legal
          punishment for certain serious crimes.

Scenario method   This will show that the argument is invalid. Imagine
that the premise is true (its actual truth is irrelevant at this stage of the
analysis). You can still imagine the conclusion to be false by imagining
that *torture* is the most severe form of punishment. Then the conclusion would be that capital punishment should *not* be the legal punishment: Torture should. The statement that torture is the most severe
form of punishment is a counterexample to the reasoning of the
argument because it will allow the premise to be accepted and the
conclusion to be denied. The counterexample shows the argument is
invalid.

Underlining method   This method shows even more easily that the
argument is invalid. The premise covers only this part of the conclusion:

   ∴ CONCLUSION 1.   Capital punishment <u>should be the legal
          punishment for certain serious crimes</u>.

Nothing in the premise covers <u>capital punishment</u> at all! So it clearly is
not valid. Why should *capital punishment* (in contrast to other possible
punishments) be the legal punishment? Nothing in the premise tells
you.

Missing premises   The missing premise in the argument is

   PREMISE 2 (missing).   Capital punishment is the most severe
          punishment possible.

Premise 2 may not be true (that is step 5), but the point is that it is
needed to make the argument valid. Premise 1 says that the punishment for serious crimes should be of a particular, unique kind — the
most severe possible — and the added premise 2 says that capital
punishment fits that particular, unique kind. It follows, therefore,
that capital punishment should be the punishment for such crimes.
Thus premise 2 connects premise 1 to the conclusion by linking
premise 1's "most severe punishment possible" to conclusion 1's
"capital punishment."
   Because the filled in argument is now valid, there will be no
counterexamples to its validity. If we accept premise 1 *and* premise 2,
we will not be able to avoid accepting the conclusion. The counterexample to the original argument isn't one any longer. Premise 2 says

specifically that capital punishment is the most severe, so it rules out torture as a counterexample. This is not an accident, of course: Missing premises are *designed* to rule out counterexamples. It accomplishes this because the two premises cover both component parts of the conclusion:

> <u>Capital punishment</u> should be the <u>legal punishment for certain serious crimes</u>.

2.   PREMISE 1.   Capital punishment is a deterrent.

   ∴ CONCLUSION 1.   Capital punishment should be the legal punishment for certain serious crimes.

(Paraphrase of the premise: Having capital punishment would cause at least some people not to commit crimes they otherwise would.)

Scenario method   Imagine that you live in Sodom or Gomorrah, and that the people there *want* crimes to be committed. They might very well believe the premise, that capital punishment deters crime, but they might use this as a reason for *denying* the conclusion. Because they could accept the premise and yet deny the conclusion, the argument is invalid. (Notice that the counterexample here is not so plausible: People usually do not want crimes to be committed. Actually this does not hurt because the counterexample is *possible,* and so it shows that the argument is invalid. Besides, by exercising your imagination, you can probably transform this counterexample into a more plausible one.)

Underlining method   The argument is shown to be obviously invalid by that method. All the premise covers is the underlined part:

   ∴ CONCLUSION 1.   <u>Capital punishment</u> should be the legal punishment for certain serious crimes.

Nothing in the premises covers what should be the legal punishment.

Missing premises   The missing premise in the argument is

> PREMISE 2 (missing).   Any punishment that deters people from committing serious crimes should be legal.

Premise 2 *connects* premise 1 ("a deterrent") to conclusion 1 ("should be the legal punishment"), so that it leaves no possible way out between them. Our earlier counterexample is ruled out by it: If the people of Sodom or Gomorrah accept that capital punishment deters people from committing crimes and that any punishment doing that should be legal (the key word is "should"), then it does not matter what other beliefs they have. They must accept, on pain of contradiction, that capital punishment should be legal. The argument is valid. To cement the issue we can note that both parts of the conclusion are covered:

<u>Capital punishment should be the legal punishment for certain serious crimes</u>.

Evaluation   Since this is one of the commonest arguments in favor of capital punishment, it is worthwhile jumping ahead to step 5 to notice how bad the argument is. Most of the controversy has centered around whether capital punishment really *is* a deterrent, that is, around premise 1. But premise 2 is clearly false. Many punishments that would be deterrents should *not* be legal: mutilation or extreme, lifelong torture, for example. The argument is unsound. Being a deterrent is not enough to show that a certain kind of punishment should be legal. People who want to argue for capital punishment along these lines will have to produce some *additional* grounds for saying that it should be legal. (A good exercise in reasoning is to try to think of reasons that would count in favor of capital punishment but not in favor of more severe punishments like extreme, lifelong torture.)

3.   PREMISE 1.   Murder is the premeditated killing of a human being.

   PREMISE 2.   Capital punishment is the planned killing of a human being.

   PREMISE 3.   Murder is not legal.

   ∴ CONCLUSION 1.   Capital punishment should not be legal.

Underlining method   We can try the underlining method first this time. Premise 1 is puzzling initially because it does not seem to cover anything in the conclusion. Premise 2 covers "<u>capital punishment</u>"; premise 3 covers "<u>not be legal</u>" because it says murder <u>is not legal</u>. Premise 3 also helps show why premise 1 does not cover anything in the conclusion; premise 1 tries to define the word "murder" as it is used in the argument. None of the premises covers the word "should" in the conclusion: Premises 1 and 2 together tell you that capital punishment is a form of murder, and premise 3 tells you that murder is not legal; but nothing tells you that capital punishment <u>should</u> not be legal. The argument is invalid.

Scenario method   It gives the same results. Imagine a society that holds all three premises. Try to imagine some attitude that would allow them to deny the conclusion. Suppose they enjoy public executions: They could agree with the first two premises and also that murder *is not* legal (premise 3), but they could still maintain that public capital punishment *should* be legal. The argument is invalid.

Missing Premises

   PREMISE 4 (missing).   Murder should not be legal.

Premise 4 covers the "should" that the stated premises omitted; it also connects both premise 1 and premise 2 to the conclusion. So it makes the argument valid. In addition, it probably represents how the arguer actually arrived at the conclusion from the stated premises. It rules out the original counterexample nicely. Even if people enjoy public executions, as long as they accept that capital punishment is premeditated killing, that premeditated killing is murder, and that murder *should not* be legal, they will also have to accept that capital punishment *should not* be legal either.

Evaluation   Here again it is worthwhile to anticipate step 5 because the argument is another common one that is nevertheless unsound. In fact, it completely evades the point. Premise 1 is false: Murder is not just any premeditated killing; when police kill a sniper, it is premeditated, but it is not murder; killing an attacking enemy soldier may be carefully planned, but that does not make it murder either. Murder is more accurately defined as the "*unjustified* premeditated killing of a human being." To prove the conclusion, the arguer will have to address the question of whether capital punishment *is justified* directly. But that is what the arguer should have been proving in the first place. The stated argument evades the issue.

4.   PREMISE 1.   Punishment should be an attempt to rehabilitate the offender.

   PREMISE 2.   Capital punishment does not attempt to rehabilitate the offender.

   ∴ CONCLUSION 1.   Capital punishment should not be a legal punishment.

Scenario method   I can't imagine a way to accept the premises and deny the conclusion. Even in Sodom and Gomorrah, if the people accept that punishment should be an attempt to rehabilitate and that capital punishment does not attempt this (the premises), they would have to admit that it should not be the legal punishment (the conclusion). Even if they enjoy public executions, they would have to accept the conclusion as long as they accept the premises. Similarly, torture, the counterexample to the first argument, is not a counterexample here: it is irrelevant. In short, I can't find a counterexample to the argument. Of course, this doesn't show the argument to be valid. Maybe I'm just not being clever enough.

Underlining method   This method shows why I couldn't imagine a counterexample: The argument is *valid*. Premise 1 covers

   Capital punishment <u>should</u> not <u>be a legal punishment</u>

because it tells what conditions <u>a</u> (<u>legal</u>) <u>punishment</u> should fulfill, namely, rehabilitation. Premise 2 covers

<u>Capital punishment</u> should <u>not</u> be a legal punishment

because it says that <u>capital punishment</u> does <u>not</u> fulfill those conditions. So all component parts of the conclusion are covered, and the premises "connect" by means of "rehabilitation." No missing premises are needed.

5.   PREMISE 1.   It is essential for society to have legal punishments that demonstrate its disapproval of certain serious crimes.

   PREMISE 2.   Capital punishment demonstrates society's disapproval of certain serious crimes with a lasting example.

∴ CONCLUSION 1.   Capital punishment should be the legal punishment for certain serious crimes.

Underlining method   The argument may seem by this method to be valid. Premise 1 tells under what conditions something <u>should be</u> ("it is essential . . .") <u>the legal punishment for certain serious crimes</u>, and premise 2 says that <u>capital punishment</u> does fulfill those conditions. So the argument may look valid, but it is not.

Scenario method   This method shows that it is not valid because we can imagine a counterexample. Think of life imprisonment. A person might think that it is essential for society to demonstrate its disapproval (premise 1) and think that capital punishment does this (premise 2), but he or she might think that life imprisonment does it just as well. Therefore, capital punishment should not be the legal punishment (denying the conclusion); life imprisonment should. Nothing in the argument gives you a reason to choose capital punishment over different methods of demonstrating society's disapproval.

Underlining method revisited   What went wrong with this method the first time is that premise 2 does not really cover <u>capital punishment</u> in the sense intended. Here it means that capital punishment, <u>in contrast to other inconsistent methods</u>, should be the legal punishment. Premise 2 does not give any reason for singling out capital punishment, so the arguer has not proved that <u>capital punishment</u> should be the legal punishment. This example shows that you cannot use the underlining method mechanically. You always have to think clearly about what the conclusion really means, what the arguer has to prove, and whether the premises actually cover the component parts of *that*.

Missing premises   The missing premise has to single out capital punishment and rule out other inconsistent possibilities. Unfortunately, the argument does not give us any clue about why the arguer favors capital punishment over these other methods. The only missing premise that will make the argument valid, then, is one that says something both vague and superlative:

PREMISE 3 (missing). Capital punishment is the *best* lasting example for society to use to demonstrate its disapproval for certain serious crimes.

We need a missing premise this vague because we have no clue what (if anything) the arguer has in mind, and we need something this superlative ("the best") because we have to rule out the other methods besides capital punishment.

Evaluation   Premise 3 connects the stated premises to the conclusion, but it also shows clearly how empty the argument is. Premise 3 (the premise the arguer *did not* mention) is nearly the same as the *conclusion* he or she was trying to prove in the first place. The stated premises hardly matter: Nearly everyone, whether for or against capital punishment, would agree with them.

You can see from the above how filling in the missing premises of an argument is so valuable. In this case, it shows that this argument for the conclusion is hardly an "argument" at all. The stated argument gives you almost no reason to believe the conclusion. The arguer has simply sidestepped the issue and *assumed* (in the missing premise) what he or she was supposed to be arguing for.

In each of these examples the filled in premises make an invalid argument valid by connecting what the stated premises say to what the conclusion says. The basic job of missing premises is this "connecting." *Missing premises are not the same as assumptions* Thus it is important not to confuse the missing premises of an argument with the "assumptions" of the argument. All missing premises are assumptions, but not all assumptions are missing premises. Missing premises are assumptions in that they state outright what the arguer *assumed* in reasoning from the premises to the conclusion. But many assumptions are not missing premises at all. For example, it is probably an assumption of all the arguments about capital punishment that human beings need some legal system, but that is not a missing premise in any of them. Similarly, all the arguments for the legalization of marijuana undoubtedly involve the assumption that marijuana is presently *il*legal, but again that is not a missing premise in any of them. Actually, any argument will have thousands of assumptions — all these arguments, for example, assume that humans exist, that marijuana exists, that people can be killed, and so forth. The only assumptions that have to be written out, however, are those the arguer *needs* to get from the stated premises to the conclusion.

How Many Missing Premises Should There Be?

The only general answer is, "as few as reasonably possible." A danger in filling in missing premises is that once you see that there is a gap between premises and conclusion, you will try filling it in piecemeal. It is easy to get yourself into a position in which you have so many missing premises that you end up lost, trying to create your own argument, instead of merely filling in the missing parts of the arguer's.

Suppose someone says,

> Of course tourists aren't being exploited at Disney World. They have a good time there, don't they?

The argument has a single premise and conclusion:

PREMISE 1.   Tourists have a good time at Disney World.

∴ CONCLUSION 1.   They are not being exploited.

It is immediately clear that the argument is invalid. You might be led into giving too many missing premises by going through a series of thought processes. Nothing in premise 1 covers the idea of exploitation, so you might begin:

PREMISE 2 (missing).   You are exploited when someone takes advantage of you.

But this does not connect to "have a good time" in premise 1. So, you might add:

PREMISE 3 (missing).   If you are having a good time, you are spending your money willingly.

But you still haven't linked this willingness to the rest of the argument. So you can now add:

PREMISE 4 (missing).   If you are spending your money willingly, then you are not being taken advantage of.

Adding these three premises does make the argument valid, but it is far too complicated. The logical connections in the argument travel from premise 1 to premise 3, then to premise 4, then to premise 2, then to the conclusion.

A better approach is to use a single missing premise:

PREMISE 5 (missing).   When tourists are having a good time, they are not being exploited.

This premise may not be true, of course, but it connects premise 1 to conclusion 1 in a direct, simple way and rules out any counterexamples at one stroke.

Finding one or two well-phrased, comprehensible missing premises to make the argument valid and cover a whole host of counterexamples (some of which haven't even occurred to you) is one of the things that makes step 4 so difficult to do well.

How General Should the Missing Premises Be?

This is a difficult aspect of filling in missing premises. It can be illustrated best by an example:

American labor unions contribute heavily to the economic decline of this country. Therefore, we should find some way of seriously limiting the power of unions.

The first sentence is the premise; the second is the conclusion. The argument is invalid: The fact that labor unions do something cannot by itself show that <u>we should</u> limit their power. A missing premise is needed to link the idea of contributing to economic decline (premise 1) with the need to limit power (conclusion 1). This missing premise can be formulated in at least three ways:

PREMISE 2 (missing).   We should seriously limit the power of anything that contributes heavily to our economic decline.

PREMISE 3 (missing).   We should seriously limit the power of any American organization that contributes heavily to our economic decline.

PREMISE 4 (missing).   If American labor unions contribute heavily to our economic decline, we should seriously limit their power.

*Three levels
of generality*   These three ways of writing the missing premise portray three levels of generality. Premise 2 is the most general: It makes a statement about *anything* that contributes to our economic decline. Premise 3 is less general: It too talks about things that contribute to our economic decline, but it is restricted to things that fit the particular topic of this specific argument; namely, to *American organizations* that so contribute. Premise 4 is hardly general at all: It does not talk about any *kind* of thing, but it is limited entirely to *American labor unions*.

Yet each of these missing premises will make the argument valid and thus rule out all counterexamples. Each connects premise 1 to conclusion 1. Which of the three you should choose as the missing premise is an important question: first because these three levels of generality are possible in almost any argument, and second because in many cases the soundness of the argument will hinge exactly on which level is chosen.

Yet answering it is hard. There is something reasonable to be said in favor of each, and so we cannot make a blanket statement that one level of generality will always be the correct one.

In favor of premise 2 is that it states a principle that the arguer would probably cite as the basis of the reasoning: If something contributes to our economic decline, it should be limited.

In favor of premise 3 is that it also represents a principle that the arguer almost certainly holds and that underlies the reasoning in the argument. It is not as basic a principle as premise 2, however.

In favor of premise 4 is that it does not go beyond what the arguer is already committed to. Premises 2 and 3 do: They attribute something to the arguer that goes beyond the actual argument, and so a degree of doubt enters about whether these premises accurately represent the arguer's thought. That is not so for premise 4. It attributes to the arguer nothing he or she is not already committed to by what has been said.

Premise 4 is the *minimal* missing premise in that it says the minimum necessary to get from the premises to the conclusion. Premise 2 is the *maximal* missing premise in that it states the principle behind the reasoning in its most general, its *maximal,* form. In this argument, and indeed in most arguments, the correct choice lies *between* the maximal and minimal forms.

Minimal vs. maximal premises

There is something wrong about choosing premise 2 or premise 4. Premise 2 reads more into the argument than premise 3 does, and we cannot be reasonably certain the arguer holds a position as general as premise 2. It is one thing to say that *American organizations* that contribute to our economic decline should be limited (as premise 3 says), but it is much more doubtful to say that *anything* that contributes to our economic decline should be limited (as premise 2 says). Premise 2 means that if the Organization of Petroleum Exporting Countries (OPEC) or the poverty programs contribute heavily to our economic decline, they should be seriously limited. That is an extreme view: It might require a war in the Middle East and starvation in America. Premise 3 is much more reasonable: It says only that certain American organizations should be limited. OPEC, even if it does contribute to our economic decline, is an international organization, and we may have no right to limit its power; poverty programs may be a *necessary* drain on our national economy. In any event, the discussion of them lies beyond the scope of premise 3, and that is as it should be.

Maximal premises say too much

Premise 3 is also a better choice than the minimal premise 4, which says too little. True, it "connects" the stated premises to the conclusion, but it does this only by repeating what the premise says and then repeating what the conclusion says. If we were doing symbolic logic, a minimal premise like premise 4 might be the correct choice; but it is not the correct choice in practical reasoning. It does not make clear the reasoning that would lead an arguer to assert the conclusion on the basis of the premise. Premise 4 merely repeats; it does not illuminate anything. It does not tell you *how* the arguer went *from* the allegation that labor unions contribute heavily to our economic decline *to* the conclusion that they should be limited. Premise 3 does illuminate the reasoning behind the argument: It spells out the general principle that led the arguer from that premise to that conclusion. *Why* should labor unions be limited? Because *any* American organization that hurts America's economy should be limited, and labor unions do that.

Minimal premises say too little

The answer then is to formulate missing premises so that they fall between the maximal and the minimal:

The missing premise should be a *general* statement, but one that is built on the specific topics mentioned in the argument.

Generality of missing premises

Missing Premises for Different Logical Arrangements

Missing premises are filled in to make the argument valid. They do this by connecting what the stated premises say to what the conclusion says. Formulating the missing premises in such a way as to make the connection correctly depends heavily on the kind of logical arrangement the argument has, vertical or horizontal.

Vertical arguments   Arguments with purely vertical arrangements are usually much easier to handle. It is easier both to locate what the missing premise has to cover and to formulate the missing premise well. The reason is simple. In an argument with a purely vertical arrangement, one single statement supports another single statement, which in turn supports another single statement, and so forth, until the conclusion is reached. Diagramed we have:

So at each stage where a missing premise is needed, it has to connect only one statement to one other statement. In this diagram there are two subarguments: one from premise 1 to premise 2, and another from premise 2 to conclusion 1. Thus each stage considered by itself will be an argument of the simplest form, with a single premise and, in effect, a single conclusion drawn from that premise.

If the individual subargument is invalid, typically, three things will happen: The stated premise will cover only part of the conclusion. It will say something additional — call it X — about that covered part. And it will leave another part of the conclusion uncovered. In this typical case the missing premise is usually easy to formulate in a single statement. The missing premise will consist of a statement linking X to the uncovered part of the conclusion.

How to formulate the missing premise

If this is done carefully, the subargument will be made valid. If you do this with each subargument, the whole argument will be made valid. So, in effect, a vertical argument is just a series of the simplest kind of argument, each of which is easy to make valid.

Horizontal arguments   Formulating missing premises for horizontal arguments is more difficult. Depending on the number of premises, an argument with a horizontal arrangement will typically look like this:

PREMISE 1   +   PREMISE 2   +   PREMISE 3   +   PREMISE 4

CONCLUSION 1

Assuming for the moment that none of the premises is simply irrelevant, each of them will contribute something to the argument, either by covering a part of the conclusion, by linking the other premises together, or by some other means. In any case each of them, in conjunction with the others, supports the conclusion.

If the horizontal argument is invalid, the missing premises will in some way have to link *the whole set* of stated premises to the conclusion. Phrasing these is often hard. You cannot link each stated premise separately to the conclusion because that would turn the arguer's single argument into four smaller (and probably weaker) arguments. You have to hold a number of distinct statements in your mind and piece together how the arguer could reason *from* them *to* the conclusion. Then you have to formulate this reasoning in understandable statements. These are the missing premises.

Linking the whole set of premises to the conclusion

Unfortunately, there are no general steps for doing this because different horizontal arguments can work in such different ways. Each argument has to be done on its own, and you have to figure out how to connect that particular batch of premises to the conclusion in such a way as to make the argument valid.

Sometimes the missing premise can be formulated simply by explicitly mentioning something from each of the stated premises. If, for example, an argument in favor of capital punishment says, in four premises, that capital punishment is relatively painless (premise 1), permanent (premise 2), a deterrent to others (premise 3), and relatively inexpensive (premise 4), the argument as it stands is clearly not valid. We have to add one premise that says, "For certain serious crimes we need a relatively cheap and painless, permanent punishment that will deter others from committing the same crime" (premise 5, missing), and another premise that says, "No other punishment has all four of those characteristics" (premise 6, missing).

How to formulate the missing premises: one case, mentioning each of the stated premises

In this type of argument all the premises are parallel, each covers the same part of the conclusion, and each mentions a different characteristic of that part. The missing premises then link all those characteristics to the part of the conclusion that is not covered. This type of argument occurs fairly frequently.

It is by no means, however, the only type of horizontal argument. In another frequent kind of case the stated premises "link together" in a train of reasoning, so that the missing premises need to mention *explicitly* only what one or two of them say. The rest will already be connected or will be connected implicitly. Argument 3 against capital punishment is an example of this. The first premise says that murder is the premeditated killing of a human being. Premise 2 says that

How to formulate the missing premises: a second case, filling in the missing link

capital punishment is the planned killing of a human being; thus premise 2 links the "murder" in premise 1 to "capital punishment." All we need to complete the argument, then, is to fill in the missing link, a premise that connects "murder" to the "should not be legal" of the conclusion. And that is the missing premise:

Murder should not be legal.

It links both premises to the conclusion, even though it mentions explicitly only something from premise 1 ("murder") and something from the conclusion ("should not be legal"). But premise 2 is connected to the conclusion implicitly. Without it the argument would not be valid. The arguer has reasoned *from* premise 1, *through* premise 2, then *through* the missing premise, *to* the conclusion.

A third kind of case is similar. It occurs when the premises, by linking together, cover most but not all of the conclusion. Here the trick is to come up with a missing premise that covers that part and connects it to the appropriate stated premise. (You can tell which is appropriate only by inspecting the individual argument being analyzed.) Consider this one (the premises are numbered; the last sentence is the conclusion):

How to fill in the missing premises: a third case, covering the uncovered part

(*1*) Bums, hobos, derelicts, and people like that contribute nothing to society. (**2**) They beg money on the streets; (**3**) they sleep in doorways; (**4**) they are drunk in public. (**5**) People who are of no use to society should not be allowed to do this. There should be some law to prevent them from disturbing people.

The logical arrangement of this argument is purely horizontal:

PREMISE 1 + PREMISE 2 + PREMISE 3 + PREMISE 4 + PREMISE 5

CONCLUSION 1

And the argument is nearly valid. We can draw lines around the component part of the conclusion covered by each premise:

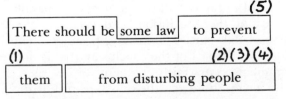

Premise 1 tells what bums, hobos, and derelicts are like; premise 5 says that people like that should be prevented from disturbing others; and premises 2, 3, and 4 show how bums, hobos, and derelicts *do* disturb others. The only uncovered part of the conclusion is "<u>some law</u>." The missing premise, then, must link "some law" with an appropriate stated premise. Here that is premise 5. The missing premise is:

> PREMISE 6 (missing).   This prevention should be by law.

Because of the already existing links among the stated premises, there is no need for the missing premise to mention anything from premises 1, 2, 3, or 4. All it must do is close the last gap between premise 5 and the conclusion.

These are three frequent ways horizontal arguments fit together. There are other ways as well (thus you might need to fill in a missing link *and* cover an uncovered part of the conclusion). And paying attention to these ways will often help you formulate clear, comprehensible missing premises. But no amount of schematizing or general descriptions of cases can replace careful, intelligent reasoning about what that particular horizontal argument needs to make it valid. In practice you have to see clearly what the stated premises say, taken all together; how they fit together to say it; and what in the conclusion they leave uncovered. Then you have to determine how that uncovered part can best be covered by missing premises.

Careful, intelligent reasoning is needed

Complex arguments   A great many arguments are neither purely vertical nor purely horizontal, but more complex. You might naturally think that it would be appreciably more difficult to fill in missing premises in long, complex arguments, and in a way it is. Long arguments consisting of many interrelated subarguments require *more* missing premises to be made valid.

But that's really the only sense in which it is harder to find missing premises for complex arguments than for purely vertical or horizontal arguments. What *is* hard for complex arguments is figuring out the logical arrangement of premises and conclusions. Once that is done, filling in the missing premises is not any harder. Diagraming the logical arrangement *simplifies* complex arguments: It breaks the long argument down into a series of smaller subarguments, and each of those subarguments is either purely vertical or purely horizontal. So if you become good at filling in missing premises in purely vertical and purely horizontal arguments, you will automatically be good at filling in missing premises in complex arguments as well. It's the same task.

Logical arrangement simplifies complex arguments

Suppose you have an argument with a complex arrangement like this:

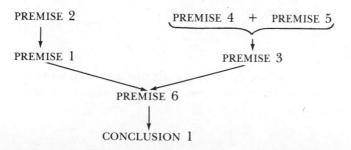

This *is* a complex argument, but it *looks* more complex than it is. By inspecting it, you can see that it breaks down into four subarguments, two of them vertical and two of them horizontal:

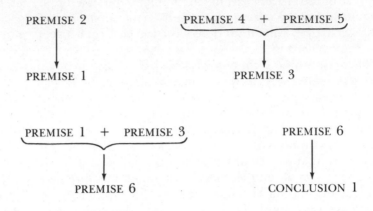

When missing premises are needed

In general, the logical arrangement (plus some careful thought) tells you where missing premises are needed:

> Missing premises are needed in every invalid, important subargument.

In this abstract example there are four subarguments. To find out where you need missing premises, you examine each subargument to find out if it is valid. If it is, no missing premises are needed there. If it is invalid, you examine it to see if it is an *important* part of the argument. If it is just a side issue, for instance, or if the premise is merely an example of something, the subargument will not need a missing premise. But any premises contributing something important toward establishing the conclusion should be part of a valid argument. So if the subargument is not valid already, you will have to add missing premises to make it valid.

Some subarguments are not important

In each subargument, whether it is vertical or horizontal, you will formulate the missing premise in the way you would if that were the whole argument you were analyzing. Doing this for each of the subarguments that needs it will make each of them valid, and that will make the argument as a whole valid. It will only remain then to evaluate the premises. If they are all true, the argument is sound and has proved its conclusion.

Problems

Problems 1–4 consist of invalid arguments (already broken down into premises and conclusions) followed by several sets of possible missing premises. Choose the best set. Justify your answer.

1. Said by someone buying liquor:

> PREMISE 1.　Alcohol is alcohol.

∴ CONCLUSION 1.　It is not going to make any difference whether you buy Chivas Regal or some cheaper scotch for the party.

Which set of missing premises below is most appropriate?

Set 1
> PREMISE 2 (missing).　The alcohol in the cheaper scotch will get people just as drunk as the alcohol in Chivas Regal.
>
> PREMISE 3 (missing).　The point of buying liquor for a party is getting people drunk.

Set 2
> PREMISE 2 (missing).　The quality of a scotch depends entirely on its alcohol content.
>
> PREMISE 3 (missing).　You want the best quality scotch at the lowest price for the party.

2.　PREMISE 1.　Only God has the right to choose between life and death.

PREMISE 2.　When man chooses to make capital punishment legal, man goes against God's will.

∴ CONCLUSION 1.　Capital punishment should not be legal.

Which missing premise below is most appropriate?

PREMISE 4 (missing).　Any act that goes against God's will should not be legal.

PREMISE 5 (missing).　Any legalized punishment that goes against God's will should not be legal.

PREMISE 6 (missing).　If capital punishment goes against God's will, it should not be legal.

3. From the end of Marx and Engels's *Communist Manifesto:*

PREMISE 1.　The Communists' ends can be attained only by the forcible overthrow of all existing social conditions.

PREMISE 2.　The proletarians have nothing to lose but their chains.

PREMISE 3.　The proletarians have a world to win.

∴ CONCLUSION 1.　Workers of all countries should unite to overthrow the ruling classes.

Which set of missing premises below is most appropriate?

Set 1
> PREMISE 4 (missing).　The ruling classes cause the problems of the proletarians.
>
> PREMISE 5 (missing).　Overthrowing the ruling classes would help the proletarians.

Set 2 $\Bigg\{$ PREMISE 4 (missing).   If the proletarians have nothing to lose but their chains, and they can win a world, then they should unite to overthrow the ruling classes.

Set 3 $\Bigg\{$ PREMISE 4 (missing).   If you have everything to win by an action and nothing to lose, you should do that action.

PREMISE 5 (missing).   The proletarians can overthrow all existing social conditions only by uniting.

4.   PREMISE 1.   If inflation is 14 percent, a person who earns $1,000,000 will lose $140,000.

PREMISE 2.   Under the same conditions a person who earns $10,000 will lose only $1,400 to inflation.

∴ CONCLUSION 1.   The rich are hurt by inflation more than the poor are.

Which of the following missing premises is really needed in the argument?

PREMISE 3 (missing). $140,000 is a considerably greater amount than $1,400.

PREMISE 4 (missing).   The amount of hurt a person sustains by inflation is measured in the number of dollars lost.

PREMISE 5 (missing).   Someone who earns $1,000,000 is rich.

PREMISE 6 (missing).   Someone who earns $10,000 is poor.

For problems 5-7 use both the scenario and the underlining methods to show the arguments invalid. Then fill in the missing premises needed to make them valid.

5.   PREMISE 1.   If men were truly superior to women, there would be no need for the social controls or taboos that foster and protect men in a superior caste system.

PREMISE 2.   There are such social controls and taboos.

∴ CONCLUSION 1.   Men are not superior to women.

6.   PREMISE 1.   The loss of a few murderers is worth saving the lives of innocent people.

PREMISE 2.   The threat of capital punishment would deter some murders of innocent people.

PREMISE 3.   The laws should deter crime and work toward saving the lives of innocent people, as long as they do not inflict physically cruel suffering on the criminals.

PREMISE 4.   The victims of capital punishment do not suffer much physically when they are put to death.

∴ CONCLUSION 1.   Capital punishment should be a legal punishment for murder.

7.   PREMISE 1.   Promoting new ideas about sex roles tends to diminish the value placed on the traditional family.

∴ CONCLUSION 1.   Traditional ideas about sex roles should be encouraged.

8. In the first argument for capital punishment (p. 211), torture was a counterexample because nothing in the premise ruled out the possibility that torture was a more severe punishment than execution. Why can't we rule this out simply by stating in the missing premise:

   PREMISE 2 (missing).   Capital punishment is more severe than torture.

2. *Criticizing Arguments*

STEP 1.   Paraphrase.

STEP 2.   Write the argument in premises-and-conclusion form.

STEP 3.   Arrange the premises and conclusions in their logical order.

STEP 4.   Fill in the missing premises needed to make the argument valid.

STEP 5.   *Criticize the argument for validity and the premises for truth.*

Validity

Invalid arguments   Suppose you are in the process of analyzing an argument, you have just completed step 4, and you are ready to begin step 5. Is the argument valid?

The answer: *"Of course it is."*

In step 4 you *made it* valid by adding missing premises. You cannot very well criticize the argument for being invalid at this stage of the analysis. If it is not valid now, at step 5, it's *your* fault, not the arguer's.

Yet in some cases the criticism does make sense. Suppose Ethel and Judith are arguing angrily.

Judith says, "There's no real freedom for blacks or women in the United States."

Ethel replies, "There sure is. You should see what it's like in Russia. There's hardly any freedom at all there — for anybody."

Ethel is arguing:

   PREMISE 1.   There is hardly any freedom at all in Russia for anybody.

∴ CONCLUSION 1.   There is real freedom for blacks in the United States.

It would be clear at step 4 that the argument is invalid. But it is not *merely* invalid: It is invalid in a way that cannot be counteracted by missing premises that are even remotely plausible. We *could* make it valid by supplying these two premises:

> PREMISE 2 (missing).   Countries with more freedom than Russia have real freedom.

> PREMISE 3 (missing).   Blacks and women in the United States have more freedom than Russians.

But premise 2 is preposterous. It's wildly implausible. Ethel is maintaining that Russians have very little freedom, so having *more* freedom than the Russians have obviously doesn't mean you're really free.

Ethel's reason is actually irrelevant to the conclusion; that is shown by how obviously false premise 2 (missing) is. It is the *reasoning* from her premise to the conclusion that is bad. Even in the back of her mind she never supposed that premise 2, or anything like it, was true.

Invalidity as a justified criticism

If it is clear that it's the arguer's reasoning that is incorrect (rather than the truth of the missing premises), then you are justified in making a charge of invalidity as a major criticism.

Though the example may seem farfetched to you, it is a kind of argument that people untrained in reasoning frequently make. They often state "reasons" that have very little to do with what they are trying to prove:

> The bookstore charges too much for its books.
> How do you know?
> Every semester I'm broke from buying them.

> E. M. Forster was a great novelist.
> Nonsense. He was a homosexual.

> Cigarette smoking causes cancer.
> Oh, they say that about *everything*.

The arguments are invalid for very clear reasons, and in these cases that is a weighty criticism. It would be easy enough to come up with counterexamples to the reasoning. There is no need in addition to fill in missing premises.

Of course if pushed, you could. And the fact that the missing premises would be so implausible is proof of the argument's invalidity.

In most arguments, though, you will not end up after step 5 with a serious charge of invalidity. In step 4 you will have filled in the premises needed to make the argument valid, and you will be ready at step 5 to evaluate the premises for truth.

Truth

The general technique for evaluating premises for truth   You have arrived at this point at an analyzed, valid argument: with its meaning interpreted, maybe alternate readings given, broken down into premises and conclusions, its premises arranged in a logical order, and made valid by the addition of missing premises. All that remains is to judge, on the basis of reasons, whether the premises, given as well as filled in, are true or false. That's all that's left to evaluating the argument's soundness, to seeing whether it proves its conclusion.

The general technique is this. You begin your evaluation with those premises (stated or filled in) that come at the top of the logical arrangement of premises (step 3). Then you work your way down. Whenever you have a sound argument or subargument in the arrangement, you draw the appropriate conclusions (you do not have to evaluate the truth of them separately). Whenever you have unsupported statements or statements that are supported only by an unsound argument, you again evaluate the truth of *those* statements, and so on, until you reach the main conclusion.

The general technique in brief

Taking each premise, you interpret it fairly, examine it carefully, and sincerely try to figure out the best reasons you can for and against it. On the basis of these reasons you decide if it is true, if it is false, or if you simply cannot say.

The function of the logical arrangement of premises   You start with the premises at the top of the logical arrangement because the logic of the argument progresses *from* them, *through* the various subarguments, *down to* the conclusion.

Suppose you have an argument whose premises are arranged logically like this:

PREMISE 1

↓

PREMISE 3   PREMISE 2

CONCLUSION 1

When you fill in the missing premises, it will probably look like this:

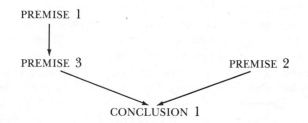

PREMISE 1   +   PREMISE 4
                  (missing)

↓

PREMISE 3   +   PREMISE 2   +   PREMISE 5
                                    (missing)

↓

CONCLUSION 1

You begin by evaluating premise 1. Is it true or false? Why? It is necessary, really, to think it out thoroughly and not just respond that it's true because, say, it's familiar. You should be able to give reasons, good reasons, to support your answer. (Suppose you have found that premise 1 is true.) You now examine premise 4 (missing) in the same way. Is *it* true or false? What *reasons* do you have for your answer?

Suppose you have found that both premises 1 and 4 (missing) are true. Because they are true, and because they constitute a *valid* argument for premise 3, you can conclude that premise 3 is true also. There is no need to evaluate premise 3 independently, and there is no requirement to give additional reasons to support premise 3. If you have found that premises 1 and 4 (missing) are true, then you *have to* accept premise 3 also. This subargument is sound — it proves its conclusion.

Now suppose instead that you have found that one of the premises in that subargument is false, say, premise 4 (missing). You still have a *valid* subargument from premises 1 and 4 (missing) to premise 3, but the subargument is *not sound.* So premise 3 has *not* been proved. It does not follow that premise 3 is false, of course; it follows only that the arguer has not proved it.

In this case you *do* need to evaluate premise 3 on its own grounds. Again, you search for reasons for it and against it and judge premise 3 to be true or false according to that evidence.

Suppose you find premise 3 to be true. What remains is to evaluate premises 2 and 5 (missing) to see if they are true also. (It doesn't matter which of these two you do first.) If you decide that each of them is true, then the conclusion has been proved. The subargument from premise 3, premise 5 (missing), and premise 2 to conclusion 1, you have just determined, is *sound.* You already knew it was valid (after step 4), and now you have found that its three premises are true. So the arguer has proved the conclusion.

Notice that it does not matter too much if something was wrong with premises 1 or 4 (missing). Even without them the arguer has proved the conclusion because premise 3, premise 5 (missing), and premise 2 are enough to prove the conclusion. Of course, in your final analysis you would want to note that the *reasons* the arguer had for believing premise 3 were wrong, and to that degree the argument suffers. Still, the main argument is sound, and that is the most important thing for proving the conclusion.

Judging truth   The preceding description of the general technique of step 5 has been abstract. The practical application, as usual, can be more complicated and less airtight. The most important practical issue is: How *do* you judge a premise to be true?

You judge premises on the basis of *reasons,* of evidence. If the reasons you have, on examination, support what the premise says, then you should judge the premise true; the more strongly they

support the premise the more certain you should be that it *is* true. If
the reasons you have, on examination, go *against* what the premise
says, then you should judge the premise to be false; again, the more
strongly the reasons go against the premise, the surer you will be that
the premise is false.

*Going
with the
evidence*

Sometimes (though by no means always) you will have some
reasons that support the premise and other reasons that go against
the premise. In such cases you still have to go with the evidence. If you
have better reasons for the premise than against it, you will give a
qualified and tentative judgment that it is true; if the reasons go more
against it than for it, you will give a qualified and tentative judgment
that it is false. In either case you will keep a healthy amount of doubt.

If the reasons for and against are about equal, then the most
reasonable judgment you can make is that *you don't know* whether the
premise is true or false. In such a case it would be unreasonable to
take a stand (especially a strong stand) that the premise is true or false.
The thing to do is to withhold judgment and be open to further
evidence on either side.

*I don't
know*

Notice that saying "I don't know" in that case is very different from
just saying "I don't know" from the beginning or because of simple
ignorance. Here you actually have reasons *why* "I don't know" is the
best answer: The evidence for and against balances out.

Ignorance, though, is also sometimes a good reason for saying "I
don't know." If the premise deals with issues that require specialized
or technical knowledge, then you may simply not know the answer.
For example, a popular book maintains that advertisers hide sexual
symbols in their advertisements so that we will not notice them
consciously but will be influenced unconsciously to buy their product.
Are people influenced by such subliminal cues? Probably, your honest
answer will be, "I don't know." You would probably give the same
answer if a premise said that people can be taught in their sleep or
that most asthma is psychosomatic. If the cases are important to you,
you will probably try to find out the answers by acquiring the
necessary knowledge.

Ignorance

Premises with multiple interpretations   Evaluating premises in practice is
also made a little more complicated when premises contain key words
or other expressions that you have found to be ambiguous. In such
cases you would have given (in step 1) more than one interpretation of
the expression. And that will mean that a premise containing the
expression will say quite different things, depending on which interpretation is under consideration.

This is not really much of a complication, though. It requires
simply that you evaluate such a premise more than once: one time for
each distinct interpretation you have given. Having specified which
meaning you are working with, you evaluate the premise in exactly
the same way you would if it contained no ambiguous words at all.

That is, you judge it to be true, or false, or uncertain, and give reasons to support your judgment. Then you evaluate the premise with the other meaning in mind.

We had many examples of this in earlier chapters. Often, giving different evaluations in this manner can be extremely important. Arthur Jensen wrote *Bias in Mental Testing* (New York: 1980), an 800-page book that argues that black children are, on the average, inferior genetically to white children in intelligence. One of the crucial premises in his argument is that IQ tests are unbiased, and Jensen gives a lot of statistical evidence to back up this claim. But Stephen Jay Gould in "Jensen's Last Stand" (*New York Review.* May 1, 1980. pp. 38–44) shows that the word "bias" is ambiguous in Jensen's argument: It has a technical sense and an ordinary sense. Roughly, a test will be "biased" in the technical sense when the same score has different meanings depending on which group earns the score; a test is "biased" in the ordinary sense when it is unfair (for example, because one group has an economic advantage over the others). Gould shows that the evidence supports Jensen only in the technical sense of "bias," not in the ordinary sense. So, given one meaning, Jensen's claim about bias is true; given the other, ordinary meaning, it is entirely unsupported. Unfortunately for Jensen, his thesis about intelligence hinges on showing that IQ tests are unbiased in the *ordinary,* not the technical, sense. Evaluating each interpretation separately, therefore, shows that Jensen's whole case falls apart.

Discovering truth   It bears repeating that in all these judgments — whether of truth, falsity, or some doubt in between — you always have to judge on the basis of *reasons.* A major part of reasoning is learning to back up your judgments with reasons. It is only slightly too strong to say that *whenever* you hear a claim, especially if it is at all important, you should ask yourself: "Is it true? What reasons are there for and against it?" And you should work to come up with reasons (plausible, relevant reasons) to support judgments and claims you make in response.

(It's shocking that a great many people don't even wonder if the statements they come across are true. Even when the statements are about things that affect their lives deeply (moral beliefs, customs, habits, institutions), people sometimes don't even question them. And when they do, it is still less usual for them to search actively for reasons for and against. The only time people do seem to feel obliged to come up with reasons is when it strikes them that a statement is false. For psychological reasons people feel more compelled to justify saying that a statement is false.)

Justification, giving reasons, is just as necessary when you think a statement is true. We saw in earlier chapters that merely questioning statements and searching for reasons can be truly enlightening.

Consider again the statement:

You should treat others as you would have them treat you.   *The golden rule*

Your tendency is just to accept it; it is something you hear all your life. If you criticize it at all, you criticize it as being too "idealistic" (a pretty weak criticism). If pressed for a reason in its favor, you are apt to say, "Well, if you want people to treat you a certain way, you should treat them that way" (which is just a rewording of the statement, not a reason for believing it).

But if you really search for the reason for believing it, you will find that it is based on a very doubtful proposition. One of the few real reasons in favor of it is that, in general, people tend to treat you the way you treat them, and therefore you will be more likely to be treated nicely if you treat others nicely. That is a real reason in the sense that if true, it would be a convincing argument in favor of the golden rule. But *is* it true? Do people generally reciprocate actions? Does that really square with your experience? Doesn't it seem instead that there are some people who generally push others around and seldom get pushed around themselves, and that there are other people who keep being pushed and seldom push back? People in reality don't seem to reciprocate very much. If this reasoning seems at all accurate to you, the golden rule rests on pretty shaky grounds. Besides, if that is your reason for believing it, the golden rule is a *selfish* principle: Why do good deeds for others? So they will do good deeds for you.

Further, there are reasons that might make you think that the golden rule is not just doubtful, but *false*. For example, the golden rule can be (and sometimes has been) used to justify atrocities. A sincere Inquisitor who thinks he should be burned at the stake if he were a heretic could use the golden rule to justify burning others at the stake; that is the way he would have others treat him if *he* were a heretic. (The same kind of justification was given appropriately by Nazis who believed sincerely that Jews should be exterminated.) Notice that the golden rule does not say, "You should treat other people well." *That* would be a generous principle. But how is what you *want* relevant to how you *should* treat people? Aren't there numerous things you might want others to do unto you (writing a term paper for you or helping you commit a successful crime) that you *should not* do unto them. Considered carefully, the golden rule often seems to go *against* morality.

That conclusion is staggering to someone who just takes the principle for granted. The golden rule rests on a highly doubtful belief that people *do* in fact treat you the way you treat them. It is selfish rather than generous, justifies many atrocities, and often seems to go against what is morally right. Even if you do not agree with the reasons given, they should be confronted, thought out, and justified by giving reasons back.

Take another example. Chapter Two contained a construction of   *Owning life insurance* the argument: "The head of a family should own life insurance." Did you then try honestly to figure out first if it was true? Clearly, you should have. Many people spend their money on life insurance, however, without giving the matter much thought. But a sober examination tends to show that most heads of families should not own life insurance. One good reason against it is inflation. You pay with today's dollars, but you will be paid back with tomorrow's dollars, which will probably be worth quite a bit less. If you are thirty years old and have contracted to get back $2000 for burial expenses when you die, chances are that that amount of money will not cover a tenth of the cost of a funeral by the time you die. But even without inflation, life insurance does not seem a good investment. There are many confusing varieties of life insurance, but think of the basic plan as a pure business transaction. Rates are computed first by guessing at what age you will die, and second by tabulating how much profit they will make on the amount of money you have paid them, given that you die when they think you will. If you die earlier than that, they will lose money on you. If you die on or after that date, they make an increasing profit on you. That profit comes out of the money *you* could have made by investing in something else. Thus it is like a bet: They are betting you will die at a certain age or older. What are *you* betting?

Now in spite of the way that may make you feel, life insurance will still be a good investment if you *do* die young. So one important piece of information you need before investing is the age when you are likely to die. Of course you don't *know* when you are going to die. Still, you could make a reasonable guess by checking the statistics on the ages at which various kinds of people (people with your background, in your part of the country, of your occupation, and so forth) on the average do die. But the trouble is that those are the statistics the insurance company has already used to figure out the age at which you are likely to die. *They* know when you are likely to die; *you* don't. So unless you have some inside information about your own bad health or hereditary diseases to which you are susceptible (or unless someone else will pay a good part of the premiums for you), life insurance will probably be a bad bet.

You should have seen this earlier when trying to build an argument *in favor of* life insurance. Essentially, you needed three premises:

PREMISE 1.   The head of a family should provide certain things for his or her family after death.

PREMISE 2.   Life insurance provides those things.

PREMISE 3.   Life insurance is the best (or at least a very good) method for providing those things.

But to evaluate premise 3, you really have to *compare* life insurance with other methods, i.e., savings accounts, treasury certificates, gold. Otherwise you have not really examined whether premise 3 is true or not. And you only need to make a few actual comparisons to find that there are a number of better ways to invest than life insurance.

To discover what is wrong with statements like the golden rule or "The head of a family should own life insurance," it is necessary to inspect them closely. That is a surprisingly hard thing to learn to do. It means not giving an automatic verdict, not being swayed excessively by your immediate reaction or by the reactions of others. It means *noticing* that there is something that needs to be figured out.

The next thing is to take the statement squarely and try to figure out on your own if it is true. It is important to take the statement squarely in its central sense. With most general statements it is usually not a very deep or fatal criticism to find a few exceptions. If someone says, "You should always give a person the benefit of the doubt," it wouldn't be much of a criticism to bring up picking up hitchhikers near the penitentiary as a counterexample. That would be an off-center criticism. Hitchhikers near the penitentiary are simply an exception, and though they may be an objection to the letter of the statement, they are not an objection to its spirit. Exceptions may clue you in to broader reasons against the statement, but to evaluate the statement honestly you have to key in on its central issue. A central objection to giving people the benefit of the doubt is that it's more reasonable to make judgments about people on the basis of the *evidence* you have, even if some of it is not certain — so you *shouldn't* always (or even in general) give people the benefit of the doubt. *That's* the important part of the statement. If the central claim is wrong, there is no need to think up exceptions. If the central claim is right, then perhaps a little rephrasing is necessary to rule out the exceptions.

A few common mistakes   People sometimes make elementary mistakes when they talk about "truth" because they think the concept of truth is harder to understand than it actually is. *Judging* a particular statement to be true or false is often hard; it depends on the statement. A sound judgment often has to take into account a good deal of evidence. But the *concept* of truth is not a particularly hard concept to understand. In fact a good case can be made for saying that the concept is confusing because it is *so easy*.

People sometimes confuse truth with opinion, or with the agreement of the majority. Or they say that a statement is not true because it is a *value* judgment. Or they mix truth up with certainty and say you can't ever *tell* if something is true. Some of these contentions touch on complex philosophic issues, but as concrete, practical answers they are all based on confusions. And you can see this by reasoning about each a little.

Is truth opinion? No. You know that you have had opinions that have turned out to be wrong. Sometimes they were deeply held opinions. You don't always simply "change your mind"; you frequently *learn* (through school, more mature thinking, someone's telling you) that your opinions were false. When you were a child, you may have believed that there really was a Santa Claus and that he, not your parents, brought you presents. But it was not true; there isn't

Exceptions

Key in on central issue

Truth ≠ opinion

(and there wasn't then) any such person. It seemed to you that there was, and it may even seem to you now that the "idea" of Santa Claus did exist or that Santa Claus does exist "in a sense" or "for you." But these are really ways of admitting that there isn't really a Santa Claus (with people who really exist, you don't have to say they exist "for you").

Truth / agreement

Similarly, truth is not the same thing as what the majority agrees on. People have agreed on things that have turned out not to be true, and there are things that are true that people don't agree on. Before Galileo, nearly everyone would have agreed that heavy objects fall faster than light objects. It seemed like common sense; to many people it still seems so. But it isn't true. If you put a piece of iron in one jar and a feather in another and drop them both, you'll see that they both will hit the ground at the same time. Today people *disagree* about whether there is life on other planets. Still, in spite of their disagreement, either there is life out there or there isn't: One side or the other is right. Perhaps we will never find out *which*, but our finding out or not, our disagreeing or agreeing, doesn't have anything to do with whether or not there really *is* life out there. The truth of the matter doesn't depend on us, but on what the universe is like.

Truth and value judgments

Another confusion arises in the differences between "value judgments" and "factual judgments." It is important to pay attention to these differences. But it does not follow that value judgments are not true or false. We certainly act and talk *as if* our judgments about right or wrong were true or false. We often change our minds about moral issues on the basis of evidence: Children *learn* that torturing cats is not all right; you sometimes condemn people without a hearing, and then you realize that your condemnation was incorrect (false) when you find out the person's real motives. We are also as certain of some moral beliefs as we are of many factual beliefs: There is something wrong with burning down an orphanage to see the color of the flames. That's *obvious*. And, that judgment is much surer than the one concerning life on other planets. It may be a value judgment, but it is a true value judgment.

Even agreed-on value judgments are sometimes found to be incorrect. In ancient Israel it was thought to be *just* to punish a wrongdoer unto the seventh generation. It doesn't seem just, though, to punish a wrongdoer's children, grandchildren, great-grandchildren, all the way down to the great-great-great-great-grandchildren. That's punishing people for things they didn't do, and that seems clearly *unjust* by any reasonable standards of justice. That means that saying it *is* justice is false. Describing it as a value judgment does not get you out of deciding, on the basis of reasons, whether it is or is not just.

Being certain

The idea of certainty is another one that is confusing on its own and often becomes mixed up with truth. Certainty is a matter of degree, and the claim that certainty is impossible is only as good as the evidence backing it up. Though there are many statements we are not certain about, there are others we *do* seem to be certain about. You may be uncertain about what grade you are going to get in this course, but you probably *will be* certain once you have actually received it. Again, you may be uncertain whether or not there is life on other planets, but you *are* certain there is life on this one.

People sometimes talk about "absolute certainty," meaning certainty without *any* possibility of error, and they claim you cannot ever be absolutely certain that statements are true or false. (What about the claim itself, though?) That seems doubtful: You are not certain whether or not there is life on other planets, but you are certain — absolutely certain — that either there is or there isn't.

Absolute certainty

But even if it were so, what you need for reasoning is not "absolute certainty," but a reasonable judgment about what is true. And truth, as the preceding examples illustrate, is not the same thing as certainty. You recognize that you are fallible, and so you *should* leave open the possibility that even the statements you feel sure of *might* be wrong. But you should go with the evidence you have. The stronger the evidence, the more certain you'll be and the more entitled to say it's true.

Truth ≠ certainty

What is hard about truth is not the concept, but the application. The concept is simply that a statement is true if it describes the way things are and false if things are not the way it describes them as being. Applying truth, figuring out if things *are* indeed the way the statements describe them as being, is often very hard. Scientists sometimes work for years trying to figure out if a particular hypothesis is true or false. There are a lot of other statements about which we are just not in a position to tell, where we do not have enough evidence to make a reasonable judgment (for example, the full effects of chemotherapy on cancer, or whether Napoleon was planning an escape from St. Helena). But we do have enough evidence to make sound judgments about a lot of important statements (for example, that smoking cigarettes causes lung cancer and emphysema, that driving 55 rather than 70 mph saves lives and gas). And sometimes it is quite easy to judge a statement to be true (for example, that animals feel pain, or that genocide is wrong).

Judging truth

In all such cases, however, the method for judging truth is the same. You have to amass evidence (reasons), and then you have to make a judgment based on those reasons. It takes ingenuity to come up with relevant, plausible reasons, and it takes honesty to judge in accord with them.

Just as you do not want to fall into the error of thinking you do not know anything, so you do not want to fall into the opposite error of thinking you know everything. It is important not to hold statements dogmatically and be unwilling to change your mind. The reasonable approach is to make the best judgment you can in the light of the reasons you have, but then to leave the judgment open to revision if any new reasons come up. This is the reasonable approach because, after all, what you are trying to do is figure out what is true, not to win arguments or defeat your opponent.

What you believe   When people think about truth in the abstract for a long time or when they argue, they are tempted to *say* they believe something even when they don't, especially when the argument is heated. It also happens in reasoning and philosophy courses when people try to defend views they ordinarily would reject.

That is often healthy because it makes people question things that should be questioned. But it is self-defeating if it makes them come to the conclusion that they don't believe anything. People do believe many things, even if they can occasionally convince themselves that they don't.

Reasoning is a *practical* skill, and a good practical way of telling if you believe something is by observing how you *act* rather than what you say. You can get yourself to doubt that the sun will rise tomorrow morning, but if you are saving money for next semester's tuition, chances are you *do* believe it will rise. A method that may strike home even more forcefully is to see how much you are willing to *bet* on what you say. Maintaining that you don't know whether the sun will rise tomorrow will be shown for what it is: a bluff. Would you be willing to bet money against someone who says it *will*? Probably not, not even with heavy odds. And if you would be willing once, you certainly would not be a second time.

Keeping a perspective on criticizing   After you have finished step 5, there is literally nothing more to do in analyzing that argument. If you have paid careful attention to what was meant, if you have seen how the premises fit together logically to make a main argument and subsidiary, supporting arguments for the conclusion, if you have evaluated all the premises fairly, then you have discovered that the argument is either sound or unsound.

But it is difficult to be sure that you have done all this faithfully, so it is a good idea to step back from the argument and look at it as a whole. Above all you do not want anything to get in the way of figuring out what is true. You do not want to hold someone to the letter, and you do not want to dismiss a basically good argument for extraneous reasons. At the same time you want to have a clear insight into what the arguer is trying to prove and whether he or she succeeds.

Your training in *constructing* arguments ought to be particularly helpful here. Ask yourself, "How would I go about trying to prove this person's conclusion?" "What would be the hardest part to establish?" "How does the person's argument differ from the one I would give?" "Does this person's argument give insights into the conclusion? Does the person bring up reasons I never would have thought of?"

Putting yourself in the arguer's place should enable you to see the argument as a whole, its strongpoints and weakpoints, and its relation to other issues.

Problems

1. Fill in the missing premises of the three invalid arguments on page 228. Tell how the missing premise of each is false.

2. Give a quick evaluation of the argument: Human mother's milk causes tumors in laboratory animals. Don't breast-feed your baby.

3. Give a quick evaluation of this argument: Aquinas's arguments can't all be wrong or he wouldn't be so famous.

4. Does the criticism of life insurance — that it is usually a bad bet — apply also to automobile insurance or hospitalization insurance? In which ways are they similar and in which ways different?

5. "You can never be absolutely certain of any statement." Is that true? Give the best counterexample you can to it.

6. Consider the following explanation from Nigel Calder's geology textbook, *The Restless Earth:* (New York, 1972), p. 16:

> We can now specify the cause of the Thera volcano which is still active from time to time. Southern Greece, Crete and the Aegean Islands are riding on a small plate, a chip of the Earth's outer shell, which is travelling south-westwards towards Africa. It can do so only by overriding part of the floor of the Mediterranean, a deep oceanic basin. That ocean floor, and the African plate of which it is a part, is bent downwards, creating a pronounced trench of deeper water off the outer coast of Crete. The ocean floor is driven at a steep angle into the body of the Earth, where it is gradually destroyed. But, in the process, the enormous friction causes earthquakes and also generates heat that melts rocks and throws up volcanoes at some distance behind the trench.

Give the most reasonable answer you can to the following questions about the truth of Calder's premises. Give evidence to back up your judgment.

(a) Are Southern Greece, Crete, and the Aegean Islands actually traveling toward Africa?

(b) Southern Greece and the rest are built on solid rock. How is it possible for them to travel?

(c) Are some earthquakes caused by mere *friction*?

(d) Can friction produce enough heat to make a *volcano*?

7. Evaluate the truth of the premises (both stated and filled in) in the

argument from the last paragraph of *The Communist Manifesto* (question 3, p. 225).

3.   Checklist for Analyzing Arguments

Step 1.   Paraphrase.

  1. Restate the argument in different words.

   (a) Is there a special context?

   (b) Is there more than one plausible interpretation?

   (c) Are there strongly connotative words?

   (d) Are there problems of scope?

   (e) Do any of these function importantly in the argument?

  2. Check the paraphrase for accuracy.

   (a) Does it make the premises obviously true or obviously false?

   (b) Does it match the original?

Step 2.   Break the argument down into premises and conclusion.

  1. Determine if it is an argument. Is the arguer trying to prove anything by giving reasons?

  2. Identify the conclusion.

   (a) Is there a special context?

   (b) Is there more than one conclusion?

  3. Identify the premises. Consider each sentence that is not the main conclusion.

   (a) Is it being given as a reason or is it irrelevant?

   (b) Does it contain more than one independent claim?

   (c) Number the premises in the order of occurrence.

Step 3.   Arrange the premises and conclusion in their logical order.

  1. Draw arrows between a statement and what it supports to form subarguments.

   (a) Which premises are supported by other premises?

   (b) Which statements are unsupported?

   (c) Which premises most closely support the conclusion?

  2. Fit the subarguments together.

(a) Are all relevant premises included?

(b) Is the argument vertical, horizontal, or a mixture?

Step 4. *Fill in the missing premises needed to make the argument valid.*

1. Determine the validity of each important subargument.

   (a) Can you imagine a scenario in which the premises would be true and the conclusion would be false?

   (b) Is some part of the conclusion not covered by a premise?

2. Fill in the missing premises in each invalid subargument. Good missing premises must fulfill these conditions:

   (a) They must make the argument valid.

   (b) They must be principles that the arguer could have used to reason from those premises to that conclusion;

      (i) they must be general enough to be a guiding principle in the arguer's reasoning, and

      (ii) they must be related to the particular details of the argument.

   (c) They must be expressed in a clear, comprehensible way.

Step 5. *Evaluate the argument.*

1. Validity: If there is no missing premise that meets the three conditions, then the argument can be criticized as *unsound because it is invalid.*

2. Truth: Consider each premise, starting at the top of the logical arrangement.

   (a) What reasons are there in favor of it?

   (b) What reasons are there against it?

   (c) Is it true or false?

   Continue until you have evaluated all the premises.

   (d) Are all the essential premises true? If no, the argument is *unsound.* If yes, the argument is *sound.*

Exercises to Chapter Six

Part A

Arguments 1–8 are from the exercises to Chapter Five (18–25). There you arranged the premises and conclusions in their logical order and found out some correct arrangements in part C.

Now take each of those arguments again, fill in the *missing premises* needed, and fit these into the logical arrangement.

Then, *evaluate* the argument by picking out the weakest or most doubtful premise.

A multiple-choice test and comments and answers concerning the missing premises of arguments 1–8 are contained in parts B and C.

1.   PREMISE 1.   There are many religions.

PREMISE 2.   All the religions believe in the same God.

∴ CONCLUSION 1.   Religions should learn to live in peace with one another.

PREMISE 2

↓

CONCLUSION 1

2.   PREMISE 1.   Singing Christmas carols in the public schools contradicts the separation of church and state.

PREMISE 2.   The practice is unconstitutional.

∴ CONCLUSION 1.   The practice should be abolished.

PREMISE 1

↓

PREMISE 2

↓

CONCLUSION 1

3.   PREMISE 1.   A sound argument is one that leads you from true premises to true conclusions.

PREMISE 2.   You can't ever tell for sure if anything is true.

∴ CONCLUSION 1.   Logic is useless.

PREMISE 1   +   PREMISE 2

↓

CONCLUSION 1

4.   PREMISE 1.   Candidate X will reduce unemployment.

PREMISE 2.   Candidate X will improve the economy.

PREMISE 3.   Candidate X will lower taxes.

∴ CONCLUSION 1.   You should vote for X.

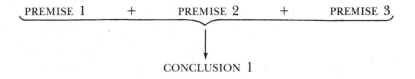

5.   PREMISE 1.   Walt Disney always made such nice family movies.

PREMISE 2.   His movies have no violence or sex in them.

∴ CONCLUSION 1.   Walt Disney was a good man.

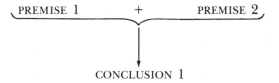

6.   PREMISE 1.   Kellogg's MOST cereal is high in bran fiber, has wheat germ and a full day's allowance of ten vitamins and iron.

PREMISE 2.   These wholesome ingredients are woven into crunchy little biscuits with the taste of honest whole wheat.

PREMISE 3.   MOST has nutritional good taste.

PREMISE 4.   You shouldn't settle for a cereal with less nutritional good taste than MOST has.

∴ CONCLUSION 1 (unstated).   You should buy MOST cereal.

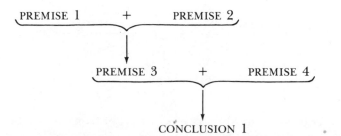

7.   PREMISE 1.   If you believe in gravity, you already believe that there are forces from the stars and planets that affect people on earth.

PREMISE 2.   Astrology says the same thing as the laws of gravity. [Paraphrase of "That's just what astrology says."]

PREMISE 3.   Astrology says the stars and planets exert forces on the people on earth.

PREMISE 4.   Astrology says that the forces exerted are different according to the configuration of stars and planets on the day you were born.

∴ CONCLUSION 1 (unstated).   You should believe in astrology.

PREMISE 1   +   PREMISE 3   +   PREMISE 4

PREMISE 2

CONCLUSION 1

8.   PREMISE 1.   Judges are too easy on first offenders.

PREMISE 2.   Giving light sentences starts criminals down the road to more serious crimes.

PREMISE 3.   It is unusual for a convicted robber who is a first offender to be given more than two years in prison.

PREMISE 4.   Light sentences are not enough.

∴ CONCLUSION 1 (unstated).   Judges should give harder sentences to first offenders.

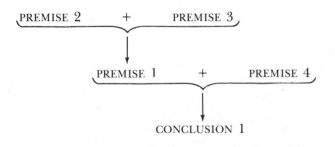

Evaluate arguments 9–15 quickly. Try to key in right from the start on the strong and weak points of each. Some brief comments are contained in part C.

9. To disprove: Taking medicine without a doctor's prescription is dangerous. Argument: Doctors do write prescriptions for medicines that are painkillers and are dangerous. Anacin, however, is considered a painkiller, but it is sold over the counter at drugstores as a nondangerous medicinal remedy. But it is not necessary to have a doctor's prescription to purchase Anacin.

10. Many people still think it's wrong for a man to cry. But crying is a sign of emotion, and a man has emotions just as women do. A man can show signs of emotional release.

11. Sources from which news media obtain information are often biased, and the media themselves sometimes give a biased account that reflects their own prejudices. Therefore, information obtained from the media is not always the truth.

12. We should not travel to the moon. Space travel is so expensive, and traveling to the moon is irrelevant to our national economy. On our previous trips to the moon we found nothing that shows we should be there or can live there.

13. Programs are unfair when one individual is forced unwillingly to support another individual. The welfare program through taxation takes money from those who have earned it and gives it to those who have not. I and many people like me are not giving up our money willingly. Draw your own conclusion!

14. Women are not inferior to men. More and more women are entering and graduating from law schools and medical schools. More women are entering military academies, once thought to be for males only, and are able to do all the assignments as well as the men. Women have formed professional ball teams, proving that women's athletics are as exciting and successful as men's are. Women have a higher threshold of pain than men. More women are filling high-paying, top-level management jobs.

15. Even today it is a prevalent belief that married women should stay at home instead of working. This despite the fact that an increasing number of married women are entering the labor market. The woman's salary contributes to the family's finances. Women work because work fills a need for achievement not met in any other way.

Part B

Multiple Choice

Missing premises   Several possible missing premises are listed after each of the arguments from part A. Select the most accurate ones. (Note that more than one missing premise from the list may be needed and that some other missing premises may be needed in addition to those listed.)

Fit the missing premises into the logical arrangement, and then criticize the weakest premise in each argument.

1.   PREMISE 1.   There are many religions.

PREMISE 2.   All the religions believe in the same God.

∴ CONCLUSION 1.   Religions should learn to live in peace with one another.

Missing premises:
(a) Religions should all believe in peace.
(b) Religions that believe in the same God have no cause to fight with one another.
(c) Other:

2.   PREMISE 1.   Singing Christmas carols in the public schools contradicts the separation of church and state.

PREMISE 2.   The practice is unconstitutional.

∴ CONCLUSION 1.   The practice should be abolished.

Missing premises:
(a) Whenever church and state act as one on a public issue, it is unconstitutional.
(b) The Constitution states that there must be a separation of church and state in public institutions.
(c) Christmas carols are religious songs.
(d) Any practice that is unconstitutional should be abolished.
(e) Other:

3.   PREMISE 1.   A sound argument is one that leads you from true premises to true conclusions.

PREMISE 2.   You can't ever tell for sure if anything is true.

∴ CONCLUSION 1.   Logic is useless.

Missing premises:
(a) Anything that is not true is useless.
(b) Anything you can't be sure about is useless.
(c) Not knowing for sure if anything is true makes it impossible to construct a sound argument.
(d) Other:

4.   PREMISE 1.   Candidate X will reduce unemployment.

PREMISE 2.   Candidate X will improve the economy.

PREMISE 3.   Candidate X will lower taxes.

∴ CONCLUSION 1.   You should vote for X.

Missing premises:
(a) You want reduced unemployment, an improved economy, and lower taxes.
(b) X's opponents will not do these things as well.
(c) X does not fall behind her opponent on other important issues.
(d) You should vote for the person who will do best on these issues.
(e) Other:

5.   PREMISE 1.   Walt Disney always made such nice family movies.

    PREMISE 2.   His movies have no violence or sex in them.

∴ CONCLUSION 1.   Walt Disney was a good man.

Missing premises:

(a) A movie without violence or sex is a nice family movie.
(b) Anyone who makes nice things for the family is a good person.
(c) Anyone who makes nice family movies is a good person.
(d) The morality of a movie reflects the morality of the person who made it.
(e) Other:

6.   PREMISE 1.   Kellogg's MOST cereal is high in bran fiber, has wheat germ and a full day's allowance of ten vitamins and iron.

    PREMISE 2.   These wholesome ingredients are woven into crunchy little biscuits with the taste of honest whole wheat.

    PREMISE 3.   MOST has nutritional good taste.

    PREMISE 4.   You shouldn't settle for a cereal with less nutritional good taste than MOST has.

∴ CONCLUSION 1 (unstated).   You should buy MOST cereal.

Missing premises:

(a) You need a full day's allowance of ten vitamins and iron.
(b) You want it in a cereal that tastes good.
(c) Other cereals are less than MOST either in nutrition or good taste.
(d) If you eat MOST cereal in the morning before starting a busy day, you can skip other meals because you will already have a full day's allowance of the vitamins and nutrients you need.
(e) Other:

7.   PREMISE 1.   If you believe in gravity, you already believe that there are forces from the stars and planets that affect people on earth.

    PREMISE 2.   Astrology says the same thing as the laws of gravity.

    PREMISE 3.   Astrology says the stars and planets exert forces on the people on earth.

    PREMISE 4.   Astrology says that the forces exerted are different according to the configuration of stars and planets on the day you were born.

∴ CONCLUSION 1 (unstated).   You should believe in astrology.

Missing premises:

(a) If two theories say the same thing and you believe one of them, you should believe the other also.
(b) You believe in gravity.
(c) Gravity also says that the forces from the stars and planets are different according to their configuration on the day you were born.
(d) Other:

8.   PREMISE 1.   Judges are too easy on first offenders.

PREMISE 2.   Giving light sentences starts criminals down the road to more serious crimes.

PREMISE 3.   It is unusual for a convicted robber who is a first offender to be given more than two years in prison.

PREMISE 4.   Light sentences are not enough.

∴ CONCLUSION 1 (unstated).   Judges should give harder sentences to first offenders.

Missing premises:
(a) Judges should not be so lenient to criminals.
(b) A sentence that starts criminals down the road to more serious crimes is too easy.
(c) Two years in prison is a light sentence.
(d) Harsher sentences for first offenders would discourage them from committing more serious crimes.
(e) Other:

Part C

The following (1–8) contain some suggested answers to the multiple-choice missing premises in part B. These are also fitted into the logical arrangement. A few comments on missing premises, their arrangements, and their truth follow each argument. (Additional questions are in parentheses and are printed in italics.)

1.

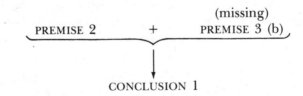

Comments:

The missing premise is the one listed in (b): Religions that believe in the same God have no cause to fight with one another. It has all the marks of a good missing premise: It makes the argument valid; it is something this arguer would reasonably believe; it is phrased clearly and intelligibly. The trouble with (a) is that it does not *connect* premise 2 to the conclusion: It does not have anything to do with premise 2.

The weakest premise in the argument could be either premise 2 or premise 3. Premise 2 needs paraphrasing for scope: Obviously, *all* religions do not believe in the same God; there are primitive religions that worship evil deities, for example. The arguer, though, may have meant "all major religions" or "all major Western religions." Even so, it seems clearly false. It is a tenet of Islam, for example, that Jesus was *not* God. It is hard to square this straightforward denial with thinking that Moslems and Roman Catholics believe in the same God. Premise 3 also may be doubtful: Historically, at least, religions have found many points worth fighting about besides belief in God. A weak argument, to say the least.

2.

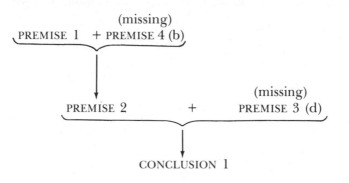

(missing)
PREMISE 1 + PREMISE 4 (b)

PREMISE 2   +   (missing)
PREMISE 3 (d)

CONCLUSION 1

Comments:

Missing premise (a) is definitely wrong. It is the kind of distorted missing premise the argument's opponent would try to foist on it. Missing premise (c) is an assumption of the argument, and an arguable one, but it is not literally a missing premise. What it says is really already included in premise 1. Missing premise (b) is needed to progress validly from premise 1 to premise 2, but it is so obvious that it may not need to be stated. Missing premise (d) is the main one underlying the arguer's reasoning.

    The argument certainly looks sound, but if a premise has to be attacked, premise 1 is probably the weakest.

3.

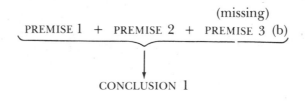

(missing)
PREMISE 1 + PREMISE 2 + PREMISE 3 (b)

CONCLUSION 1

Comments:

Missing premise (a) does not connect: Premise 2 talks about lack of certainty, not straight-out lack of truth. Missing premise (b) connects perfectly, whereas (c), like (a), fails to make the argument valid. (*Find a counterexample to the argument consisting of premises 1, 2, and (c).*) Another missing premise could be added, saying "Logic is built on the idea of a sound argument." This seems to be part of the meaning of the word "logic," and part of the paraphrase, rather than a missing premise. But including it as premise 4 does not hurt the argument.

    The argument is certainly no good at all. It would prove its point only if it itself were *sound*. (*Why is premise 3 false?*)

4. *Comments:*

All four of the missing premises are needed to make the argument valid.
The one you are most likely to leave out is (c). The logical arrangement of
all the premises, given and missing, is purely horizontal. (*Give a brief reason
or a counterexample to show why each of the missing premises listed is needed.*)

5.

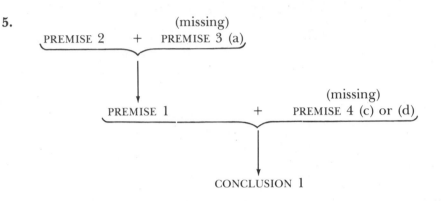

Comments:

Missing premise (a) is needed to reason from a movie's having no violence or sex
(premise 2) to its being a nice family movie (premise 1). To reason validly from
premise 1 to the conclusion, you need (b), (c), or (d). If you weigh (b) against (c),
(c) comes out better. Missing premise (b) talks about "nice things for the family,"
whereas (c) confines itself to "nice family movies." Because premise 1 talks only
about movies, (b) goes too far beyond the stated argument. (*Because it is more
general, it is easier to find a counterexample to it. Give a plausible counterexample to (b)
that is not also a counterexample to (c).*) Choosing between (c) or (d), however, is
harder. Either will make the argument valid, but (d) is more general than is
literally needed. In particular, the arguer only talks about good movies and good
persons, as in (c), and has not said that a person who makes *bad* movies is a *bad*
person, and (d) in effect does say this. So, by the guidelines laid down in Chapter
Six, (c) is a better choice. Still, in this argument it seems psychologically likely that
a more general relation between people and the movies they make lies behind
the arguer's reasoning about Disney. This relation could be stated in other words
as well: "People express their personalities through their movies" or "You should
judge a moviemaker's character by the kind of movie that person makes." Either
(c) or (d) is correct: (c) more from the point of view of logic and (d) from the
point of view of psychology.

It is hardly necessary to say that premise 4 (missing), in whatever form, is the
weakest link in the argument. People make family movies for many motives
(money is a major one), and there is no justification for drawing a conclusion
about the person's character. The reasoning in the argument is shoddy.

6.

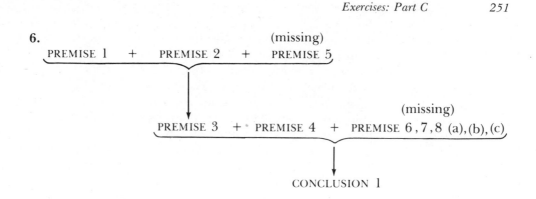

Comments:

The subargument from premises 1 and 2 to 3 is nearly valid, needing only premise 5 (missing): Whole wheat tastes good. You need (a), (b), and (c) to reason to the conclusion. Notice how many different kinds of premises are needed to establish a conclusion that you should buy a product. In addition to claims about what the product delivers, it has to be shown that you *want* what the product delivers, that no other product delivers it better, and that the best way to get the product is to buy it. Most advertisements don't even come close to showing this much. Look, for example, at (c). Kellogg's does not *say* this (it would be a lie for which they could be sued), but unless it is true, nothing they do say gives you a reason to buy MOST over other brands. Though (a), (b), and (c) are the major missing premises, the argument still is not quite valid for reasons that may be important in particular cases. (*Try to think up a counterexample to the validity of the whole argument. Then formulate a missing premise to cover it.*) Missing premise (d) is not a missing premise at all. Kellogg's does not say this and is not committed to it. Claiming this is a missing premise is cheating by turning Kellogg's argument into a straw-man argument. The argument is easy enough to refute legitimately without distorting it.

7.

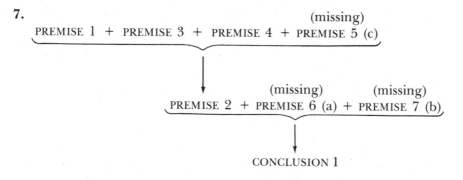

Comments:

Let's inspect this argument from the bottom up to see how deceptive it is. The arguer is trying to show that you should believe in astrology. The stated reason in the bottom subargument is that astrology says the same thing as the laws of gravity. Let's suppose for the time being that it is true. To get from there to the conclusion, the arguer needs missing premises 6(a) and 7(b). Together, these cover all parts of the conclusion: Premise 6(a) says what <u>you should believe in</u>; premise 2 covers <u>astrology</u>; and premise 7(b) neatly connects premise 2 to premise 7 by saying you do believe in gravity. Moreover, the missing premises here are undoubtedly true: Belief in gravity is an eminently reasonable belief, and premise 6 is so obvious it could be left unstated. So the truth of the conclusion rests entirely on the truth of premise 2. And the arguer gives a subargument to back up premise 2. Premises 3 and 4 cover the component part "<u>astrology</u>"; premises 1 and 5(c) cover the component part, <u>the laws of</u> gravity; and reading the premises shows that they <u>say the same thing</u>. So all parts of premise 2 look covered. And premises 1, 3, 4, and 5 are all true: That *is* what the laws of gravity and astrology say. But if these premises are true, and if they cover all component parts of premise 2, then the top subargument is sound, then premise 2 has been proved. And if premise 2 has been proved, the lower subargument will be sound also, and the conclusion is proved.

How could it be, though? Astrology is at least highly questionable. It has no scientific backing. Gravity, on the other hand, is a well-established concept. What went wrong is that we did not paraphrase. The deceptive word in the argument is "forces." The forces talked about in the laws of gravity are precisely measurable and act on all objects in the same way; the gravitational forces from the stars and planets acting on people are extremely small and certainly do not vary appreciably from time to time. None of these qualities characterize the "forces" that astronomy talks about. Paraphrase would have distinguished the two different interpretations of the ambiguous word "force," and this argument would not have seemed valid. (*Taking account of this ambiguity could also have been accomplished in a missing premise. Formulate one that will make the argument valid. Fit it into the logical arrangement. Is it true?*)

8.

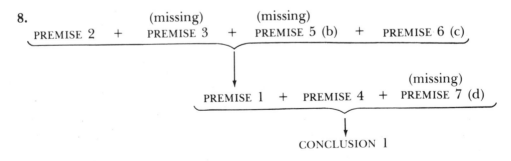

Comments:

Missing premise (a) is not a missing premise; it is a restatement of the conclusion. For the sake of completeness, (b), (c), and (d) are all needed in the places indicated, but (d) is the crucial missing premise and needs independent corroboration. (*Actually, it looks like a statement that can be experimentally tested fairly easily. What kind of test can you make up?*)

(Validity: Is "should" in the conclusion covered? If so, how? If not, what would you add to cover it?)

There is another point to be understood about paraphrase. Notice the easy connotation of "a couple of years" in the original argument. We paraphrased that in premise 3 as "two years," which is considerably more neutral. It still sounds easy, though — that is, the missing premise in (c) sounds clearly true. Comparatively, of course, two years is easy, easier than five or ten or life. But that doesn't show it is easy in itself. Sometimes, by hearing words often, people become unimaginative. If you hear about atrocities often enough, for instance, you tend to stop thinking of them as so bad. "A couple of years in prison" means over 700 nearly identical days, waking up in a dismal cell, being at the mercy of often brutal guards and other prisoners. It means monotonous, unproductive, humiliating, terrifying days, without any real liberty at all.

Using your imagination this way is sometimes very important, and it is a crucial aspect of understanding many arguments. Otherwise, a critical point (like the truth of missing premise (c)) in the argument may go right by you. The argument about light sentences and first offenders may or may not have merit, but it is important that neither side base its case on a lack of imagination.

Comments on arguments 9–15 from part A follow.

9.   PREMISE 1.   Doctors do write prescriptions for medicines that are painkillers and are dangerous.

   PREMISE 2.   Anacin is considered a painkiller.

   PREMISE 3.   Anacin is sold over the counter at drugstores as a nondangerous medicinal remedy.

   PREMISE 4.   It is not necessary to have a doctor's prescription to purchase Anacin.

∴ CONCLUSION 1.   It is false that taking medicines without a doctor's prescription is dangerous.

Comments:

The argument desperately needs paraphrase. To prove the conclusion, the arguer would at least have to say that Anacin *is not* dangerous. But all the arguer says is that it is sold "as a nondangerous medicinal remedy" (premise 3). That only means that it is *presumed* to be safe, not that it is in fact safe. That's a kind of cheating you have to watch out for in advertisements. But the main fault of the argument is that the arguer takes the conclusion to mean, "It is false that taking *any* medicine without a prescription is dangerous." *(How do you know this is what the arguer takes it to mean? What does it actually mean?)*

10.   PREMISE 1.   Crying is a sign of emotion.

   PREMISE 2.   A man has emotions just as women do.

   PREMISE 3.   A man can show signs of emotional release.

∴ CONCLUSION 1.   It's all right for a man to cry.

Comments:

The premises may be true, but the argument is invalid as it stands. Nothing in the argument says that it is *all right* for a man (or a woman, for that matter) to release emotions, and, more importantly, nothing says why it is all right for a man to release his emotions in *that* way, by *crying*. Thus some of the component parts of the conclusion are not covered by the premises.

11. PREMISE 1. Sources from which news media obtain information are often biased.

PREMISE 2. The media themselves sometimes give a biased account that reflects their own prejudices.

∴ CONCLUSION 1. Information obtained from the news media is not always the truth.

Comments:

The argument is valid. It assumes that a biased account is not true, but this is probably part of paraphrase rather than a missing premise. Not only is it valid, but it appears to be sound. (*Explain how it is valid and sound.*)

12. PREMISE 1. Space travel is so expensive.

PREMISE 2. Traveling to the moon is irrelevant to our national economy.

PREMISE 3. On our previous trips we found nothing that shows we should be there.

PREMISE 4. On our previous trips we found nothing that shows we can live there.

∴ CONCLUSION 1. We should not travel to the moon.

Comments:

The argument presents four reasons in favor of the conclusion. It is invalid, though, because nothing in the premises covers the idea that we <u>should not</u> travel to the moon. We need to add a missing premise that connects this idea to the stated drawbacks of traveling to the moon. We could make the connection by either of these two missing premises:

PREMISE 5 (missing). We should not make trips unless they will be useful.

PREMISE 6 (missing). We should not make expensive trips unless they will be useful.

(*Which of these two missing premises states the assumption the arguer is making here? Why?*)

13. PREMISE 1. Programs are unfair where one individual is forced unwillingly to support another individual.

PREMISE 2. The welfare program through taxation takes money from those who have earned it and gives it to those who have not.

PREMISE 3.   Many people do not give up their money to such taxation willingly.

∴ CONCLUSION 1 (unstated).   The welfare program is unfair.

Comments:

A good, valid argument. All component parts of the conclusion are covered. The premises in the argument are also quite plausible. (*What if someone objected to premise 3 by saying that taxes are imposed only with the consent, by voting, of the people taxed?*) (*Is premise 1 really fair, though?*)

14.   PREMISE 1.   More and more women are entering and graduating from law schools and medical schools.

PREMISE 2.   More women are entering military academies, once thought to be for males only.

PREMISE 3.   The women are able to do all the assignments as well as the men.

PREMISE 4.   Women have formed professional ball teams.

PREMISE 5.   Women's athletics are as exciting and successful as men's.

PREMISE 6.   Women have a higher threshold of pain than men.

PREMISE 7.   More women are filling high-paying, top-level management jobs.

∴ CONCLUSION 1.   Women are not inferior to men.

Comments:

The main fault of the argument is that the arguer does not know what he or she is trying to prove. The conclusion needs paraphrase: "inferior" in what respect? Because of this unclarity, the premises go in different directions. Premises 1, 2, and 7 all say "more women," but they are not comparing women *to men* (needed to prove the conclusion) but today's women to yesterday's. But there were so few women before in these institutions that an increase does not prove too much about equality. Only premises 3 and 6 compare women directly to men, and premise 6 looks irrelevant to most ideas of equality. (*What if someone says that women's equality to men does not need to be argued for?*) (*Does men's equality to women need to be argued for?*)

15.   PREMISE 1.   Increasing numbers of married women are entering the labor market.

PREMISE 2.   The woman's salary contributes to the family's finances.

PREMISE 3.   Women work because work fills a need for achievement not met in any other way.

∴ CONCLUSION 1.   Married women should not stay at home instead of working.

Comments:

This is a good foundation for an argument because premises 2 and 3 give such plausible and relevant reasons in favor of the conclusion. Moreover, premise 3 gives a *general* reason why anyone should work. Premise 1 does not contribute much: It says that women *do* work; it is not a reason why they *should*. The argument as it stands requires a missing premise to say that achievement (premise 3) and financial contributions (premise 2) are more important than what is done in the home.

Part D

Arguments 1–10 have relatively simple logical arrangements. Evaluate each of them for *validity*. Then fill in the *missing premises* needed in each.

1. The purpose of our government is to act for the benefit of its citizens. Therefore, the only kind of scientific research our government should support financially is research that will be beneficial to humanity.

2. If a woman becomes pregnant as a result of rape, she did not *choose* to be pregnant. She was forced into it. Having an abortion, then, at least in the case of rape, is a woman's right.

3. The purpose of a university is the dissemination of knowledge. Therefore, admission to a university should be based solely on academic potential.

4. Less than one hundred years ago, the most prominent scientists denied that airplane flights would ever be possible. Surely it is reasonable to believe that humans eventually will journey among the stars.

5. Criminals typically come from impoverished homes. Therefore, to eliminate crime, eliminate poverty.

6. The family that prays together, stays together.

7. "There's no country as great as the smallest city in America. I mean, you can't watch television. The water won't even run right. The toilets won't flush. The roads, the cards ... They're trying to make it all right, but there's nothing as great as America." — Muhammed Ali.

8. It is Ralph's twelfth birthday. He is five feet, three inches tall and has grown two inches in the past two months. If he continues to grow at this rate, he will be more than eight feet tall by the time he is fifteen.

9. Vitamin A deficiency causes night blindness. If you want to see better in the dark, eat foods rich in vitamin A.

10. A $100 fine is a much greater punishment to a poor person than to a rich person. This is unfair. So, fines as punishments should be replaced by uniform jail sentences, the same for all.

11. Go back through arguments 1–10 and evaluate the missing premises you filled in for *truth*. Give reasons to back up your judgment.

Analyze and *evaluate* 12–40 in detail.

12. Each species of plant or animal occupies a unique place in the environment. If one becomes extinct, there is no telling what impact that will have on the rest of the environment. The loss will be irreplaceable. We cannot allow any species to become extinct if we can help it.

13. Computers are coming to dominate our society, and this is only the beginning. Every educated person ten years from now will need to know how to do at least simple programming. Therefore, computer programming should be a required course in universities.

14. Washington (AP) — President Carter on Friday vetoed legislation that would have given the Ute Indian tribe 3,000 acres of California land and $5.8 million for economic development.

"This legislative relief is unwarranted," he said in a written message to the house, "because it would give special advantages to the Ute Mountain Tribe over others whose circumstances may be similar."

15. Nuclear energy is safe because, on a percentage basis, fewer people have died from it than from any other form of energy in any given year to date.

16.   PREMISE 1.   Nuclear power, if used in the wrong way, is extremely dangerous to all life.

     PREMISE 2.   Many procedures must be used to ensure the safe use of nuclear power.

     PREMISE 3.   If any of these procedures is not done, or is done inadequately, the chance of disaster increases.

     PREMISE 4.   Shortcuts are being taken in building the plants themselves to save time and money.

     PREMISE 5.   These shortcuts sometimes involve safety procedures.

     PREMISE 6.   As a result some safety procedures are sometimes not done and others are done inadequately.

∴ CONCLUSION 1.   Man's use of nuclear power is not safe.

17. In the United States guns are easy to buy. In European countries it is much harder to obtain a gun. There are far fewer shootings per capita in European countries than in the United States. Guns should be controlled more closely in the United States.

18. I'm as free as a bird, and a bird can't change. So there's no point in trying to change me.

19. In *Science Digest* (December, 1980, p. 27) there is a brief article that suggests that altruism "is always selected against in nature" and "is a behaviour trait that is doomed to die out." To support this claim, we are told about how the male starling tries to prevent his mate from sexual contact with other males. According to the writer, "It could be an advantage to the female to have genetic diversity in her young. The chicks might inherit disease resistance or some other valuable trait, and as a result fewer would die. But for the male, genetic continuity is crucial."

20. "CENTRUM. The vitamin supplied to the 1980 Winter Olympics. A more complete formula than any other brand."

21. In the introduction to his anthology, *Sociobiology Examined* (Oxford, 1980, p. 4) Ashley Montague writes: "Scientists are human begins with their full complement of emotions and prejudices, and their emotions and prejudices often influence the way they do their science. This was first clearly brought out in a study by Professor Nicholas Pastore ... in 1949. In this study Professor Pastore showed that the scientist's political beliefs were highly correlated with what he believed about the roles played by nature and nurture in the development of the person. Those holding conservative political views strongly tended to believe in the power of genes over environment. Those subscribing to more liberal views tended to believe in the power of environment over genes. One distinguished scientist (who happened to be a teacher of mine) when young was a socialist and environmentalist, but toward middle age he became politically conservative and a firm believer in the supremacy of genes!"

22. PREMISE 1.   Medical care is a necessity for survival.
    PREMISE 2.   All necessities for survival should be available to everyone.
    ∴ CONCLUSION 1.   Medical care should be made affordable to everyone.

23. PREMISE 1.   All people need medical care at some point in their lives.
    PREMISE 2.   Medical care assures society of health protection.
    PREMISE 3.   A healthy society benefits not only the individual but the society as a whole.
    PREMISE 4.   A healthy society is more likely to be an industrious society.
    ∴ CONCLUSION 1.   Medical care should be made affordable to everyone.

24. PREMISE 1.   Many people need medical care to keep their health.
    PREMISE 2.   Some people need medical care to live.
    PREMISE 3.   Health and life are everyone's rights.
    PREMISE 4.   A person should not lose his or her right because the person cannot afford it.
    ∴ CONCLUSION 1.   Medical care should be made affordable to everyone.

25. "Because of wind resistance and engine efficiency, 55 is a critical speed for your car. Pass it, and you're using more gas to travel the same distance.

    "By slowing down from 70 to 55, you could actually increase your gas mileage by up to 39%, depending on your car. And over a 10-mile stretch it would cost you only 3 minutes more." *(Reader's Digest,* October, 1979, p. 48.)

26. You should clean up your own table in the cafeteria. Don't leave it so messy. What if everyone did the same? The cafeteria workers would never get their work done.

27. You shouldn't clean up your own table in the cafeteria. Don't leave it so neat. What if everyone did the same? The cafeteria workers would be fired because there would be no work for them to do.

28. University rules against nepotism are designed to prevent the unfair privileges that might be granted to the spouses of employees. But what the rules actually do is discriminate against women, and like all sexist rules they should be abolished. Men, because they are usually older than their wives, generally have jobs already. This means that a woman will be unable to teach at a particular university simply because her husband teaches there, even is she is the best qualified for the position.

29.   PREMISE 1.   The world has much violence in it.
　　PREMISE 2.   Everyone, including children, should be aware of it.
　　PREMISE 3.   Banning violence from television is a form of censorship.
　　PREMISE 4.   If a parent believes a program is not suitable for his or her
∴　　 child, it should be up to that parent to turn the set off.
　　───

　　CONCLUSION 1.   Violence on television should not be banned.

30.   PREMISE 1.   Violence is a fact of life.
　　PREMISE 2.   Television is mainly entertainment.
　　PREMISE 3.   People seem to find violent shows entertaining.
　　───

　∴ CONCLUSION 1.   Violence on television should not be banned.

31. History is not an accurate report or account of events that have occurred. It is biased because the people retelling the story are going to recount it from their own point of view, which is slanted. The Japanese reported World War II from a different point of view than the Americans. The same can be said about the American Indian wars.

32. The right to vote is more than a right. It is a duty. Voting is the way the people in a democracy express their views most forcefully. It is not important whether you vote Democrat or Republican. What is important is that you vote.

33. How would you feel if someone raped your sister? Rapists should be "fixed" so they cannot rape anyone ever again.

34. Absence makes the heart grow fonder. Therefore, one good way to remain happily married is to take separate vacations occasionally.

35.   CONCLUSION 1.   Humanity is not basically good.
　　PREMISE 1.   People are the only creatures on earth that kill other
　　　　 animals, just for the fun of it.
　　PREMISE 2.   Humanity has created weapons capable of destroying all
　　　　 life.

PREMISE 3.   People like to inflict physical damage on one another (there are always street fights in which people use chains and knives to cause extreme physical damage).

PREMISE 4.   People like to watch others get hurt (they watch violent sports like boxing and football; the bloodier the movie, the more popular it is; they always slow down to see traffic accidents).

36. Rome fell because of internal decay. Its citizens were addicted to vice and carnal pleasures. They became soft. They no longer paid attention to religion. There was no respect for law and order. And now America is traveling down the same easy path. Look at our sexual degeneracy, atheism, and crimes. It is imperative that we get tough with ourselves — before it is too late.

37. Birth control pills are bad for one's health — but pregnancy is worse.

38. Psychiatrists have a higher suicide rate than any other occupational group. Clearly, many emotional unstable individuals are attracted to psychiatry.

39. "There's an unprecedented smoker move to Merit. No other new cigarette in the last 20 years has attracted so many smokers as quickly as Merit."

40. It would be foolish and dangerous even to consider letting children vote, as some unrealistic liberals recommended. *Psychology Today,* itself as a liberal magazine, had to admit in the November, 1980 issue that "most 11-year-olds are not yet capable of understanding the way law and government work" because their minds "have trouble with abstract notions of justice, equality, or liberty and are rather largely confined to the concrete. ("Children and Other Political Naif," Joseph Adelson interviewed by Elizabeth Hall, p. 56.)

Chapter Seven

Reasoning
Things Out

1. The General Worth of Reasoning in Life

Except for some questions and examples in Chapter One, this text has concentrated on reasoning primarily as it applies to arguments, either in constructimg them or analyzing them. This is right and natural. Reasoning is particularly fitted to dealing with arguments because what reasoning should do best is analyze *reasons*. We have many other ways of reacting to an argument besides reasoning. We can react emotionally, for example, and see whether we like or dislike what the premises and conclusion say. But this does not seem like a good way of getting at the *truth* of the conclusion: There are unpleasant truths as well as pleasant ones. Emotional responses seem an even worse guide to understanding the *relation* between reasons and conclusions. The usual emotional reaction is to ignore reasons and act simply on one's feelings about the conclusion.

Reasoning is fitted to arguments

In reasoning, though, you are searching actively for the truth, and the method you use while reasoning is to see where the evidence leads you. Thus the field in which reasoning applies most directly is the search for truth and the relation between premises and conclusion.

It is a mistake, though, to think that reasoning deals *only* with handling arguments. You also reason when you try to figure out which move you should make in a game of chess or how much you should bet on filling an inside straight in poker. Doing mathematics problems well or scoring high on reading-comprehension tests clearly involves reasoning. The same thing is true when you try to understand one of your teacher's lectures or the implications of a psychology experiment; or when you try to figure out how to trim your budget or whether you should continue in school; or if euthanasia, abortion, and suicide are right or wrong. All these activities need not involve arguments straightforwardly (though there is some relation between them and dealing with arguments), yet they are all instances of reasoning.

What they have in common is that they all involve figuring things out: strategies in games, solutions to tests, answers to problems. In the most central sense that's what reasoning is; it is figuring things out.

The central sense of reasoning

That means understanding the issues, examining them carefully, and thinking hard about them.

Skill in reasoning functions in at least four important areas. You are well acquainted with two already.

First, it enables you to construct arguments for beliefs you hold, and, second, it gives you the means to evaluate other people's arguments. You are already familiar with the worth of reasoning in these two areas. Virtually the whole text has concentrated on them. But there are two other areas that have not been covered much. Not because they are less important, but because a foundation in handling arguments is probably necessary to acquiring any kind of skill in them, and also because they are more complex and have too many ramifications to be covered well in a short space.

Third, then, reasoning can help you get an understanding of *strategies* in arguing and a knowledge of *issues* you are concerned about. And, fourth, reasoning is of prime importance in helping you to question, examine, and deal with *your life* and the things in it. These two essential uses, though built on an understanding of how to analyze and construct arguments, go beyond arguments.

2. Beyond Arguments: Issues and Strategies

Issues

In Chapter One we covered briefly twelve arguments in favor of legalizing marijuana. By examining the arguments and how they fail to work, you learn a lot about the *issue* of legalizing marijuana. You learn, for example, that many aspects of marijuana use, including many of the reasons people give generally for its legalization, are usually only minor, secondary reasons, not reasons that would *justify* legalizing marijuana. That it is medically useful and nonaddictive, that legalizing it would hurt organized crime and generate tax revenue, that it is not as harmful as tobacco or alcohol — even taken all together, these reasons do not seem sufficient to justify legalizing a substance. In one way or another they all miss the central problem about the conditions under which a substance should be legalized. Other reasons were found to be even further from this central problem. That smoking marijuana doesn't merit a prison sentence or that many people (including, perhaps, a president) *say* there is nothing wrong with it — such reasons seem not just off the main point, but irrelevant.

After going through the arguments, you will have a good idea of what the central questions are likely to be: Is marijuana harmful? To whom is it harmful and to what extent? How much testing needs to be done to establish a substance's harmfulness? Do people have a right to harm themselves as long as they don't harm others? (This comes from the missing premise.)

Strategies

Knowledge of the central problems in this argument is not developed fully primarily because it wasn't necessary to examine the arguments in greater detail. Nevertheless, the knowledge gives you a strategy for dealing with arguments about the legalization of marijuana that you did not have before. If someone gives you a new argument, one that you haven't heard, you're not likely to be greatly surprised. You will quickly be able to see how it fits into this grid of arguments and how it attempts to answer the central question, and you will be able to respond intelligently to it.

Strategy and knowledge

This is even clearer with capital punishment. You are now familiar with that issue in a way that goes beyond the particular arguments considered in Chapter Six. You can handle other arguments that get tossed around about it. You know that anyone who wants to give a solid argument in favor of capital punishment has to say (a) what function punishment in general is supposed to serve, (b) how capital punishment serves that function, and (c) how it differs from clearly unreasonable punishments like mutilation or extreme, lifelong torture. This approach gives you a powerful strategy in arguing: You can easily understand new arguments on the subject and immediately fire off questions and objections that are right to the point. The same kind of strategy applies to arguments *against* capital punishment. You know the conditions that will make them good or bad, relevant or irrelevant. Do they say (a) what precisely are the negative effects of capital punishment and (b) why having that kind of effect makes something wrong?

You know how to handle these arguments because you now have come to know the issue. Even more than that, you are now in a good position to generalize the problems and questions to other related issues:

The inter-connection of issues

Punishment: How about punishing one's children? What's that supposed to accomplish, and does it? What about the ultimate punishment — the concept of Hell? When does a punishment "fit" the crime?

Unreasonable punishments: What makes mutilation and extreme, lifelong torture unreasonable as punishments? *Are* they unreasonable? (This brings up Hell again.)

What makes an act *wrong*? What is the difference between private wrongs and wrongs done by law? Why shouldn't you take revenge on people? *Should* you ever take revenge?

You probably do not have answers to these questions, but just thinking of them as being related gives you a hold on a network of issues and problems that you never had before.

Questioning Presuppositions

One of the most effective strategies when arguing with people is not to object to the reasons they give, but to object instead to the *presuppositions* of their arguments. A presupposition is something that is taken for granted but not stated. For example, in the debate about gun control, opponents of gun-control legislation contend that such laws will not prevent criminals from getting guns, but that they will prevent ordinary citizens from defending themselves. Now it is debatable whether legislation would prevent criminals from getting guns: Wouldn't it make it *harder* to get them? At least for small-time criminals? Isn't that a positive gain? But instead of debating about the truth of the premise, you can question a presupposition the argument rests on: Is crime prevention the only major point of gun-control legislation? The answer is No; one of the goals of gun control is the prevention of accidental shootings (by children playing with their father's gun, for instance). This objection undercuts much of the basis of your opponent's argument, and it is discovered by using the strategy of questioning presuppositions.

Presuppositions are not always missing premises

The presuppositions of an argument are often contained in the missing premises, but not always in a way that allows you to discover them very easily. This person's argument can be written out with two stated premises and one filled-in premise:

> PREMISE 1.   Gun-control legislation will not prevent criminals from getting guns.
>
> PREMISE 2.   Gun-control legislation will prevent ordinary citizens from defending themselves.
>
> PREMISE 3 (missing).   If a potential law will not prevent crimes but will prevent defense against crimes, it should not be passed.
>
> ∴ CONCLUSION 1.   Gun-control legislation should not be passed.

Missing premise 3 looks plausible, and that is what leads you to center the debate around premise 1 or premise 2. Even examined closely, you are likely to conclude that premise 3 is true. But the objection based on the prevention of accidents is actually an objection to premise 3. The objection says, in effect, that sometimes laws *should* be passed even if they do not prevent crime and do prevent self-defense against crime, namely, in cases where some other good is accomplished (the prevention of accidental shootings). *Maybe* you would have come up with this objection by questioning premise 3, but a more likely procedure is to ask yourself consciously: "Is that the only important thing the debate is about? What is the whole argument presupposing?"

There is a sense in which questioning presuppositions does not go beyond analyzing the argument. A thorough analysis should bring out many of them. But it is helpful to think of this as a separate strategy because it focuses your attention on basic points that may underlie both your and your opponent's statements. Noticing those points gives you a powerful tool when arguing with someone.

Advertising is an enterprise that frequently tries to keep presuppositions as far in the background as possible. Ads often don't give arguments or reasons at all; they merely try to hold your attention. When they give reasons, they usually mention things their products do, or do well. They will say that Ban or Arrid stops perspiration odor, or how much garbage a Sears Trash Compactor will hold, or that Cheer gets your clothes white. At best they give arguments comparing their product with other products (usually just leading brands though — another presupposition?). Ban may say that it is better at stopping odor than Arrid; Sears may show how much more its trash compactor will hold than its competitors'; Cheer may have people tell you they prefer Cheer to Tide. The conclusion of these arguments is that their brand of product is good, or better than others, or best. Is it true? Maybe, maybe not. Check it out if it's important to you.

But there is another conclusion to their arguments, in a sense the real conclusion: that you should buy their product. Coming to *this* conclusion requires much more than knowing even that the product is the best. Other presuppositions are that you need the product, that you want it, that it is good for you, and that the amount of good is worth the price.

Americans buy many products they do not need. Companies spend a lot of money trying to make you think you need their products. They are most effective when they play on your guilt (giving your children "the best" — life insurance, the newest toys and clothes) or your image in the eyes of others (dandruff remedies, breath fresheners). Too often people buy products out of habit, or because it is the accepted thing to do, or because they simply never question whether they should. They may question which product to buy (presumably the best for the price), but often not whether they need that *kind* of product at all. Not long ago it was taken for granted that a newly married middle-class couple would buy a new house within a few years (ads always call them "new *homes*" — paraphrase needed?); similarly, it was a habit among many car owners to buy a new car every other year. Those are expensive purchases to take for granted.

Attacking the presuppositions of advertisements is important even when the product isn't that expensive. In fact, most people who shower once a day and eat a halfway reasonable diet don't smell bad enough to need a deodorant; it's a rare household that needs a trash compactor, best or not; and it seems silly for Americans to attach so much weight to getting clothes white (instead of merely clean).

Questioning the Entire Basis of an Argument

A more radical way of attacking an argument or a set of arguments on a topic is to question the whole basis on which the arguments, positive as well as negative, rest. This strategy differs from questioning the presuppositions of an argument only in degree, but the degree is great enough to mark it off as a distinct way to meet an argument. Actually, it is not so much a strategy for opposing others' arguments as it is a way of opening up new perspectives for yourself on controversial issues and explanations.

A historical example

Take a historical example. There was much debate about the treatment of slaves long before the idea of abolishing slavery became popular. Slave owners who thought deeply about the matter would argue about the best way to treat slaves. And some slave owners were genuinely humanitarian: To them, the "best" way to treat slaves meant not just "the most efficient," but "the morally best." Should one be a strict disciplinarian or an understanding and forgiving master? Under what conditions is corporal punishment justifiable?

Points were raised in favor of each side. One side said, "Discipline is what teaches slaves right from wrong. If you are too forgiving, slaves will get out of hand. And if that goes far enough, they will end by bringing down on their own heads worse punishments than those you did not give them out of misplaced 'understanding.' It is a hard lesson to learn, but early leniency hurts the slave more than it helps."

The other side says, "Mercy and understanding are an essential part of all morality. Your slaves are human, even though they are slaves, and should be treated as humans. If you are too strict with slaves, too quick to punish, you will make them afraid to take any initiative or make any decision on their own. That is not even a good way to make an efficient worker, much less a morally responsible person."

What is hard for us to see today is how any humanitarian who was concerned about morality could have justified slavery itself. Holding mature, reasonable people against their will — owning them and having control over all aspects of their lives — seems one of the clearest examples of injustice. It seems so clear that it is hard for us to get enough historical perspective to understand how slave owners could ever have honestly thought it *was* just.

It seems to us today, by hindsight of course, that a rational examination would have shown slave owners that slavery was not justified; at least it would have had a chance if they had examined the idea closely. The institution of slavery underlies the opposing arguments on each side, and hence both arguments are wrong for the same basic reason. Thus it is only by questioning the whole basis of the arguments that slave owners were likely to get to the truth of the matter.

It's harder to find examples in our own contemporary culture where questioning the whole basis of an argument will lead us to such a drastically new position. It's difficult to step back from one's culture sufficiently to examine it by reason. (It is a little jolting, for instance, to realize that the slave owners' arguments on either side are the same as ones often given in our society; only we give them about raising *children*.)

Controversies take place *within* certain cultural situations, guidelines, and ways of thinking. Arguments are given on one side and the other. Often it is not only right but necessary to decide, on the basis of reasons, for one side or the other. But stepping back and questioning the situations, guidelines, and ways of thinking themselves can give you new strategies for dealing with the problem, deeper reasons to prefer one side of the argument, or sometimes a fresh perspective that lets you step outside the whole issue.

For example, a lot of debate has gone on recently about reverse discrimination. Because whites have had unfair privileges for so long, one argument goes, white children are, in general, in a much better position socially, economically, and educationally than black children. So if from this moment forward we prohibit all racial discrimination, blacks still will not have equal opportunity; being completely non-discriminatory at this stage merely makes the present *inequalities* last longer. What is needed, the argument continues, is temporary discrimination *in favor of* blacks until they reach a position of general social, economic, and educational equality. Only then will they have equal opportunity.

A contemporary example

The opposite side in the controversy maintains that all racial discrimination is unfair because it means judging people not on the basis of their individual merits, but on the basis of irrelevant characteristics like skin color or national origin. Discriminating against whites today is like punishing twentieth-century Jews for actions that other Jews may have committed 2000 years ago. The better-qualified person, this side maintains, should always get the job or the admission to law school, regardless of past discrimination.

This is an intriguing controversy, with widespread practical consequences. You grasp the problem only if you feel the pull in both directions. If one side seems wholly wrong to you, you're probably not interpreting it fairly. Both sides have plausible, relevant arguments; that's what makes the case so intriguing.

It is interesting to analyze the arguments in detail. But stepping back from the argument and examining the whole foundation of it may lead to some unexpected results. Part of that foundation is the assumption that human beings have rights, in particular, the right to equality of opportunity. That assumption lies at the root of our condemnation of racial and sexual discrimination. But is that assumption correct? What is it about people that makes them have rights? And, in particular, equal rights? It pays off, in deeper understanding, to try to answer this hard question.

A number of possible answers come to mind: People have rights because they have intelligence, or because they have the ability to reason, or because they have future goals and interests, or because they can feel pain when deprived of what they need to maintain life or well-being.

Logic does not always dictate that you choose a particular answer, but it does dictate that you accept the consequences of the answer you choose. And in this case all the answers have unexpected consequences. If intelligence or the ability to reason gives people rights, then some people just do not have rights and some animals do: There are chimps and dolphins that are more intelligent and better able to reason than infants and many retarded adults. The same holds true for having goals and interests: The chimp who picks and strips a branch to use it later to capture ants pretty clearly has a goal in mind, more of a goal than some humans. (These answers also have consequences for abortion.) Again, if the ability to feel pain is related to having rights, then many kinds of animals have rights.

These preliminary answers are superficial and far more needs to be said, but they open up surprising areas of enquiry. If humans have rights in virtue of such properties, don't animals have rights also? Even stronger, if having properties like these gives humans *equal* rights, will not many animals, by the same reasoning, be entitled to the same rights we have?

The fact that these questions may sound contrary to common sense doesn't automatically count against them. Slave owners said the same thing against the abolition of slavery. Indeed, whenever you question underlying cultural assumptions, your ideas are liable to sound contrary to common sense.

Questioning cultural assumptions can sound bizarre

This is not a defense of the thesis that animals have rights. Whether they do, or whether they have the same rights as humans, is a matter for argument, evidence, and reasoning. But it's a topic that may be enlightening to examine, and it gets exposed by questioning the whole basis of our arguments about human rights.

Constitutionality

A different kind of answer to the question of equal rights is that we (human Americans) are guaranteed equal rights by the Constitution. *Within* the context of a society that accepts the constitution, constitutionality is the deciding factor in judging rights and obligations. *Within* that context, this argument is valid:

PREMISE 1.   It is unconstitutional.

∴ CONCLUSION 1.   It shouldn't be allowed.

The Constitution, though useful, is not sacred. We change it periodically by adding or subtracting amendments, by letting the Supreme Court reinterpret it (itself an action not sanctioned by the Constitution), or simply by ignoring it sometimes when it gets in the way (if you try to exercise your constitutional right to bear firearms by carrying an unconcealed rifle down the street, the police will simply arrest you for disturbing the peace). On a deeper level, then, we will have to question whether the Constitution is correct in what it says about rights. We will want to see the evidence it rests on, the reasons that persuaded the authors of the Constitution that all humans do have equal rights, the reasons we agree. And that again means questioning the whole basis of arguments.

Problems

Comment on the following:

1. If you're so smart, why aren't you rich?

2. Who is better genetically fitted to survival, women or men?

3. Observe people carefully and you'll notice that when they scratch their noses while they're saying something, they're usually lying.

4. Which people are more forceful and domineering, Libras or Pisces?

5. What's the difference between a pure-bred dog and a mongrel?

6. Arthur Schopenhauer showed what was wrong with sex acts between humans and animals: " . . . Bestiality is a wholly abnormal offense that is very rarely committed, and so is really something exceptional. Moreover, it is so revolting and contrary to human nature that it condemns itself and deters more effectively than could any rational arguments."

3. Beyond Arguments: The Examined Life

Topics like capital punishment and the legalization of marijuana are controversial. That means that there are arguments given on both sides. If you want to defend or oppose one of the sides, questioning presuppositions or the whole basis of an opponent's argument is a useful strategy. It is a useful strategy even if you have no actual opponent and are simply trying to get at the truth of the matter on your own.

But there are many aspects of life that don't present themselves in the form of arguments or even controversies. There may be ways of looking at them in terms of arguments, but that's not how they present themselves. Rather, they seem to be just "things": goals, *Analyzing* desires, cultural traditions, social institutions, habits, fears, ways of *"things"* thinking and reacting. Yet these "things" need rational examination as much as arguments do. They are parts of your life that may heavily influence whether you'll be happy or sad, successful or unsuccessful, and it's important that you reason them out. You may not want to take the results of your reasoning as the only factor in making important decisions (emotional responses, for example, also have to be weighed in), but it would be foolish to make the important decisions in your life without at least doing your best to reason them our first.

Actions

School: Should you continue in school? What do you hope to gain? Is going to school an effective way of gaining that? In relation to those goals, what is the significance of grades?

Exams: What are the final exams in your courses likely to cover? When should you begin studying? How should you study? What's the smartest way to divide up your time? Can you fit in both study and enjoyment?

Marriage: Should you marry so-and-so? Or even before you have anyone particular in mind, what kind of person do you want to have for a spouse? Where are you most likely to meet such a person? Is that the kind of place you go to frequently?

Habits: You realize that you shouldn't smoke cigarettes. What's the best way to get yourself to quit? Should you just do it by trial and error? Quit cold turkey? Taper off? Pay money to have someone hypnotize you? How important is quitting to you? How important should it be?

Fears: You are afraid of heights. What should you do to get over it? What concrete steps can you take? Any? Or is learning to accept the fear and live with it a more realistic alternative? What steps can you take toward that?

These are all merely questions, not answers. But there are answers — solid, realistic, maybe surprising answers — to many of them. And many answers can be discovered by reasoning. The mere act of asking yourself these questions seriously is sometimes enlightening. At the least it brings before your mind goals you have, and it makes you wonder about the means for achieving those goals. It may make you reevaluate your present behavior to see if it's likely to help or hinder achieving those goals. And reasoning the things out will almost certainly help you make better decisions about what to do.

Decisions

This is true even of small decisions. If you are playing chess, you'll want to reason out your moves in advance. You have to figure out what the effects of *this* move will be, what alternative moves you have, what the range of your opponent's responses are, what responses you will have to each of *those* moves, and so on, for as many moves in advance as you can keep track of. But you have to make these calculations while keeping directly in mind your long-range goal (winning the game) as well as your shorter-range goals (this particular gambit or piece of strategy). And you have to make sure that the shorter-range goal does not conflict with the long-range one: Winning a piece may cause you to lose the game.

Reasoning is crucial in less "intellectual" games as well. If you play poker and rely primarily on luck or hunches, you're probably not going to win much money. At least not for long. There are many factors in playing well and winning consistently, but an essential one is knowing the odds against drawing a card you need and balancing that against the bet you must make to stay in. And that involves careful reasoning.

Even in "physical" games you can benefit from reasoning things out. If you have trouble catching a football, say, because it often bounces off your hands, reasoning about what's involved in catching can actually help you. Practice, of course, is the principal help, but you have to know *what* to practice. One thing that makes a ball bounce off your hands is that it's traveling fast while your hands are standing still. You can remedy that by having the passer throw the ball more slowly (that's no good — it's more likely to be intercepted) or by moving your hands faster. So *that's* what you should practice: moving your hands in the same direction the ball is moving when you're trying to catch it.

Reasoning out physical things like this is not as farfetched as it may sound at first. It is one of the functions of good coaches: They reason out strategies and ways of playing, and they teach mediocre players how to improve by telling them what to do. Good coaches needn't be able to do the actions themselves; they need to *know* which things to do and get their players to do them. And one of the best ways to come to *know* what to do, even in physical acts like catching a football well, is by reasoning it out.

Notice how much the reasoning in this last case is like constructing an argument. You see a problem; you break it down into parts; you envision various solutions; you bring up reasons for and against some of them; and you draw a conclusion (based on the reasons) about which solution is best.

4. Reasoning Out Your Actions

The same method of reasoning will help you figure out good answers and make intelligent decisions for more important questions and problems. Before trying to write out this method in a general form, though, let's examine a topic in which coherent reasoning seems essential but is not very often employed and from which a general method will emerge.

Consider marriage again. There are many worthwhile questions to ask yourself about marriage: Is it still a necessary institution in our society? What is the relationship between marriage and children? What's wrong with having more than one spouse? Should you get married at all? Why? Let's confine ourselves to a more personal one: "Whom should you marry?" Or in the more immediate situation where you are already contemplating marriage with a particular person, "Should you marry X?" *An example*

This seems like a question that sorely needs reasoning right at the moment, yet it's probably true that many people marry their spouses without reasoning it out very much. They *feel* a lot about it and react to their emotions. Maybe they even analyze their emotions. But they generally don't reason out the positive and negative aspects of marrying X.

This is not to exclude emotions or passions. Passions may be the right thing to act on in a lot of situations, and they may be a part of the decision to marry X. But marriage is supposed to be a long-term, maybe lifelong, commitment. An optimal decision needs reasons behind it.

What reasons do people have for marrying the people they do? Probably the most frequent reason is *love*.

Because you've become so well trained in reasoning, the question that springs immediately into your mind is, "Is love a *good* reason for marrying somebody?" (That is a question about *validity*. The other critical questions that occur to you (again, as a reasoner) are about truth and paraphrase: "Do I really love X? What makes me think so? What *evidence* do I have?" and "What do I mean, roughly, by 'love' in this case?")

To judge by the divorce rate, love doesn't seem to be a particularly good reason for marriage; at least it doesn't seem to make the majority of marriages last. But how about you specifically? How often are you misled by your feelings into thinking people are better than they are? How long does the feeling of love typically last for you?

If love doesn't seem to be a good reason, you're still stuck with finding one. The answer, clearly, is to be found by figuring out certain things about you, about marriage, and about X. First, you have to figure out what your *goal* is in getting married. What do you want specifically? (This will not automatically have a selfish answer; the things you want may include X's welfare.) Second, you have to figure out what sort of person is likely to fit in with and aid attaining those goals. Third, you have to figure out if X is that sort of person and if marrying X is the most suitable action. Fourth, you have to recognize the drawbacks to marrying X and calculate how serious they are. (Serious enough to cause divorce later?) Finally, it may be worthwhile to question whether your goals in getting married, and specifically in marrying X, are good ones, ones that are worth pursuing.

These questions can be turned into a rough method for reasoning things out. Provided you adapt it to fit the particular circumstances under consideration, it is a useful framework for analyzing any number of your actions.

A Method for Analyzing Actions

STEP 1. What are your goals in this activity?

STEP 2. How do your present actions contribute to or detract from achieving these goals?

STEP 3. What are the ways best suited to achieving these goals?

STEP 4. What costs and disadvantages do those ways have?

STEP 5. Are the goals worth achieving?

Step 1   Knowing your goals in an action is so obvious a step in reasoning that it seems unnecessary to write it down. Why are you doing something if you don't know what you want from it? Yet it's very easy to engage in activities without ever thinking out the goals beforehand. It is especially important that you think out *specific* goals like getting a raise or losing ten pounds, not just general ones like being successful and healthy. What in particular do you want to gain from *this* action?

Specific goals

Doing this effectively requires that you be honest with yourself. Honesty is not enough, though. It also requires some intense thinking out; it requires reasoning. It is important to find out what you really want, not just what you think you want. Many goals are foisted on people from the outside — by movies, television, advertisements, peer pressure. If you work for and achieve one of these, and it's not something you really want, attaining it is likely to make you feel empty. So it's necessary to think your way through your actions and your motives.

Real goals

Why are you going to school? Or, more specifically, why are you taking one particular course? Questions like these can't be answered in a textbook, of course; they depend too much on your personal desires. But look at a few possible goals. You might have taken the course to fulfill a requirement, or to earn a high grade, or to gain knowledge of that subject, or because it was a challenge, or to be with your friends, or for some combination of these.

Examples

Notice how merely considering these alternatives closely makes you realize how inadequate some of the goals are. It also should make you see interconnections between the specific goals and others you may have. Why should fulfilling a requirement, for example, be impor tant? What is the good of that, of graduating? High grades are a clear, specific goal; what in turn do they get for you? As an end in itself a grade soon becomes just a small, unremembered part of your grade-point average; as a step along the way toward, say, getting a job, it seems unrealistic; as an index of how much you learned, though, a grade can give you a valuable, objective assessment. Knowledge of a subject is an appropriate goal, especially if you are interested in the subject or think you might become interested (broadening your horizons), but also if the knowledge will be useful to you in your practical life (like reasoning). Being with your friends seems like a paltry goal in taking a course (you can be with them before and after class), and it feels uncomfortable just to consider it as a possible main motive. But examine your behavior. If you find yourself taking classes with your friends, classes you don't particularly need or care about, then the desire to be with or be approved by your friends may in fact be your real goal. If so, your goals probably need some careful reexamination.

Step 2   Once you know what you want, you have to figure out if your actions help you get it. That is, you want to know how much of what you do contributes to achieving your goals and how much detracts from achieving them. In detailing what your present course of action accomplishes, it's again necessary to be as specific as possible.

You might think that once people realize what they want, their actions will just turn in that direction. It doesn't seem to be so, though. Many times peoples' actions seem to be at cross-purposes with their goals.

Suppose you want to quit smoking. It is clear that many of the activities you ordinarily engage in are not conducive to quitting smoking, and since it seems like an important goal, it's probably necessary to sacrifice some other pleasures to attain it. Quitting shortly before a time of stress, for example, is going to be counter-productive because each foiled attempt makes it harder to believe that you'll ever succeed. Other actions are dictated as well: You should (at least temporarily) stay away from friends who smoke and from situations during which you typically smoked before. That means you may have to skip satisfying meals and drinking alcohol for a while; avoid parties, friends who smoke, and long car rides; and cultivate actions that make smoking difficult or less desired (swimming, watching scary movies about lung cancer, drinking water, brushing your teeth). Performing ordinary actions, the ones you do without thinking, will make it all the more likely that your attempt will fail.

This means you have to be exceptionally conscious of the things you do during such times. If you have unsuccessfully tried quitting smoking before or breaking some comparable habit, make a list of your activities and see how many of them go against what you are trying to accomplish and how many go toward it.

Step 3   Thinking up alternative ways to achieve the goals you have in mind is the process in which reasoning comes in most purely. Reasoning is sometimes *defined* as a problem-solving ability. The problem to be solved is how *best* to achieve your goals.

*Problem
solving*

Many of the arguments analyzed in earlier chapters required a missing premise of a particular kind. The arguments had a form like this:

PREMISE 1.   You want X.

PREMISE 2.   Doing Y achieves X.

∴ CONCLUSION 1.   You should do Y.

The argument is invalid. It needs a missing premise saying that doing Y is not just *a* way of achieving X, but that it is the *best* way (or the best all-around way, or the most effective or most feasible way). This kind of argument bears a close relation to analyzing your activities. In step 1 you figure out what you want; in effect you fill in premise 1. In step 2 you detail what means you are now using to get it; that, in effect, is premise 2. In step 3 you search for other, better ways of achieving your goals, that, in effect, is testing the missing premise.

Finding better ways calls for clear thinking and ingenuity. You are unnecessarily limited if you confine yourself to standard ways of pursuing goals; indeed, step 3 is supposed to remind you to search for unconventional ways. You have to keep in mind not only what you want to achieve, of course, but also what is feasible, effective, and in accord with other goals and limitations (like morality, for instance). But even within such limits it is surprising how many new ways you can come up with once you set yourself to thinking them out.

Suppose you are nearing the time for final exams in your history course. One very specific goal you may have is to do well on the test (that's step 1). You can get evidence of how effective your present test-taking activities are by looking at your grade-point average and your performance on previous tests in this and similar courses (that's step 2).

In step 3 you examine other ways to do well on the test. What are some more effective ways? The stock answers, "Study a lot" or "Know the material," are not very helpful. They're too general, and they don't dictate any definite strategy. You need to know what *specifically* to study, and that means wondering what the final exam will cover. Trying to figure out what the final will cover is a good, incisive, answerable problem for almost any course, and it is something that reasoning should help you answer. By examining the teacher's earlier tests and noting which material in the course has been emphasized in the lectures, you will probably gain an insight into the kind of thing the teacher thinks is important in the course, and that's a good bet for test questions. But you can come up with a more concrete answer than that. Ask yourself: If I were the teacher, what would I ask? And try to put yourself in the teacher's place. What knowledge would you be trying to get across to students (goals again)? How would you go about doing it (means to the goals)? How does one teach history?

Some hard thinking will reveal that there are probably two main approaches to teaching a course like history: You can emphasize the *details* or the *overview*. Emphasizing the details aims at getting students to know a historical period intimately, from the inside. If it is a course on the Italian Renaissance, it means knowing the various principalities, their rulers, families, and alliances, their geographical limitations, and their economic situation. If it is a course in art history, it means being able to identify a great many paintings, statues, and buildings. If it is a course in literature, it means knowing the individual poems, novels, and plays, and, perhaps, characters and individual passages.

The overview approach, on the other hand, tries to get students to see a historical period as a whole, with certain dominant trends and preoccupations. It's a more theoretical approach and uses selected details only as illustrations of larger points. The Renaissance course would emphasize the rediscovery of Greek or Roman models or else the continuity with the Middle Ages; the art history course would emphasize the earmarks of the periods being covered and how they fit together; the English literature course would emphasize common themes of the writers and comparisons and contrasts between them.

It is easy to recognize which of the two approaches your teacher tends to emphasize. And knowing the tendency of your teacher is likely to give you much more specific information about what will be on the test; it will also dictate the most reasonable way to study for the test. The most efficient way to learn a mass of detailed facts is to memorize them: Make up lists out of your notes and readings, and quiz yourself until you can rattle off the facts almost instantly. This is the way vocabulary is studied in a foreign language course. Memorizing is not the best way to study for the overview sort of test, though. For this type of test understanding is necessary (seeing how the parts fit together); outside reading will also probably help quite a bit. You will still need to learn some individual details, but not a whole lot of them. Rather, you'll now have to search for ones that most perfectly support the broad perspective.

Of course, the best way to study would be to do *both*: memorizing masses of facts and understanding the period as a whole. Reasoning certainly doesn't rule that out. What it does, though, is tell you the most *effective* way to study for your test. Figuring out the approach to the test will give you a head start that you wouldn't have had if you simply tried to "know the material." Reasoning out new, effective ways to achieve your goals can give you a much better chance of succeeding.

Doing step 3 need not be this elaborate. Sometimes thinking out the simplest procedures for doing the simplest tasks can be absurdly practical.

The authors of *Cheaper by the Dozen* joke about the methods they had to use to raise twelve children. Giving twelve baths, for example, required a very fast procedure. Fill the tub, they say, soap a washcloth, then: zip, down the front of an arm, up the back; Zip, down the front of a leg, up the back; and so forth. Two strokes for each part of the body and you're finished in four minutes. Now that's *not* brilliant. Anyone could think of it. What is amazing is that people don't think of it. Some people (adults, not just children) can't shower in five minutes to save their lives. Even the simplest reasoning, if you can remember to do it, can teach you things.

Step 4   It is not enough to recognize your goals and then figure out the best way to attain them. You also have to assess the disadvantages of your actions, both with regard to yourself and others. This often calls for some sensitivity. Reasoning things out is not the same as being heartless, though a bald description of the process may make it seem that way.

You don't want merely to find the most effective way of getting what you want, you also want to be sure that it fits in with your other goals, desires, and beliefs. If the most effective way to pass your history test is by cheating, reasoning probably does not yield the verdict that you should cheat. Passing the test is only *one* goal, not the most important one either, and cheating will go against another goal of being honest. Reasoning will thus direct you to another way to pass the test, maybe less effective, but more in keeping with the rest of your life. Thus you should not get the impression that the reasonable thing is to get what you want regardless of the consequences; that would be foolish in most instances. The reasonable thing is to take account of the consequences.

Step 5   One traditional view of reasoning is that it is properly confined to discovering *means* to achieve goals, that it cannot be used to set the goals themselves because they are a product of psychological and environmental factors, not of rational choice. If you happen to hold that view, then step 5 is a distinctly odd one; it requires you to examine your goals directly and figure out if there are reasons why they are worth achieving.

One way of doing this is to weigh one set of goals you have against another set you also have. You may belong to a fraternity or a sorority for any number of reasons. But it is true for the most part that such organizations interfere with learning. So if learning is important to you, the rational thing will probably be to drop fraternities and sororities.

This may sound like merely recognizing disadvantages of certain activities (thus step 4), rather than questioning the goals themselves (step 5). Take it a little deeper, though. One of the things a college education is supposed to give you is new values, richer ones than those with which you entered school. This is especially true of a liberal-arts education: By exposing students to art, music, literature, other cultures and languages, it is possible for students to change their perspectives and ways of thinking for others that are richer. And in many cases this sort of education works: Many liberal-arts students do leave college with a different outlook from the one with which they entered. It is a mistake to think that all a university education does, or is supposed to do, is fill you up with new *facts*; it is also supposed to give you new ways of looking at the old facts. *[Changing values]*

One of the perplexing things about changing values, though, is that *you* do not seem to be exactly the cause of the change. You typically cannot just make up your mind and say, "I don't like Shakespeare or Picasso or Beethoven, but from now on I'm going to." Your actions and attitudes, however, *can* consciously help or hinder the transformation of values. You can say, "I'm going to take a good course in Shakespeare and really try to see what's there"; you can look hard and closely at one of Picasso's cubist paintings and try to understand and appreciate its complexities; you can take a music-appreciation course — not because you are already interested in classical music but, in a sense, because you're *not*. *[Being open to new values]*

Doing this is placing yourself open to new values, and in a way it is a form of questioning your old ones, of wondering if they should indeed *be* your values. Step 5 contains a reminder that sometimes you should change your goals. One of the gravest charges against fraternities and sororities is that they tend to foster the same set of values you had before you entered the university, and thus they make it less likely that you will be open to other possibilities. This may not be so of all fraternities and sororities, of course; you have to judge in the individual case. But if you find it is so, then you may decide rationally not just to give up the organization, but to try to give up the goals for which you joined the organization in the first place.

Step 5 is radical

This is a much more radical thing than giving up one goal because it conflicts with another. And indeed step 5 should be thought of as a step that may lead to radical conclusions. It directs you to examine your goals themselves.

Newspapers periodically contain stories of people who wake up one day and change their whole way of life. They decide to abandon the job they have held for twenty years, perhaps their family, or their whole way of life. One striking thing such people often say is that the possibility of leaving their established way of life never occurred to them before. Their problems and the solutions always were thought of *within* the way of life they were living. Probably, far larger numbers of people never do consider alternate manners of living or, if they do consider them, do it just as a pleasant dream, not as a serious possibility. You are not likely to throw away what you are doing for a whole different set of values, but that should be a reasoned decision, not the product of blindness. Under step 5, questioning your way of life and envisioning alternatives seriously becomes an integral part of the examined life.

Doing the steps takes concentration

In doing any one of these five steps, the most important thing is to do it. That means not just answering quickly, not giving the automatic non-thought-out response. Look beneath the surface of your acknowledged goals to find other ones that are easier to overlook. Inspect your activities closely: Do they make you happy? Are they steps on the way to being happy? If not, you should be able to account for why not. Experiment in your head with alternative plans; search for them actively and then add up their advantages and disadvantages. Finally, evaluate your goals. How does having them make you feel? What conflicts do you have among them? Are they, considered as objectively as possible, *worth* pursuing?

Problems

Use the appropriate part of the method for analyzing actions on the following topics.

1. To what extent should people show allegiance to their country?

2. To what extent should people show allegiance to the symbols of their country, for example, flag, national anthem, etc.

3. "Flight Insurance: Before you hastily buy last-minute flight insurance from an airport vending machine (as many, many travelers do), consider the question in the light of your total insurance coverage. Do you really need more insurance coverage? (And remember, American domestic lines are demonstrably the safest in the world; you are safer in the sky in an airplane than in your bathtub at home. Don't be panicked into a needless purchase.)" (Birnbaum, *United States 1979*)

4. On pages 271-272 we went through a number of questions about whether *love* was a good reason for marrying X. Some people think it takes the spontaneity and joy out of a relationship to analyze it that much. Is that true?

5. Is "love" hard to paraphrase?

6. What is the difference between a rational analysis of a relationship and a psychoanalysis of a relationship?

5. Reasoning Things Out: A Broader Method

The method just discussed applies primarily to personal activities and goals. But you may also wonder about broader aspects of our society and culture.

You may become interested, for example, in questioning such social institutions as trial by jury or our adversary system of justice, or such economic institutions as private property, or such cultural taboos as eating horsemeat, or other institutions, habits, cultural traditions, legal tenets, moral injunctions. Reasoning is the prime tool for questioning such things because you want to figure out the *truth* about them: what they are for, how they work, whether they fall short, how much they can be improved.

A method for dealing with things like these can be readily developed out of the method for analyzing personal activities.

A Method for Analyzing "Things"

STEP 1.   What is the thing *supposed* to do? What is its purpose or goal?

STEP 2.   What does the thing in fact do? How does it actually work?

STEP 3.   How close does it come to what it is supposed to do?

STEP 4.   What drawbacks or harmful side effects does it have?

STEP 5.   Are there better ways to achieve the same end? What are they?

STEP 6.   What drawbacks do these ways have?

STEP 7.   If the thing doesn't accomplish its end very well, how did it come about historically, and why does it persist?

STEP 8.   Finally, is it an end worth pursuing? At what cost?

These steps are adapted from the earlier set, but there are a few important differences.

In step 1 you are again figuring out goals and purposes. This is an obvious first step to seeing if something works, but it often requires that you go beneath the surface. What is the purpose of trial by jury? What is it supposed to accomplish? If you say *justice*, either you are not familiar with our court system or you haven't thought it out enough. Juries are not allowed to decide what is just (that is supposed to be contained in the laws, which juries may not tamper with); they are supposed to decide what is *true*. It is up to the jury, for example, to decide if A in fact killed B, what A's motives were, and whether A was sane at the time. Those are *factual* questions, not moral ones. The jury doesn't get to decide whether insanity should or should not make a person guilty. That's already decided. The jury only decides what happened.

Correctly recognizing the jury's actual purpose, though, can make you decidedly uneasy about the institution of trial by jury. It might make sense to rely on the *moral feelings* of twelve normal citizens, but it doesn't look like such a trustworthy method to get at the *truth* of what happened. Imagine that we did physics that way: One group of scientists would present its case that the earth orbits around the sun; the other group of scientists would present its case that the sun orbits around the earth; then both groups of scientists would leave it up to twelve untrained people to decide which side was true! That would be a terrible way to do science. What makes us think it's a good way to come to true findings about ballistics, complex tax problems, and psychiatric diagnoses? Does it sound like a trustworthy method to you?

You have to be careful where you apply step 1, though; not everything has a purpose or goal. Natural things, for example, don't. You can't legitimately ask, "What is the purpose of Pikes Peak? Or the ocean?" They don't have *any* purpose, though we can *use* them to accomplish a purpose *we* have in mind. So it is advisable to question purposes only when the thing is made or invented by humans.

Achievements and shortcomings

To ask about the shortcomings of trial by jury is to go on to steps 2 and 3. You have to examine what an institution accomplishes and how close that comes to what it is designed to do. So many of the institutions of our society fail, to a greater or lesser degree, to fulfill their purpose that you can illustrate the point with some of your own examples.

Harmful side effects

In step 4 you consider not only the shortcomings but also the harmful effects a thing has and whether it achieves its purpose or not. In a world like ours, in which many events are interconnected, it's sometimes difficult to perceive the harm. Changing the maximum highway speed from 70 to 55 mph does save lives in traffic accidents. Many lives. It's necessary to be honest about that. But the change has negative effects also. By increasing traveling time, it increases the price of goods, and in the long run that will probably also result in deaths. It is very doubtful that the number of such deaths comes close to the number of people saved in accidents, but it's important to recognize the costs on both sides. And that's true for most actions in our society. Experimenting on fancy transplant techniques saves lives, but it uses money that could be used for research for cures that are much more widely applicable, though not as attention-getting.

Steps 5 and 6 are again the ones that require the greatest amount of ingenuity. It is in step 5 that you try to think of better ways of accomplishing set goals. That calls both for original thinking (so you won't be confined to the old standard solutions to problems, solutions that may not work well) and for an ability to balance factors realistically so as to come up with a new approach that is likely to work in practice. *New approaches*

Take the way our lawyers function in the courtroom. It is called an adversary system because one lawyer argues *for* the accused and the other lawyer argues *against* the accused. One lawyer asks questions only to bring out information *favorable* to the accused; the other asks only what will be *unfavorable* to the accused.

The hope behind the adversary system is that the two one-sided ways of presenting the case will balance each other out and the result will be truth. That's step 1. But a little reflection will show that the system will not always work that way: When the lawyers are not equal in ability and interest, and the evidence is at all close, the system is as likely to lead to falsehood and an incorrect verdict based on it. (That's a partial treatment of step 2.) Of course, there is more involved in the system than this quick examination reveals. For example, lawyers defend their clients whether they think they are innocent or not, so under our system *someone* will defend the accused even if everyone thinks he or she is guilty. A trial system that used only judges hired by the state would be more open to corruption and bias. Thus the adversary system by its nature sometimes leads to incorrect verdicts, but it also generally avoids certain types of corruption and bias. (That's a partial treatment of step 3.)

To find an alternative courtroom system (in step 5) that would work in practice would be a hard and complex undertaking. One factor making any wholesale change of systems difficult is simply the cost of changing over. Our present system works, even if imperfectly, and people are familiar with it. To start a change from the ground up might involve too many unforeseen compensatory changes in other aspects of our lives. (This is doing step 6.) Now maybe a change from the ground up is undesirable for reasons like this (the point needs a lot more argument), but there are many changes that do not have such drawbacks. Wouldn't it be a fairer system, for example, if in addition to one-sided questioning by the lawyer-adversaries, someone else who was simply interested in the truth could *also* ask questions, say, the judge, or someone appointed by the court, or (better yet) the jurors themselves? That seems like a more effective way of revealing important information that might otherwise have remained hidden.

Wouldn't it be better similarly if witnesses were allowed to tell their stories in full instead of merely responding to the lawyers' questions? They could *also* be grilled by the lawyers, but surely it doesn't aid truth-finding to have essential information left out simply because it wasn't asked for.

Specific changes like these in an institution are often of more benefit than wholesale ones. And thinking out new ones gives you an insight into how things work, fail to work, and can be improved. That is a prime job of reasoning.

Step 7 is a different sort of question from the other steps. It asks not for reasoning so much as for research. It directs you to ask how an institution or a custom got to be here. It is thus a question in history, but it is related closely to reasoning, especially if the thing in question does not work well. Knowing the history of a thing can help you understand the thing's point or lack of one. It can also help you to appreciate how well it does work.

Our legal system (including trial by jury and the adversary system) developed partly by conscious planning; partly from a tradition reaching back into medieval England and beyond; partly by adaptation to very concrete, practical cases; partly by recognition of new principles of justice (like racial equality); and partly because of many other factors. That is why it is doubtful that a purely invented system would work as well as ours in so many areas. More specifically, our system of trial by jury (instead of by judge), with lawyers (not judges) questioning witnesses, came about partly as a reaction to the medieval English system in which the judge was a *Lord* who could *profit* directly from the verdict and who already wielded too much *power*. Knowing this little bit of history can then help in reasoning about our legal system because it illustrates that there is not anything intrinsically necessary about trial by jury or lawyers as advocates, that both institutions arose in reaction to a problem that no longer exists in the same form.

Step 7 requires some care in interpretation. A historical explanation of how a thing came about is not the same as giving a rational justification for it. Knowing how Nazism grew as a response to the conditions in Germany after World War I does not show that Nazism was a good solution to Germany's problems. That is a kind of mistake sometimes made by social scientists.

Similarly, the fact that a practice *did not* occur in history does not show automatically that there is something wrong with it. For instance, some people have argued that the same principles we use to justify raising animals for food would justify raising human babies for food also (for example, provided we butcher them painlessly and before they reach the age of reason!), and that therefore raising animals for food should be stopped. It is *not* an adequate objection to this statement to say that people *do not* raise babies for food and never have. That people do not do something doesn't show that there is anything wrong with it. (Therefore, the missing premise involved in the objection is false.) There are only three adequate positions: Reject butchering animals, accept butchering babies(!), or find some principle that shows what is wrong in the one case and not wrong in the other.

Step 8 is like the last step in analyzing your personal activities. Evaluating goals themselves and wondering if they are worth pursuing are important parts of having a reasonable view of the world. It enables you to choose wisely among goals; understand how social, political, economic, moral, and educational practices fit together (or fail to); and gives you a defensible perspective from which to accept or reject principles and points of view.

Evaluating goals

One trouble in doing this well is that social and cultural goals, like personal ones, are deeply embedded in us. So many of our customs and habits just seem right — indeed, the only right thing — that it is difficult to get yourself to question them cogently. A very good way to do it, however, is to take a position you believe in or a custom you follow and try to construct the best argument you can *against* it. That means taking, as the conclusion to be proved, the direct contrary of what you believe, breaking it down into its component parts, and thinking hard about the best reasons you can to cover each part. It is necessary to *work* at finding new reasons because what a person believes in seems so *natural* (paraphrase?) that it is hard to envision its being wrong.

This is a valuable exercise, both because it is good practice at constructing hard arguments and because it may broaden your point of view. It may even help you to discover things you never thought of before.

It is sometimes said that people cannot step outside their culture to evaluate it and its goals. Some cultures are deeply committed to human sacrifice or cannibalism; ours is not. But, it is argued, that does not give us the right to condemn their culture and their goals. *We* are simply committed to other things.

There is some truth in this claim. Certainly it would be difficult, maybe impossible, to evaluate one's *whole* cultural heritage, and there may be some specific cultural taboos that are too deep to be evaluated by reason.

But *most* cultural attitudes and beliefs are not like that. It may be difficult to bring oneself to evaluate them, but it is possible rationally. To do it, you have to analyze them not on the basis of feelings or responses or what seems natural or right, but on the basis of reasons.

A good example is the one just mentioned of "human sacrifice or cannibalism." Notice, from the point of view of *reasons*, how different the two acts are. There are many reasons why human sacrifice should not be practiced: Innocent people are made to feel pain; it takes away people's ability to choose what will happen to them; and the sacrifice doesn't accomplish anything. (These may not, of course, seem like good reasons to the person who believes in human sacrifice, but they do to me.) On the other hand, I can't really think of any good reasons against cannibalism. I can think of reasons against *killing* people to eat them, but not against eating them if they happen to have *been* killed. Reasons against violating someone's wishes are also easy to find, but not against doing it when a person has consented. The act *feels* wrong to me — and I'm revolted by the mere idea of eating another person's flesh — but I can't think of any *reasons* that make it wrong; it doesn't inflict any pain; it doesn't harm others; it doesn't violate anyone's rights. I would hope to be able to convince a rational native that human sacrifice was wrong, but I don't have any such hope with regard to cannibalism.

Maybe there *are* solid reasons why cannibalism is wrong, and I just can't think of them. But it seems more likely that this is one feeling that is merely a cultural prejudice.

The active search for reasons does enable you to come to rational conclusions even about deep-seated cultural attitudes and goals.

Problems

For topics 1-7, use the appropriate part of the method for analyzing "things."

1. Name some prominent social institutions, other than those mentioned in the text, that fail to fulfill their purposes. Explain.

2. Are vocabulary tests a legitimate part of measuring intelligence in standardized IQ tests? Why or why not?

3. Genetic engineering.

4. George Will is a nationally-syndicated columnist. The following is from a column entitled, "There's No Argument For Incest:"

I cannot catalog all the disagreeable potentialities of the modern mind, but an article attempting to make incest less abhorrent deserves attention because it illuminates, like a flare of sulfurous gas, the darker recesses of that mind. [The middle of Will's column is a report on the contents of that article, of some findings in favor of incest by other researchers, and of the efforts of some groups to make anti-incest laws less severe.]

The co-author of the original Kinsey report says: "It is time to admit," among other things, that incest between children and adults "can sometimes be beneficial."

"It is time . . . . " This incantation moves the modern mind: change is natural, therefore change is progressive, therefore the natural progression of mankind is through expanding "emancipation" from "taboos" and other "hang-ups" that inhibit "self-fulfillment." The nonsequiturs clang together like empty freight cars on a railroad to barbarism.

There is no labyrinth as unconquerable as a simple mind: An idea, once in, stays. The simplemindedness of the modern age manifests itself in the worship of "change."

5. Alcoholism is a disease.

6. Name at least two purposes of giving parking tickets. Can these purposes come into conflict? How?

7. American paper money all has the same size, same color, and same basic design for all denominations. Paper money in most countries comes in different sizes, colors, and designs for different denominations.

People are often fond of the way their own money looks and prefer it to the money of other countries. In many cases this is simply liking what is more familiar, and there is no right or wrong to the matter. But is that true here?

With American bills all the same size, how does a blind person tell the difference between a $10 bill and a $20 bill? What function does it serve to have different colors?

6. *Judging Your Ability to Reason*

By this point you have been learning methods of reasoning and you have been practicing using the skills. You should be able to judge your improvement by comparing your skills to what they were before you began studying reasoning. And you should compare your skills primarily on two grounds. The first is essentially the ability to *answer* questions more skillfully, to *solve* problems better. The second consists not so much in answering questions as in *asking* the right questions to begin with; it is *noticing* that there are problems to be solved.

Answering Questions

The first ability in practice relies on being able to make good, sharp criticisms. You should have noticed a marked improvement in this. Whether people are good at reasoning or not, they criticize things they hear, but it is often in a vague, sometimes empty way. Consider the following negative criticisms:

What he said wasn't very clear.
It was so unclear I couldn't understand it.

I disagree with what she said.
I don't like it.
The book didn't hold my interest.
Who is to say if she is right?

He left something out. What he says might be right, but it doesn't convince me.

Each of these is an example of criticism, but none is a very good criticism. They are altogether too general and uninformative. Some of them could just as easily be saying something against *you* as against the arguer (such as, "You're not very good at understanding things

then, are you?" or "You must have a pretty limited range of interests.").

*Precise
criticisms
needed*

If you have become better at reasoning, your stock of criticisms
should have become much more precise than this. You should now
find yourself keying in on exactly what is wrong. Instead of merely
saying that his argument was too unclear to understand, you will say:

> It was so unclear that I couldn't tell if he meant X or Y or some
> other thing. But if he meant X, then he is wrong for this reason; if
> he meant Y, then he is wrong for this other reason. And those seem
> the only plausible interpretations of his words.

Paraphrase

That is a formidable and precise way to criticize, and it is one that is
built on a skill of *paraphrasing*. It begins by actually trying to help the
other person's argument by clarifying it: If under each of the various
clarifications it still turns out he is wrong, then it doesn't look like he
has any real position left open to him. He can't any longer simply
reply, "That's not what I meant"; since you've given various readings
of his argument, he is at least obliged to say what he did mean.

Truth

Besides paraphrasing, you have learned to criticize for *truth,* and to
do this with precision also. Saying, "I disagree," is not really offering
any criticism. Why should anyone care if you disagree? Disagreeing
with a statement is not what is important; what is important is
producing *reasons* why the statement is *false.* That is a trenchant
criticism because it goes right to the heart of the matter. A person
cannot rationally ignore reasons against her position. She has to show
either that your reasons are wrong or that they do not oppose her
argument (truth and validity again).

Validity

Along with criticisms of meaning and truth, then, are precise
criticisms based on *validity.* That involves stating the arguer's missing
premises and evaluating them. If you have become better at reasoning, you will find yourself asking much more often, "Now what has
been *left out* of the argument? What is the arguer assuming but not
stating?" To evaluate someone's argument by saying, "That doesn't
convince me," is again not really to criticize the argument at all. Maybe
it *should* convince you; maybe you are just being stupid about it. The
solid criticism is to say instead:

> This argument doesn't convince me because his argument is in-
> valid. What he needs to prove his conclusion is *this,* and *this* is false
> because. . . ."

That is a criticism that is not only precise, but almost impossible to
escape. You have said what the arguer needs, and why what he needs
is wrong.

Paraphrasing, giving reasons for truth or falsity, and spotting
invalidities and missing premises are the major ways your ability to
criticize should have improved. Used well, they make an impressive
set of skills for evaluating arguments.

Asking the Important Questions

There is a second way in which your reasoning power should have improved. That's not only being able to come up with good criticism, but also finding points to criticize in the first place. You should have become more dubious, skeptical, and questioning. That doesn't mean you should be skeptical about people or their motives. It's not that people are out to fool you: Some of them are, but most are probably not. People fool *themselves,* or they get fooled by common ways of thinking. You should be skeptical about those ways of thinking. Statements, positions, habits, social institutions — things you would have taken for granted before — should now seem problematical to you. A reasoned life involves not just solving problems, though that by itself is a hard skill to attain, but actively looking for the problems you (and others) have overlooked.

Exercises to Chapter Seven

I. Identifying Issues

The arguments in 1–5 each revolve around an issue. Identify the focus of the issue by analyzing the arguments. What are the *key* claims in each issue? What parts of the conclusion are covered by the arguments? Is any part left uncovered by all?

1. (a) "After the 1925 Scopes Monkey Trial, public school textbooks in all subject areas gradually begin to deal with evolution as an unquestionable fact. Evolutionists insisted that creation was too religious to be presented in the public school. However, evolution cannot be observed in operation, so it must be accepted on faith also. It is a philosophy of life, a religion. Neither model [creation or evolution] can either be tested or repeated, so neither can qualify as a scientific theory. The evidence favoring both models can be studied so that the student may decide which model correlates the most data, with fewer contradictions."

   (b) " . . . the purpose of an English class is to teach English, of a math class to teach math, and of a science class to teach science. And to teach science means to inform students of the best available theories based on the scientific principles of empirical evidence and logical reasoning. The purpose of a science class is NOT to disseminate certain religious convictions in clear contravention of the constitutional guarantee of separation of church and state. You may as well teach woodcarving in history class or barnstorming in typing.

   "The point of this letter is not to argue the merits of evolution over those of any religious theory, but rather to ask that things be kept in their proper places. Science belongs in the science class; religion belongs in the Sunday School."

   (Both of these arguments were contained in letters to the editor of *The Times* of Shreveport, Louisiana, June 19, 1980.)

2. (a) A university is an institution dedicated to the dissemination of knowledge. Appreciation of our own language and traditions is a real part of an education. Studying a foreign language is an excellent way to gain such an appreciation. Besides that, it is often a real asset in getting a job. So university students should be required to master a foreign language.

(b) PREMISE 1.   A second language gives you access to more knowledge, literature, etc.

PREMISE 2.   Often, other languages are better suited to expressing specific ideas than your own is.

PREMISE 3.   Communication and interchange with other cultures is crucial to the maintenance of world peace as well as to the exchange of technological advances or important discoveries.

PREMISE 4.   Language is the most efficient means of communication.

∴ CONCLUSION 1.   It is necessary to learn one or more languages besides your own.

(c) "In order to get a college degree today, mere competence in one's field will not suffice. As many students are painfully aware, one has to take a mishmash of English literature, science, social science, humanities, foreign languages, and math.

"We are told that this is necessary to further some sort of nebulous idea of an educated man. But at a time when a college degree is often recognized as poor preparation for a career, can we really afford to spend one fourth to one half of our college career taking courses entirely unrelated to our major? Easing course requirements would allow a student to double the hours in his major.

"Further, it is evident that little is gained from these required courses. Students forget what they "learned" before they get final grades. They didn't want the course; they have no use for the course material; they may easily learn to actively hate the subject. You simply can't forcefeed unnecessary, unusable knowledge to students and realistically expect it to have any educational value.

" . . . If a student has adequate background, he should not be required to take any courses. If not, a pass-fail survey course might be appropriate. Best of all, no student should be required to take any course not directly applicable to his major." (*The Driftwood* (University of New Orleans), 11 October 1979. Reprinted by permission.)

3. (a) CONCLUSION: Couples should live together before getting married.

PREMISE 1.   Marriage is a lifelong contract.

PREMISE 2.   Living together allows a couple to test their relationship before getting married.

PREMISE 3.   By testing their relationship, they will have a better idea of whether it is sound enough to last a lifetime.

PREMISE 4. It is better to find out that information before marriage than after.

(b) Living together without being married is immoral. It's as simple as that.

(c) "The main truth about marriage is concealed from lovers because it cannot be experienced beforehand or even conceived by them — the daily grind in terms of self-interest. When an ordinary man and woman decide on marriage the step is remarkable enough. Two people who do not know each other to any extent (they cannot!) invite each other to all meals, and to bed, and to house, for the rest of their lives. It sounds crazy. If often works. Even so it is an extraordinary venture, no matter how often or universally done." (Collier, *The Carlyles,* New York: 1971, p. 36)

4. (a) When an animal goes mad and is endangering the lives of others, the animal is destroyed because it is no longer functioning in a normal society and is threatening the safety of others. This is true of those guilty of violent crimes, such as murder and rape, most of whom are multiple offenders. Capital punishment is not wrong, because it is putting a mad and dangerous animal away and setting an example to others like himself to protect the majority of people who lead relatively nonviolent lives.

(b) People often display their disgust with the death penalty. This is one of the reasons violent crimes are so prevalent in today's society.

These people say, "How many more human beings will we kill before our thirst for vengeance is finally quenched? Doesn't it make you feel good to know we've begun executing felons again?"

These people try to make those in favor of the death penalty seem guilty, and after headlines of bloody murders in our homes and neighborhoods, why shouldn't the average citizen have a thirst for vengeance?

Opponents of the death penalty should realize that if a person did not commit murder, he or she would not have to worry about the electric chair. A simple fact — but people often can't seem to understand this simplicity, especially when they are blinded by their feelings for a murderer.

5. (a) There's nothing bad about death. After all, when you're dead, you can't feel anything, not pain, not loss. You can't feel unhappy because you're not there. So if there is no unhappiness, no pain, no feelings of loss, there's nothing *bad* about it. It's simply not existing.

(b) There is nothing worse than death. When it comes to *my* death, nothing can be more important to me. Compared with it, bravery, honor, love, morality don't mean anything. To die in order to preserve them doesn't make any sense, for once I die, bravery, love, and the rest will stop existing for me. *Everything* will stop existing for me. As far as my feelings are concerned, my death is the same as the destruction of the whole universe.

II. Topics for Reasoning

The topics or issues in 6-22 are to be reasoned out. Where the methods in the chapter are appropriate, use the method for analyzing personal actions (p. 272) or the method for analyzing "things" (p. 279-280). (Some comments and further questions follow 6-12, so be sure to answer them before going on.)

6. *Race:* Are some races intellectually inferior to others?

7. *Divorce:* What can be said for and against it?

8. *Fear of heights:* A practical plan to overcome its effects.

9. *Treason:* What precisely is it, and is it bad?

10. In the exercises to Chapters Five and Six there were questions concerning the fact that European countries have an astonishingly lower rate of violent crimes than the United States and Canada. How good an explanation can you give of this?

11. *Abortion.*

12. *Passions:* Sometimes people are blinded by their passions for others. Because they love or hate someone, for example, they are unable to come to an unbiased view of that person's character. This happens frequently to parents, lovers, close friends, and bitter enemies. Sometimes this inability is disadvantageous (though in some situations it may be beneficial).

    Problem: How to get an accurate view of the person's character.

Comments:

6+ to 12+ concern topics 6 to 12 above. Be sure to answer the questions above before going on.

6+. Because race is a natural (not a man-made) phenomenon, it does not have a purpose. So it can't be analyzed by the methods in this chapter without rephrasing the question into one about the reasonable *attitude* to take toward racial differences. The important thing is to notice that the major issue is not the one asked in question 4, but one that is associated in many minds with the question of "racial inferiority." Doesn't it seem unlikely that two races will have exactly the same average intelligence? (They don't, for example, have the same average *height*.) They have such different backgrounds you would think that just as a matter of chance, intelligence would have been affected. A more important question is: "Is there a *significant* difference?" That's another matter entirely. The *most* important question, however, is one that is not asked directly in question 4, but is a crucial part of the issue raised and the reasonable attitude to take toward it. It's this: Suppose for the sake of argument that there is a difference, even a significant difference in the average intelligence of races; so what? What follows from that? What, if any, ramifications does it have legally, morally, educationally, socially? A good case can be made for saying *none*. (*Reason out some of the possible ramifications by using the method on p. 272.*)

7+. If you took the question to ask, "What can be said in favor of divorce as a necessary evil in our society?" then you have not gone far enough. That divorce is bad is a presupposition that needs to be analyzed. You should also have examined at least the possibility of its being a positive good. It does what it is designed to do — terminate undesired marriages — fairly efficiently. Steps 1, 2, and 3 probably reveal nothing against the institution of divorce. Maybe it should be thought of as a kind of graduation. True, under step 4 it has some undesirable side effects. Two main ones are deeply hurt feelings and the harm it does to children. But these do not really account for why people think of divorce as a bad thing. The partners involved do tend to suffer deeply, but there is something backward in using this as a reason for concluding that divorce is bad. Part of the cause of the hurt feelings is the belief that divorce is something *bad*. If divorce were a fairly probable occurrence — no hard feelings, you shake hands and walk away — then the people would not be hurt so much, or it would be a short-lived hurt the way it is when nonmarital relationships end.

Much of the harm that is done to the children may also be a product not of the divorce itself, but of thinking of divorce as a bad thing. These alternatives are worth exploring. But divorce in childless marriages or in marriages with grown children is still viewed as something saddening.

In fact it is hard to see what rational basis there is for thinking of divorce as bad. It does involve breaking a contract, but there aren't such bitter feelings when business partnerships are dissolved. And the civil contract of marriage like all contracts, has the possibility of terminating it built in.

Again, this is not an argument in favor of divorce. It is an argument in favor of examining deeply held ways of life to see if they are built on cultural prejudices. (*Try to figure out — historically? sociologically? — why divorce is viewed as a necessary evil (step 7). Is it a cultural prejudice or is there a firmer foundation? What practical, alternative methods are there of ending long-term relationships (steps 5 and 6)?*)

8+. Here step 3 (in the method for analyzing personal actions) is the one that needs to be thought out the most: What ways are best suited to overcome the effects of the fear of heights. But it is also important to get quite clear about step 1, the goal to be achieved. A natural goal is to get rid of the fear. But that may not be possible. A different but related goal is to minimize the negative effects the fear has on your behavior. This may not be the ideal goal — it would be easier if you were fearless — but it is a realistic backup.

One good way of finding a method is to look at other situations in which people are taught to operate in spite of fear (or other strong emotions). Wartime armies are a good example. It is remarkable in a way that ordinary men can be taught to risk their lives so completely — for instance, to charge an enemy position knowing that more than half of them will probably be casualties.

They are taught to overcome the effects of intense fear by many means. One of the main ones is sheer rote behavior: Recruits are made to practice the same action over and over again until it is done automatically, without thinking.

That method can be adapted to getting someone who is afraid of heights (or has some other phobia) to perform similar actions. It may not work for you in the end, of course (some soldiers still freeze), but it is a good plan. (*Step 5, however, needs to be examined also.*)

9+. One important lesson in reasoning is not to examine things from a perspective that is too narrowly personal. Examine your answer. Does it account for these facts: (a) treason can be committed out of deep conviction as well as other motives; (b) it can be committed against harsh and repressive governments as well as freedom-loving ones.

According to your answer, are Soviet defectors traitors? How about the refugees from Nazi Germany who wrote against Germany in our newspapers during World War II? Ezra Pound, an American poet, was later convicted of treason for broadcasting anti-American sentiments on Italian radio. How is he the same as, or different from, the German refugees? Are there circumstances under which you would feel a moral obligation to commit treason? Why or why not?

(*Are you willing to accept the logical consequences of your answer? If not, what can you do?*)

10+. This is a difficult phenomenon to explain, and plausible answers require some research, probably historical research. You have to look for possible contributing factors that are prevalent in the United States but not prevalent in Europe. (*This will in itself eliminate many popular explanations. Give a few that are ruled out.*) Examine: gun control, the amount of personal freedom, the training of policemen, the American dream of becoming rich, the lack of a solid family life, higher divorce rates, political and social dissatisfaction.

11+. There are a number of questions which you may not have considered explicitly, but which should at least not be confused in your answer:
Is a fetus alive?
Is it human?
Does it have rights?
What is the difference between a fetus, an embryo, and an infant?
Is abortion killing?
Is abortion murder?
Some of these questions are easy to answer. (*Which?*) Some are difficult to answer. (*Which?*) Some are often confused. (*Try to answer the questions if your analysis does not contain the answers.*)

12+. There are really two problems, both centered around step 3. First, how to come up with an assessment uninfluenced by your personal bias, and second to get yourself to believe the assessment. For what we tend to do when passions are involved is to make excuses and distort the evidence (unconsciously, of course) to suit our biases. This also applies to assessments you make of yourself.

If you wonder about whether your fiance is actually generous, you can ask a trusted friend (you want to make sure the friend has nothing to gain or lose by either answer). Under certain conditions, you might even get the most objective answer from a stranger. If your child's intelligence is in question, you can pay close attention to the results of intelligence tests and the assessment of teachers. If the United States is to interpret the U.S.S.R.'s actions and motives, a good place to start is with the opinions of America's European allies. In each case this evidence will not by any means be conclusive, but it is important to take it very seriously. Because it is not subject to the distorting influence of your passions, you should discount it only on the basis of clear interfering circumstances. That so many third-world countries resent the United States is evidence that the United States (or its representatives) is being oppressive. It is only evidence, of course, not proof: The resentment *may* be a result of something else, like jealousy of American affluence. *(Are other affluent nations, like Sweden, resented?)* But the evidence calls for a close self-examination, which we should strive to make as objective as possible.

Some further topics for reasoning out (without additional comments). Use the step methods whenever appropriate.

13. *Paternalism:* You are being paternalistic if you act as if you know what is better for a person than that person does. Under what conditions, if any, are you justified in being paternalistic? Give the clearest example you can of a case in which it is right, and the clearest example of a case in which it is wrong. Take a concrete example and analyze it carefully according to the five steps.

14. In Western Europe about 12 percent of the college-age population goes to college. In California the percentage is almost 85 percent. What is the *point* of a university education?

15. *Sperm banks.*

16. John Paul Getty, who became the richest man in the world, was a philosophy major in college. He said that if you want to become rich and successful, the worst subjects to major in are business or accounting. What steps should you take if you want to become rich?

17. *Horsemeat:* In many states it is illegal to sell horsemeat unless it is made unfit for human consumption. What is wrong with eating horsemeat? (Do you think it doesn't taste good?

18. *Pride:* What reasons do you have for preferring the professional sports team that happens to be located in your area? Why should *you* be proud of their victories?

19. *Honoring the dead:* What reasons are there for and against going to funeral services for relatives?

20. *Inherited traits:* The story of "The Princess and the Pea" is an exaggeration of a belief that was widely held: that children of the nobility, even if they are raised by commoners, have a greater sensitivity (of skin, feelings, and morals) than children of commoners raised the same way. Many people thought that nobility was an inherited trait. Isn't such a belief easily disproved by ordinary experience? How, do you suppose, did people keep the belief if it is so easily disproved?

What *are* some traits that are generally inherited? How do you know?

Which of the following traits seem clearly inherited? Which seem clearly not inherited? Which are more doubtful? (Give reasons to back up your judgments): Being tall, smiling when you are happy, being able to reason well, being a good dancer, having a tendency toward criminality, ducking when an object is thrown at your head. Give a counterexample whenever you can.

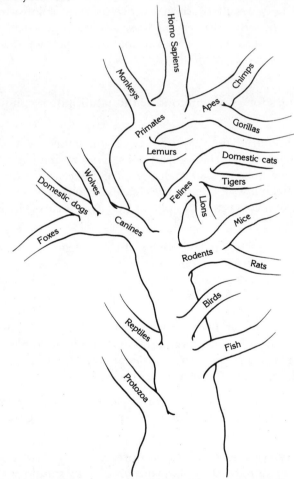

21. This is a drawing of the tree of evolution. It is the kind of drawing that often appears in books on biology and nature for beginners. How is it unreasonable to represent evolution this way, as a progression *upward*? What principle, if any, would justify putting Homo sapiens higher than chimps or monkeys? What principle, if any, would justify putting primates above rodents? Or birds above fish? Is there any single principle that will justify all the rankings in the tree?

22. *Monogamy:* What reasons are there for and against monogamy? Why should it be illegal to have more than one spouse?

Give a reasonable and well-thought-out analysis and evaluation of selections 23–30. (What point is being argued? Is the evidence true? Does the evidence given establish the point? How close does it come?)

In addition, try to get a larger perspective on the issue being discussed: What, precisely, are the most fundamental presuppositions involved? How do they relate to other important issues?

23. "Amid the arguments of what is and isn't brainwashing, stand those who argue *everything* is brainwashing. 'For a long time brainwashing was what the other guy did; our side did purely informational work,' says Henry Ebel, editor of *Behavior Today* newsletter. 'But when you get beyond the us-them part, you realize that education, religion — everything — is brainwashing in a sense.'

"It sinks so deep, he says, 'that we no longer realize we're brainwashed. We just happen to share the same basic ideas, obsessions, habits, tastes, assumptions — we are human sponges soaking up cues and programming.' Each culture, he maintains, creates its own 'cultural trance,' by which it sets the rules for society. And everyone, no matter what society, needs those rules — something — to believe in." (Chicago *Tribune*. January 3, 1979.)

24. "When we study the behavior of lower animals, we find abundant evidence that they do change their behavior on the basis of experience. The earthworm conquers a maze, the cockroach learns to avoid a shock, the fish learns to withdraw from a shadow at the edge of a stream. When a motivated organism encounters blocks or barriers or problems, it proceeds with some degree of effectiveness to learn those new responses that get it where it wants to go. In lower animals, the adaptive change in behavior come about very gradually and on the basis of repeated experience." (Fillmore Sanford, *Psychology* (Belmont, California: 1965) p. 403.)

25. "Too many people still think that the Middle Ages are merely a stagnant pit which lies between the heights of classical and of Renaissance civilization, and that all our legacy from the past was carried over the bridges which Renaissance thinkers threw across the medieval pit to the firm ground of Graeco-Roman learning. This is true even of people who deposit money in a bank, who elect representatives to a national assembly, who rely on the precedents of the English common law, who receive degrees from universities and believe that science is an important part of education, who worship in Gothic churches, and who read books written in modern European languages. They would find their lives rather limited and unsatisfactory if they could do none of these things, and yet the basic idea of every one of these activities was worked out in the Middle Ages and not in ancient Greece or Rome. Our civilization has roots in the Middle Ages as well as in the classical period, and the medieval roots often contribute more nourishment than the classical ones. The story of medieval civilization is worth knowing, and it is that story which is told, in its barest outlines, in this book." (Joseph Strayer, *Western Europe in the Middle Ages* (Pacific Palisades, California: 1974), p. 10. Reprinted by permission at Goodyear Publishing Company.)

26. John R. Bormuth of the University of Chicago "argues that there is no good evidence that the level of reading and writing skills is lower than it used to be and is declining, and that on the contrary a large and growing proportion of the population have attained a high level of literacy and the volume and economic value of written communication have been increasing.

    "Bormuth defines literacy as the exchange of information through the written word. . . .

    "As evidence of an 'increasing level of literacy in a large and growing fraction of the population' in the past 25 years or so, Bormuth cites such statistics as these: The number of items checked out of libraries rose from 2.5 per person to 4.4; white-collar workers (whose jobs depend on reading and writing) rose from 36 percent of the work force to more than 50 percent; estimated time spent reading on the job rose from 104 minutes per person per day to 141 minutes; the number of books and pamphlets purchased rose from 6.8 to 8.6 per person per year; although newspaper circulation increased less than the number of households, newspapers now have more pages, so that the volume of newspaper material purchased increased from 38 to 52 pages per household per day; 235 pieces of mail (air, priority and third-class) per person were mailed in 1950 as against 349 in 1975; in addition to the well-known increase in high school and college attendance, there has been an increase in the school year and therefore presumably in the amount of literacy instruction per student." (*Scientific American*, March, 1979. Reprinted by permission.)

27. JUDGE AND JURY FACE THE MUSIC:
    "Music has charms to soothe a savage breast" — and to sway a reluctant jury, it seems. Nancy Larson, 18, was suing her mother and another driver over a 1971 automobile accident in which she had been injured and left with a scarred face. Larson's lawyer, Alexander Goldfarb of Hartford, Connecticut, was demanding damages of $12,000; the best settlement offer he had received was for $6,000.

    "Things looked grim for the plaintiff until Goldfarb began his summation, in which he compared the beauty of a woman's face to fine Italian drawings and to the haunting visage that is the subject of the song "I've Grown Accustomed to Her Face," from *My Fair Lady*. He then surprised judge and jury alike by proceeding to sing the song to the court. Everyone agreed that he was a good singer, the judge said it was the best summation she'd ever heard, and the jury was moved to award Nancy Larson $59,125." (*Student Lawyer*, October, 1980.)

28. Dr. Peter Steincrohn, who writes a syndicated newspaper column on medicine, devoted a column to criticizing television. A vice-president of

NBC replied by letter: "You state that television commercials benumb the public. Breed procrastination. Keep people from going to the doctor on time. It seems to us that this casts the American television viewer in the role of an utter nincompoop, incapable of deciding when his health appears endangered and when he needs treatment. We do not share this patronizing view of our fellow Americans.

"You ask why the American Medical Association, American Cancer Society, any of our diversified lifesaving institutions don't 'do something about what's going on in TV?' The answer is they turn to television as the most effective means today to get their messages to the American public.

"Far from numbing the public, television has proven to be the most effective means of alerting the public to the need for better health and care. It is regrettable that your attack on television did not at least refer to some of these readily available facts."

29. "The *Grosse Politik* approach has been used up. Besides, it is misleading because it allows us to rest on the easy illusion that it is 'they,' the naughty statesmen, who are always responsible for war while 'we,' the innocent people, are merely led. That impression is a mistake." (Barbara Tuchman, *The Proud Tower*, New York: 1966, p. xiv.)

30. Condensed from *Fortune* Magazine, December 4, 1978:
Despite the broad acceptance of the view that the poor and elderly are the principal victims when inflation rises, it is almost certainly wrong. The *relative* position of these groups seems to have improved in the high-inflation years, while the relative position of high-income people, especially those with capital, has deteriorated. Or so a few indicators would suggest.

The real value of stock has dropped to about half of what it was in 1967, and dividends are off 12 percent in real value.

Payments that primarily benefit the poor and elderly have risen about 340 percent since 1967, while wages have risen only 160 percent. Social Security benefits, the primary source of income for Americans 65 and over, have risen 40 percent in real terms, while wages have risen only 2 percent in real terms.

Medical care, the component of the consumer price index that has risen most rapidly of all, is essentially free to the poor and elderly (because of Medicare and Medicaid). Prices paid by high-income people — executive living costs — have risen 30 percent between 1975 and 1978, while consumer prices generally rose only 21 percent.

Information and psychology in reasoning   Reasoning is not just a logical activity. To use it effectively in practice requires that you succeed in going through certain thought processes (psychology), that you draw conclusions, make good criticisms, and so forth (logic, pure reasoning), and that you do so on the basis of whatever information you have (knowledge). Your practical reasoning can be rendered much less useful, therefore, if you are prevented from going through the thought processes (by being intimidated, for example), or if the information you have is wrong or distorted.

Information   One of the prime sources of information for many people is newspapers. Yet the information and opinions contained in newspapers is affected by many factors: the point of view (or even biases) of columnists, the "editorial philosophy" of the newspaper, the abilities of local reporters, the national news services, the influence of advertisers. It is worthwhile to investigate, by means of reasoning and some research, these potential sources of distortion.

31. There are about ten or twenty major columnists in the country. Their opinions are carried by most newspapers. Consequently, they are enormously influential in shaping public opinion. To evaluate what these columnists say, it is important to know where they stand in general.

   Buy a copy of a newspaper from your area for a week. (It might be unfair to generalize after reading only one or two of a person's columns.) Arrange a list of columnists and try to make an intelligent and reasonable appraisal of the general point of each.

   You would probably want to answer such questions as these: Are the columnists liberal or conservative? What are their stands on the major controversial issues of the moment? Do their columns invariably defend business, or unions, or any other special group? Do they seem sensitive to actual problems people have or are they doctrinaire?

   Many of the syndicated columnists are *not* good at reasoning. You would want to examine this also: Is the column usually an intelligent one? Do the columnists evaluate opposing positions fairly or do they set up strawmen to argue against (a frequent fault)? Does the columnist get to the heart of an issue?

32. Many newspapers have an avowed "editorial philosophy." Examine the editorials in your newspaper over a period of time and try to formulate any consistent patterns in the opinions. Once you know the philosophy behind the editorial, you will be better able to check for possible distortion.

33. Once you have isolated the editorial policies, check the part of the paper that has letters from readers. Are all (or most) of the letters chosen on the same side as the editors, or is there a divergence of point of view? Consider the letters that disagree with the editorial philosophy: Do they present a strong case or might they have been chosen because the case they present is so weak (straw-man arguments again)?

34. How about news *stories* that have controversial overtones (for example, ones dealing with pornography, capital punishment, abortion, patriotism, political meetings)? Are they presented in loaded language or objectively? Find examples of stories in which the point of view of the reporter comes through.

35. AP and UPI are the major wire services. Do some research into how they work: Are their stories written by ordinary reporters? Where do the writers live? Does your newspaper print the whole story as wired to them, or do they cut it down? Does the local paper add anything?

36. Most of the revenue of newspapers comes from advertising rather than from subscribers. Can you find any evidence that sensitivity to an advertiser's concerns affects what is said in the paper? In which sections of the paper is this most likely to occur?

37. Buy copies of out-of-town newspapers and compare them to the coverage in your own. What is the difference in editorial policy? In letters to the editor? In reporting? In objectivity?

   How do they compare with respect to coverage of international news? Are there important events that are not covered at all by your local papers? How can you explain this?

Psychology   Reasoning is a psychological activity as well as a logical one. If you are intimidated or flustered or ignorant, you can be prevented from taking practical advantage of even good reasoning ability.

38. One good technique to combat this is to practice a few psychological exercises intended to overcome feelings of intimidation. With each of them it is necessary actually to do it, consciously, having planned it out beforehand. The point is to acquire the habit of reasoning on your feet, and this is best done by conscious repetition.

   For each of these exercises write a paragraph describing the experiment and the result.

(a) Practice keeping eye contact while arguing with someone.

(b) Some people have difficulty in disagreeing openly with others. The next appropriate time when someone says something you think is incorrect, say, "I think you're wrong about that," and give your reasons. (It is not at all necessary to say it belligerently, but it *is* helpful to *say* it outright.)

(c) Related to (b) is the feeling of humiliation you may get when you have to admit that a position of *yours* is mistaken. It is, of course, an unreasonable feeling; there is nothing humiliating about having been wrong. What is more unreasonable in most situations is to continue holding on to a position that you know is wrong. The reasonable thing to do is to go along with the best reasons and simply admit you were wrong. A useful exercise, the next time you find you have been mistaken, is to do precisely that: Say, "Oh, you're right. I'm wrong about it."

(d) A thing that often happens when people argue is that they tend to leave the main issue and get caught up in discussing side issues. The main controversy in this way tends to be "fogged" by smaller questions. One aspect of arguing well is to keep the discussion focused. You cannot usually do that by instructing your opponent. So a useful technique is to practice *conceding* points. Have a premeditated rational argument with someone about an issue on which you disagree. Whenever you find that the issue is being fogged (you will be surprised at how often it occurs), simply *concede* that point and argue your side without it.

(e) Figure out some other techniques to counteract your personal psychological weak points. Practice using the techniques.

39. One situation in which it is particularly easy to become intimidated and flustered is when you are going against the normal flow of selling and buying, for example, if you are trying to return a defective item, or complaining about service, or your food at the restaurant is cold. The danger in such a situation is that you will be cowed by the person in authority or that you will lose your temper and make your case weaker.

   With a friend or a classmate, practice returning a new pair of shoes in which the stitching is coming loose. Your friend can be the manager ("we cannot accept returned shoes once the soles are dirty"). While you try to combat the objections, present the strongest case you can for a refund, and remain assertive and reasonable.

40. Invite an opponent or proponent of ERA, abortion, capital punishment, or one of the issues of the day to address the class. Beforehand, assemble the main lines of your positions so you will know which points to stress, where to concede, what the key issue is likely to be. Arguing with a controversial speaker is useful both logically and psychologically. (It is also a good place to practice the psychological exercises in question 40.)

Reasoning skills are useful in any enterprise that calls for figuring things out mentally. Some of the following questions parallel questions asked in Chapter One. Apply your improved reasoning skills to these areas. And, as a sidelight, compare your reasoning ability now with your ability then.

41. In the exercises to Chapter One, you had to come up with three beliefs that a lot of people hold but which you think are false. Then in Chapter Four you had to think up an argument against your side. Now go back and inspect the arguments on both sides. How would you go about improving them? How effectively are you able to criticize both sets of arguments? How much has your skill in reasoning increased between Chapter One and Chapter Four and now?

42. When you read something, you are doing something very much like analyzing arguments, especially if you are reading it closely. That is clear when you are reading textbooks or editorials that consist of arguments, but it is true when reading other things, too. If you are reading a novel closely, for instance, and if the novel is carefully written, you can ask and answer questions of roughly the same kind as when analyzing an argument. You can take a sentence and ask what does it mean? What point is the author trying to convey in this description? (That is, what conclusions does the author want you to draw?) For example, if a character is described as going into a restaurant with a hole in his pants, it ought to mean something in the context of the novel. It might mean that he is sloppy, or easy going, or opposes the standards of society, or some such thing. (*Which* alternative will be established by other details in the novel.)

The going hypothesis is that the novelist had a reason (not just a cause) for describing the character that way. If not, if it is irrelevant, it may very well be a defect in the novel. But, in many novels, the answers can be reasoned out.

This is the second paragraph of a short German novel:

> May had begun, and after weeks of cold and wet a mock summer had set in. The English Gardens, though in tenderest leaf, felt as sultry as in August and were full of vehicles and pedestrians near the city. But towards Aumeister the paths were solitary and still, and Aschenbach strolled thither, stopping awhile to watch the lively crowds in the restaurant garden with its fringe of carriages and cabs. Thence he took his homeward way outside the park and across the sunset fields. By the time he reached the North Cemetery, however, he felt tired, and a storm was brewing above Föhring; so he waited at the stopping-place for a tram to carry him back to the city.

Operate under the hypothesis that the novel is tightly constructed and that the novelist is preparing you for what will happen later on.

Aschenbach is the main character. From the progression of this little walk of his, what is likely to happen to him at the end of the story? There are two phrases that convey it almost directly. What are they?

What are the connotations of the word "sultry" in the second sentence? Saying that things are "in the tenderest leaf" implies that they are young. The second major character in the novel is a young adolescent. From just the information in the second sentence, what kind of character is he likely to have?

43. Go back and criticize the arguments about student drinking in the exercises to Chapter One. How much have you improved in your ability to reason your way through arguments?

44. In the exercises to Chapter One, there was a selection from a study guide to the Law School Admissions Test. Go back and try the test again. Or, better yet, get a copy of an LSAT Guide and answer the questions. Has your skill increased?

INDEX